Paul McCartney

ALL THE SONGS

Rick Swan

Paul McCartney
ALL THE SONGS

Rick Swan

WYMER
PUBLISHING
Bedford, England

First published in Great Britain in 2020
by Wymer Publishing
www.wymerpublishing.co.uk
Tel: 01234 326691
Wymer Publishing is a trading name of Wymer (UK) Ltd

ISBN: 978-1-912782-43-7

Typeset and Design by Andy Bishop / 1016 Sarpsborg

A catalogue record for this book is available from the British Library.

CONTENTS

CONTENTS

INTRODUCTION

The 1950s. Liverpool, a grim coastal city in the UK, was suffering through the aftermath of World War II, re-assembling broken neighborhoods, comforting the bereaved, and looking ahead to what had to be a better future.

Nestled in his modest Forthlin Road home, budding musician Paul McCartney, a reject from the Liverpool Cathedral Choir, took a seat at the family piano. He hit a few chords, hit a few more, and in a few minutes, gave birth to "When I'm 64." This song would eventually become part of *Sgt Pepper's Lonely Hearts Club Band*, a multi-million hit and the forefront of a cultural revolution. McCartney wrote it when he was a teenager.

Flash forward to 1979. Paul McCartney, one of history's most prolific artists, was declared by the Guinness Book of World Records to be the most successful songwriter of all time. He was 37.

Impressive? Absolutely. But the *quality* of those songs? That was a different story. During the Beatle days, roughly 1963 to 1970, he had the golden touch, not only for his string of unforgettable classics – "All My Loving," "For No One," and "Let It Be," to name a few – but also for his nearly supernatural ability when it came to polishing his band's work. There are almost too many moments to count: his haunting keyboard riff on John' Lennon's "Lucy in the Sky with Diamonds," the psychedelic swirl linking sections of "A Day In The Life," the breakthrough sound collage on "Tomorrow Never Knows." Music poured out of him, virtually unprecedented, all of it breathtaking.

It came to a halt in 1970. The Beatles called it a day and went their separate ways. Although all of them struggled with their new status – it was tough being an ex-Beatle – none of the other three struggled harder than McCartney, who was rattled for an uncomfortably long time. He could no longer depend on his comrades to steer him away from questionable material. Now he had to do it himself. He no longer could depend on Lennon to turn the acceptable to the spectacular ["We Can Work It Out," "Michelle", McCartney songs for which Lennon supplied the middle eight]. McCartney's production excesses used to be tempered by his fellow Beatles. No more. Now he had to do it alone.

From 1970 and beyond, the songwriting McCartney seemed to be saddled with a rickety who-cares system that generated iffy results. Gone were "Eleanor Rigby" and "Penny Lane." Instead, came the thought-free "Mary Had a Little Lamb" and "Bip Bop," songs the Beatles wouldn't have considered for a second.

Troubles swarmed around him as he searched for his place. The Beatles had theirs – where was his? Was he overly obsessed with perfection? Maybe. Or was it insecurity? His next record couldn't be a forward-thinking experiment, with sales falling wherever they may. It had to – *had* to – be a chart topper adored all over the world.

Beneath the facade of the happy-go-lucky hit-maker seemed to be a man enduring a battle between artistry [his painful and honest "Here Today"] and the commercial [duets with Michael Jackson]. Outsiders had to wonder – did the years, perhaps decades, of drug use damage his ability to distinguish the good from the bad? Had he been *that* dependent on input from the Beatles, Lennon in particular? Did the giddy enthusiasm from fans, who were determined to like *everything,* warp his self-image, paving the way for endless "Bip Bop"s?

Navigating McCartney's solo career can be maddening. He's certainly not lazy – he defines "workaholic" – but he has a frustrating habit of releasing nearly everything he touches. Sometimes, it's half-finished [the medley on *Back to the Egg*]. Sometimes, it's a collaboration more casual than serious ["What's That You're Doing" with Stevie Wonder on *Tug of War*.] Sometimes, it's exasperating ["Hey Diddle"]. But on occasion, it can be brilliant ["Daytime Nighttime Suffering"] or as magnificent as it was when he was with the Beatles ["Maybe I'm Amazed"]. To paraphrase Forrest Gump, when it comes to McCartney's output, you never know what you're going to get.

Thus, the premise of this book: to sift the gems from the chaff and examine what's driven McCartney up and down for nearly fifty years. There are plenty of tracks suitable for casual fans, adolescents, even preschoolers. But there are tracks for an older audience too, tracks so good they can supply grown-ups with a rewarding soundtrack for a lifetime. It's these that make for a playlist worth keeping.

What's Included

As humanly possible, this book attempts to evaluate every track that Paul McCartney has released on a major label. Bootlegs aren't included, nor are irrelevant variations of existing tracks [such the party version of "Say Say Say" from *Pipes of Peace*] nor are performances exclusive to DVD, TV, or other video sources [only records and CDs here, with the rare exception]. Special cases are made for the odd, the fascinating, and the head-scratchers, including the alternate mono *Ram* [featuring an assortment of revisions] and *Thrillington* [which must be heard to be believed]. Fragments of songs, dialog, and bits of instrumentals are mostly ignored. Although remixing can improve the sound, often considerably, this book sticks to the originals, with occasional examinations of noteworthy anomalies.

Songs not included on McCartney albums, but which he recorded and released, are listed in the bonus sections. These include B-sides, contributions to anthologies, and various songs that were lost along the way. Songs which he produced and/or performed on, but credited to someone else, are also included; the performer is given in parenthesis at the beginning of the entry, such as his collaboration with Alice Cooper ["Come and Get It," a Badfinger track no less] and his production of the Bonzo Dog Band ["I'm the Urban Spaceman"].

Like McCartney's album tracks, bonuses are assigned to the approximate year they went public, not the year they were made. Each entry concludes with one likely place you can find it, also given in parentheses, but keep in mind that songs tend to pop up in multiple formats and editions, and no effort has been made to list them all.

Artists who've covered McCartney aren't included; that is, tracks on which McCartney may have written, but didn't contribute as a performer or producer. An example: Guns 'n' Roses covered "Live and Let Die" on their 1990 *Use Your Illusion I* album, but McCartney is nowhere in sight [a shame, as that would've been great]. There are a couple of exceptions here and there, but these are reserved for the truly unusual.

As in high school, all entries have been assigned a letter grade: A [exceptional], B [acceptable], C [forgettable], D [substandard], and F ["Bip Bop"].

Charts and Songwriting Credits

Highest chart positions, both for the US and UK, are indicated for each album, though I wouldn't swear to their accuracy. The *Official Charts Company [OCC]* provides data for UK albums, *Billboard* magazine is the source for US ratings. The OCC does their best with less than reliable results from radio play and self-reported ratings from retailers, not to mention the seemingly ever-changing methods for tallying streams from computer subscription services. But really, how can you be certain if one album is two points [or three or whatever] higher than another? It seems an impossibility. The determination of US positions shares similar problems.

What they're good at, however, is determining approximate ratings, valuable in accessing the *relative* popularity of a particular song or album. So instead of pondering the meaning of #1 vs #3, consider chart positions as a general guide. That is, if *Paul Grows Up* [a title I made up] charts at #1, you can be pretty sure you've got a hit on your hands. If it never gets higher than, say, #100, it's a flop.

The official songwriters are given in parenthesis after the song title, but be aware that they may not be strictly accurate. If two writers are given, this doesn't mean the creation was a 50/50 split, but rather a legal decision, a friendly one, or an arbitrary one. [You give me credit for A, I'll give you credit for B.] Even the famous Lennon-McCartney credit line should be considered skeptically. After all, "Yesterday" is considered to be 100% Paul, but is credited to both Lennon and McCartney. Take writing credits with a grain – or two – of salt.

Personnel

To the endless frustration of fans and critics alike, the official album credits for performances and technical aid aren't always accurate. Musicians come and go seemingly at will, credits are muddied, guessed at, or forgotten. A record label may hunt down someone from the artist's staff to gather up missing credits "but this might happen weeks or months after the production was complete," wrote Mark Levine for *Mix* magazine. "So getting the crediting information about the musicians and engineers who worked on the project could very well be incomplete."

In this book, significant credits are given where applicable and seem reasonable, such as the composition of the ever-changing Wings teams or the appearance of notable guest stars like Ringo Starr. Further, since a fussy McCartney was generally intent on doing it his own way, and since he was an instrumental whiz, when in doubt, it's a good a bet as any that Paul is probably playing a given instrument himself.

Other Books

For those interested in the dishy details of McCartney's life, I recommend the excellent *Man on the Run: Paul McCartney in the 70s* by Tom Doyle. *Paul McCartney: Many Years from Now* by Barry Miles is also a must-read. For music transcripts, try *Paul McCartney – Out There Tour Songbook* which provides a good, but by no means complete, overview of his catalogue.

PROLOGUE:

BEATLES ERA EXTRAS

In theory, this book begins around 1970, the year the Beatles were over and McCartney began his career with his first solo album. But during the late 1950s and throughout the 1960s, McCartney – usually with his partner John Lennon – had a flourishing moonlighting career outside of the Beatles, writing, performing, and occasionally producing for a wide range of artists, sometimes un-credited. Generally, these songs weren't considered strong enough to be Beatles records. Some are outside productions. Some are performances contributed on a lark or as a favour. A few of them are little known, some are interesting in their own right, and a couple are too goofy to ignore, like the Beach Boys' "Vegetables." Consider these to be sort of a bonus to the bonus sections.

Owing to their unusual origins, the songs don't strictly adhere to the guidelines applicable elsewhere in this book, but each involves McCartney on some level as writer, producer and/or performer. His contributions are noted after the title.

1958
"In Spite of All the Danger" [Paul McCartney and George Harrison]
Featuring the Quarrymen, sort of a proto-Beatles. Their ever-changing membership for this recording includes McCartney, Harrison, John Lennon, Colin Hanton, and John Lowe. With vocals influenced by the Everly Brothers and instrumental support by the nervous group, the song crawls through a surprisingly sophisticated structure – surprising, that is, for amateurs – with McCartney doing his tentative best to carry the simple tune. Interesting historically, substandard as a song. [*Anthology 1*] **C-**

1960
"Cayenne" [Paul McCartney; guest performer: Paul McCartney]
An instrumental demo from the Quarrymen, composed here of McCartney, John Lennon, Stu Suttcliffe, and possibly George Harrison. Sloppily performed with a weak melody, this justifies its existence by hinting at what's to come, providing charitable listeners are willing to provide the requisite benefit of the doubt. [*Anthology 1*]. **D**

"You'll Be Mine" [John Lennon and Paul McCartney]
With the same Quarrymen membership as "Cayenne," this snippet was a survivor of a session that sounds like it was recorded in a bathroom, owing to the avalanche of echo dumped all over it. A novelty tune replete with nutty voices and a nonsense spoken section, it previews the Goon Show humour beloved by Lennon and McCartney, on full

display in "You Know My Name" on the B-side of 1970's "Let It Be" single. On its own, "You'll Be Mine" reveals a whiff of good natured whimsy and a growing confidence in their own voices, but not much else. [*Anthology 1*] **C**

1963

"Bad to Me" [John Lennon and Paul McCartney]

[Billy J Kramer and the Dakotas] Kramer was getting nowhere until he hooked up with the Dakotas, a band also going nowhere, whose career took off when the refurbished group signed with George Martin. After their version of Lennon-McCartney's "Do You Want to Know a Secret" [from the Beatles *Please Please Me* album] hit the top, Martin arranged with Lennon and McCartney to supply Kramer with a new, non-Beatles tune. They quickly came up with the amiable "Bad to Me". It smelled like a hit, its Beatle-y touches ringing out all over the place. The weak point was Kramer himself, less a virtuoso performer and more of a mannered innocent along the lines of a thrift store Bobby Vee. But he had a terrific smile, and the record, with its irresistible charm, soared to the top of the UK charts. [*The Best of Billy J Kramer*] **B**

"I'll Keep You Satisfied" [John Lennon and Paul McCartney]

[Billy J Kramer and the Dakotas] On the heels of "Bad to Me," this was a lesser but plausible hit, with second-rate lyrics sitting on an okay tune, enough for a #4 [UK]. The Beatles played around with this, avoided recording it, but occasionally included it on their radio broadcasts. [Kramer: *Best of Billy J Kramer;* Beatles*: Live on the BBC.*] **B-**

"I'll Be On My Way" [John Lennon and Paul McCartney]

[Billy J Kramer and the Dakotas] Another Lennon-McCartney scrap, eagerly scooped up by Kramer for a single B-side. Folk-ish, awkward lyrics, and a rickety melody, its hit status was unlikely. The Beatles recorded one version, a live one, and apparently never did it again, an acknowledgment of its triviality. [The Beatles: *Live on the BBC*. Kramer: "Do You Want to Know a Secret" single] **C**

"Tip of My Tongue" [John Lennon and Paul McCartney]

[Tommy Quickly] *Who wants to be a star?* [Hands up, eagerly.] *We have here a Lennon-McCartney tune, never recorded by the Beatles.* [Hands waving, crowd excited.] *It's called "Tip of My Tongue."* [Crowd's enthusiasm sinks.] *It's like Tommy Steele, but not as good.* [Crowd heads for the door.] *Well?* [One has remained behind.] *Speak up son.* [He hesitates, grabs it, runs away. Later, he's hospitalized for a nervous breakdown.] [*The Songs Lennon and McCartney Gave Away.*] **F**

"Hello Little Girl" [John Lennon and Paul McCartney]

[The Fourmost] When the Beatles exploded, record companies sucked up British groups like vacuum cleaners on a dirty carpet. The Fourmost was among them. They auditioned for Beatles manager Brian Epstein, passed, auditioned for George Martin, passed. Martin rewarded them with an unrecorded song by Lennon-McCartney. "Hello Little Girl" could've been worse, but still, it's an obvious toss-off. The Fourmost did their best navigating the sappy lyrics and fair melody, and – surprise – up to #9 [UK] it went. It may strike the modern listener as hopelessly dated, but archeology students might like it. [The Fourmost: *The Songs Lennon and McCartney Gave Away*; The Beatles: *Anthology 1.*] **B-**

"I'm in Love" [John Lennon and Paul McCartney]

[The Fourmost] The Fourmost fell short with this minor Lennon-McCartney piece, a tune so insubstantial you wonder if they were fully awake when writing it. Billy J Kramer also took a crack at it, but recorded it as album filler, its natural home. [The Fourmost: *The Songs the Beatles Gave Away*] **C-**

"Love of the Loved" [John Lennon and Paul McCartney]

[Cilla Black] With a delivery as smooth as a puppy's belly, cabaret singer Black was a good match for McCartney's ballads, but as for the rockers, or even the semi-rockers, she couldn't be more wrong. "Love of the Loved" isn't the Rolling Stones, but it isn't "And I Love Her," either. Though she performs like a show biz trooper, "Love of the Loved" doesn't cut it. [*The Songs Lennon and McCartney Gave Away*] **C**

"I Wanna Be Your Man" [John Lennon and Paul McCartney]

[The Rolling Stones] Reports differ regarding the birth of "I Wanna Be Your Man." In one version, Mick Jagger was rehearsing while John and Paul looked on. During a break, Jagger [or manager Andrew Loog Oldman] lamented that the Rolling Stones needed a hit. While the dumbfounded Rolling Stones watched, John and Paul more or less wrote "I Wanna Be Your Man" on the spot. In another version, McCartney implied that the Beatles had already written and recorded it, and since there was zero chance they'd use it as a single – Ringo sang it, after all – off it went to the Stones, who recorded a sloppy but infectious rendition that gave them a UK hit [#12] and kick-started their career. John and Paul settled for filler on *With the Beatles*. And royalties from the Stones. [*Singles Collection: The London Years*] **B**

1964

"From a Window" [John Lennon and Paul McCartney; guest performer: Paul McCartney]

[Billy J Kramer and the Dakotas] More energetic than usual, this tale of a window peeper boasted a bit – a tiny bit – of maturity, though it was still aimed at adolescents. It didn't hurt that in addition to George Martin, Lennon and McCartney were in the studio too, cheering Kramer on. But it's still an inferior Beatles tune, and if it expanded his audience, well, stranger things have happened. It clawed its way to UK #10 and marked the beginning of the end of Kramer's perch at the top. McCartney, with Kramer, sings the last word. [*Best of Billy J Kramer*] **B-**

"It's For You" [John Lennon and Paul McCartney]

[Cilla Black] Lennon-McCartney still clung to their gems, tossing down third-raters to the anointed few. Black took what she could get and gave "It's For You" an honest shot. But this clunky waltz collapsed under the weight of grand orchestrations and tempo shifts, and became a non-deserving Top 10 [UK] that left next to no impression. Considering the female singers of the time, Black remained in the back seat, Petula Clark drove the bus. [*The Songs Lennon and McCartney Gave* Away] **C-**

"A World Without Love" [John Lennon and Paul McCartney]

[Peter and Gordon] Would you like some fresh Paul McCartney to launch your career, but don't know how to get it? Try this: [1] Smile when McCartney falls in love with a high profile girlfriend, like movie actor Jane Asher from *The Masque of the Red Death*. [2]

Be the girlfriend's brother [like Peter Asher]. [3] Become pals with McCartney. [4] Jump for joy when your parents invite McCartney to move in. [5] Make sure there's a piano in McCartney's room. [6] Graciously accept "A World Without Love," a tune the Beatles weren't going to touch. Though the rest of the Beatles mocked McCartney's dopey lyrics, "A World Without Love" sported an indelible melody that transcended the words. Peter and Gordon, sort of a bargain basement Simon and Garfunkel, gave the song a wide-eyed, lost kitty approach that pushed the song to #1 in the US and UK. [*The Songs Lennon and McCartney Gave Away*] **B**

"Nobody I Know" [John Lennon and Paul McCartney]

[Peter and Gordon] McCartney, ever the entrepreneur, apparently intended this to be a follow-up smash to "A World Without Love." It was, sort of, rising to #10 in the UK and #12 in the US. Chirpy and mildly sickening, "Nobody I Know" resembles "Do You Want to Know a Secret," though "Secret" is a classic by comparison. [*The Songs Lennon and McCartney Gave Away*] **B-**

"I Don't Want to See You Again" [John Lennon and Paul McCartney]

[Peter and Gordon] Another Beatle gift to P&G, and a decent one, sung with passable panache. Stumbling towards a style they could call their own, they're like your younger brothers, only wimpier. Speaking of wimpy, an eye-rolling instrumental break sets it back a few yards. [*The Songs Lennon and McCartney Gave Away*] **B-**

"Like Dreamers Do" [John Lennon and Paul McCartney]

[The Applejacks] A British band with a female drummer, the Applejacks had a relatively brief career highlighted by a modest run on the charts, followed by a quick decline. By 1966, they were performing on cruise ships. Along the way, they met Lennon and McCartney at a TV show and found themselves recipient of an original song by the skyrocketing songwriters. Of course, Lennon and McCartney weren't about to part with anything good, and "Like Dreamers Do" is near the bottom of the barrel. A cheery, empty tune that cobbles together a string of British Invasion clichés, the song bombed, and the Applejacks began to scan cruise ship schedules. The Beatles tried "Like Dreamers Do" on a pre-contract tape, though they never formally recorded it. [The Beatles: *Anthology 1*; The Applejacks: *The Songs Lennon and McCartney Gave Away*.] **C+**

"One and One is Two" [John Lennon and Paul McCartney]

[The Strangers with Mike Shannon] Next to "Tip of My Tongue," the worst Lennon-McCartney song ever. Rejected by the Beatles, Billy J Kramer, and the Fourmost, the orphaned "One and One is Two" was scooped up by Shannon and his mates, eager to be associated with anything the Beatles breathed on. Bad call. The limp recording of this lifeless song failed to significantly chart anywhere in the world. [*The Songs Lennon and McCartney Gave Away*.] **D-**

"I Knew Right Away" [Alma Cogan and Stan Foster; guest performer: Paul McCartney]

[Alma Cogan] Popular 50s singer, famous for her rendition of "I Had a Golden Umbrella" where she accidently giggled, leading to her tag as "The Girl With the Giggle in Her Voice." She got her ticket to oblivion when the Beatles appeared and more or less wiped conservative songbirds off the map, though she remained friendly with them. [Lennon was rumoured to have had an affair with her.] Martin produced this unenthusiastic, get-it-over-with song featuring McCartney [reportedly] on tambourine. Sadly, Cogan succumbed to ovarian cancer at age 34. [Single B-side] **D+**

1965
"That Means a Lot" [John Lennon and Paul McCartney]
[PJ Proby] The Beatles struggled with this during their *Help* sessions, but its awkward construction made it unsalvageable. PJ Proby, his "Niki Hokey" a here-and-gone on the US charts, snatched it up. No dice. A ballad nearly devoid of classy Beatle trappings, it's doubtful anyone could have saved it. [The Beatles: *Anthology 2*, PJ Proby: *The Songs Lennon and McCartney Gave Away*] **C**

"Mellow Yellow" [Donovan Leitch; guest performer: Paul McCartney]
From folk to jazz to psychedelic to pop to rock, Donovan has persisted for decades, changing with times, usually for the better. Of his many phases, psychedelic is his most interesting, the peak of which came with the squirrely "Mellow Yellow." Based on a rumor that you can get high smoking bananas, which a legion of pissed college students will swear isn't true, it sounds like tripping hippies having a party, with this simple anthem carrying the day. Supposedly, somewhere among the flower children is McCartney, yelling along and adding to the merriment, most likely in the fade out. Can't hear him? Me neither. [*Mellow Yellow* album] **B**

1966
"Woman" [Bernard Webb aka Paul McCartney]
[Peter and Gordon] A sophisticated tune that blossoms into a memorable Phil Spector-ish heartbreaker, thanks to the rich voice of Gordon Waller. Plunging full speed ahead into the murky world of melodrama, Gordon aches and cries and wails about a woman who did him wrong, resulting in terrific fun for the listener and a minor triumph for the composer. Speaking of the composer, McCartney used a pseudonym so as not to give the record a biased reason to succeed. The plan was successful for about two weeks. [*The Songs Lennon and McCartney Gave Away*] **B+**

"You've Got to Hide Your Love Away" [John Lennon and Paul McCartney, guest performer: Paul McCartney]
[The Silkie.] A left field hit for a British folk group, who gave it a hard-to-forget performance. Following an appearance at the Cavern Club, the Silkie – from Hull University and an English version of the Seekers – Brian Epstein saw them, liked them, signed them, and hustled them into a studio. It was there the stunned Silkie found themselves face-to-face with Lennon, McCartney, and Harrison, ready to help. Under the watchful eye of producer Lennon, with McCartney on guitar and Harrison on percussion, the Silkie created a stately, eerie take on Lennon's *Help* soundtrack contribution. Highlight: the ghostly voice of Sylvia Tatler, a star who never was. The Silkie attempted a couple more singles without the Beatles' help and failed, leading to the group dissolving. "You've Got to Hide Your Love Away" hit the US Top 10. [Single] **B+**

"Got to Get You Into My Life" [John Lennon and Paul McCartney; producer: Paul McCartney]
[Cliff Bennett and the Rebel Rousers] McCartney's salute to the joys of marijuana soared to #6 in the UK. An r&b combo that fizzled soon after, the Rebel Rousers' members went on to join Toe Fat and Uriah Heep, with Bennett eventually taking up the shipping business. With McCartney as producer, the Rebels studiously followed the version of

the song as appearing on *Revolver*, with some showbiz schmaltz thrown in to make it worse. [Single] **B**

"From Head to Toe" [Smokey Robinson; guest performer: Paul McCartney]

[The Escorts] What's Paul McCartney doing here? Well, the Escorts were from Liverpool, McCartney adored Smokey Robinson, plus he was probably nervous that his tambourine skills were getting rusty. Never fear, Paul whacks the tambourine with precision on this peppy but minor number. [Single] **B-**

1967

"Catcall" [Paul McCartney; guest performer: Paul McCartney]

[Chris Barber Band] A spooky instrumental, out of character for the light jazz Chris Barber Band. But, come on, it's Paul McCartney, and only the insane would turn him down. Aside from the lead line, spooky unto itself, the human [?] chorus is genuinely weird, sounding like ghouls preparing for Sunday brunch. McCartney joins a choir of creeps yelping it up at the end. [*The Songs Lennon and McCartney Gave Away*] **B**

"Step Inside Love" [Paul McCartney]

[Cilla Black] Custom-written for Black's TV show, *Cilla*, "Step Inside Love" became her signature song. Part of it is actually inscribed on her tombstone. One of McCartney's near-flawless ballads, Black floats over the tricky melody, making it her own – almost. You can't get rid of the show biz that's buried in your bones, and Black succumbs to the temptation to show off when it isn't necessary. McCartney knew this instinctively and showed us how it's done on an impromptu version when he and the boys were fooling around with the *White Album*'s "I Will." [Black: *The Songs Lennon and McCartney Gave Away*. Beatles version: *Anthology 3*] **B**

1968

"Thingumybob" [Paul McCartney; producer: Paul McCartney]

[Black Dyke Mills Band] A brass band, older than your grandpa, was the oddball choice to inaugurate the sparkling new Apple Records. "Thingumybob" was one of four singles in the initial Apple package, which also included "Hey Jude" [Beatles], "Those Were the Days" [Mary Hopkin], and Jackie Lomax ["Sour Milk Sea"]. A quaint instrumental that would have been rejected from *The Family Way* soundtrack, lacking any of McCartney's appeal. It bombed. [Single] **C**

"I'm the Urban Spaceman" [Neil Innes; Producers: Apollo C. Vermouth aka Paul McCartney and Gus Dudgeon]

[Bonzo Dog Band] McCartney met these razor-sharp satirists on the set of *Magical Mystery Tour* and decided to give the struggling group what they needed most: a hit single. Into the studio they went, replete with a banjo [played by Paul], a tuba, and a bizarre device made of what looked like a long hose with a funnel stuck on the end. Reportedly, you blew into the funnel while you swung the hose around your head, and it emitted honks like an ambulance crashing into a boy scout troop. The clever song proved irresistible to McCartney, who quickly polished it up, creating a tight showpiece featuring a hooky recorder and Innes' friendly vocals. It shot up to #5 [UK]. Their only hit, the Bonzos hung on for three more albums before calling it a day. [*Tadpoles*.] **B+**

"Those Were the Days" [Boris Fomin and Gene Raskin; producer: Paul McCartney]

[Mary Hopkin] This obscure tune dates back to the early 20th century. Beginning as a humble folk song, it bounced from Russia to France to Greenwich Village where it caught the ear of McCartney, who, after failed attempts to interest established performers, brought it to newcomer Mary Hopkin, a teenage Welsh unknown and a recent signing to Apple Records. The could-do-no-wrong McCartney, whose sharp ear heard something ordinary humans could not, transformed "Those Were the Days" into a grandiose, technicolour spectacular, using production techniques miles ahead of his contemporaries. Incorporating a sparkling arrangement that blended instruments as diverse as a string quartet, a clarinet, and a children's choir, the song unfolded in a dreamlike collage. Though Hopkin sings like an angel, this is McCartney's baby all the way. [*Those Were the Days* album] **A**

"Turn Turn Turn" [Pete Seeger; producer and guest performer: Paul McCartney]

No one expected the flip side of "Those Were the Days" to set the world on fire, and they weren't disappointed. Following the Byrds' definitive monster hit, only a few years old and still fresh in the minds of all, the track was doomed from the start. Which is a shame, because the track is friendly enough, Hopkin sings like she loves it, and McCartney, as always, keeps the arrangement tasteful. Of course, if you shoot at the Byrds, it helps to hit them. [B-side of "Those Were the Days" single] **B**

Postcard [Produced by Paul McCartney]

On the heels of the impressive "Those Were the Days," hopes were high for Mary Hopkin's debut album. But a seemingly random selection of material made it merely okay. It opens with Donovan's gorgeous "Lord of the Reedy River," and also features his excellent "Happiness Runs" and "Lullaby of the Moon." Other first rank selections: Harry Nilsson's "The Puppy Song," George Martin's "The Game," and George and Ira Gershwin's "Someone to Watch Over Me." But these don't even cover half the album. The rest of it consists of oldies both dreary ["Young Love"] and creaky ["There's No Business Like Show Business"], all selected by McCartney, who seemed to be bored with the project before it was finished. **B-**

"Carolina in My Mind" [James Taylor; guest performer: Paul McCartney]

[James Taylor] Taylor was among the early signings of Apple Records. His first album, loaded with great songs, pointed the way to worldwide success, which came when manager Peter Asher [the Peter of Peter and Gordon] coaxed him off Apple and onto Warner Brothers, a move that rocketed him to superstardom with the album *Sweet Baby James* ["Fire and Rain"]. The highlight of this album is "Carolina in My Mind," a Beatle-esque sparkler that, in another dimension, might have been considered for *The Beatles* [1968]. "Carolina in My Mind," though dated, remains one of the best of the 60s. McCartney adds tasty bass. [*James Taylor*] **B+**

"Atlantis" [Donovan Leitch; guest performer: Paul McCartney]

As the McCartney connection is questionable, put an asterisk by this one. An ode to the joys of living underwater, "Atlantis" is memorable for the catchy – almost annoyingly so – chorus repeated endlessly in the coda, sung by a squadron of singers which may or may not include Paul. If he's there, he's impossible to single out, as the choir's a blur. Donovan later claimed Paul was elsewhere, but others say he was belting it out with the rest of them. Hmm .... sounds fishy. [*Barabajagal*] **B+**

"And the Sun Will Shine"/ "The Dog Presides" [Barry, Robin, and Maurice Gibb/Paul Jones; guest performer: Paul McCartney]

[Paul Jones] The singer of Manfred Mann covered this Bee Gees tune from the album *Horizontal*, with drummer McCartney who sounds a little uncertain. That aside, it's a huge anthem of a song, typical Bee Gees, with Jones risking a sore throat from singing too loud. The flip, on the other hand, is crazed and vibrant, albeit a little too casual to be a classic. With Jeff Beck on guitar and Paul McCartney on drums [better here] both playing like mad. [Single] **B – /B**

1969

"Penina" [Paul McCartney]

[Carlos Mendes] Named after a Portuguese hotel, "Penina" took about as long to write as it does to say. Based on a standard 1950s chord sequence, the flabby melody barely has the strength to be sung. Carlos Mendes, a Portuguese singer and TV actor, took it straight to the bottom. [*The Songs Lennon and McCartney Gave Away*] **F**

"Come and Get It" [Paul McCartney; Producer: Paul McCartney]

[Badfinger] On a break in the recording of *Abbey Road*, McCartney whipped out all the parts of this demo, which he gave to new Apple band Badfinger with instructions to copy the demo exactly. They did. It landed at #5 in the UK and #7 in the US, a spectacular and surprising showing. Part of Badfinger's debut *Magic Christian Music*, "Come and Get It" features a satisfactory hook and does indeed sound like a McCartney piece, much to Badfinger's dismay. [McCartney: *Anthology 3*; Badfinger: *Magic Christian Music*.] **B**

"Rock of All Ages" [Pete Ham, Tom Evans, and Mike Gibbons"/ "Maybe Tomorrow" [Pete Ham and Tom Evans] [co-producer: Paul McCartney with Mal Evans; guest performer on "Rock of All Ages": Paul McCartney]

[Badfinger] Two more songs from *Magic Christian Music* with McCartney at the helm. "Rock of All Ages" is a generic rocker, amiable but forgettable. "Maybe Tomorrow" is a sweet ballad, heavy with strings. McCartney's footprints: all but non-existent. He adds piano and background vocals to "Rock of All Ages," which don't amount to much. ["Rock of All Ages" **B –** ; "Maybe Tomorrow" **B**; *Magic Christian Music*]

"Goodbye" [John Lennon and Paul McCartney; producer: Paul McCartney]

[Mary Hopkin] A low-key, pleasant track composed by McCartney, who also added bass and knee slapping while Hopkin provided an engaging but distracted vocal. "Goodbye" is a fond farewell from a lover taking a trip to a not-to-be named locale. An inventive verse goes to sleep on the blah chorus, the track's downfall. Best guess is that McCartney knocked this off in a hurry and that Hopkin, who preferred the older-style "Those Were the Days," wasn't crazy about it. ["Goodbye" single] **B**

"Sparrow" [Graham Lyle and Benny Gallagher; producer and guest performer: Paul McCartney]

[Mary Hopkin] A Hopkin favourite, highlighted by chimes and a choir with a sax sneaking in near the end. Not exactly Top 40 material, but hardly embarrassing. Gallagher and Lyle, signed to Apple Records as songwriters, would go on to better things with the group McGuinness Flint in 1970, but for now polished their chops on the odd Hopkin track, like "International," the gorgeous opener to Hopkin's second Apple album *Earth Song/Ocean Song*. [Single B-side] **B**

"Que Sera Sera" [Jay Livingston and Ray Evans; producer and guest performer: Paul McCartney]

[Mary Hopkin] Nostalgia nut McCartney wanted Hopkin to do this favourite of the false teeth crowd, but Hopkin flatly – and wisely – refused. McCartney put his foot down, Hopkin put her foot down, but since McCartney's foot was bigger, he won. Besides, he knew what'd work, and she didn't, right? Wrong. It managed a dismal #77 in the US. That's Ringo on drums, Paul on essentially everything else. ["Que Sera Sera" single] **C**

"Fields of St. Etienne" [Graham Lyle and Benny Gallagher; producer and guest performer: Paul McCartney]

[Mary Hopkin] Anti-war, always good to hear. Hopkin had been groping for a comfortable style after "Those Were the Days," but with "Fields" she's getting close to a nice fit: melancholy old-fashioned folk songs updated with interesting chording. Paul played some gentle guitar on this, but apparently had one foot out the door as *Abbey Road* was calling his name. [Single B-side] **B**

"Sour Milk Sea" [Jackie Lomax; guest performer: Paul McCartney]

[Jackie Lomax] In pre-production for the Beatles *White Album* [1968], George Harrison submitted several songs that fell by the wayside, among them "Not Guilty," "Circles," and this one, a rousing rocker that should've replaced the un-funny "Piggies." Harrison, producer of Lomax's first Apple album, resurrected it and rounded up an all-star band to record it, including himself, Ringo Starr, Eric Clapton, and on bass, Paul McCartney. That they played the hell out of it is no surprise, but the hero is Lomax himself, who belted it out with a ferocity that matched Joe Cocker and Steve Winwood. Incredibly, the single managed only #145 on the US chart. **B+**

"Thumbin' a Ride" [Jackie Lomax; producer: Paul McCartney]

McCartney helped Lomax with this toss-off for an American single release. Unspectacular, with neither man fully engaged and mainly interested in getting it over. A light soul-ish track destined to vanish. [Single B-side] **C**

"We Love You" [Mick Jagger and Keith Richards; guest performer: Paul McCartney]

[Rolling Stones] Recorded during *Their Satanic Majesties Request* and inexplicably left off the final album, "We Love You" was a reaction to the drug arrest of Jagger and Richards and the outrageous penalty imposed on their conviction. This is a thrilling performance from the Stones at their best, from the clang of prison bars to the controlled chaos in the coda. It's powerful, funny in spots, and features one of the most sizzling piano riffs in rock. Lennon and McCartney, fully supporting Jagger and Richards, agreed to sing on the chorus. If you strain a bit, you can hear them wailing away. [*The Complete Singles Collection: The London Years*] **A**

"My Dark Hour" [Steve Miller; guest performer: Paul McCartney]

[Steve Miller Band] McCartney had a hissy fit over a legal argument with Lennon, Harrison, and Starr, and the trio stomped away, leaving McCartney alone in the studio. Who should wander by but American bluesman Steve Miller, who invited McCartney to blow off steam by sitting in on a jam. "My Dark Hour" emerged from this session, with McCartney beating the hell out of the drums, also adding guitar, bass, and backup vocals. It's competent laid-back blues rock, typical for Miller. McCartney does an adequate job. [*Brave New World*] **B**

"Celebration Song" [Steve Miller and Ben Sidran; guest performer: Paul McCartney]

A shade lighter than "My Dark Hour," with McCartney guesting on backup vocals. Unimpressive. **B**

"Vegetables" [Brian Wilson and Van Dyke Parks; guest performer: Paul McCartney]

[Beach Boys] Brian Wilson, tragically, gave up on the breakthrough *Smile* album, of which "Vegetables" was a component. But for a time, *Smile* was chugging along at full speed. McCartney, a fan, was hanging around at the time, and inevitably was given permission to participate. He did, but neither as a singer nor an instrumentalist. Instead, he chewed carrots [and possibly celery] as a percussive effect. Possibly the finest version of carrot chewing on record. [*Smile Sessions*] **B**

"Rosetta" [Earl Hines and William Henri and Woode; guest performer: Paul McCartney]

[The Fourmost] Still hanging in there, the Fourmost gratefully accepted McCartney's suggestion that they record this 1930's Earl Hines creaker, plus he offered to play piano. A deal hard to refuse. Not half-bad, reminiscent of the New Vaudeville Band's "Winchester Cathedral," only less corny. Now you know where McCartney's whispered "Rosetta" on the Beatles "Get Back" [album version] might have come from. [Single] **B**

"Give Peace a Chance" [John Lennon and Paul McCartney]

[Plastic Ono Band] Recorded on second rate equipment, the primary vocalist in bed and surrounded by celebrities and regular folk, all of whom were thrilled to be part of an actual recording session with an actual Beatle. Lennon's simple plea for peace, little more than a 4-bar chorus and a couple of acoustic guitars, rose to a remarkable #2 in the UK charts [#14 in the US] and became an anthem for the Vietnam-hating generation, which basically meant everyone under 30 and more than a few beyond. McCartney isn't present, but his name is emblazoned on the writers' credits. Lennon later declared that McCartney had nothing to do with it, implying that he added Paul's name as sort of a favour or a thank you [or something]. McCartney performed "Give Peace a Chance" in his 1990 tour along with "Help" and "Strawberry Fields Forever." **B+**

Unreleased: Rumours and Uncertainties

Rumoured Lennon-McCartney songs that were never recorded by them or anybody else continue to persist. Some are verified, sort of, by McCartney, others exist as brief fragments, often little more than a sung title. Though there's no hard evidence that any of these mystery songs exist, that's not to say that McCartney might suddenly remember one or two [it happened with Unplugged's *"I Lost My Little Girl"]. And there's his legendary notebook from the pre-Beatle days containing who knows how many Lennon-McCartneys.*

Titles lacking references mean that legitimate, verifiable sources are too vague or are next to impossible to find. Bootlegs don't count.

"Calypso Rock," "My Love is Like a Bird," "Thinking of Linking," "Just Fun," "Too Bad About Sorrows" [the previous three briefly heard during the sessions for Get Back, *which eventually morphed into* Let It Be*], "That's My Woman," "Fancy Me Chances," "Because I Know," "That's My Woman," "Winston's Walk," "Looking Glass," "Well Darling," "Some Days," "Write Every Day," "Years Roll Along," "I Don't Know," "Keep Looking That Way," "Fallen For Someone," "Falling In Love Again," "Tell Me If You Can," "Pinwheel Twist," "Won't You Please Say Goodbye," "My Little Book," "I'll Wait Till Tomorrow," and "Now and Then" [an attempted but abandoned Lennon song, part of the* Anthology *sessions that produced "Free as a Bird" and "Real Love"].*

CHAPTER ONE:

THE FAMILY WAY [1967]

Produced by George Martin
Did not chart [US], did not chart [UK]

In November 1968, the soundtrack for *Wonderwall*, composed and produced by George Harrison, was released in the UK. Recruiting musicians as varied as Eric Clapton and Peter Tork [of the Monkees] and utilizing first-class studios from London to Bombay, Harrison took the production seriously and worked on it like a man possessed. The all-instrumental album, a meticulous 19 tracks of Harrison-composed Indian and Western music, was Beatle-worthy, all of it listenable, some surprisingly good ["Red Lady Too" and "Party Seacombe" are standouts]. Though the movie was so-so, *Wonderwall Music* was impressive, one that holds up today, some fifty years later.

Back in January, 1967, the soundtrack for *The Family Way*, composed by Paul McCartney, was released in the UK. This project was approached more casually.

A few months earlier, Beatles producer George Martin had been approached by the creators of the forthcoming *The Family Way* film for soundtrack music, which he agreed to do. He was pretty sure that McCartney would jump at the chance to become involved as well. Martin approached McCartney with the project, only to be confronted with a superstar whose initial interest bordered on the indifferent. Martin pleaded with McCartney to contribute something, anything to the film, a black and white soap opera starring Hayley Mills who'd recently appeared in *That Darn Cat*.

Ultimately, McCartney relented. He knocked off a brief theme lasting less than 30 seconds. Declaring himself finished, McCartney returned to planning *Sgt. Pepper* or watching television or whatever else he was doing.

A short time later, Martin returned to McCartney, saying that *The Family Way* folks wondered if he could contribute something else to be used in the movie's love scene. A song maybe? Anything? Again, McCartney resisted, but in the end, agreed. He spontaneously knocked off another brief fragment, gave it to Martin, then turned his attention to other projects. And, a tribute to his skill, McCartney's themes were reasonably satisfying and betraying not a bit of his limited interest in the film.

Still, the themes were frustratingly short. In its original format, *The Family Way* soundtrack existed as a 45 rpm single with one theme on each side. But reportedly, the record company knew a good thing when it was staring them in the face and coaxed Martin into handling an expansion. Sensing that McCartney was indeed finished with *The Family Way*, Martin labored – with occasional doses of McCartney's assistance – to expand, develop, and arrange McCartney's two miniscule chunks of music. McCartney's brief themes were stretched and squeezed into every permutation Martin could think of, resulting in an album that runs about 25 minutes. [The 2011 reissue is longer, but fundamentally the same.]

"Theme from the Family Way [and Variants]" [Paul McCartney]
[George Martin Orchestra] A grandiose brass band, reminiscent of the instrumental break in the opening track of *Sgt. Pepper*, meanders here and there long after the listener gets the message. George Martin does what he can with not very much. Dated and quaint. **B-**

"Love in the Open Air [and Variants]" [Paul McCartney]
[George Martin Orchestra] Amazingly, considering how little effort the composer gave to its creation, McCartney's off-the-cuff "Love in the Open Air" is a haunting, melancholy theme reminiscent of the Beatles' "She's Leaving Home." Approximately 16 bars with no lyrics or much of anything else beyond the

melody line itself, arranger George Martin had his hands full, and the resulting album felt bloated and overcooked. With luck, the single might turn up at a yard sale near you. **B+**

CHAPTER TWO:

McCARTNEY [1970]

Produced by Paul McCartney
Charted at 1 [US], 2 [UK]

Why a full-length album from an emotionally wounded artist who didn't seem up to it? Why not an EP? Short for Extended Play, an EP looks like an album, but contains about half the music. EPs been used successfully by a diverse collection of artists – Prince, Elvis Presley, Cheap Trick, even the Beatles [*Beatles Hits*, 1963] – and was made to order for McCartney, who at the start of his solo career had plenty of talent but a shortage of songs and an attitude that probably wasn't sufficiently healthy for the focus an album requires. The obvious solution: jettison the five [!] instrumentals and a couple of also-rans [like "Teddy Boy"]. You've got yourself an EP.

But perhaps McCartney wasn't in the mood to contemplate alternative formats. When the Beatles collapsed, a devastated Paul trudged off to the wilds of Scotland, taking up residence in a remote rural cottage to settle in for endless, dreary weeks of brooding, sleeping, and drinking, wondering what to do, coming up empty, then crawling back to bed.

With him was the long-suffering Linda, who was running out of patience for her glazed, semi-comatose husband. This was not pleasant. This could not continue. She pleaded, reasoned, and coaxed, but Paul ignored her. It was like talking to mud.

But Linda persevered, and eventually, her urgings won the day. McCartney began to show signs of life, emerging from his grimy sheets in his dirty shirt and scraggly beard. Slowly but determinedly, Linda re-introduced her dazed husband to his tape recorder, a 4-track Studer, which could be, *had* to be the key to recovery.

Uncertain at first, McCartney's self-pity began to fade to a manageable level as he tentatively, then more confidently, started to fool around with the Studer, a reasonably sophisticated machine similar to the tape recorders used on *Sgt. Pepper*. He had no mixer and only a single microphone, but he adapted to his equipment's limitations, knocking off ditties like "The Lovely Linda" just like he did on *Abbey Road* fragments, not that long ago.

It gradually dawned on him that next to the Beatles, he now had the perfect band: himself. Maybe he wasn't, for instance, the greatest drummer in the world, but he was good enough. Nobody could tell him what to do or how to do it. And didn't he record "Wild Honey Pie" all by himself? He did it once, he could do it again.

With a bundle of half-finished experiments under his belt, McCartney was off to suburban Morgan Studios, then the familiar Abbey Road Studios, both of them professional and comfortable facilities, where he polished off his recovery project, not acknowledging – or caring – that his legendary propensity for dreaming up new songs in an instant had temporarily abandoned him. In the meantime, there were enough of his old songs that had been rejected or mocked by the Beatles that he could share with a curious world.

McCartney, as is his nature, buried himself in work. The album was completed quickly. The might-have-been EP? Lost forever in the mists of time.

"The Lovely Linda" [Paul McCartney]

Back in the Beatles days, Lennon and McCartney developed an effective way of working, where one of them composed the verse, the other tackling the middle eight [or bridge]. "We Can Work It Out," "And

I Love Her," and "Michelle" were among the classics employing this deceptively simple technique. But with Lennon now gone, McCartney had no partner to help him finish songs that clearly needed another element. His solution: he had no solution. Songs in need of a middle eight section didn't get them, and the verses stood or fell on their own. "Lovely Linda" badly needs something other than its simple verse, because as it stands, it's a forgettable snippet instead of a complete composition. And what's with that irritating giggle near the end? Haven't we heard that before? Yes we have, on the bargain basement "Maxwell's Silver Hammer" from *Abbey Road*. **C**

"That Would Be Something" [Paul McCartney]
A promising instrumental intro that loses its promise when the critical listener realizes how little there is to it. McCartney's charming vocal redeems it somewhat, but doesn't compensate for the lack of substance. It begs on its melodic knees for a middle eight [see the previous "The Lovely Linda"] but help is not on the way. **B-**

"Valentine Day" [Paul McCartney]
The first of five instrumentals, each one as crappy the next. The dull melody doesn't even work as a guitar exercise. And using an amateur drum track doesn't mean you're kind of adorable. It means you're kind of arrogant. **D**

"Every Night" [Paul McCartney]
During the Beatles reign, gonad-less tunes like "Maxwell's Silver Hammer" and "Ob-La-Di Ob-La-Da" were easier to swallow when scorchers like "Happiness is a Warm Gun" and "I Want You [She's So Heavy]" were right around the corner. Alas, on this album – and basically for the rest of his career – testicles are too often on vacation. The listener must adjust his or her expectations – no balancing heft from a "Happiness is a Warm Gun" – and weigh the songs accordingly. So "Every Night" stands as a strongly melodic piece, one of the best on *McCartney*, but deprived of a "Happiness is a Warm Gun" to harden it up, it deflates pretty fast. The better-than-average lyrics focus on his real life problems of Beatles-induced restlessness and agoraphobia. This is the only song on the album that attempts to face these personal problems, though it's telling there's nothing here, even a hint, about his drinking. Although his reference to wanting distance from his troubled brain comes close. **B**

"Hot as Sun" [Paul McCartney]
This one is revived from the pre-Beatle days. Why McCartney thought it was worth digging up is a mystery, other than a need for filler to avoid an EP. A bland instrumental playable by middle-schoolers, with amateur lead guitar by somebody you'd never suspect of being one of earth's premier performers. Rather than a warm summer day in the Bahamas, as this title suggests, it instead evokes a rattling air conditioner in a Motel 6. Incredibly, McCartney included this for a while in his live set lists. Careful, buddy. The patience of Beatle fans only goes so far. **D**

"Glasses" [Paul McCartney]
A few seconds of noise, created by running a finger around the rim of a wet glass of water. You can duplicate this yourself in your own kitchen. When McCartney claims responsibility for coming up with avant garde touches on Beatles records ["Tomorrow Never Knows"], is this what he's talking about? **F**

"Junk" [Paul McCartney]
Another Beatles throwaway, this one from the *White Album* [and available as a demo on *Anthology 3*]. A dreamy tune, but one lacking the strong hook necessary to make it memorable. Still, McCartney performs it tastefully, with soothing acoustic guitars and psychedelic imagery to spare. The musical equivalent of an ice cream cone, sweet, melting, then gone. **B**

"Man We Was Lonely" [Paul McCartney]
A catchy verse, a ho-hum chorus, and wife Linda wrestling with a simple harmony. And the awkwardly titled "Man We Was Lonely" sports the usual inane, grammar-free lyric. Too slight for someone of McCartney's stature, but in the context of his first solo release, you take what you can get. And what you get is a pseudo country chorus coupled with a promising but underdone bridge. Also covered by Davy Jones, lead cutie of the Monkees. **B-**

"Oo You" [Paul McCartney]

This is more like it. McCartney leaves the Beatles behind, sends middle-of-the-roaders to their room, and proceeds to channel Count Five. Every note – the vocals, guitar, everything – screams "garage," and for lovers of "96 Tears" [Question Mark and the Mysterians] this is a ticket to heaven. The opening riff crushes its garage competition, and McCartney's casual, snotty vocal finishes them off. For once, the sloppy drums provide a perfect accompaniment to the go-for-broke performance. Who'd have thought McCartney had it in him? And imagine this: wouldn't it have been awesome if he'd set aside *Kisses on the Bottom* [the old folks' music box], and instead had given us a whole album of garage band tunes? **B+**

"Momma Miss America" [Paul McCartney]

A demo of a demo. **D-**

"Teddy Boy" [Paul McCartney]

This began as an offering to the Beatles to beef up *Get Back* [the album that became *Let It Be*]. A version appears on *Anthology 3*, with a snarky John Lennon adding hillbilly square dance calls near the end. Why did Lennon do this? Could it be that "Teddy Boy," with its clumsy rhymes, jerky rhythms, and nursery school melody, had about as much chance of becoming a Beatles song as "She'll Be Coming Round the Mountain"? Not one to let a song die, McCartney resurrected it, with his Beatles arrangement more or less intact. Interesting, that in his seemingly endless tour schedule which found him performing virtually everything his catalogue – including "Bip Bop" and "Mary Had a Little Lamb" – he's never found room for "Teddy Boy." **C+**

"Singalong Junk" [Paul McCartney]

If McCartney was in need of material, as he clearly was, why not go back to the Beatle days, by-pass the rejected ["Teddy Boy"], and revive some of the tunes the band never got around to completing? "I Lost My Little Girl" and "Back Seat of My Car" were attempted and abandoned during the *Get Back* sessions, and either one would have been preferable to the instrumental version of a song we heard a few minutes ago. What's different about this? How about the xylophone plinks? How about we don't do this? **C**

"Maybe I'm Amazed" [Paul McCartney]

A brilliant composition with a stellar performance, his best ever. It's a marvel it turns up on an album as spotty as *McCartney*. But here it is, an exquisite masterwork about McCartney's desperate love for his wife. The soaring melody rivals "She's Leaving Home," "Hey Jude," and virtually anything he came up with for the Beatles. With beautiful, stunning vocals, McCartney shifts effortlessly between sorrowful hushes and raging loneliness. And this time, playing everything himself adds a touch of winsome amateurishness that makes the piece all the more unforgettable. Best moment: the bridge, where McCartney's voice rises higher and higher to notes he can barely reach, climaxing in a hopeless plea of anguish. This is the same guy who did "Momma Miss America?" I can't believe it either. **A**

"Kreen-Akore" [Paul McCartney]

Let's see. How to end this album? How about some filler? Better yet, how about a drum solo? By an amateur drummer? Begin with a snare performed by a lazy novice who's skipped his drum lessons. A few guitar strums, followed more tedious drumming, this time with a labored roll or two. Then, settle in for a dull rhythm pattern that doesn't really go on all day, it just seems like it. The piece gets its name from the Kreen-Akore Indians of Brazil, a tribe who stays hidden from the world. That is, until they arrive to beat the hell out of the guy who dreamed this up. **F**

[bonus]

"Suicide" [Paul McCartney]

Wouldn't you know that a song called "Suicide" is the song that can't be killed, attempted by McCartney at least four times over the years, most famously during the *Get Back* album sessions where it was presumably laughed out of the room. In 1974, McCartney submitted it to Frank Sinatra, whose response was basically, "Is he kidding?" before it was flatly rejected. Here, accompanied only by his own piano, McCartney croons away, using his lounge lizard voice for this finger poppin' tune that tells a story about a poor woman trapped in a destructive relationship, who sees no way out other than snuffing her own life. A breezy song with you-gotta-be-kidding me lyrics. [*McCartney Bonus*] **B-**

"Maybe I'm Amazed [One Hand Clapping]" [Paul McCartney]

One Hand Clapping was a barely seen TV documentary allegedly about a sanitized Wings, but the focus clearly was on McCartney, performing songs like "My Love," "Live and Let Die," and this one, employing an electric piano, way too much echo, and an off-key background singer [I'm looking at you, Linda]. Slipshod, unengaged, and in need of more rehearsal, "Maybe I'm Amazed" is inferior in about every way to the studio version, although a great song is tough to kill. [*McCartney Bonus*] **B**

"Every Night [Live 1979]" [Paul McCartney]

More suited to a parlor room than a concert hall, "Every Night" was doomed to failure in this venue, as it's aimed at an audience preferring "Hi Hi Hi" to intimacy. McCartney, probably sensing this, hesitates as he plays it, puzzled, perhaps, why the crowd has trouble responding. [*McCartney Bonus*] **B-**

"Hot as Sun" [Live 1979] [Paul McCartney]

Does anyone outside of the hardest of hardcore Beatlemaniacs think a live "Hot as Sun" is a fantastic idea? A fair idea? An idea? [*McCartney Bonus*] **F**

"Maybe I'm Amazed [Live 1979]" [Paul McCartney]

Better than *One Hand Clapping*, but McCartney's mind is elsewhere, possibly on his worsening throat which makes one wonder if he'll hit the troublesome high notes [he does, kind of]. The scat singing sounds forced, the piano trill is pointless, and McCartney tries hard to sell it. Luckily, it sells itself [*McCartney Bonus*] **B+**

"Don't Cry Baby" [Paul McCartney]

In a spoken word intro, McCartney tries to soothe his baby with the promise of a song. The baby cries, fearing it's "Bip Bop." Instead, it's essentially a useless version of an instrumental "Oo You," boring the baby to sleep. [*McCartney Bonus*] **B-**

"Woman Kind" [Paul McCartney]

Maybe he's just fooling around, but he's offering it up as a real tune, so he's asking for it. "Puerile" is too kind. If he claimed a preschool kid wrote this, it'd still flunk. Additionally, "Women Kind" treats us to a selection of McCartney's goofy and exasperating voices, resulting in an extra-goofy and exasperating mess. **D**

"Stardust" [Hoagy Carmichael and Mitchell Parish; arranger: Paul McCartney]

[Ringo Starr] So McCartney arranged the orchestra? A guy who can neither read nor write music? What'd he do, hum it? Anyway, Ringo sings it, sort of, in the style of Frank Sinatra, sort of. This from a guy who could barely make it through "A Little Help from My Friends"? Can you say "vanity project"? [*Sentimental Journey*] **D-**

CHAPTER THREE:

RAM [1971]

Produced by Paul and Linda McCartney
Charted at 2 [US], 1 [UK]

Though *McCartney* sold like crazy, critics were not impressed, dismissing it as a disengaged collection of Beatles rejects and sloppy instrumentals, light years away from "Hey Jude" and "Golden Slumbers" which appeared a mere handful of months ago. McCartney couldn't have been pleased. But deep down, he had to realize that *McCartney* didn't represent his best work.

Still, that was then. Gone would be half-realized tunes. Gone would be homemade productions from a homemade studio. Gone would be all the vocal-less clutter. The new album would require all the Beatles magic he could muster.

The songs came tumbling in an avalanche, twice as many as he'd ultimately use, but they supplied a range of options from which he could skim the cream. The songs covered a variety of styles – whimsical, sentimental, melancholy, not unlike his Beatles work. All new, complete with lyrics and melodies, ready to record. And yes, there were a *lot* of them, by some counts well over two dozen.

He considered musicians, who they'd be, where he could find them. This time out, he'd draw from a pool of the planet's top session players, any of whom, presumably, would jump at the chance to work with a musician of McCartney's stature.

Only there wasn't much jumping. As McCartney hadn't had much experience with recruiting musicians for his own album, he was more or less feeling his way in the dark, auditioning candidates in a New York basement, occasionally using, for reasons unknown, broken-down equipment. Fortunately, because he was fishing in a professional pond, McCartney ended up with pretty good choices: David Spinozza [guitarist who worked with Herbie Mann and David Sanborn], Denny Seiwell [drummer, worked with Liza Minnelli and Billy Joel], and Hugh McCracken [guitarist who replaced Spinozza midway through the sessions when summoned elsewhere; McCracken was guitarist for James Taylor].

Next, the actual recording, which would no longer include his living room, but instead would utilize state-of-the-art locations such as A&R Studios in New York and Sound Recorders Studio in Los Angeles. As money was no object, McCartney took whatever time a particular song required, at one point hiring the New York Philharmonic Orchestra for overdubs. All told, with vacations here and there, *Ram* took about five months to wrap up.

Satisfied at last that he'd created his *piece de resistance*, McCartney unleashed *Ram* to an expectant world, a world willing to set aside *McCartney* as an ill-conceived experiment. And initially, the reaction was positive. Fans gobbled it up, awarding it a platinum status in the US.

Critics, however, were not so kind, almost universally awarding *Ram* with a thumbs- down – *way* down. They hated it, thoroughly, with all the venom they could muster. Robert Christgau, arguably the genre's most respected critic, called it "a major annoyance." *Rolling Stone*'s Jon Landau, the eventual manager of Bruce Springsteen, called it "incredibly inconsequential." Though opinion has softened somewhat over the years, in 1971 the critical verdict was in, and it was incontrovertible: *Ram*, the product of a Beatle with all his Beatle jets blasting away, was a dog.

"Too Many People" [Paul McCartney]
A mall-friendly opening, followed by a flat verse with the melody dutifully following the major chords, leads to a catchy middle eight, then back to the so-so verse. In other words, McCartney came up with a

solid half of a song, leaving the rest to a co-composer who wasn't there. "Too Many People" makes a case for having a respected partner that – just as he'd had for his entire career to date – could provide lyrical feedback and melody suggestions to make his song stronger. And Lennon was clearly on McCartney's mind, as "Too Many People" scolds the big bully for being a nag, whining about how John shouldn't have done – sniff, sniff – what he did. An uneasy preview of disappointments to come. **B**

"3 Legs" [Paul McCartney]
Judging from his music, this is a guy who's rarely felt blue, ever. McCartney merrily sings about swallowing flies and an amputee puppy, all of it nonsense. Some Beatle detectives have wondered if McCartney's commenting abstractly about the Beatles breakup – a trio of limbs, the fourth limb gone – but that's not only stretching it, but gives the author more credit than he deserves. Musically, we're in routine territory, with McCartney whacking away on three chords while his long-suffering wife chimes in on the chorus. A preliminary *Wild Life*? Gulp. **D –**

"Ram On" [Paul McCartney]
Opening with a surprising ukulele, this goes psychedelic in a hurry: a muted kick drum, spooky background vocals, weird reverb, and a plea from a soothing McCartney to love everyone you see. Then it's over. Half done and a shame, as this deserved to be developed into a real verse-and-chorus song. Instead, a truncated verse, then bye bye. **B**

"Dear Boy" [Paul and Linda McCartney]
The surprise addition of Linda McCartney as a co-composer might have surprised her too. A second writer didn't help much here, as its amicable melody is buried in piles of vocal sludge, a hint that an insecure producer didn't know when to quit. If the vocal snowstorm had been shoveled away, a small but pleasant tune would've been found underneath. But that didn't happen. **B-**

"Uncle Albert/Admiral Halsey" [Paul and Linda McCartney]
McCartney paid attention during the recording of Lennon's "Happiness is a Warm Gun" [*White Album*] where fragments of several incomplete songs were knitted together to form a whole. Under McCartney's supervision, the concept was blown up to nearly a full album side in *Abbey Road*, a 16-minute medley hailed by fans and critics as a masterpiece. Seizing on the medley idea, McCartney tried it again on *Ram*, more modest this time, coming up with a shorter, lighter, and unashamedly silly piece with vague seagoing images and bathing instructions. Even though it requires the listener to swallow indigestible words, it's hard to resist, since McCartney employs strong melodies throughout, making the nursery rhyming forgivable. McCartney's never performed this live. Strange, as this #1 hit is a sure-fire crowd pleaser, meatier than "Til There Was You" or "All Together Now," which he plays every now and then. **B**

"Smile Away" [Paul McCartney]
A throwaway rocker with clever backup vocals [by Munchkins?] spoiled by a cutesy pie McCartney raving about body odor. I like ridiculous lyrics as much as the next lunatic. But there's ridiculous, then there's stupid. **D+**

"Heart of the Country" [Paul and Linda McCartney]
I'm not sure McCartney makes a convincing farmer, but here he is, extolling the virtues of the great outdoors. The song screams filler, cheery and thought-free, and the yodel at the end of the chorus sounds like Roger Miller's "Dang Me." Hey Paul – if you really want a peaceful snooze, you might rent a room at the Hilton. Or if you prefer, you can buy the building. **C**

"Monkberry Moon Delight" [Paul and Linda McCartney]
I guess this is about milk, but I prefer to believe it's McCartney's LSD song. Although drugs aren't mentioned [neither is getting high], he does touch on shoving instruments up his nostrils, a storm playing scary songs, and an angry vegetable that makes creepy sounds. He pounds the piano like a maniac and sings like a deranged mental patient, both encouraging signs for a don't-rock-the-boat star. A simple melody, catchy and fun, and McCartney lights up for five full minutes [two minutes too long]. By the way, on the last verse, does he mention a pair of guys puffing on their Monkberry hookahs? **B**

"Eat at Home" [Paul and Linda McCartney]

A nifty riff opens to a tight 50s-influenced rock tune, seasoned with subtle *double entendre* word play. This pleasant Buddy Holly-influenced song buzzes along nicely until the middle section, which climaxes with a surprising and terrific four-bar trill, rocketing the tune into Beatle nirvana. This, like "Smile Away," is basically brain-free, except one is clever and the other is dumb. **B+**

"Long Haired Lady" [Paul and Linda McCartney]

Tied with "3 Legs" and "Smile Away" for the worst song on the album. A tedious paean to his wife, "Long Haired Lady" features a prominent Linda [on vocals, by herself], nearly six minutes of top-of-his-head orchestrations, a coda that never ends, and precious husband and wife mannerisms in need of a nausea shot. Could it have been saved? Yes, provided it also had new lyrics, new backings, new melodies, and cut in half. In other words, if it had been "Oh Woman Oh Why." **D**

"Ram On [Reprise]" [Paul McCartney]

Heavy on bizarre – but not too bizarre – noises at the expense of a melody, meaning it serves better as an introduction to "Back Seat of My Car" than a stand-alone piece. A half-baked idea that could have been better if McCartney had exerted some effort instead of just fiddling with effects. A bonus that almost but not quite saves it: a brief preview at the end of "Big Barn Bed," coming soon on *Red Rose Speedway*. **B-**

"Back Seat of My Car" [Paul McCartney]

A lush heartbreaker, masterfully sung by an unusually passionate McCartney. Compare this to, say, "My Love," a shameless bid for the Top 40 where he sounds like he's singing into a mirror. Here he means business, smartly capturing the angst of teenagers groping each other in the back seat, trivial to others, but life-and-death to them. The music alternately sweeps from the subtle to the grandiose, avoiding schmaltz but touching on melodrama exactly where it's appropriate. "Back Seat of My Car" was by-passed way back when during the *Get Back* sessions. Bad call, Beatles. **A**

[bonus]

"Another Day" [Paul and Linda McCartney]

McCartney's first post-Beatles single echoes his former group's style, what with its sharp production and well-chosen special effects, such as the squawking birds. But it's not hard to see why the Beatles passed it up during the *Get Back* sessions. With a static opening – the first few bars ride the same note – the song lacks the strong melody of "Two of Us" or "The Long and Winding Road" and fails to really take off until the middle eight. Lyrically, it recalls the superior "Eleanor Rigby," not a good idea. Instead of "Eleanor"'s stark imagery and original setting, "Another Day" relates the tired tale of a forlorn secretary who longs for a noble man to whisk her away, thus solving her problems. Not exactly a feminist anthem. [*Ram Remaster*] **B**

"Oh Woman Oh Why" [Paul McCartney]

The blood brother of *McCartney*'s "Oo You." More garage-y rock from a guy who didn't seem to care much for that style during the Beatles. But McCartney demonstrates an easy aptitude for the grungy side. The listener pines for more, much more of this approach – guitar and drums banging away, a sneering nut on vocals, a gun shot out of "Hey Joe" – that could've been used to liven up *Ram*. [*Ram Remaster*.] **B+**

"Little Woman Love" [Paul and Linda McCartney]

The flipside of "Mary Had a Little Lamb," McCartney tickles the ivories while wailing away about how about how good a fit his lover is. This is filler, through and through, despite the spot-on band performance and McCartney's candy cane vocals. He probably tossed it together because he got a kick out of that irritating piano riff. If so, is that a definition of inspiration? Or an excuse for fluff? [*Special Edition Ram*] **C**

"A Love for You" [Paul McCartney]

An up-tempo winner that "Smile Away" could never be, not with a hundred Pauls playing a hundred guitars for a hundred hours. With a from-the-gut twang, McCartney rocks his way through this like a swaggering 20 year old. Crisp guitars, enthusiastic background voices, and as catchy as the flu. It also sounds a bit under-produced, which, compared to the insecure instrumental layers ladled on *Ram*, is a plus. [*Special Edition Ram*] **B+**

"Hey Diddle" [Paul and Linda McCartney]

From the sublime [*A Love for You*] to the horrible. A nursery rhyme from a place where nursery rhymes are used as torture. If it was for his kids, I'm sure they don't want to hear a note of it again, ever, a reaction shared by his pet sheep. A speck worse than "Mary Had a Little Lamb" or [shudder] "Bip Bop," it makes my diddle ache. [*Special Edition Ram*] **F**

"When the Wind is Blowing" [Paul McCartney]

A cluster of atmospheric chords pillows a haunting lyric-less melody, a thoughtful and unique construction that McCartney would do well to display on an album as desperate for material as, say, *Wild Life*. This reminds us, again, that McCartney is indeed a one-of-a-kind composer when he forgoes laziness and whatever it is that possesses him to barf up something as asinine as "Bip Bop." [*Ram Archive Edition*.] **B+**

"The Great Cock and Seagull Race" [Paul McCartney]

From "Blackbird" to "Another Day" to this – McCartney really likes to hear those birdies sing. Chirping turns out the be the most appealing part of "Great Cock," what with its all-too-familiar Chuck Berry lines, and a jam that ran of ideas an hour ago. In other words, it's filler. I bet those birds are turkeys. [Also known as "Rooster."] [*Ram Archive Edition*] **D**

"Complain to the Queen" [Paul McCartney]

Bluesy, inane fragment of a backstage improv in Amsterdam. Doubtful if McCartney was too interested in releasing this, but considering "Bip Bop," you never know. [Internet Only] **D**

"Uncle Albert Jam" [Paul McCartney]

The near-rockabilly jam extract by McCartney, Hugh McCracken, and Denny Seiwell makes the studio cut sound turgid by comparison. Although to be fair, it's much too sloppy to be taken seriously. Listen once, chuckle, forget it. [*iTunes*] **B-**

"Rode All Night" [Paul McCartney]

A chunky upbeat guitar showcases "A Love for You," a much superior tune buried in this mess where the musicians don't appear to have a clue as to what's going on. McCartney mumbles a few lyrics, the guitar is briefly energized before petering out, and McCartney gropes for a feel that never comes. But he presses on, curious if this will blossom into a genuine song. It barely blossoms into a jam. If this is meant to demonstrate where songs come from, we get the picture in the first 30 seconds. But it keeps going. And going. And going. [*Ram Archive Edition*] **D**

"Sunshine Sometime" [Paul McCartney]

This combines elements of "When the Wind Blows" and the Beatles' "I Will," a surefire formula for success in McCartney's skilled hands. A soothing bossa nova that should have been included on *Ram* with "A Love for You" and "When the Wind Blows" in place of "Long Haired Lady," "3 Legs," and "Smile Away." [*Ram Archive Edition*] **B**

"Now Hear This Song of Mine" [Paul McCartney]

Brung To Ewe By is on an obscure disc intended as promo for radio stations, featuring over two dozen takes of "Now Hear This Song of Mine." Most of them lasted 15 seconds, a few went all the way to a minute. They're all variations of piano-driven tripe. With farm animals honking, screeching, and yowling for help. [*Brung to Ewe By*] **D**

Mono Ram

Mono records were on their way out in the sixties, owing to expanded sound possibilities from the techies and the swelling numbers of audiophiles investing in stereo equipment. But a few records, like Ram, *slipped through and pressed for mono, most of which were manufactured for radio stations. Mono versions tend to pack more of a punch – all of the elements are consolidated into one channel instead of stereo's two – but individual instruments may be harder to isolate. Since they featured the same performances, however, the differences between mono and stereo versions are minor, especially to the casual listener.*

That said, there were exceptions, with some mono versions carrying unexpected edits, brand new sections, and mysterious studio effects, all unheard in the stereo versions. Incidentally, the Beatles lay claim to first prize in mono/stereo manipulation. The lower key in "She's Leaving Home" [Sgt Pepper], the absence of ghostly voices in "Blue Jay Way" [Magical Mystery Tour], and Ringo's vanishing complaint about his blistered fingers [White Album] are just a few of the mono goodies ready to be excavated by determined listeners.

Those digging into the mono Ram *will find the entire album filled with differences, none of them major, but all of them fairly interesting. ["Heart of the Country" is omitted from the following list, as both the stereo and mono versions are essentially the same.] Owing to consumer interest, the mono version is included as part of the massive* Ram Remaster.

"Too Many People [Mono]" [Paul McCartney]
The mono "Too Many People" dials back the special effects and minimizes the harmony voices. Result: a focused, less cluttered track, with fewer instruments fighting for their share of the musical spectrum as they did in the stereo version. Mono here is cleaner and tougher, making it preferable to the official stereo. [*Ram Remaster.*] **B**

"3 Legs [Mono]" [Paul McCartney]
The mono version attempts a rescue mission by flattening the answering voices, bringing the guitar up a bit, and shortening the whole thing, but this patient can't be revived. **D**

"Ram On [Mono]" [Paul McCartney]
Psychedelia is played down in mono. A bad move, since the fewer the effects, the more the track suffers. Plus Linda's too loud. **B-**

"Dear Boy [Mono]" [Paul and Linda McCartney]
This cries out for the swamp of background vocals to be reduced by, say, 80%. It was not to be. This version cut the background by a good 40% or so, a step in the right direction, but it needed a mono engineer wielding a butcher knife. **B**

"Uncle Albert/Admiral Halsey [Mono]" [Paul and Linda McCartney]
Effects seem to be missing, taking the song's nutty swirl of sound with them. Vocals aren't as full – maybe a harmony or two has been sliced off? Less fun than stereo. **B-**

"Smile Away [Mono]" [Paul McCartney]
"Smile Away" benefits from the mix, as it's harder hitting, the guitars seem ballsier, and the Munchkin voices more in your face. Too bad about the lead vocal, which is the same old cutesy Paul. **D**

"Monkberry Moon Delight [Mono]" [Paul and Linda McCartney]
A touch of reverb creates more of a haunted house, with McCartney as the lead demon. The songs gains atmosphere, but loses detail [wasn't a tambourine in there someplace?]. A toss up; both stereo and mono are pretty good. **B**

"Eat at Home [Mono]" [Paul and Linda McCartney]
Intriguing mumbles near the beginning, maybe McCartney ordering lunch. Other than that, the entire song sounds a bit off-balance. The guitar is unnecessarily boosted a bit, and the drums are too reserved, as are the backing vocals. Stick with stereo. **B**

"Long Haired Lady [Mono]" [Paul and Linda McCartney]

What appears to be random reverb messes up the vocals here and there. Plus a sloppy edit near the end screws with the flow. A second rate song becomes third rate. **D-**

"Ram On [Reprise] [Mono]" [Paul McCartney]

A few seconds shorter than stereo. So mono is better. **B-**

"Back Seat of My Car [Mono]" [Paul McCartney]

Mono whisks away the grandeur, pushing it into more restraint, making this less than the technicolour spectacular this was meant to be. Grandeur is preferable. **B+**

CHAPTER FOUR:

WILD LIFE [1971]

Produced by Paul and Linda McCartney
Charted at 10 [US], 11 [UK]

After trying it himself on *McCartney* and flirting with session men on *Ram,* a determined McCartney at last finalized a dream he'd had in the back of his mind for a long time: a rock group that was all his. Wings – a name he dreamed up, no particular reason – included drummer Denny Seiwell, guitarist Denny Laine [formerly of the Moody Blues and famous for the hit "Go Now"] wife Linda on keyboards, and himself. Four members, just like the Beatles. Linda's keyboard skills were shaky, but McCartney was confident she'd get better.

For the most part, the shiny new group was cheery, supportive, and gung ho to hit the road. Of course, they might have been less cheery if they'd known what was coming up: travelling the back roads of London in a ramshackle bus, receiving less than stellar wages, and having to endure "Mary Had a Little Lamb" and "Bip Bop" over and over till their brains began to crack. But for now, enjoying the camaraderie and anticipating a hard-to-believe adventure with a genuine Beatle, it was all good.

First, though, an album. Still smarting from *Ram*'s critical drubbing, McCartney had decided on a new approach to making records, one that might soothe the critics without alienating his fans. Taking his cue from his hero Bob Dylan, McCartney was convinced that short and fast was the best way to capture the electric energy of music that demanded the same. For reasons unknown, McCartney by-passed the work required to generate the ton of *Ram* songs, instead starting more or less from scratch.

Following a brief rehearsal at McCartney's house, off went the band to Abbey Road Studios. They adjusted their instruments, cleared their throats, then knocked off the new tunes one after the other in a musical blur. Wings, a band that barely existed, completed the album in about a week. [*Sgt Pepper* took roughly four months.] Many of the tracks were first takes, a production rate that McCartney hadn't tried since *Please Please Me* in 1963.

Did it work? Not really. With a limited supply of fully developed songs, McCartney resorted to improvised fragments ["Mumbo"], sketchy ditties ["Wild Life"], and kiddie songs that were breathlessly awful ["Bip Bop"]. When the song list inevitably fell short, McCartney went back for a *Ram* leftover, finishing off the album with the pleasant but slight "Dear Friend." Arrangements were little more than bare bones rhythm tracks, giving the record the feel of a demo collection. Production was non-existent, with the Beatle magic of using unusual instruments and unexpected studio tricks not to be found. Plus, the songs were way too long. For example, "Wild Life" runs an excruciating 6:48, "Some People Never Know" drags on for 6:35. Did McCartney extend the tunes so he'd have to write less? Even the cover was second-rate. Wings standing in a pond?

The critics wasted no time in bringing out the nooses. *Sputnikmusic*: "Sappy and goofy." *Rolling Stone*: "vacuous, flaccid, impotent, trivial, and unaffecting." Fans headed for the hills. According to *Chart Masters*, *Wild Life* sold about 1/3 as many copies as *Ram*, an abysmal drop.

McCartney's reaction? Load up the bus and hit the road.

"Mumbo" [Paul and Linda McCartney]

Maybe it's not a good idea to open your album with an impromptu jam, heavy on what-was-that backups, groan-inducing instrumentation, a couple of major chords toggling back and forth, and a singer hollering in improvised Sanskrit. Maybe listeners will think the band isn't sure of what they're doing. Maybe they'll suspect the band has no songs. Maybe they'll think a crappy album is coming up. Maybe they'll be right. **D**

"Bip Bop" [Paul and Linda McCartney]
The musical equivalent of a spike jammed into your skull. Or maybe that's an exaggeration, giving "Bip Bop" more power than it deserves. Its aesthetic crimes are many: the melody's endless sway, back and forth, between two notes; the cloying performance; the timid and painful commentary by a superstar's wife; the teeth-grinding repetitions of nonsensical snippets. "Bip Bop" is the annoyance that keeps on giving. **F**

"Love is Strange" [Mickey Baker, Sylvia Vanderpool, Ethel Smith]
A 1956 hit by Mickey & Sylvia and a favourite of McCartney's, which he performs like an adolescent with a schoolboy crush. He may like it, but it's easy to dismiss as a trifle compared to more substantive oldies, like "Long Tall Sally" or "All Shook Up." The dull backing just sits there and rots, the vocalists sound like they're falling asleep. On the plus side, McCartney left off the cooing-at-your-lover section, which is as sickening as a tubful of saccharine. Does it justify its nearly five minutes' playing time? Maybe two minutes, tops. **C+**

"Wild Life" [Paul and Linda McCartney]
A kid's song that lumbers along like a wounded brontosaurus. I wonder, did they bother to check their tuning before they started? Did they consider that maybe a handful of uninteresting chords couldn't sustain a piece this tedious? Did they consider that maybe a new band might be better off practising in a basement instead of on a record? Questions to ponder while waiting for "Wild Life" to hurry up and finish. **D –**

"Some People Never Know" [Paul and Linda McCartney]
Linda was a nice person who served as an advocate for common sense when her husband was, shall we say, elsewhere. But there ought to be a law against her trying to sing harmony, which wrecks what little substance exists in the verses of a bauble like this. The middle section is another matter, a clever melody sung by McCartney – by himself – successfully using vocal elasticity that would've have come in handy on "Dear Friend." At over 6:30, though, "Some People Never Know" wears out its welcome before reaching the halfway point. **B-**

"I Am Your Singer" [Paul and Linda McCartney]
Linda stands alone, at least for a verse or two. Sit down, Linda. On the verge of crumbling to dust before your very ears, "I Am Your Singer" is the worst that *Wild Life* has to offer. [Next to "Bip Bop." And "Mumbo." And "Wild Life."] The hopeless lyrics defy analysis, as does the tepid tune that any self-respecting newbie folksinger would've flushed, fast. **D**

"Bip Bop Link" [Paul McCartney]
A surprisingly neat instrumental by McCartney on the acoustic guitar. In contrast to most of *Wild Life*, it makes you pine for a longer version, complete with another section or two which it sadly lacks. **B+**

"Tomorrow" [Paul and Linda McCartney]
In a garden of weeds, a flower. "Tomorrow," an irresistible tune, delicate and sweetly-sung, is one of McCartney's best, a stand-out of a career that thus far has been lost in the desert. He sounds like the McCartney of old, a little melancholy on the verse before launching into a sky-high hook of a melody that doesn't quit. True, "Tomorrow" suffers from a too-sparse backing that plagues *Wild Life* throughout, but with a song this strong, a could-be-better background is easy to overlook. **B+**

"Dear Friend" [Paul and Linda McCartney]
McCartney whimpers about being treated like dirt from John Lennon. Which makes this sound a lot more interesting than it is, as McCartney thumbs through his mental dictionary for the appropriate words to express himself, fails, and settles for vague accusations that scratch but don't cut. A pretty tune, with a vulnerable, appealing performance. But a pretty song doesn't deserve six minutes when it consists of lyrics this meager. And needs more than a verse. **B**

"Mumbo Link" [Paul McCartney]
Less than a minute of instrumental nonsense based on scraps of "Mumbo." But isn't "Mumbo" a scrap? **F**

[bonus]

"Give Ireland Back to the Irish" [Paul and Linda McCartney]

Critics pounced on John Lennon's 1972 *Sometime in New York City* for its shallow commentary on the news of the day. McCartney, too, thinks of himself as a political commentator, at least every decade or so, even though his commentary tends to make Lennon's seem sophisticated. In "Give Ireland Back to the Irish," Wings' first single, McCartney advised his green brothers and sisters to join him in the pursuit of freedom, quickly adding that their British oppressors are great guys too. The clunky playing supports a noodle of a tune, proving that McCartney needs a more practised group and more time to ponder his songs. He quietly backed away from political themes – save animal rights, for which he demonstrated a genuine passion – until 2001's 9/11 attack on the US which inspired "Freedom," which was dopey too. [*Paul McCartney Collection*] **C**

"Give Ireland Back to the Irish [Version]" [Paul and Linda McCartney]

A semi-amateurish instrumental, where the vocals take a back seat to gargling woodwinds played over a garage band merrily launching itself over a cliff. [*2007 iTunes Bonus Track*] **D**

"Give Ireland Back to the Irish [Alternate]" [Paul and Linda McCartney]

A practice run of the single. I thought the single *was* practice. [*Paul McCartney Collection*] **D**

"Mary Had a Little Lamb" [Paul and Linda McCartney]

Wings single number two. Perhaps McCartney believed that the hummable song would trick listeners into overlooking the nursery rhyme. It does not. Perhaps he believed it would re-capture the lovable whimsy of "Yellow Submarine." It does not. Perhaps he believed a record this juvenile would infuriate his audience, frustrate his audience, and make them grind their teeth till their incisors fell out. Bingo! [*Paul McCartney Collection*] **F**

"Mama's Little Girl" [Paul McCartney]

Is McCartney nuts? How else to explain his inexplicable decision to hold this small but sweet tune until 1990 [for the b-side of the inferior "Put It There"]? A near-perfect example of what McCartney does best: a strong melody with lyrics that don't give you a migraine, intelligent backgrounds, and an intimate production that seems like he's whispering in your ear. [*Paul McCartney Collection*] **B+**

"Good Rockin' Tonight [Home Recording]" [Roy Brown]

For a minute, McCartney unburdens himself from the world's "Bip Bop"s and rocks through a too-brief acoustic version of an ancient Elvis tune. He'd do it again on *Unplugged* [1991]. Fun but too short. [*Wild Life Deluxe Edition*] **B**

"Bip Bop" [Home Recording]" [Paul and Linda McCartney]

In-your-face rendition of this yechhh-fest, played for a baby. [*Wild Life Deluxe Edition*] **F**

"Hey Diddle [Home Recording"] [Paul and Linda McCartney]

The home concert continues, featuring McCartney diddling away while his audience frantically hunts for the "off" button. [*Wild Life Deluxe Edition*] **F**

"She Got It Good [Home Recording]" [Paul and Linda McCartney]

A fragment that not only fails to provide insight into McCartney's songwriting, it also fails to entertain even a teensy bit during its few seconds of existence. [*Wild Life Deluxe Edition*] **D**

"I Am Your Singer [Home Recording]" [Paul and Linda McCartney]

This could only be enjoyable if it was funny. It's not funny, however, just painful, as Paul and Linda fumble along, finding their way. More of a practice for a demo, not intended for human beings. [*Wild Life Deluxe Edition*] **F**

"Outtake I, II, III" [Paul McCartney]

Junk from McCartney's tape collection, not of interest musically or sociologically or humorously. Remember, you're paying real money for this. [*Wild Life Deluxe Edition*] **F**

"Dear Friend [Home Recording I, II]" [Paul and Linda McCartney]
McCartney at the piano, trying out "Dear Friend," basically the same as the *Wild Life* cut except for some minor fluffs and brief improvisations. Hearing him all by his lonesome, it's hard not to marvel at the guy's near-superhuman voice, evidenced by his holding a note, perfectly in key, forever. [*Wild Life Deluxe Edition*] **B**

"Indeed I Do" [Paul and Linda McCartney]
A demo of a McCartney and Linda duet, drunk on love. It's slightly endearing, hearing the lovebirds bill and coo over some pleasant acoustic guitar. But the coo-ing exceeds the statute of limitations which, for a trifle like this, lasts about 30 seconds. [*Wild Life Deluxe Edition*] **C-**

"African Yeah Yeah" [Paul McCartney]
One-chord jam on a single guitar and a drum set on the verge of falling apart. McCartney idly bangs away on a dimly recalled African rhythm, shouting nonsense all the while. If you like this, you're probably the mother of a band member, someone who's never heard music before, or McCartney himself. [*Wild Life Deluxe Edition*] **F**

"Dear Friend [Orchestra Up]" [Paul McCartney]
McCartney wisely backed off the orchestra on the album version, but for this, he turned them up to let the curious know what they missed: the same track, swallowed by woodwinds and strings that soften a tune already too mushy. [*paulmccartney.com*] **B-**

CHAPTER FIVE:

RED ROSE SPEEDWAY [1973]

Produced by Paul McCartney
Charted at 1 [US], 5 [UK]

"After I had heard Wild Life, I thought, 'Hell, we have really blown it here.' And the next one after that, Red Rose Speedway, I couldn't stand."
PAUL McCARTNEY, THE BEATLES: OFF THE RECORD 2

With new guitarist – Henry McCullough from Joe Cocker's group, intended to add a lick or two of the blues to the feather-light Wings – they were off, the ramshackle double-decker loaded with instruments, children, and organic food galore. At McCartney's instructions, Wings would head for British universities to give spontaneous performances suitable for bored and [hopefully] enthusiastic students.

To the Universities of Nottingham, York, and Newcastle they went, setting up in student cafeterias and student unions, playing for audiences occasionally under 1,000. Reaction was overall positive. Still, though generally satisfied, McCartney couldn't shake the occasional pang of disappointment. Students seemed thrilled to see a genuine Beatle playing in the places where they ate chili. But they were puzzled by the near-amateur performances of McCartney's new band. And they weren't crazy about the repertoire either, light on Beatle songs – only one in fact, a perfunctory version of "Long Tall Sally" – and heavy on throwaways like "Bip Bop" and "Seaside Woman."

But the band persevered, rolling on to Leeds, Sheffield, and Birmingham. With the bus huffing and puffing its way through the British back roads, sometimes at 35 mph, McCartney had plenty of time to mull over his next album. He knew his previous albums hadn't fared with the discerning crowd as well as he'd hoped, but this one – fingers crossed – would be different. And McCartney had cranked out so many songs that he began to visualize the album as a double, just like he'd intended for *Ram*.

Though far from definite, McCartney temporarily sketched out a lineup or two, one the earliest looking like this [destinations of unused tracks and old recordings are also indicated]:

Side A
    1. Night Out [Red Rose Speedway Archive Edition]
    2. Get on the Right Thing [leftover from Ram]
    3. Country Dreamer [b-side to 1973's "Helen Wheels" single]
    4. Big Barn Bed
    5. My Love

Side B
    1. Single Pigeon
    2. When the Night
    3. Seaside Woman [1977 single by Suzy and the Red Stripes, a Wings pseudonym]
    4. I Lie Around [b-side to 1973's "Live and Let Die" single]
    5. The Mess [b-side to 1973's "My Love" single]

Side C
1. Best Friend [Red Rose Speedway Archive Edition]
2. Loup (1st Indian on the Moon)
3. Medley: Hold Me Tight / Lazy Dynamite / Hands of Love / Power Cut

Side D
1. Mama's Little Girl [b-side to 1990's "Put It There" single]
2. I Would Only Smile [*Red Rose Speedway Archive Edition*]
3. One More Kiss
4. Tragedy [*Red Rose Speedway Archive Edition*]
5. Little Lamb Dragonfly [leftover from *Ram*]

[A later acetate re-ordered this list and also included "The Mess," "Jazz Street," and "1882." All are on *Red Rose Speedway Deluxe*.]

Despite McCartney's good intentions, *Red Rose Speedway*, as it came to be called for reasons unclear [maybe after Rose, his housekeeper?], was fraught with difficulty. McCartney was determined to make it a group effort, with each band member contributing more or less equally. But McCartney's delusion of equality was ridiculous, as were his clumsy attempts as making it an actual band rather than a backing group, which it clearly was. Fed up with McCartney's endless jamming and apparent difficulty in making musical decisions, veteran Glyn Johns [his resume included The Rolling Stones, The Who, and Led Zeppelin] resigned, leaving McCartney to produce all by himself.

Reluctantly – or maybe to get the troubled project finished – he chopped the double album into a single, most likely to the relief of EMI executives who may have questioned a double in light of the less than fantastic sales of *Wild Life*. Surviving tracks tended toward the softer and lighter ["When the Night"], and harder, more aggressive tracks [like another "Hi Hi Hi"] were nowhere in sight.

Thanks to the success of "My Love," a middle-of-the-road cut and a #1 in the US, *Red Rose Speedway* sold satisfactorily. But again, it met with critical scorn that bordered on disgust. *Rolling Stone*: "safe and familiar." *Village Voice*: "aimless whimsy." *AllMusic*: "deliberately slight." In time, even McCartney denounced it.

As for the band? Maybe McCartney was in denial, but the end of Wings was right around the corner.

"Big Barn Bed" [Paul and Linda McCartney]
McCartney previewed "Big Barn Bed" in the coda to *Ram*'s "Ram On," and it was enough of an intriguing tease to make us salivate for more. Here it is, and it barely qualifies as okay, with all of the intrigue sucked out as McCartney spins the hazy tale of a pal who snoozes in a shack with a leather-shelled mammal. The band bops along, not too hard, but just enough to sustain the undemanding sing-along, witless lyrics and all. **B-**

"My Love" [Paul and Linda McCartney]
Lyrically reminiscent of the Beatles' "Don't Let Me Down," but with nowhere near the emotional resonance, this dreary ballad is hard to categorize as anything but a cynical effort at a hit single. Tolerable melody aside, it's as empty as most of the rest of *Red Rose Speedway*; it just happens to be about his wife rather than lambs or dragonflies or pigeons. The highlight: Henry McCullough's ethereal guitar solo, improvised on the spot. McCartney, who usually dictates the solos note for note, had nothing to do with it. **C+**

"Get On the Right Thing" [Paul and Linda McCartney]
After an ascending melody, a familiar device that McCartney uses on "My Love," "Live and Let Die," and a few others, this drops depressingly into a pseudo-soul chorus, predictable and lazy. Too often, the song relies on cheap melodies that the old McCartney – that is, the Beatle McCartney – would have dumped in a second. **D**

"One More Kiss" [Paul and Linda McCartney]
An attractive but incidental tune by a McCartney who, as always, can generate minor leaguers like McDonald's generates hamburgers. Though it feels unfinished, as if missing a bar or two at the end of the verses, it reaches a zenith when it unveils the minor chords of the chorus, a simple but clever musical trick that barely qualifies as innovative. **B**

"Little Lamb Dragonfly" [Paul and Linda McCartney]

If you can get past the dorky title, what remains is a captivating song that oozes charm, easily the best on an otherwise thin album. Two songs are cleverly combined to make a long one. The first – about a sheep on its way to the slaughter – is serviceable, but the second – starring an insect that represents the ache of loss – draws on the Beatle-ish skill we were afraid was gone forever. As a singer, McCartney demonstrates genuine sincerity, a quality in short supply on *Red Rose Speedway*. **B+**

"Single Pigeon" [Paul and Linda McCartney]

A snatch of what might have been, before McCartney lost interest and it fluttered away. Sure, the words are meaningless, but they'd surely be repaired in the song's finished version. Er, wouldn't they? **C+**

"When the Night" [Paul and Linda McCartney]

Hidden away near the end of the album, this banal track hauls itself to a place where infirmed tunes go to die. A clunky chord-beating piano lesson, a nest of clichés, and an uncharacteristic performance by a seemingly bored singer. Does McCartney have to release *everything*? I'm surprised he didn't try to pawn it off on Ringo. **D**

"Loup [1st Indian on the Moon]" [Paul and Linda McCartney]

Back in the Beatle days, McCartney tended to get a bit peeved when he didn't get credit for the avant garde touches he felt he deserved. It was he, after all, who came up with the psychedelic insect effects preceding "Sun King." And on "Tomorrow Never Knows," generally considered to be John's baby, McCartney contributed the tape loops that sent the track into another dimension.

The most successful avant garde pieces tend to go for broke, as evidenced by heavyweights John Cage [*Sonatas and Interludes*, using a prepared piano with objects lodged between its strings] and Edgard Varese [*Ionisation*, all percussion]. But McCartney is too conservative to go that far, possibly fearing the real wacky stuff could offend his fans. He might try to emulate the softer side of, say, Brian Eno. But Cage or Varese? Not going to happen. Thus, "Loup," a prime example of McCartney's don't-rock-the-boat attitude, exists as an uneasy combination of conservative progressive rock [the shopping mall side of Pink Floyd] with a few Eno-light sound effects [bleeps and blips as heard on TV commercials]. It doesn't work, of course, sounding like a cheap soundtrack for a low-budget science-fiction film. It's a gross understatement to point out that this isn't the Beatles. **D**

"Medley: Hold Me Tight/ Lazy Dynamite/ Hands of Love/ Power Cut" [Paul and Linda McCartney]

One of rock's most majestic moments occurred in 1969 with *Abbey Road*'s ending, a 16-minute wonder that McCartney supervised and largely composed. It worked once, so why not try it again? Bad idea. The *Abbey Road* medley used top-of-the-line tunes from Lennon/McCartney. McCartney in particular, was in top notch form, with "Golden Slumbers" as an example. Here, McCartney links four songs destined for b-sides, if that. So we have the fluffy "Hold Me Tight" burdened with annoyingly redundant lyrics; "Lazy Dynamite," a lyric tangle not worth the effort to translate; "Hands of Love," a puffy duet; and "Power Cut," a dumb ode to electricians. The performance is so-so, the production dry, and the songwriting off the cuff and colourless. A disappointing ending to an underwhelming album. **B-**

[bonus]

"I Lie Around" [Paul and Linda McCartney]

Anyone remember 1967's "The Happening" by the Supremes? How about "I'm Only Sleeping," the Beatles' dreamland tribute from *Revolver*? Take bits from each, mush them together, and you've got the emaciated skeleton of "I Lie Around." Where Diana Ross sounds giddy and John Lennon sounds like he's needing a nap, McCartney sounds distracted, as if he's pondering what to wear while the tape rolls. Once past the intro, which echoes the Beatles' "Polythene Pam," McCartney croons about being worn out. From what? [*Red Rose Speedway Deluxe*] **C-**

"Country Dreamer" [Paul and Linda McCartney]

Cute, 5%. Exasperating, 95%. [*Red Rose Speedway Deluxe*] **C-**

"The Mess" [Paul and Linda McCartney]
This feeble rocker came from the same guy who gave us "Helter Skelter." Say it isn't so. The live b-side to "My Love," it plays like the band learned it an hour ago and the singer's making up words as he goes along. Slowing it down near the end was not a good move, nor was the brain-dead riff, nor were the thin backing vocals, nor was gluing together disparate sections that have nothing to do with each other. As for the title ... too easy. [*Red Rose Speedway Deluxe*] **D+**

"Hi Hi Hi" [Paul and Linda McCartney]
Tapping into his love for 50s rock and finding the switch that activated "Back in the USSR," McCartney pops out this infectious shuffle, accompanied by a band weeping for joy at the chance to play anything that isn't "Mary Had a Little Lamb." Bizarrely, the track was banned by the BBC for its sexual and drug overtones, bringing back the hysteria over "Yellow Submarine" [fundamentalist Christians just *knew* it was a drug reference] and "Puff the Magic Dragon" [Satan strikes again!]. As if any of McCartney's flighty words had anything to do with anything. The overdrive near the end rockets into outer space, making me want to drop some yellow submarines, right now. [*Red Rose Speedway Deluxe*] **B+**

"C Moon" [Paul and Linda McCartney]
The flip of "Hi Hi Hi," marketed as a double A-side, this pales before "Hi Hi Hi" as it drifts too far into the land of the brain dead. A light reggae, "C Moon" explains how it's better to be a circle [a "C" and a "moon"] than a square [your finger and thumb making the appropriate shape]. As the sappy sing-along lumbers to the coda, McCartney complains about being misunderstood by old-timers, then wanders back to two buddies who can't tell their dad or each other or someone ... anyway, we're all "C Moon," right? [*Red Rose Speedway Deluxe*] **B-**

"Live and Let Die" [Paul and Linda McCartney]
McCartney may be winsome, he may be cheery, he may have a superhuman talent for melody. But sinister and dry witted, traits you might expect from a James Bond anthem, he is not. Opening with a lift from his own "Here, There, and Everywhere," McCartney slides into a gentle tune which quickly blossoms into his version of spy-ish excitement, which means frantic xylophones exploding all over the place, all of which has as much to do with cartoons as with Sean Connery. Thankfully, producer George Martin supplies the right amount of good taste, keeping a lid on an arrangement [Paul's?] that threatens to get out of hand. This is less a McCartney classic than a Martin spectacular. Martin, incidentally, was the producer of Shirley Bassey's "Goldfinger." [*Red Rose Speedway Deluxe*] **B**

"Live and Let Die [Group Only]" [Paul and Linda McCartney]
The group in an early rehearsal. If you think it'd be illuminating to hear Wings practise, think again. Instead, consider that McCartney just might be wondering if this track – him singing, no overdubs, no exploding xylophones – would be good enough to release. [*Red Rose Speedway Deluxe*] **C**

"1882 [Home Version]"/ "1882" [Paul and Linda McCartney]
Having made a demo of this for 1970's *McCartney*, McCartney allegedly thought it over, then decided it wasn't good enough to sit beside "Momma Miss America." A grindingly slow waltz telling the who-cares tale of a kid who swipes food from his mom. The demo was sluggish enough, but the studio version incredibly slows things down to a sub-crawl. I guess McCartney's punishing us, as it drags on for a hard-to-believe six-plus minutes. [*Red Rose Speedway Deluxe.*] **D –**

"1882 [Live 1972]" [Paul McCartney]
No one expects every composition to be a masterpiece. But to detonate your bombs on stage, well, that's a lot to endure for even the hardest of the die-hards. This is the tale of a kid who swipes food, is executed, and is confused, as are we all. Imagine a waltz, reduce the tempo by half, then reduce it again. And again. [*Red Rose Speedway Deluxe.*] **D**

"Thank You Darling" [Paul and Linda McCartney]
Makes *When the Night* seem substantial. [*Red Rose Speedway Deluxe*] **D-**

"Jazz Street" [Paul and Linda McCartney]

Red Rose Speedway instrumentals are a definite improvement over *McCartney* instrumentals. Then again, you don't have to go far to beat "Momma Miss America." A piano noodles along, pleasantly enough, but as it rolls along its non-committal way, a better title would be *Middle of the Road Street*. Why does McCartney like instrumentals? Maybe because music is easy, words are hard? [*Red Rose Speedway Deluxe*.] **B-**

"Night Out" [Paul and Linda McCartney]

Considered as an opener for the never-to-be double *Red Rose Speedway*. An up-tempo instrumental featuring a non-threatening guitar and occasional chants of the title. Hard to loathe, but tough to like. [*Red Rose Speedway Deluxe*.] **B-**

"Seaside Woman" [Linda McCartney]

Linda was a photographer, a chef, and a business woman, but never a serious musician. Then she met Paul. Just like that, she's a singer. My, the things we do to keep our mate happy. Linda wrote and performed this slip of a tune, released as a single by Suzy and the Red Stripes [i.e. Wings]. She does her best with her thin voice and curious relationship with a tonal scale. It's not half-bad, considering the source, a serviceable albeit forgettable effort about a beachcombing female, all supported by a dinky melody. [*Red Rose Speedway Deluxe*] **B –**

"B-Side to Seaside" [Paul and Linda McCartney]

Linda chants the verses, warbles the chorus, and waits for somebody, probably McCartney, to finish his dreary solo. Criticizing this is like kicking a puppy. [Flip of "Seaside Woman" single] **C-**

"I Would Only Smile" [Denny Laine]

Denny Laine's contribution to *Red Rose Speedway*, booted to the curb. Too bad, because this is an agreeable – not to say great – rocker, featuring Denny's friendly vocals and a reasonably catchy hook. The band apparently was fond of it too, as it showed up regularly in early concerts. Denny also included it on *Japanese Tears*, his hard-to-find solo album from 1980. [*Red Rose Speedway Deluxe*.] **B-**

"Tragedy" [Gerald H. Nelson and Fred B Burch]

Some rockers want to be Jimi Hendrix or Bob Dylan. Apparently, McCartney wants to be Eddie Fisher. This lounge favourite was written by Gerald H. Nelson and Fred B. Burch, then turned into a Top Ten single by Thomas Wayne and the DeLongs. If a 1950s weeper is something you might enjoy, dive right into this ultra-lush mushfest. But be forewarned: McCartney's done weepers a lot better than this, such as "She's Leaving Home" and "Here, There, and Everywhere." [*Red Rose Speedway Deluxe.]* **C-**

"Hands of Love [Alternate]" [Paul and Linda McCartney]

Sluggish attempt, same arrangement as on *Red Rose Speedway*. Pointless. [*paulmccartney.com*] **D**

"The Bruce McMouse Show" [Paul McCartney]

An hour-long animated/live film starring McCartney, the rest of Wings, and a pipe-smoking cartoon mouse who lives under the stage. The film features some elementary school acting [by Wings], some concert footage [also by Wings], and some song and dance routines [also by – sob – Wings]. It vanished, probably because it stunk. The soundtrack showcases snippets of live pieces, such as "My Love." It also has cartoon mice playing violins. [On *Red Rose Speedway Deluxe*.] **F**

James Paul McCartney TV Special

McCartney's declaration that Linda would serve as his new writing partner raised a few eyebrows. This new policy began with his assertion that Linda co-wrote "Another Day" for which she'd receive 50 per cent of the publishing money, a considerable sum owing to Paul's astronomical popularity. Speaking for Northern Songs, which McCartney had attempted to circumvent, Sir Lew Grade claimed that awarding songwriting credit [and the money] to a virtual unknown gave McCartney an unfair share of the royalties. Lawyers for McCartney maintained that he was entitled to write with whomever he liked. The case went to court. Lo and behold, McCartney prevailed. To make everyone happy, McCartney agreed to star in a one-hour TV special for Grade's company.

From all the legal ins and outs came James Paul McCartney, *a 55-minute television broadcast in May,*

1973 which ranks as one of the worst vanity projects ever to grace a TV set. Among the highlights: a sugary performance of "Big Barn Bed," McCartney and the guys frolicking with sheep to the tune of "Mary Had a Little Lamb," and Paul entertaining fellow workingmen at the neighborhood pub with "You are My Sunshine." The low point was reached in a remarkably inane production number "Gotta Sing Gotta Dance," where Paul stumbled through a dance routine, with the ghost of Fred Astaire hiding behind the curtains, throwing up. [Red Rose Speedway Deluxe Edition]

"Gotta Sing Gotta Dance" [Paul McCartney]
A new song from McCartney's abominable *James Paul McCartney*, this 1920s-style stunner features McCartney wearing a fake moustache, non-dancer McCartney in a dance routine, and a couple dozen backup hoofers wearing half-tuxedos/half-gowns, thus ending their careers. When you think of Paul McCartney, I'm betting you don't associate him with vaudeville, but vaudeville it is, on display for all the world to see. By the way, the set consists of giant, cut-off-at-the-thigh ladies' legs. [*Red Rose Speedway Deluxe Edition*] **F**

"Six O'Clock" [Paul McCartney; guest performer: Paul McCartney]
[Ringo Starr] For Ringo's third album, McCartney attempted to duplicate the playful charm that brightened "A Little Help from My Friends" and "Yellow Submarine." He failed. This is hammered-together crud, long on forced nostalgia, short on inspiration. Ringo sings wearily, as if he's fulfilling an obligation to producer Richard Perry to round up his three old pals for sort of a Beatle reunion. That he did, but so what? Ringo – and McCartney for that matter – would have been better served to wait for McCartney come up with something smarter. [*Ringo*] **C**

"You're Sixteen"
[Ringo Starr] McCartney solos on the kazoo. What is he, five? Meanwhile, Harry Nilsson added doo-wop vocals, half serious and half spacey, and sounded like a grown up. As for the song, it's an oldie warbling an oldie, with dubious implications. [*Ringo*] **B**

CHAPTER SIX:

BAND ON THE RUN [1973]

Produced by Paul McCartney
Charted at 1 [US], 1 [UK]

Trouble was brewing with new Wings-men Henry McCullough and Denny Seiwell. Though they admired McCartney, certain aspects of the band were grating. Why, they wondered, were they touring universities in a barely drivable bus – a bus! – when a star of McCartney's stature could sell out auditoriums anywhere on the planet? Why were they performing sub-standard material like "Give Ireland Back to the Irish" and "Mary Had a Little Lamb"? With rare exceptions [like Henry's solo in "My Love"], why was school marm McCartney dictating virtually every note they played? And though they genuinely liked Linda, she was far from a professional musician. Yet there she was, every night, sharing equal billing with the far more experienced pros, inevitably affecting the performance.

But perhaps the biggest sticking point was money. To say that McCartney had a lot of it would be putting it mildly. Beatles publishing, real estate, his growing art collection, all of it continued to swell McCartney's net worth. And with the depressing aftermath of the Beatles more or less behind him, he wasn't against spending it, investing in lavish houses, luxury cars, unlimited studio time, pricey jewelry for his wife, basically anything and everything he wanted, whenever he wanted it.

Meanwhile, the Wings boys got by on comparatively meager wages. True, McCartney was the mastermind and they were sidemen, replaceable on a moment's notice. But he was also a *rich* mastermind. His sidemen had a hard time understanding why he couldn't cough up a bit more cash. Things came to a boil when McCartney made a vague promise to share more royalties as the band progressed, but this never seemed to happen. Following a dustup in the studio over who played what and when, Henry left and never returned. Shortly thereafter, a phone disagreement with Seiwell ended with the drummer also resigning. Though loyal Denny Laine remained, with only the three of them left – Denny, McCartney, Linda – the band was effectively over.

McCartney was not happy. But it began to occur to him that maybe, at least for now, he didn't need anyone else. He could handle bass, drums, guitar, keyboards, all of it, with Denny and Linda chipping in now and then. The new album, for which he'd come up with terrific new tunes, would be like *McCartney*, only better. This time, instead of struggling with an album while fighting off depression and confusion after the end of the Beatles, he felt strong, focused, and confident he could do it all.

A studio in Nigeria had already been booked. As to why Nigeria, it was a place he'd longed to visit, plus it'd be an exciting new locale for his new project. Once the three of them settled in, Nigeria would be perfect.

Except, er, for that studio. McCartney in his haste had failed to investigate it thoroughly. Once there, he found it to be little more than a ramshackle lean-to with makeshift baffles and little in the way of state-of-the-art equipment, requiring a hasty overhaul.

And except for the locals, some of whom were suspicious that McCartney was a potential music thief, setting the stage for a wary relationship.

And except for the civil unrest, where Nigeria, coming off a violent civil war, had factions who hated each other and were competing for government rule, which threatened to explode at any time.

And except for a near-fatal robbery. McCartney, venturing out at night against the advice of friendly Nigerians, found himself staring at a knife wielded by a gang of thugs who demanded he hand over his stuff. An unhurt but terrified McCartney gave them everything he had, including, unfortunately, a cassette containing demos of his new songs. [The cassette has never been recovered.]

Incredibly, the determined McCartney pressed on, completing new demos where needed, making the best of an iffy studio, and doing his best to smooth over any misunderstandings with wary locals. Eventually, the album was completed, with only a few overdubs needed back in London.

To say that it was a hit would be an understatement. *Band On the Run* was filled with his best songs to date. It there were any flubs in the one-man performance, either they were impossible to hear or, on the basis of terrific material, didn't matter. The public snapped it up. Critical response was generally supportive. *AllMusic*: "Sophisticated nuanced arrangements and irrepressibly catchy melodic hooks." *Classic Rock Review*: "His arrangements are spectacular."

To be fair, not all critics were on board. *Christgau's Record Guide*: "Pop masterpiece? This?" Cynical listeners noted that the best songs were up front ["Band On the Run," "Jet"] and the weaker ones ["Picasso's Last Words," "No Words"] were hidden towards the end, making the album sound better to casual fans who made up their minds after hearing only a few tracks.

But these complaints were in the minority. *Band On the Run* eventually became a triple platinum seller. It spawned two gold singles ["Jet" and "Band On the Run"], and received near-unanimous praise. It took him five albums, but McCartney had done it. And like he planned, practically by himself.

"Band On the Run" [Paul and Linda McCartney]
With the exception of "Maybe I'm Amazed" [*McCartney*], this is probably McCartney's best-known non-Beatles song and one of his most beloved. By stitching fragments together – a template used in "Happiness is a Warm Gun" [*The Beatles*], "You Never Give Me Your Money" [*Abbey Road*],, and "Uncle Albert/Admiral Halsey," [*Ram*] – the charm of "Band On the Run" largely comes from three sections that rise dramatically in quality as the song progress. The first and worst finds McCartney crooning nonsense about going to jail accompanied by the lamest synthesizer line of 1974. It picks up a bit in part two with a muscular guitar riff, helped if you ignore the lyrics [when he gets out of prison, he gives his riches to poor people – sure you will]. Following a laboured orchestra comes a driving acoustic guitar, McCartney singing like a man possessed, and a verse/chorus that dares you not to like it. It's this, the final third that makes its appearance after a lousy intro and an okay middle section, that lifts "Band On the Run" off the ground and firmly implants itself in our collective memories. **B+**

"Jet" [Paul and Linda McCartney]
McCartney's best rocker, and I don't mean just on *Band On the Run*. I mean, ever. McCartney, more self-assured than he's been on previous albums, sings and plays like he's winding up for the knockout punch, which arrives in the blistering coda. The backing track is note-perfect, better than expected for what is basically a pop song, transformed here into a guided missile. What do the words mean? Who cares? With a track this good, McCartney could be singing the phone book. McCartney will attempt rockers in the future – "Angry" [coming up on 1986's *Press to Play*] comes to mind – but they sound forced, fussy and decidedly inferior next to the superb "Jet." **A**

"Bluebird" [Paul and Linda McCartney]
The gorgeous "Bluebird" is McCartney-esque bliss, the first in a long while that keeps the sentimental gobbledygook under control while letting the melody soar. Background vocals are kept at arm's length, which is good, as are all temptations for over-production, which is very good. The lyrics falter, and the comparisons to "Blackbird" are obvious, and this, truth be told, doesn't come close. But for a solo McCartney, this is a prime example of inventive beauty, a moving song that hits home, quietly and powerfully. **B+**

"Mrs. Vandebilt" [Paul and Linda McCartney]
Yeah, I know, "Mrs. Vandebilt" is fun for all. But it seems it's aimed at nursery school kids. The up and down melody is right out of *Sesame Street*. The backing vocals are ladled with playroom inanities, colourful but hardly for grown-ups. McCartney finds kiddie music irresistible and he has a tough time with adult themes, but considering his time spent with John Lennon, you'd think he would've learned. **B-**

"Let Me Roll It" [Paul and Linda McCartney]
Round One: McCartney makes a frontal attack on John Lennon with "Too Many People" [*Ram*]. But the attack fails due to McCartney's pixie dust lyrics.
Round Two: John fires back with the clever but mean-spirited "How Do You Sleep" [*Imagine*], a direct hit.

Round Three: McCartney responds with the pity party of "Dear Friend" [*Wild Life*], which staggers Lennon with its dorkiness. Lennon tries to respond, but can't stop giggling.

Round Four: McCartney slams it home with "Let Me Roll It," combining a riff reminiscent of Lennon's "Cold Turkey" [*Shaved Fish*] and Lennon's savage *Plastic Ono Band*. John wobbles, swoons, collapses. Victory: McCartney. **A**

"Mamunia" [Paul and Linda McCartney]

"Mamunia" shares its title with a Nigerian hotel, in case you were hoping for something mysterious. Or interesting, which this song about the perils of rainfall [it falls on you, you get wet] sorely lacks. Is rain an allegory? Please. The verse crawls along like a worm searching for its wormhole. The chorus modulates up a notch, encouraging you to wake up and sing along. I wonder if "Mamunia" is actually Nigerian for "filler." **C+**

"No Words" [Paul McCartney and Denny Laine]

Dubious harmonies, shaky guitars, and Denny lost in the mix. One waits for "No Words" to take off, but it never happens. Rather, it sort of stops and starts, heading for a not particularly appealing chorus, and ending with an uninspired guitar solo. I'll go out on a limb and bet this is not anyone's favourite *Band On the Run* track. **C**

"Helen Wheels" [Paul and Linda McCartney]+

Snappy, great fun, and impressively, almost all one chord, sort of like "Paperback Writer" [*Revolver*]. Pushed along by McCartney's aggressive bass, "Helen Wheels" slaps you in the face after the anesthesia of "Mamunia" and "No Words." Could this have been a Beatles song? Hmmm... **B+**

"Picasso's Last Words [Drink To Me]" [Paul and Linda McCartney]

"Loup" [*Red Rose Speedway*] squirts out a son. Opening with a verse evoking a dying artist while drunks whoop it up in a bar, it switches to one of the drunks falling sleep, who favours us with an excerpt from "Jet." Also: a clarinet solo, an orchestral rendition of the drunk verse, a vocal drunk verse [drunker than before], and a chunk of "Mrs. Vandebilt." Where did this all come from? A guess: Dustin Hoffman, present at its informal composition, was so delighted with McCartney's on-the-spot creation of an embryonic "Picasso" that McCartney decided he was too, ultimately coaxing himself to slap something together. The recording also features Ginger Baker, late of Cream, playing a bucket of gravel. **D**

"Nineteen Hundred and Eighty Five" [Paul and Linda McCartney]

This is more like it. McCartney beats the hell out of his piano and sings like a maniac about nothing [per usual]. Grinding fluff like "Picasso's Last Words" into the dirt, the long-ish tune sounds like the keyboard will blow up any second and McCartney will run away cackling. Powerful melody, unforgettable piano riff. The only fault: a couple of slow sections filled with dorky "ooo"s and "ahhh"s, presumably so McCartney can catch his breath. Once that intermission is over, he rants and raves, the arrangement gets more frantic, more intense. Then, out of nowhere, it swings into a bit of the jolly "Band On the Run," an unexpected finale that neatly ties up McCartney's most accomplished album. **B+**

[bonus]

"Band on the Run [Barn Rehearsal]" [Paul and Linda McCartney]

Semi-sloppy run-through you can keep in the barn. [*Band on the Run Deluxe*] **D**

"Bluebird [Live 1975]" [Paul and Linda McCartney]

Sparse take on a *Band On the Run* highlight. Just a snatch, here and gone. [*Band On the Run Deluxe*] **C+**

"No Words [Original]" [Paul McCartney and Denny Laine]

Irrelevant, worse than the original. Which is saying something. [*Band On the Run Deluxe*] **F**

"Band on the Run [Original]" [Paul and Linda McCartney]"

Just the last third of the single, played on an acoustic guitar, with McCartney experimenting with the melody. He doesn't seem to care. So why should you.? **C –** [*Band On the Run Deluxe*] **C-**

"Jet [Original]" [Paul and Linda McCartney]
Still powerful, even in this crude version. If McCartney tried harder, this version could be a winner. But he didn't, and it isn't. [*Band On the Run Deluxe*] **B-**

"Nineteen Hundred and Eighty Five [Original]" [Paul and Linda McCartney]
Ineffectual rendition, basically the same as the released track. If it the melody and lyrics don't really change, and the performance doesn't really change and the arrangement doesn't really change, what, pray tell, is the point? [*Band On the Run Deluxe*] **C**

"Mrs. Vandebilt [Original]" [Paul and Linda McCartney]
A slight version of a song doesn't need one. [*Band On the Run Deluxe*] **C-**

"Picasso's Last Words [Drink To Me] [Original]" [Paul and Linda McCartney]
As this mostly was a studio creation, hearing the early version provides a couple of insights. That's not to say the insights are worth hearing. [*Band On the Run Deluxe*] **D**

"Jet [1993 Soundcheck]" [Paul and Linda McCartney]
A soundcheck sample, when McCartney is under no pressure to perform, seems to prove that "Jet" not only is a great song, it's one that's pretty hard to screw up. Still, it's inferior to the record, as you can't pick out the details that make it sparkle. [*Band On the Run Deluxe*] **– B**

"Let Me Roll It [Rehearsal 1993]" [Paul and Linda McCartney]
If this was the only version that existed, it'd earn a thumbs-up. Therefore, thumbs- down. [*Band On the Run Deluxe*] **B –**

"Helen Wheels [Crazed]" [Paul and Linda McCartney]
McCartney has his own meaning for "crazed." That would be "not crazed." [*Band On the Run Deluxe*] **C-**

"Picasso's Last Words [Drink To Me] [Acoustic]" [Paul and Linda McCartney]
If you stripped this down the chorus, you might have something. This, however, remains fully clothed. [*Band On the Run Deluxe*] **C-**

"Band on the Run [Northern Comic Version]" [Paul and Linda McCartney]"
Not funny. Not anything. [*Band On the Run Deluxe*] **F**

One Hand Clapping
One Hand Clapping, a self-produced McCartney film, was assembled from what look to be McCartney's home movies, largely using impromptu scenes of the new improved Wings fooling around in Abbey Road Studio. Allegedly, they were rehearsing for a tour, but the tour never happened. Why? Because drummer Geoff Brittan was out the door, as was the 20-year-old guitarist. [More about this in the Venus and Mars *chapter]*
Not exactly a sunny premise, but you'd never know it from One Hand Clapping, *where everything seemed hunky dory and conflicts apparently were left on the cutting room floor. The film, seldom seen at the time but now available as a DVD curio, shows the band going through their paces, happy and professional, with McCartney firmly in charge. As a movie, it's awful. As a souvenir of a rehearsal, it's acceptable, but no more than that.*

"One Hand Clapping Theme" [Paul and Linda McCartney]
The movie's theme song lays an electric guitar and a simple synthesizer over a plodding drum beat, none of it interesting. Instant movie music, instantly forgettable. [*Band On the Run Deluxe*] **D**

"Jet" [One Hand Clapping]" [Paul and Linda McCartney]
McCartney seems strangely subdued for this competent but lifeless run-though of *Band On the Run*'s best number. Maybe his distracted new group can't cut it against his [practically] one-man performance on the album. Maybe this is a sign of things to come. Or maybe after Take 900, McCartney wants to end it already. [*Band On the Run Deluxe*] **C**

"Soily [One Hand Clapping]" [Paul and Linda McCartney]
A surprise, or it would have been if *One Hand Clapping* would have come out as planned. A middling rocker, appearing again on McCartney's 1976 blockbuster *Wings Over America*, the band feels its way through it, not sure if to go for the throat or lie back for a snooze. The snooze wins, but it's not entirely the band's fault, as this uninspired throwaway should've been left in the trunk. [*Band On the Run Deluxe*] **D**

"C Moon [One Hand Clapping]" [Paul and Linda McCartney]
Whatever its faults, the studio "C Moon" at least was lively. Not here. Sleeping pills on film. [*Band On the Run Deluxe*] **D+**

"Little Woman Love [One Hand Clapping]" [Paul and Linda McCartney]
Mediocre tune brought to semi-life in a bland performance. [*Band On the Run Deluxe*] **C-**

"My Love [One Hand Clapping]" [Paul and Linda McCartney]
McCartney the crooner, ready for Las Vegas. In the DVD, interspersed with McCartney looking cute, is drummer Geoff Brittan dressed in a karate suit, demonstrating how to inflict fatal blows. Is he going to kill "My Love?" [*Band On the Run Deluxe*] **C-**

"Bluebird [One Hand Clapping]" [Paul and Linda McCartney]
A virtual duplication of the album. Why would you need two? Oops, forgot the sax solo. Like I said, why would you need two? [*Band On the Run Deluxe*] **C**

"Let's Love [One Hand Clapping]" [Paul McCartney]
McCartney favours us with a solo take of what will become Peggy Lee's title track of her 1974 album. McCartney arranged, produced, and wrote it, and Peggy sang it employing her trademark come-hither voice. A pleasant, conventional number that begs the question: What's McCartney doing with Peggy Lee? [*Band On the Run Deluxe*] **B**

"All of You [One Hand Clapping]" [Paul McCartney]
McCartney pulls out another middle-of-the-roader, an upbeat – but not too upbeat – love song, drawing us uncomfortably close to the lounge. This one seems to have vanished. A shame. Not. [*Band On the Run Deluxe*] **C+**

"I'll Give You a Ring [One Hand Clapping]" [Paul McCartney]
A piano-based version of what would become one of McCartney's best B-sides, but you wouldn't know it from this slovenly misfire. As if McCartney needed to kill some time while the crew fussed with the camera, he seems to have idly popped this off. [Flip side of 1982 single "Take It Away." Also on *Band On the Run Deluxe*.] **C**

"Band On the Run [One Hand Clapping]" [Paul and Linda McCartney]
Flubbed guitar on the opening indicates this might be interesting. Ditto on bridge number one: more minor flubs. Wraps up with a strained vocal and indifferent backing. Doesn't sound like a hit to me. Then again, this is practice. [*Band On the Run Deluxe*] **C+**

"Live and Let Die [One Hand Clapping]" [Paul and Linda McCartney]
You think McCartney crammed an orchestra in the studio for an "informal" performance? McCartney could make all his whims come true – most of them anyway – and, besides, he had money to burn, so what the hell. However, you can't whim-away your wife's backing vocals, nor can you whim-away your apathetic group's hit-or-miss performance on a tune they may or may not be enjoying. You can, however, insist on formal attire for your session violinists. [*Band On the Run Deluxe*] **C**

"Nineteen Hundred and Eighty Five [One Hand Clapping]" [Paul and Linda McCartney]
McCartney flawlessly accompanies himself on the piano as the rest of the group checks their watches. His voice carries the day, effortlessly nailing the tricky melody. Still, the studio version decimates it. [*Band On the Run Deluxe*] **B-**

"Baby Face [One Hand Clapping]" [Harry Akst and Benny Davis]
Written in 1926 and performed by everybody, including Bobby Darin, Little Richard, and the Muppet Chickens. McCartney probably heard this song around the house when he was a kid and never forgot it. He played it over the credits of *One Hand Clapping* and, of course, it's a frivolous throwaway. And you know what do to with a frivolous throwaway, don't you? [*Band On the Run Deluxe*] **D**

"Jet/Mrs. Vandebilt/Band on the Run [Live 2009]" [Paul McCartney]
Inexplicable inclusion on *Band On the Run Bonus* [which used to be available at your local Best Buy], taken from McCartney's *Good Evening New York City*, 30 years in the future. **C**

"No Words [Live 1979]" [Paul McCartney and Denny Laine]
It's fun to hear McCartney tackle an obscurity in a live setting. Unfortunately, the obscurity is "No Words." [*Band On the Run Deluxe*] **D+**

"Band On the Run [Live 1979]" [Paul and Linda McCartney]
A headache to play, but what else can you do with one of the biggest singles of your career? A problem also faced by Queen ["Bohemian Rhapsody"] and the Beach Boys ["Good Vibrations"]; you stumble through it, ignore the parts only playable in the studio, and watch the audience go crazy anyway. [*Band On the Run Deluxe*] **B**

"Zoo Gang" [Paul and Linda McCartney]
The lead on this instrumental trifle sounds like a short-circuited duck. The rest: a clip-cloppety rhythm, somebody practising a guitar, and that's pretty much it. Destined for a B-side, since nobody makes C-sides. [B-side of UK single "Band On the Run." Also on *Band On the Run Deluxe*.] **D**

"Rock 'n' Roll Music is Now" [James Taylor; guest performer: Paul McCartney]
[James Taylor] Taylor seemed to be nearing the end of his creative rope circa 1974, as his fifth album *Walking Man* made painfully clear. Gone were the crystalline melodies and intimate lyrics, replaced by mundane funk like "Rock 'n' Roll Music is Now." McCartney's singing along somewhere in this embarrassment, but who'd blame him if he couldn't recall it? [*Walking Man*] **D –**

"Let's Love" [Paul and Linda McCartney]
[Peggy Lee] McCartney's affection for swing era singers is part of his core, and to him, a collaboration with Peggy Lee is like a gift granted by a genie, but head-scratching for his rock fans. The melancholy "Let's Love" successfully caresses, smooths, and dabs the tears away, but it owes more to Lee's effortless style than McCartney's melodic dazzle, which tends to come up short when he's fumbling with seduction. I bet Peggy Lee could teach this boy a thing or two. [*Let's Love*, 1974] **B**

Mike McCartney/Mike McGear
The name change, McCartney to McGear, is so Mike won't take advantage of his older sibling's fame, a gambit I doubt worked too well. Mike had a decent career going before he decided to take a shot at show business, resulting in the moderately successful comedy/music group Scaffold [1966-1974], which later morphed into Grimms, a group he stayed with for a couple of years. After attempting a low-key solo album [Woman], he hooked up with Paul for McGear, a solo album that wasn't quite a solo, as Paul did everything but sweep the floors. In fact, musicians from Wings – under Paul's direction – play virtually everything, effectively becoming McGear's group for the album. So is McGear a practice album between Band on the Run and Venus and Mars? Could be.

The extra tracks discussed near the end of this section are from the 2-CD Deluxe Reissue, released in the summer of 2019. This may not be the last we've heard from McGear. Rumour has it that all or most of the McGear songs exist with Paul's vocals, intended as a guide for his brother, which would make this a genuine, sort of, Band on the Run sequel. This is unsubstantiated but not unprecedented, as Paul had a habit of cutting vocal demos for artists he was producing, clear back to Mary Hopkin's "Goodbye" [1969] to the Everly Brothers' "On the Wings of a Nightingale" [1984]. Maybe someday, we'll find out.

"Sea Breezes" [Bryan Ferry; producer and guest performer: Paul McCartney]
[Mike McGear] From the first Roxy Music album comes this simple tune about love's fragility that Bryan

Ferry turned into a majestic ode from another dimension. Here, it reverts to the ordinary, with a tentative vocal and fairly sophisticated production, nothing fancy but passable. Probably too intense for Mike, as he seems more comfortable with lighter fare, and less so with songs overflowing with melodramatic Ferry-isms. [*McGear*] **B**

"Leave It" [Paul McCartney; producer and guest performer: Paul McCartney]
[Mike McGear] "Leave It" is far and away the best track on an otherwise hit or miss album. It's bouncy, catchy, and reasonably short. Based on an enthusiastic acoustic riff – think "Things We Said Today" in a major key – it's one of McCartney's finest from this period. He was either generous or crazy to give it up to a singer with McGear's limited vocal skill, but then again, brothers are often nice to each other. Lyrics are nonsense, which is par for the course. [*McGear*] **B+**

"What Do We Really Know" [Paul McCartney; guest performer: Paul McCartney]
[Mike McGear] A backwards guitar promises an off-the-wall extravaganza, a promise that falls apart when the thin vocal begins and the promise collapses. McGear does what he can, which is not very much. [*McGear*] **B-**

"Norton" [Paul McCartney and Mike McGear; producer and guest performer: Paul McCartney]
[Mike McGear] Derivative of the Grimms, Mike's old band, Mike chants un-funny poetry while Wings dully riffs away. [*McGear*] **D+**

"Have You Got Problems" [Paul McCartney and Mike McGear; producer and guest performer: Paul McCartney]
[Mike McGear] A reject from *Red Rose Speedway*? Imagine a song that couldn't stand up to "Single Pigeon," then head for the hills. [*McGear*] **D+**

"The Casket" [Paul McCartney, Mike McGear, and Roger McGough; producer and guest performer: Paul McCartney]
[Mike McGear] McGough is an old pal of McGear's, having served with him in Grimms and later honoured by the Royal Society of Literature. No surprise, then, the lyrics to "The Casket" rise above the average. A so-so musical performance sabotages this otherwise solid composition, supported by a tasteful piano and hushed background choir. It deserves to be rescued for use elsewhere. But 30-plus years later and still entombed, it probably is fated to rest in peace. [*McGear*] **B**

"Rainbow Lady" [Paul McCartney and Mike McGear; producer and guest performer: Paul McCartney]
[Mike McGear] By now, the listener should get the distinct feeling that this is [1] basically a second-rate Wings album, [2] filled with second-rate songs, and [3] McGear may be a nice guy, but a world-class singer he is not. The mediocre and dated "Rainbow Lady" is not entirely McGear's fault. The fault more likely lies with his brother, who seems reluctant to give up the goods. Perhaps one "Leave It" is the best Paul can do, a reasonable presumption considering the ups and down of his own career. [*McGear*] **C**

"Simply Love You" [Paul McCartney and Mike McGear; producer and guest performer: Paul McCartney]
[Mike McGear] A nursery rhyme transformed into a musical snoozer by employing a worn-out chord progression. A history lesson: "Here There and Everywhere" begat "Hey Jude," which begat "Golden Slumbers." A few years later, "I Am Your Singer" begat "Mary Had a Little Lamb," which begat "Simply Love You." [*McGear*] **D+**

"Givin' Grease a Ride" [Paul McCartney and Mike McGear; producer and guest performer: Paul McCartney]
[Mike McGear] Predictable and half-done. An intriguing title doesn't make it intriguing. [*McGear*] **C-**

"The Man Who Found God on the Moon" [Paul McCartney and Mike McGear; producer and guest performer: Paul McCartney]
[Mike McGear] Routine melody, impenetrable lyrics, lackadaisical performance, ending the album not on a high note, but with a thud. [*McGear*] **C**

"Dance the Do" [Paul McCartney and Mike McGear; producer and guest performer: Paul McCartney]
[Mike McGear] Originally an A-side backed with "Norton." Endless repetition of the title, yelped over a jam session. Vivian Stanshall from the Bonzo Dog Band is supposedly in there too. Imagine: a record executive okayed this as a single because he thought he heard a hit. [*McGear Reissue*, 1991] **D**

"Sweet Baby" [Paul McCartney and Mike McGear; producer and guest performer: Paul McCartney]
[Mike McGear] Another extra, this one the B-side to "Leave It." Sufficiently terrible – flat melody, hopeless lyrics – to make you hate babies, sweet or otherwise. [*McGear Reissue*, 1991] **D+**

[bonus]

"Luxy" [Paul McCartney]
What passed for heavy metal around the Wings headquarters, this riff-heavy – but not too heavy – shout-a-thon is interesting for the garbled, borderline insane vocals and that repeating riff, playing over and over until either you start to like or give up and jump out the window. An oddity, but before you search for it, a reminder that other oddities from this era – "Picasso's Last Words," "Zoo Gang" – weren't really too odd at all. [Internet Only] **C+**

"Proud Mum" [Paul McCartney]
The soundtrack for Mother's Pride bread, mid-1974. Whether this was actually broadcast remains a mystery for us with faulty memories, but let's assume it was, as it demonstrates a strange sense of humour that compelled McCartney to associate himself with groceries. Anyway, it was actually recorded, and a two-minute version exists on *YouTube*. Similar to the lame "Lunch Box Odd Sox," "Proud Mum" mainly consists of McCartney thumping out a thin melody on the piano, sort of like a mental patient struggling to remember "Lady Madonna." You can almost visualize bread slices marching to the toaster. [Mother's Pride commercial soundtrack] **D**

"Sea Breezes [No Orchestra]" [Bryan Ferry] [Produced by Paul McCartney]
[Mike McGear] The same track as on the original album, minus the violins sawing away. Paul knows what he's doing when it comes to arranging, and the violins reinforced what was already there without distracting from or overwhelming the performance. Hence, let the sawing resume. [*McGear Deluxe Reissue*, 2019] **B**

"Leave It [Extended]" [Paul McCartney and Mike McGear; producer and guest performer: Paul McCartney]
[Mike McGear] Unedited track, complete with minor fluffs of no consequence and an occasional sax squawk. Far too long with nothing much happening. [*McGear Deluxe Reissue*, 2019] **C**

"Paddy Pipes 1,2,3" [Paul McCartney and Mike McGear; producer and guest performer: Paul McCartney]
[Mike McGear] Somebody who can't improvise tries to improvise anyway. [*McGear Deluxe Reissue*, 2019] **F**

"Do Nothing All Day" [Paul McCartney and Mike McGear; producer and guest performer: Paul McCartney]
[Mike McGear] Brother of "I Lie Around," a lazy semi-charmer about a favourite pastime. Surprisingly strong arrangement with minor but interesting touches, such as a low vocal background, a sax choir, and whistling. A song suited for McGear, to whom whimsy comes naturally, this should've been on the original album. [*McGear Deluxe Reissue*, 2019] **B**

"A to Z" [Paul McCartney and Mike McGear; producer and guest performer: Paul McCartney]
[Mike McGear] Kids singing the alphabet, cute as intended, introduce McGear who sings it too, this time over a light funk background. Back to the kids, back to McGear, solo at the end to stretch it out. Imaginative? Or filler? How about both? [*McGear Deluxe Reissue*, 2019] **B-**

"Girls on the Avenue" [Paul McCartney and Mike McGear; producer and guest performer: Paul McCartney]
[Mike McGear] Generic light rock about watching women, with a castanet making an appearance for no reason other than it was in the studio during the recording. Vanishes in a snap of the fingers. [*McGear Deluxe Reissue*, 2019] **C**

"All the Whales in the Ocean" [Paul McCartney and Mike McGear; producer and guest performer: Paul McCartney]
[Mike McGear] A demo-ish waltz, pleasant, unremarkable. The kids from "A to Z" must've had some time left on their session, as they get to perform on the coda. Highlight: some whale noises near the end. So we have a waltz, children, and whales, adding up to water-logged filler. [*McGear Deluxe Reissue*, 2019] **C-**

"Blowin' in the Bay" [Paul McCartney and Mike McGear; producer and guest performer: Paul McCartney]
[Mike McGear] A record exec says, "We've *got* to get 'Blowin' in the Bay' out there!" Earlier, "We've *got* to get "Bip Bop" out there!" [*McGear Deluxe Reissue*, 2019] **D**

"Keep Out" [Paul McCartney and Mike McGear; producer and guest performer: Paul McCartney]
[Mike McGear] Mild wordplay, but too brief. Two takes with radically different backgrounds, one sparse, the other punchy. But neither exceeds a minute. Hearing studio experiments might be fun for fanatics, but those who demand unused scraps are fated to get bunches of half-done bits like these. [*McGear Deluxe Reissue*, 2019] **C-**

"I Just Want What You Got – Money" [Paul McCartney and Mike McGear; producer and guest performer: Paul McCartney]
[Mike McGear] A proper song exists in here, but it's hard to tell from what's essentially the same verse repeated over and over against a draggy rock background. Probably a studio jam abandoned because, as these things often do, it reeked. [*McGear Deluxe Reissue*, 2019] **D**

"Let's Turn the Radio On" [Paul McCartney and Mike McGear; producer and guest performer]
[Mike McGear] Filler cleverly disguised as a song. Except it's not clever. [*McGear Deluxe Reissue*, 2019] **D**

CHAPTER SEVEN:

VENUS AND MARS [1975]

Produced by Paul McCartney
Charted at 1 [US], 1 [UK]

Glory days for McCartney who, in the aftermath of the triumphant *Band On the Run*, could release just about anything he wanted. Assuming, of course, he stuck to his don't-rock-the-boat philosophy of creating hits: radio friendly songs [a breeze for him] and a positive outlook [a no to "Cold Turkey," a yes to "Mary Had a Little Lamb"]. Plus, he'd proven that he could do it all – songwriting, performing, arranging – and hold his own with any popstar on the planet.

But there were, as always, problems. First, there was the essentially completed *One Hand Clapping* film, featuring McCartney in the studio walking through a spotty repertoire. The project was aborted for no apparent reason other than it wasn't any good. It was buried for a good part of a century, one of the most expensive all-for-naught rehearsals in rock history.

Next, McCartney's fantasy of an ideal band was again on the rocks. Guitarist Jimmy McCullough and drummer Geoff Brittan squabbled throughout the *One Hand Clapping* sessions, climaxing with Geoff heading for the door, leaving McCartney drummer-less for the second time [Denny Seiwell wasn't coming back]. Scrambling for a replacement, McCartney quickly settled on John English from Georgia, a solid percussionist who, in 1977, eventually would hear the call of the lord and become a born-again Christian. But at least for now, the drum seat was filled, and Wings would fly on.

Domestic annoyances also plagued McCartney, the most notorious of which was a California encounter with the law. While driving with Linda in Los Angeles, he whizzed through a red light and was promptly pulled over by a policeman, who smelled marijuana. Sure enough, the drug was found in Linda's purse. She was hustled off for questioning. After McCartney paid a fine, the legal matter was put to rest, but the publicity wasn't. Although a drug bust – three of them in as many years – probably didn't hurt him with the bohemian crowd, it apparently did little good with their disapproving moms and dads, a key component of McCartney's audience. [This wasn't Paul's only brush with the law. In 1972, Swedish authorities nabbed him and Linda for marijuana possession for which he coughed up a penalty of roughly two grand. In 1973, Scottish authorities arrested him for growing pot plants. In court, Paul claimed he didn't know what they were.]

Finally, there was the new material. Though McCartney likely was oblivious, his new batch of songs were a step or two down from *Band On the Run*, many of them lazily written, some seem dashed off in a few minutes, and a few showed a curious – some might say troubling – fascination with the trivial. Comic books weren't exactly a popular song topic ["Magneto and Titanium Man"], nor were recipes for turning love into soup ["Spirits of Ancient Egypt"].

His casual fans wouldn't care. They were tickled pink with easy listening numbers they could hum on the way to work. Critics, however, were another matter. Though McCartney claimed indifference, critics – after a temporary truce following *Band on the Run* – would probably have their knives out, which couldn't have been comforting. But that, more or less, is exactly what happened. Though *Mojo* and *Christgau's Record Guide* were receptive, *Rolling Stone* wasn't, with Paul Nelson opening his stinging review with, "As time goes by, John Lennon's importance to the Beatles becomes more and more self-evident."

"Venus and Mars" [Paul and Linda McCartney]
John Lennon in *Playboy*: "McCartney doesn't think he's a good lyricist ... I don't think he's made an effort." If McCartney had followed John's advice – which he was not inclined to do, regardless if the advice came

from John or anybody else – he might have produced a song with lasting impact, something that would resonate genuine emotion. But this was not to be, as he offers instead this antiseptic opening, a mish-mash of half-baked images, woozy motifs, and an obvious prelude to his live show. **B-**

"Rock Show" [Paul and Linda McCartney]
The mini-medley beginning with "Venus and Mars" proceeds with "Rock Show" a by-the-books Chuck Berry clone containing some of the most wince-inducing rhymes of McCartney's career. It rocks – make that "rocks" – like toddlers rocking their dolls. Plus the band sounds embarrassed. Or maybe I'm projecting. **C+**

"Love in Song" [Paul and Linda McCartney]
A generic ballad. McCartney holds the melody on the same couple of notes for the first four bars, creating a static line that does nothing to enhance its romantic potential. Not that there's much to start with, if we prefer our love songs to be comprehensible and grammatically accurate. Plus, the middle two bars sound like "Rudolph the Red Nosed Reindeer." **C**

"You Gave Me the Answer" [Paul and Linda McCartney]
McCartney longs for the Age of Vaudeville and can't resist dabbling in the genre. Sometimes, the results are good ["When I'm 64," *Sgt Pepper*]. Sometimes, not so good ["Honey Pie," *The Beatles*]. This is a fair one, an amiable dance number that hops along merrily to a neat piano riff backed by a teatime orchestra. He sidesteps the corn – most of it anyway – by delivering his vocal as if he's in on the joke too. One of the few bright spots on *Venus and Mars*. **B**

"Magneto and Titanium Man" [Paul and Linda McCartney]
For those of you not up on Marvel Comics history, Iron Man took on Titanium Man and the Crimson Dynamo in *Tales of Suspense* #46 & 68. This apparently was an important event in the life of McCartney, as he was moved to write about it. Yes, it's a kid song, better than "Mrs. Vandebilt" but a lot worse than "Yellow Submarine." Sometimes, don't you wish McCartney would record an album of nothing but kid songs, just to get them out of his system? Incidentally, Marvelphiles may wonder what Magneto is doing here, as he was allied with the Brotherhood of Evil Mutants, not Titanium Man. C'mon Paul – get it together! **B-**

"Letting Go" [Paul and Linda McCartney]
A dreary slog through the mud. Next to no melody, and no lyrics, as least none that makes sense to an English-speaking human. An inexplicable single following "Listen to What the Man Said," it blew up like an over-inflated balloon. On the other hand, what else from *Venus and Mars* had a shot as a single? "Spirits of Ancient Egypt"? **C**

"Venus and Mars [Reprise]" [Paul and Linda McCartney]
The "Reprise" takes another shot at the title track. The only reason for its existence I can think of is that McCartney had two arrangements with minor differences, couldn't decide between them, so he used them both. Good thing he had only one of "Letting Go." If you're the type who easily forgives dismal lyrics, wait till you get to the name of the rocket. **B-**

"Spirits of Ancient Egypt" [Paul and Linda McCartney]
McCartney name-checks Egyptians. Does this mean he's concerned about the Middle East? Nope. He learned from "Give Ireland Back to the Irish" [*Wild Life*] to give world affairs a wide berth. Instead, he pontificates here about [1] driving a car across water, [2] an Italian ghost choking on a phone cord, [3] selling buildings to Indians. I think. Musically, it's a collage of crappy ideas, none of which had the legs to stand on its own, and destined to be questioned by any competent producer. Except McCartney. **D-**

"Medicine Jar" [Jimmy McCullough and Colin Allen]
Jimmy McCullough steps up to the mic and delivers one of the album's stronger songs, so good you wonder if McCartney regrets letting the new guy show off. Jimmy wasn't a novice by a long shot, having played with One in a Million [a support band for the Who], then rose to fame with Thunderclap Newman, who earned their place in rock history with the anthem "Something in the Air." Here, he writes frank and vivid lyrics about his deceased pals, simultaneously warning and sympathizing with them, making him credible and a little scary. Musically, "Medicine Jar" features a tough riff and a guitar-driven punch that

McCartney himself rarely achieved, although he's an inventive player throughout this track. Jimmy died from a faulty heart, a condition aggravated by drugs, in 1979. Age: 26. **B**

"Call Me Back Again" [Paul and Linda McCartney]
Somewhere in the muddle of "Call Me Back Again" is a decent song, but it'll take some work to find it. First, kill the blaring horns, too grandiose for a tune this light. Next, scratch the backing vocals, which drift off key in spots. Finally, cut it in half; 2:30 is about right, not the seemingly eternal 5:00-plus. What's left is an enticing performance and a relaxed composition, with a touch of the 1950s for good measure. But this isn't that. **B-**

"Listen to What the Man Said" [Paul and Linda McCartney]
A perfect song for Billy Joel. Buffed and scrubbed until the last drops of sincerity and spontaneity were sucked down the drain, "Listen to What the Man Said" was made to order for the Top 40, circa 1975. The opening riff, played incessantly, is undeniably catchy and easily the highlight. As for the rest – McCartney's professional vocals, Tom Scott's phone-it-in sax solo – well, Billy would like it. To no one's surprise, "Listen to What the Man Said" hit #1 in the US, not exactly discouraging McCartney from cranking out more of the same. **B-**

"Treat Her Gently – Lonely Old People" [Paul and Linda McCartney]
Two tunes competing for the album's worst, stuck together to make an endurance contest for masochists. Kids won't care for it [too boring], teenagers won't care for it [too dumb], old folks won't care for it [too condescending]. Bizarre images abound. She's demented? Boozed up? At the same time? And this time, a by-the-books "pretty" tune won't save it. **D**

"Crossroads Theme" [Tony Hatch]
An unobtrusive buttress for a TV show. McCartney didn't write it – credit goes to Tony Hatch, who did music for a variety of projects including 1960's *Circus of Horrors* – but Paul thought it'd be great commentary on "Lonely Old People." See, old people like soap operas, and this was a soap opera and – oh never mind. **D**

[bonus]

"Lunch Box/Odd Sox" [Paul and Linda McCartney]
Putrid instrumental knock-off with McCartney on piano and various elves clanking away on percussion. This was for a TV show? Does McCartney know that "Odd Sox" is an actual company that specializes in novelty socks such as "Hey Arnold" and "Ghostbusters Slime?" Maybe Odd Sox the Company will send him a sample of "Hulk Hogan Varsity." [*Venus and Mars Deluxe*] **D**

"My Carnival" [Paul and Linda McCartney]
A jam turned into a song that should've stayed a jam. Its awfulness increases as it trudges towards something like an ending. [*Venus and Mars Deluxe*] **D**

"Bon Voyageur" [Paul McCartney and Tony Dorsey]
If you think that this DVD-only entry is a secret McCartney composition, guess again. It's actually bits and pieces of various *Venus and Mars* tracks ["Listen to What the Man Said," "Magneto and Titanium Man"] accompanying a short collection of home movies about McCartney and Linda's New Orleans vacation. However, near the end, a one-minute section shows McCartney jamming with his buddies on some indecipherable up-tempo debris, so I guess that counts. Horn player Tony Dorsey is supposedly in there someplace. [*Venus and Mars Deluxe*] **D**

"Junior's Farm" [Paul and Linda McCartney]
McCartney's reputation as a balladeer may be somewhat overblown. Aside from the heartbreaking "Maybe I'm Amazed," quality ballads from his solo career seem few and far between. Compare that to his growing list of first-class rockers: "Hi Hi Hi," "Jet," "Helen Wheels", and now this one, another irresistible barn burner. While superficially similar to "Helen Wheels" – check the tempo and McCartney's delivery – it's a winner without question, filled with stylish hooks and raging guitars. [*Venus and Mars Deluxe*] **B+**

"Sally G" [Paul and Linda McCartney]
McCartney at his most ingratiating. Recorded in Nashville, he goes country, limply, with this tedious tale of a good girl gone naughty. Somebody thought it was OK, as it crawled its way to #17 on the US charts, the flip side of the many times superior "Junior's Farm" at #3. [*Venus and Mars Deluxe*] **C-**

"Bridge On the River Suite" [Paul and Linda McCartney]
Horn-driven, leisurely, and yawn-inducing instrumental, which sounds like the accompaniment to the end credits of a pastoral travelogue. [*Venus and Mars Deluxe*] **C+**

"Going to New Orleans" [Paul and Linda McCartney]
An embryonic take of "My Carnival" with different lyrics, essentially the same melody, and a stripped-down band. If a first draft of "My Carnival" sounds appealing, here you go. The stripped band improves somewhat on the dull "My Carnival" by emphasizing its silly side. **D+**

"4th of July" [Paul and Linda McCartney]
A demo for John Christie, presented here as a slow-ish [think "Blackbird"] acoustic guitar piece, sung by an introspective McCartney. Clearly not intended for public consumption – too many missteps – but with a bit of work, this could have been a *Venus and Mars* highlight. Surely someone pointed this out to him. Or maybe he really and truly can't tell the promising from the mediocre. [*Venus and Mars Deluxe*] **B**

"Rock Show [Old Version]" [Paul and Linda McCartney]
Demo time. Slower, much less production, no backing vocals, ends with a garage band jam. Ugh. [*Venus and Mars Deluxe*] **C-**

"Letting Go [Extended]" [Paul and Linda McCartney]
Keyboard heavy, echo all but gone as are background vocals, and a weary lead vocal. Still, this version is more intimate, making it a worthy alternate. Those interested in the genesis of "Letting Go" have an interesting specimen to examine, and, except for McCartney's vocal, one with more to offer than original. [*paulmccartney.com*] **B-**

"Love My Baby" [Paul McCartney]
Less than a minute and a half long, this 1974 *One Hand Clapping* outtake features McCartney, his electric piano, and a flimsy improvisation that vaguely sounds like "Little Woman Love," only worse. If this slipped by you, worry not. You haven't missed a thing. [*paulmccartney.com*] **C-**

"Rock Show [New Version]" [Paul and Linda McCartney]
Perhaps the realization that "Rock Show" is one of McCartney's lamest rockers, ever, inspired McCartney to try this. A fraction more energy from the vocals and elimination of the backgrounds are essentially all the differences, as it otherwise just curls up and dies. [*paulmccartney.com*] **C**

"Night Owl" [James Taylor; guest performer: Paul McCartney]
[Carly Simon] Taking a break from fretting over *Red Rose Speedway*, McCartney dropped by Simon's session to lend his throat to Taylor's tune, presumably a nod to Taylor's association with Apple Records [he was one of Apple's early discoveries]. A mediocre Taylor song, benefitting only slightly from McCartney's contribution. [*No Secrets*] **B –**

"Walking in the Park with Eloise" [Jim McCartney]
[Country Hams] Lawrence Walk-type number written by McCartney's dad, Jim. Credited to the Country Hams, an impromptu band from Nashville [allegedly featuring Chet Atkins and Floyd Cramer], the instrumental bounces along as happy as can be, its jaunty melody carried by trumpets and rinky-dink piano. Great for what it is: nostalgia for gray beards. [*Venus and Mars Deluxe*] **B**

CHAPTER EIGHT:

WINGS AT THE SPEED OF SOUND [1976]

Produced by Paul McCartney
Charted at 1 [US], 2 [UK]

McCartney the Stubborn was determined to solidify his long-held dream of being a part of a band and to cement Wings in the public consciousness. He longed for this, even though he was doing fine, pretty much all on his own. *Band On the Run*, largely a solo project, not only sold millions, it generated critical respect which must've warmed the Stubborn One's heart. And true, other superstars – Elton John, Bob Dylan, George Harrison – saw no need to draw extra attention to their backing bands, touring [as McCartney planned to do] on the strength of their own names.

Didn't matter. In spite of his formidable musical skills, McCartney hungered for the camaraderie of musicians on a mission, one for all, all for one. He ached for the exchange of ideas, the discussion plans, the back and forth involved in developing songs. That his point of view and his alone was the one that prevailed rarely clouded his fantasies.

So Wings it was. There, emblazoned on the cover of the new *Wings at the Speed of Sound*, in big block red letters: WINGS, with not a McCartney in sight. The back, inadvertently echoing the front of *A Hard Day's Night*, were the band members making loopy faces. Not insignificantly, everyone was the same size. For this album and the mega-tour to follow, Wings would be a group of equals. Of course, McCartney was likely the only human being on the planet who felt this way.

Response to the new album wasn't surprising – fans: delighted, critics: stomach aches – but McCartney's enthusiasm for Wings overwhelmed the reaction, which he seemed to regard as old news. He stayed focused on Wings and their upcoming tour. What he had planned would go a long way towards making the band a household name. Public support – inevitably he hoped, fingers crossed – would follow.

So, in preparation for *Wings Over America*, more edicts from the Stubborn One were falling in place:

1. Since this was a Wings project, all the members would sing.

2. Since the tour would be all about Wings, the set list would be mostly Wings songs, with a few Beatles' numbers tossed in to keep long-time fans from ripping up the seats.

3. "Silly Love Songs" would be the new single. With luck, maybe "Silly Love Songs" would be a hit on the disco circuit, because, after all, it *was* a disco song.

"Let 'Em In" [Paul and Linda McCartney]

If you imagine this being sung by a drug-addled hippie, it works, big time. McCartney plays the part of the hippie, so stoned that he can't even drag himself out of bed to see who's come to visit. In march a parade of weirdos – old relatives, a famous minister, the Everly Brothers – and McCartney still can't get up. It's all wired to the eccentric, imaginative accompaniment of a doorbell, heavenly flutes, and a drum corps from the military outpost next door, making this one of his most off-the-wall tunes ever. McCartney snuck this dope-drenched tune onto Top 40 radio, where it reached a deserved #2 in the UK and #3 in the US. **B+**

"The Note You Never Wrote" [Paul and Linda McCartney]

It begins with roughly eight counts of the same note, an alarm bell that McCartney is coasting. Singer Denny Laine handles it as well as he can, but face it: this sentimental tripe is a long way from the Moody Blues' enduring "Go Now." As is true of so many McCartney compositions, a good song lurks somewhere inside, but burdened with inane lyrics and random instruments [jingle bells?], it can't get out. **B-**

"She's My Baby" [Paul and Linda McCartney]
An off-the-cuff song with atrocious lyrics and a where-have-I-heard-that-before melody. McCartney sings like he's looking at his cute face in the mirror. The quality of *Wings at the Speed of Sound* wouldn't have been affected a bit if "She's My Baby" never existed. **B-**

"Beware My Love" [Paul and Linda McCartney]
Once past the weak opening – McCartney adores choirs – we're off and running on the album's sole rocker. Guitars take off, the piano bangs away, and McCartney fires on all cylinders as if he's being chased by pot cops. The bass effectively leads the band through a series of pounding, descending chords as McCartney's vocal reaches a level of intensity that sweeps him away. But the lyrics don't work – so what else is new? – and the band is held back by a conservative mix that, prominent among other crimes, nudges the guitars too far back. It's no "Jet." But it's no "Silly Love Songs" either. **B+**

"Wino Junko" [Jimmy McCullough and Colin Allen]
Re-write of *Venus and Mars'* "Medicine Jar," which is plain sad. A painful list of degradations, agonies, and health disintegrations endured by a junkie, making one wonder what this grim song is doing on an album with the helium-light "Cook of the House." Morphine and alcohol killed the talented Jimmy at age 26. You think "Wino Junko" is the testament he wanted? **B-**

"Silly Love Songs" [Paul and Linda McCartney]
A slick outing sporting a terrific bass line and let's-be-friends vocal is a flat-out bid for recognition at the world's dance parlors, dating it irrevocably as a disco song. These days, it's all but impossible to hear this and not think of those superficial times of John Travolta, the Hustle, and Disco Duck – that's what McCartney wanted? Fixating on a single note is a warning sign for lazy writing, McCartney's smiley-face counterpoint is nauseating, and not counting the bass [not bad, the best thing on the record], the arrangement comes right off the Disco Dollar Store. McCartney seems to be daring us to criticize his ditty in the lyrics. Okay, here it is: you could do a lot better than this cynical commercial for a fleeting dance craze. **C**

"Cook of the House" [Paul and Linda McCartney]
Is coercing your non-singer wife to sing a lousy song grounds for divorce? Linda attempting "Seaside Woman" was sort of okay, but that was a novelty song assumed by all to be a one-shot. This is different. This is awful. Over the sizzle of an electrocuted eggplant and Linda, on the edge of exasperated, recites/sings a list of odds and ends in the kitchen cabinet destined for the next pot of vegetarian soup. Would you rather have a bowl or, perhaps, another grocery song? **F**

"Time to Hide" [Denny Lane]
Denny overstays his welcome with this retro-sixties mediocrity. Yes, he sings well, and yes, the band performs like a passable early Moody Blues, lurching toward barely acceptable filler for *Magnificent Moodies* – make that *Moody Blues: The B-Sides*. You have to do better than this, Denny, or McCartney won't let you write another one. **C-**

"Must Do Something About It" [Paul and Linda McCartney]
This is where filler lives, fertile land for the seeds of sleep. This wearisome lullaby is brought to you by first-time singer Joe English, performing on a track that doesn't sound like it'd be of interest to anybody else in the band except the new guy. **C-**

"San Ferry Anne" [Paul and Linda McCartney]
Cute flute trills and trumpet flutters kill the melancholy that gave this slight song its appeal. If McCartney had backed off the corny flourishes, maybe. The moody mid-section and restrained vocals help, but not enough. **B**

"Warm and Beautiful" [Paul and Linda McCartney]
Though it opens with a dull five-note motif, the sweet chords beneath save it before the vocal takes over, guiding us though one of the strongest melodies of McCartney's career. A restrained McCartney sings effortlessly as always, but this time he's got a challenging run of notes to deal with – the middle eight jumps over an octave – and it's a thrill to hear him wrestle it to the ground. Why McCartney has

neglected this poignant gem in concert is a mystery. And why hasn't it been absorbed into the repertoire of standards, like "Yesterday?" **A-**

[bonus]

"Silly Love Songs [Demo]" [Paul and Linda McCartney]
McCartney at the piano delivering a modest version of "Silly Love Songs," halfway interesting, halfway the same old crap. Without the musical distractions, we notice the weak melody, the fairly active chord sequence, the strained vocalisms [when accompanied by Linda], and the lack of a strong bass line, which, as the demo proves, serves as the heart of the song. Just hearing the demo, it's difficult to imagine this would be a smash single. But times were different then, allowing so-so material to flourish too often. **C-**

"She's My Baby [Demo]" [Paul and Linda McCartney]"
Singing to himself, a subdued McCartney walks through this forgettable number. Nothing hidden is revealed, except the monotonous sing-song up-and-down quality of the verse, which gets old, real fast. **C-**

"Let 'Em In [Demo]" [Paul and Linda McCartney]
Livelier than the studio track and filled with unused tidbits, making it a kick to hear. McCartney's enthusiasm awakens, he comes to life, and his glee is infectious. Points for the giggling baby at the end. **B**

"Message to Joe" [Paul and Linda McCartney]
Thirty seconds of electronic piffle that sounds like parakeets choking each other. **F**

"Beware My Love [John Bonham Version]" [Paul and Linda McCartney]
You'd expect a thunderstorm from the Led Zeppelin drummer. And you'd be right. Bonham [the Led Zeppelin guy] holds back a bit so as not to steamroll the hapless Wings on this alternate take, but he's out in front and confident all the way. McCartney livens up, which is fun, and some bizarre guitar riffs electrify the end. **B**

"Must Do Something About It [McCartney Version]" [Paul and Linda McCartney]
Same song, different – and better – singer. But does McCartney improve it? Not much. Another would-be B-side for a middle-of-the-road single. **C**

"Warm and Beautiful [Instrumental]" [Paul and Linda McCartney]
Music box version of the album's best track. An okay way to kill a couple of minutes, but compared to the vocal track, it's just passable. **B**

"Liverpool Lou/Ten Years After On Strawberry Jam" [Dominic Dehan; guest performer and writer: Paul McCartney]
[The Scaffold] A low budget Monty Python, the group consisted of McCartney's brother Mike, comedian Roger McGough, and poet John Gorman, who issued records from the late 60s through the 70s. Once in a while, the gods smiled, and they landed a hit. A predictable waltz, dominated by Mike, it's aimed at oldsters who like their comedy easy on the brain; that is, without a whiff of surrealism or cynicism. Paul provided the backing, but largely stays out of sight. He also furnished the throwaway B-side, some lazy noodling to accompany a Scaffold comedy routine. [Both on *The Scaffold's Singles A's and B's*: "Liverpool Lou" **C** ; "Ten Years After on Strawberry Jam" **F**]

"Mine for Me" [Paul and Linda McCartney; guest performer: Paul McCartney]
[Rod Stewart] By the time Stewart reached the end of his fifth album for Mercury Records, ennui was the name of the game. So when McCartney offered him this song, sounding like something Ringo Starr would reject, Stewart snapped it up. Plasticized McCartney tunes exist. This is one of them. [*Smiler*] **C**

"Change/Goodbye/Never Say Goodbye/Star Song" [Adam Faith; guest performer: Paul McCartney]
[Adam Faith] Faith was a successful UK pop singer and TV personality who was heading toward the end of his recording career when McCartney volunteered to turn a few synthesizer knobs [first three songs] and sing background [last song] on his new album. Faith sounds professional but tired. [*I Survive*] **C**

CHAPTER NINE:

WINGS OVER AMERICA [1976]

Produced by Paul McCartney
Charted at 1 [US], 8 [UK]

Hey, what happened to "Cook of the House?" The set list for this 1975-76 gargantuan tour – which began as a three-month sweep through Europe and Australia, followed two months in North America, then back to Europe for another two months – included roughly half of the *Wings at the Speed of Sound* and even more of *Venus and Mars*. Present were the unmemorable "Spirits of Ancient Egypt" and "Call Me Back Again," but no "Cook," certainly to the relief of Linda who'd be on stage for the entire tour, banging away on her rudimentary keyboard parts. Also notable in their near-absence: a handful of Beatle songs, which to the cynic seemed like an obligatory gesture and a disappointing one.

McCartney's insistence on including so many Wings songs was puzzling, since there was hardly a demand to hear deep-cut Wings. Although a sizeable percentage of the massive audience – tickets sold out everywhere almost instantly – wanted to hear "Band On the Run," "Silly Love Songs," and other recent hits, it's a good bet they were spending good money to hear a genuine Beatle perform genuine Beatles songs. After all, Wings were mortals. The Beatles were gods.

Still, fans took what they could get. To no one's surprise, the response to the Beatles' five songs was ecstatic. As for the rest, well, the audience liked them too, but who's kidding who? This was as close to a Beatle concert as anyone would ever get.

The first US concert took place on May 3, 1976 in Fort Worth, a sell-out of course, then off they went, filling stadiums, coliseums, and sports arenas from coast to coast. The band travelled first class on a modern jet airline with the Wings logo emblazed on the fuselage. Inside, space was cleared away for sort of a club room, capable of satisfying the band's whims. The jet was loaded with musicians [including four brass players], McCartney and Linda's kids, the kids' babysitter, McCartney's bodyguard, and various staff members, with marathon poker games – in which McCartney participated periodically – to help pass the time. No drugs, no groupies. This was strictly a family affair.

The state-of-the-art show employed the best light and sound systems money could buy. When McCartney suddenly appeared on center stage, nattily dressed, smiling away, cooing "Venus and Mars," the crowd erupted, screamed, then erupted some more. McCartney was in his element.

The music was tight, energetic, and professional. Flubs, miscues, mic problems, wrong notes – typical for a rock show – were scattered throughout the performances and bothered no one.

Except McCartney. When the tour ended, he hustled his musicians into a recording studio to fix the tapes, a process often grueling owing to McCartney's desire for perfectionism. How long did it take to get the live tapes into a state acceptable to the Stubborn One? Drummer Joe English: "Forever."

And there were movies for McCartney to fuss over. The first, *Rockshow*, was a documentary of the concert, assembled from various US venues. Basically, it was a standard 30-song concert film with an abundance of close-ups of McCartney. [To be fair, it *was* McCartney's movie]. The theatrical release was held until 1980 and McCartney, busy in the studio, couldn't attend, and *Rockshow* more or less vanished. It was re-released in 2013, all 120 minutes-plus of it.

The second film, *Wings Over the World*, consisted of excerpts from *Rockshow*, along with rehearsal clips, backstage antics, and a few home movies. Released as a TV documentary to the BBC in 1979, it contains few surprises but remains a pleasant diversion for hardcore Wings lovers. It was released again in 2013 as part of the *Wings at the Speed of Sound Deluxe* package.

As for the album, *Wings Over America*, a three-record set, received mixed reviews. *Pop Matters*: "...does little in the way of providing fresh or even different perspective on the material." But its spectacular sales rocketed it to #1 on the US Top 10 and earned it platinum status. It also ended McCartney's run of #1 albums for a long time to come.

"Venus and Mars [Live 1976]" [Paul and Linda McCartney]
Ever the showman, McCartney designed this unremarkable but effective show opening, most likely when he was putting together the *Venus and Mars* album. It began with a delicate "Venus and Mars," virtually identical to the studio track, which lit the fuse for ... **B-**

"Rock Show [Live 1976]" [Paul and Linda McCartney]
...the band springing into action, rocketing into "Rock Show," which blew the top off an arena full of gawking and screaming spectators. More of a settling-down number instead of a sure fire killer, "Rock Show" clunked its way to an anti-climactic finish, then... **C**

"Jet [Live 1976]" [Paul and Linda McCartney]
...the band blasted into "Jet," upping the ante with the best from *Band On the Run*, using the stripped down ensemble to propel the concert into nirvana. **B**

"Let Me Roll It [Live 1976]" [Paul McCartney]
Another good one, and time for the audience to take a breath and bask in McCartney's clever John Lennon imitation. Would this persist all night? Well ... **B**

"Spirits of Ancient Egypt [Live 1976]" [Paul McCartney]
...no. Head scratching from the crowd who were primed for a Beatle tune but got a slice of sludge instead. **D+**

"Medicine Jar [Live 1976]" [Jimmy McCullough and Colin Allen]
A change of pace as Jimmy steps up to the mic and reels off a competent but enjoyable number about dropping dead. **B**

"Maybe I'm Amazed [Live 1976]" [Paul McCartney]
Are you alone? Lower the lights. Put on "Maybe I'm Amazed" from *McCartney*. McCartney sounds sad, desperate, compelling. Now turn up the lights, invite some partying pals over, and put on "Maybe I'm Amazed" from *Wings Over America*. McCartney sounds excited, buoyant, eager to please. Your preference? Released as a single, it rose to #10 in America, making the *McCartney* track, its emotional intensity dwarfing *Wings Over America*, resonate even more. **B**

"Call Me Back Again [Live 1976]" [Paul McCartney]
Way too slow for a concert like this, a trial for those who haven't heard it before, and not much fun to play whether you're a guitarist, horn man, or tambourine whacker. Maybe McCartney likes it. **C**

"Lady Madonna [Live 1976]" [Paul McCartney and John Lennon]
Those credits – McCartney and Lennon? If you say so. But the odds of public perception changing because of *Wings Over America* – which awards credit to McCartney first, Lennon last, when about a zillion Beatles albums beg to differ – are slim to none. As for the performance, what can be said except that it's the dream of every Beatles fan come true. A solid effort by McCartney, who must be thrilled and a bit stunned at the response to this classic. **B+**

"The Long and Winding Road [Live 1976]" [Paul McCartney and John Lennon]
McCartney hated the *Let It Be* version with all those sappy Phil Spector strings, so this is the chance for him to get it right. Listening to him glide over the melancholy melody, it's hard not to get caught up in that enduring Beatle magic, and remind yourself there was a time, not that long ago, when music wasn't just a disposable product but a religious experience. Too bad that a few extraneous notes, especially near the end, indicates that McCartney doesn't take it as seriously as his audience. **B+**

"Live and Let Die [Live 1976]" [Paul McCartney]

Fireworks, smoke bombs, laser beams. If you liked James Bond – for a brief time, the only serious rival to the Beatles – McCartney is here for you. Tough to concentrate on the song if you were in the audience, what with all the extraneous noises, but if you're home, you'll notice the music seems a little thin and the effects a little obnoxious. It stayed in the show forever as a guaranteed crowd pleaser. And you know how McCartney loves to please the crowds. **B-**

"Picasso's Last Words [Live 1976]" [Paul McCartney]

This opened the acoustic set. Because the special effects were left in the studio, it's superior here. Consider it a warm-up piece for the meat of the set, coming right up. **C**

"Richard Cory [Live 1976]" [Paul Simon]

A mystifying choice. Not because it's bad, but because there's a good dozen or so obscure Paul Simon songs made to order for Wings as they sport stronger melodies [like "April Come She Will," "At the Zoo," "So Long Frank Lloyd Wright"]. A joke in the middle jolts us with the uncomfortable fact that this is a song about suicide. **C**

"Bluebird [Live 1976]" [Paul McCartney]

Acceptable with or without the effects, possibly because the album decorations were so subtle. Danger: we seem to be wandering dangerously close to the middle of the road. **B**

"I've Just Seen a Face [Live 1976]" [Paul McCartney and John Lennon]

A Beatles song with the balls whacked off. But the music is basically intact, making this a warmly played cover of a terrific tune. **B+**

"Blackbird [Live 1976]" [Paul McCartney and John Lennon]

Since the original was acoustic, this is the most accurate reading of a Beatles number, and, of course, it's gorgeous. Thanks to McCartney for not mangling it with electric guitars or his wife's harmonizing. **A**

"Yesterday [Live 1976]" [Paul McCartney and John Lennon]

Not a dry eye in the house as McCartney launches into the most covered tune of all time. He sings it like he just learned it, an accomplishment when you consider that a walk-though would have satisfied the crown. It sounds like an iffy idea, but the substitution of horns for the strings not only works, but elevates the song as well. If only they were all like this. **A**

"You Gave Me the Answer [Live 1976]" [Paul McCartney]

Identical to *Venus and Mars*, except the horn section covers the tea time orchestra heard on the album. No big loss. Dedicated to concert goers who want their artists to sound exactly like the record. **B**

"Magneto and Titanium Man [Live 1976]" [Paul McCartney]

A zip through the wasteland. Some of "Magneto" is spoken, and McCartney sounds embarrassed when it's time to recite. **C+**

"Go Now [Live 1976]" [Larry Banks and Milton Bennett]

A left field hit in 1964 by the Denny Laine version of the Moody Blues, this is the second surprise [after "Richard Cory"] and a welcome one. Doubtful if the kids in the crowd knew the connection between Denny and the Moodies, but McCartney did, Denny did, and everybody over 25 did. The kids could stand to wait five minutes. **B**

"My Love [Live 1976]" [Paul McCartney]

There ought to be a law against doing "My Love" and "Yesterday" in the same show. Fess up, Paul – you know, deep down, "My Love" ought to be set outside and left to rot, right? Right? **C+**

"Listen to What the Man Said [Live 1976]" [Paul McCartney]

For dancers, not for analysts who will have a hard time finding anything of substance. Except that seductive, worm-like riff burrowing into your brain, for which you'll need to hunt down an exterminator. **C+**

"Let 'Em In [Live 1976]" [Paul McCartney]
Another near-exact album copy. Denny, however, brightens things up by donning a military drum and a three corned hat to play the snare cadence. Adults in the crowd may be uneasy, fearing they've wandered into a children's concert by mistake. **B-**

"Time to Hide [Live 1976]" [Denny Lane]
Denny approaches the mic, opens his mouth, and out crawls a sleeping pill. Instead of this, about another Moody Blues tune? **D+**

"Silly Love Songs [Live 1976]" [Paul McCartney]
McCartney should've paired this with "Listen to What the Man Said" and let the dancers boogie their hearts out. Amuse yourself with the thought of simultaneously playing the intricate bass line while singing the melody exactly on key. McCartney sounds like he could do it half asleep. **C-**

"Beware My Love [Live 1976]" [Paul McCartney]
A welcome rocker that not only accurately duplicates the album cut, it actually nudges it the right direction. Though the album vocal was pristine, this is the winner, due most likely to [1] the crazed audience cheering him on, and [2] a better-than-average song earning its surprising response. This was made for a crowd, and should have been revived for future tours, as it was essentially dropped after *Wings Over America*. **B+**

"Letting Go [Live 1976]" [Paul McCartney]
This changes the tempo but lowers the energy, considerably. Maybe McCartney thought that he needed to calm down the crowd. Success! **D**

"Band On the Run [Live 1976]" [Paul McCartney]
So iconic is this memorable song that crowd was with him at the first note. He'd have to muff it completely to blow it at this point, but of course he doesn't, letting it play out in all its glory, every note in place, more or less. The crowd cheers, McCartney beams. As for the performance, it trails the album version in precision and enthusiasm. McCartney beams anyway. **B**

"Hi Hi Hi [Live 1976]" [Paul McCartney]
Fierce rocker, McCartney having a blast. Makes you wish you were there, a goal "Spirits of Ancient Egypt" failed to achieve. **B**

"Soily [Live 1976]" [Paul McCartney]
Dumb song, with wince-inducing vocals and a flaccid performance. Plus it's too easy to mix up with "The Mess." My nominee for the most breathtakingly bad lyrics in the McCartney catalogue. And that includes "Bip Bop." Uh, possibly. **F**

[bonus]

Live at the Cow Palace
A bonus CD accompanying *Wings Over America Deluxe* containing different live versions of eight songs, which are basically the same as on the un-deluxe version. Utterly superfluous, unless you think you'd enjoy a sloppier "Picasso's Last Words." **B-**

"Pure Gold" [Paul McCartney; guest performer: Paul McCartney]
[Ringo Starr] Another Ringo album, another McCartney half-baked potato. Pseudo-nostalgia over the oldest chord progression in the catalogue. Consider that this is half of the World's Greatest Band at work. [*Ringo's Rotogravure*] **D**

CHAPTER TEN:

THRILLINGTON [1977]

Produced by Percy "Thrills" Thrillington [Paul McCartney]
Did not chart [US], did not chart [UK]

On a whim, oblivious to the growing British punk scene and the increasing popularity of the anarchic Sex Pistols, McCartney decided to release the six-year-old *Thrillington* album, an instrumental take on *Ram*, vaudeville style. A curious world noticed for a second, then returned to their Clash albums. At this point, not many were interested in McCartney's bonkers projects, particularly ones as precious as an album of sitting room covers. That he was really producer Percy Thrillington came as a surprise to virtually no one, and his tepid revelation of the "secret," mentioned in a *Rolling Stone* piece, landed with a thud.

Thrillington stands as an album nobody asked for and, aside from collectors, nobody much wanted. A re-visit to *Ram*, performed in a non-revelatory style, much worse than the original, it's instantly disposable. Despite the involvement of top musicians – Steve Gray and Herbie Flowers, to name two, with Richard Anthony Hewson helping on the arrangements – this is McCartney's baby all the way, revealing his exasperating eccentricity or how far he'd follow his whimsical self-indulgence, no matter how stupid. And fans complained about Lennon's *Two Virgins*?

"Too Many People [Thrillington]" [Paul McCartney]
Tuning up, mumbled chatter – hey, it's *Sgt Pepper*! My mistake. It's a track from *McCartney Plays for Preschoolers*. **D**

"3 Legs [Thrillington]" [Paul McCartney]
Sleazy sax-driven strip tease by hamsters. **D+**

"Ram On [Thrillington]" [Paul McCartney]
Be still my heart, an attractive opening. Then a schmaltzy sax slithers in and wrecks it. **D**

"Dear Boy [Thrillington]" [Paul McCartney]
Basically a choir excursion, the voices aren't as overwhelming as they are in the original. But then, instruments lumber in, and it's blahhh time. **D+**

"Uncle Albert/Admiral Halsey [Thrillington]" [Paul McCartney]
A lazy arrangement with a handful of players. Which isn't terrible, but a few seconds in, you wonder, what's the point? Too thin, too slow, too anemic, forget it. **D**

"Smile Away [Thrillington]" [Paul McCartney]
"Sentimental Journey" crossed with a potato chip commercial played in a tempo for slugs. **D**

"Heart of the Country [Thrillington]" [Paul McCartney]
If it's a joke, I got it after the first few measure of "Too Many People." Ever had an annoying kid tell you tell the same joke over and over and over? **D-**

"Monkberry Moon Delight [Thrillington]" [Paul McCartney]
An ailing trumpet hacks up a scrawny melody. **D-**

"Eat at Home [Thrillington]" [Paul McCartney]
Made to order for the hearing impaired. **D-**

"Long Haired Lady [Thrillington]" [Paul McCartney]
Instead of the identical approach again and again, a salvageable version of this album would attempt different styles. Examples: a country "Eat at Home," a punk rock "Heart of the Country," a baroque "Ram On," an electronic "Smile Away." Since this would require effort and multiple styles would spoil the "joke," there is zero chance this could have happened. **D-**

"Back Seat of My Car [Thrillington]" [Paul McCartney]
At last, a saloon piano from a 1950's B-western tells us it's time to go. Before we go, may we torch the saloon? **D**

[bonus]

"One of Those Days in England" [Roy Harper; guest performer: Paul McCartney]
[Roy Harper] Renowned musical hero who's scooped up virtually every honor the industry has to offer, Harper has produced dozens of well-received albums, including this one featuring vocals by Paul and Linda on a single track. But what a track. Nearly 20 minutes long, the sprawling mini-masterpiece touches on a fond nostalgia for an England that used to be. The McCartney couple tends to be buried, but for a piece that shines like this, no big deal. [*Bullinamingvase*] **B+**

"Giddy" [Paul McCartney]
[Roger Daltrey] McCartney fiddled around with the *Ram*-era "Rode All Night," coming up with this music hall ditty. Daltrey blasts his way through it, trying to do his best with not very much. "Rode All Night" was a poor song – actually, more of a jam fragment – to begin with, but one supposes that Daltrey took what he could get. The backing supergroup [including Mick Ronson, Eric Clapton, Pete Townsend, Keith Moon, John Entwistle, but no Paul] adds some muscle, but this isn't worth the lift. [*One of the Boys*] **C+**

Holly Days [Producer and guest performer: Paul McCartney]
[Denny Laine] The second solo album by Laine, the first being the inoffensive *Ahh ... Laine*, consists of Buddy Holly remakes, all performed by Laine and McCartney, with incidental assistance from Linda. Songs include the expected: "Heartbeat," "It's So Easy," "I'm Gonna Love You Too," and seven others. Knowing McCartney's fondness for Holly – he bought Holly's entire catalogue – this seems to be more of a McCartney project than a Laine project, but whatever. As a Laine album: ehh. As a Holly album: double ehh. As a McCartney album: z-z-z ... **C**

CHAPTER ELEVEN:

LONDON TOWN [1978]

Produced by Paul McCartney
Charted at 2 [US], 4 [UK]

Why was 1977 a meaningful year for McCartney? It wasn't because of the *London Town* recording, although that had its problems. For reasons unknown, McCartney decided to move the sessions for *London Town* to the Virgin Islands and record on three boats bobbing on the Caribbean Sea. After the initial bliss of vacation wore off, troubles began: electrical mishaps, psoriasis from sun exposure, a broken foot, a marijuana bust from the Coast Guard. McCartney decided to cut his losses and move the recording back to the UK.

It wasn't because his next tour had been postponed. Preparation for his follow-up to *Wings Over America* were derailed when, to McCartney's surprise and delight, Linda announced she was pregnant. If Linda couldn't perform, a tour was out of the question. In spite of the opinions of the inner circle, the negative critical reaction to her musicianship, and the tears of agony from fan-sensitive promoters, he wanted – he *had* – to have Linda there, on stage a few feet away, for her support and reassurance.

It wasn't because of the abrupt departures of his musicians. Jimmy McCullough was shown the door for one too many squabbles. Drummer Joe English hit the road because of stingy wages. Down to just three – McCartney, Linda, the ever-loyal Denny. It was *Band On the Run* all over again.

So what was meaningful in 1977? It was the release of a single," Mull of Kintyre." This song wasn't especially bad. In fact, it was stylish in its own way, a waltz derived from old Scottish folk tunes, complete with bagpipes, and lyrics espousing the beauty of the rural country. Sentimental, friendly, and nostalgic, it rang out in pubs, eateries, everywhere that common folk would gather for a drink or two and sing their cares away. The single rose to #1 on the UK charts, stayed there, and outsold the UK's biggest single to date. Which was, ironically, "She Loves You" by the Beatles.

Problem was, a large segment of the British populace, mainly lower class youth, didn't respond to this nostalgia for a Britain they never knew. The Britain they knew – and loathed – was swamped with growing unemployment, indifferent adults, empty promises, and a tomorrow as bleak as a blank slate. They weren't in the mood for a multi-millionaire rock god crooning about a beautiful green peninsula he probably owned.

Then, out nowhere, sprang the Sex Pistols, a rock group like no other and the antithesis of Paul McCartney. With their permanent sneer, clothes from the trash can, and an inability to play more than a handful of guitar chords, the Sex Pistols were embraced by the outsiders – the punks – in a celebration of defiance. Incredibly, the punks pushed the Sex Pistols' debut single "Anarchy in the UK" to the lower ranks of the British charts, and their second "God Save the Queen" to a stunning #2.

At the age of 34, McCartney felt like an old man. The division between the old and the young hadn't been this stark since 1967's Summer of Love. Only this time, McCartney was on the wrong side. British kids, some of them anyway, had no use for McCartney, not with his mansions, his jets, or his hokey "Mull of Kintyre." He didn't belong to them. He belonged to their parents. Would the division last? Who knew? But for now, it was here, and it was real.

Reaction in the US wasn't as extreme, but it was still troubling for the commercially conscious Paul. *London Town* failed to reach #1, an eye-opener that suggested all was not well. Though the subsequent single, "With a Little Luck," hit the top, the previous "Mull of Kintyre" barely registered, an embarrassment for which McCartney apparently blamed Capitol Records, with whom he parted company. [Columbia quickly signed on.] Critical reaction to *London Town* was savage: *MusicHound*: 2 stars out of 5, *Rolling*

Stone Record Guide: 2 stars out of 5. *Ultimate Classic Rock*: "...scattered, unfocused .... lazy and bored ...."*London Town* would have been less of a one way ticket to the landfill if the writing had been stronger, but a feeling of get-it-done-and-get-it-out hung over the record like a dense fog. For many, *London Town* was a letdown, all of it cautious, generally unimaginative, and displaying little growth since *Ram*. It felt like McCartney couldn't wait to get the writing finished, so he could immerse himself in recording and playing on his Caribbean boats. And really, who cared about the here-today-gone-tomorrow Sex Pistols anyway?

Heather, his daughter, did. She was a fan.

"London Town" [Paul McCartney and Denny Laine]
Perhaps it's McCartney's insecurity that prevents him from taking chances, why he polishes his songs until the spontaneity has been scrubbed away, all the while remaining inoffensive to everyone within hearing range. This is in spite of the fact that as a rock musician, and as former member of the most innovative group on the planet who took radical turns with virtually every release, you'd think he'd feel compelled do the opposite, at least once in a while. But it's not happening. "London Town," which supposedly evokes his home's lonely streets, instead flits from here and there evoking nothing but ridiculous images that rhyme whether they like it or not. Falling back on the lazy man's static opening [eight-plus notes, all the same], the meandering "London Town" fails as both as rocker and a ballad, falling in the gray space in between. **C**

"Cafe on the Left Bank" [Paul McCartney]
Add a sprightly rhythm to a refrained production, and the result is the promising "Cafe on the Left Bank," But the result is fleeting. After the second verse, you're left waiting for an imaginative touch that never comes. Again, McCartney has squeezed out anything resembling a human emotion, leaving an empty shell as he scampers away to the next empty tune. **B-**

"I'm Carrying" [Paul McCartney]
Another static opener – five quarter notes, all the same – and you wonder why McCartney songs are starting to sound alike. No bridge or middle eight to speak of, just the same monotonous verse and chorus, over and over. Yes, he sings well, and yes, it's an attractive production. But songwriting? Isn't this where McCartney is supposed to excel? **C+**

"Backwards Traveller" [Paul McCartney]
Though "Soily" sports the worst lyrics McCartney ever let dribble from his pen, "Backwards Traveller" is a close second [or third – there's a lot of competition]. A grade schooler leafing through a dictionary might have better luck. Beyond the usual lyrical disappointment, what's left is ponderous folk song, barely a minute long. **D**

"Cuff Link" [Paul McCartney]
Delighted by a new keyboard effect, McCartney gets down with a semi-funky instrumental. Improvised, or close to it, it's doomed to be purged from the collective musical consciousness, substituted by vague memories of McCartney's temporary obsession. Which is a fair summation of *London Town* as a whole. **C-**

"Children Children" [Paul McCartney and Denny Laine]
A folk tune, odd because folk has never been McCartney's strong suit. He's a melody guy, modern and far-reaching, at least in theory. "Children Children" is about jolly elves, jolly kids frolicking in the jolly woods, and other jolly clichés. **D**

"Girlfriend" [Paul McCartney]
Made to order for Michael Jackson, who snapped it up for his monster *Off the Wall* album. "Girlfriend" avoids the overt cuteness that causes so many other McCartney songs to choke. A solid melody, the first on *London Town*, leads to a clever instrumental break that shift from major to minor and back again. And McCartney's falsetto is a welcome change. Nice, but Jackson beats it. **B**

"I've Had Enough" [Paul McCartney]
The second cousin of "Smile Away" [*Ram*] with a dash of "I've Got a Feeling" [*Let It Be*]. Bob your head to

the infectious rhythm, sing along with the addictive chorus, and dread the coming of the final verse in which McCartney favours us with a self-conscious recitation. **B**

"With a Little Luck" [Paul McCartney]
A #1 single in the US, #4 in the UK, and one of the album's stand-outs, thanks to McCartney's slick performance and the in-check production. Of course, McCartney's breezy optimism is what made Sex Pistols fans want to burn down his house. I wonder if the beaten down street punks wonder if their problem is they're not optimistic enough. **B**

"Famous Groupies" [Paul McCartney]
A good-natured trot through Groupie Land, citing nothing your mother would disapprove of. Too bad, as I bet McCartney has some stories he could tell. As presented, McCartney's groupies might as well be the Girl Scouts. The song itself sounds improvised, melody-free, with McCartney singing in an intentionally dumb voice. More filler, as if *London Town* needed it. **D+**

"Deliver Your Children" [Paul McCartney and Denny Laine]
The rhythm and acoustic guitars remind one of "Famous Groupies," not the best sign. Nor is the use of "children," a redundant reminder of "Children Children," a song we just endured. Nor is the co-credit for Denny Laine, who's not exactly batting a hundred. Nor are the lyrics, something a bunny rabbit might write. Nor is the lifeless production. On the plus side, the melody is – no, that sucks too. **D+**

"Name and Address" [Paul McCartney]
McCartney imitates Elvis, or more accurately, imitates Andy Kaufman imitating Elvis. Hopelessly un-musical and decidedly un-funny. Maybe Kaufman would like to take a crack at it. **D-**

"Don't Let It Bring You Down" [Paul McCartney and Denny Laine]
Better than average folk tune with semi-melancholy vocals and simple guitar strumming. In this case, better than average isn't a recommendation. **B-**

"Morse Moose and the Grey Goose" [Paul McCartney]
This mess features an annoying buzz throughout, a sea shanty in the middle, and a piano riff that disappears from your consciousness the second after you hear it. While McCartney croons about a moose, he might wonder where his audience went. Oh, there they are, singing "Anarchy in the UK." **D-**

[bonus]

"Girls' School" [Paul McCartney]
McCartney was apparently bent out of shape because this single flopped [it stalled at #33], but it's easy to see why it did. The awkward structure made it hard to follow, and the flat melody just laid there and twitched. Worse, the subject matter – naughty instructors flirting with female students – made it a tough sell to the stodgy Mr. and Mrs. America, who, sadly or not, comprised a major chunk of his audience. [1993 *London Town* reissue.] **B-**

"Mull of Kintyre" [Paul McCartney and Denny Laine]
Soothing as a lullaby, masterly produced down to the last detail, "Mull of Kintyre" is McCartney at his conservative best. But though it roped in the old timers with its sentimental message, it alienated many teenagers who couldn't care less about verdant meadows and foggy oceans. The single sold by the tons, something on the order of two million in the UK, but it also solidified McCartney's image as a stodgy parent, a guy who'd rather have a bottle of expensive wine than a ticket to a Clash concert. Also, it reached a mere #45 in the US – on the Easy Listening chart no less – owing to the abundance of Scottish nostalgia in "Mull" which didn't translate well. [1993 *London Town* reissue.] **B**

CHAPTER TWELVE:

BACK TO THE EGG [1979]

Produced by Paul McCartney and Chris Thomas
Charted at 8 [US], 6 [UK]

The late 70s was a troubling time for superstars. In the early 70s and late 60s, rock gods like the Rolling Stones and the Who had the musical world at their feet, drowning in money and women and every indulgence they wished for. They were oblivious to the problems of mortal man, confident that this dream that would go on forever.

But then, disaster. In blinding succession came a slew of trends – disco, punk, new wave, all of them spawning music that mowed down established norms like road kill. Disco swapped the loose blues of old-time rock for rigid rhythms, sometimes generated by machines instead of drummers. New Wave emphasized garish fashions and tended to employ keyboards in place of electric guitars. And punk, the most radical trend of all, produced snarling new groups who substituted defiant attitude for technical proficiency. To the superstars' shock, record buying youth – the superstars' audience! – were gobbling up the new sounds, loading the charts with tracks by the Sex Pistols ["Pretty Vacant"], the Clash ["London Calling"], and the Damned ["Neat Neat Neat"].

What was a poor superstar to do? Some ignored it, hoping it would go away. Many, however, struggled to various degrees to incorporate elements of the new sound into their own music. Results ranged from the adequate [Rolling Stones: "She Was Hot"], to the awful [the Beach Boys remake of "Here Comes the Night"], to the head-scratching [James Brown: *The Original Disco Man*]. Regardless of quality, the old-timers were no longer setting trends. They were chasing them.

McCartney was not immune. As he wrestled with this existential dilemma, his career seemed to wallow on automatic pilot. Though the time had come to recruit new members for Wings, his interest often was elsewhere, allegedly leaving the bulk of decision making up to Denny Laine. Denny, following a few perfunctory auditions, picked drummer Steve Holley [session man for Elton John and Joe Cocker] and guitarist Laurence [session man for Cleo Laine and Charles Aznavour], whom McCartney accepted without much question.

The new album, *Back to the Egg*, had plenty of material awaiting, but not much of it top drawer. There were the usual where-have-I-heard-it-before ballads ["Love Awake"], a too-cautious experiment ["Reception"], an oldies retread ["Baby's Request"], and a couple of better-late-than-never punk-ish tunes ["Spin It On," "Old Siam Sir"]. The latter was a nod to the Clash-types, but only a nod, and McCartney didn't seem to have his heart in it.

Originally, McCartney had vague plans to make the album a cohesive tale of a struggling band, supported by energetic performances. But the plan went down the toilet when, true to form, McCartney's near-obsession with perfection resulted in endless amounts of studio time necessary to clean it all up. Reportedly, *Back to the Egg* required about three times as much studio work as *Abbey Road*.

For the first time, McCartney hired a co-producer. Veteran Chris Thomas, a classically trained violinist who got his break when EMI hired him as an assistant to Beatles producer George Martin. Since then, he'd worked with a long list of rock groups, including Roxy Music, Pink Floyd, Procol Harum, and, ahem, the Sex Pistols. He tried, the band tried, McCartney sort of tried, but it didn't add up to much, at least as far as the critics were concerned. *Robert Christgau's Consumer Guide*: " .... he's just hoping something will stick." *AllMusic*: " .... no spark whatsoever." *Rolling Stone*: " .... grab bag of dreck...." Another year, another – yawn – album.

"Reception" [Paul McCartney]
If you spin the dials on a bunch of radios at the same time, dump the results on an abandoned Bee Gees bass line, and add a puking guitar, this is what you get. **D**

"Getting Closer" [Paul McCartney]
Is this a track dedicated to an amphibian buddy? The rest of it can't be this screwy, can it? Jesus – it's about cementing your pinkies together. Or something. At least the music's good. Er, right? **C-**

"We're Open Tonight" [Paul McCartney]
An uninspired guitar riff, two lifeless verses, and some improvised chicken strangling. Done. Somebody should've told him the song wasn't finished and that the lyrics needed serious revision. But do you get the feeling that McCartney isn't inclined to listen? **C-**

"Spin It On" [Paul McCartney]
High energy, semi-snotty delivery, guitars up front where they belong. A million miles away from the Clash, but at least he's on the right road, veering off from the ditch that, naturally, is filled with lyrical bull crap. However, it's tuneless in spots and needlessly sloppy, meaning he was too lazy to clean it up, unusual for McCartney. But before the Sex Pistols get too cocky, remind them of McCartney's "Helter Skelter" [*The Beatles*], recorded over 10 years ago when Johnny Rotten was in the principal's office. **B**

"Again and Again and Again" [Denny Laine]
Denny comes across as a nice, cooperative guy, a 40 watt bulb in a 100 watt room, who creates dependable, singable tunes. "Again and Again and Again" fills the Denny slot nicely, pleasant to hear, which slips away into the atmosphere the second it ends. **B-**

"Old Siam Sir" [Paul McCartney]
Marching to war with militant Smurfs. McCartney, furious, McCartney, screaming. McCartney, trying to out-yell that toy piano. Of course it's nonsense, but that aside, it resembles the concept he'd had initially, sort of the rise of a made-up punky band, before it was squashed by "Baby's Request" and a half-dozen other wimp-a-thons. A few more of these, and the all-new, all Clash-are-my-brothers McCartney would've had an album to make the punks sit up rather than ignore it like they would a snoozing bum. **B**

"Arrow Through Me" [Paul McCartney]
Coherent words make this a cut above your average McCartney song. But still weak, owning to non-specificity and – well, let's just say it's not as vivid as "Anarchy in the UK" or "London Calling" or "Mull of Kintyre." A decent vocal, an odd melody that floats here and there, and a possibly, a plea to a disagreeable Linda. **B**

"Rockestra Theme" [Paul McCartney]
Round up as many fellow superstars as you can, then put them all in a studio at the same time for an instrumental designed especially for the occasion. Among the invited: David Gilmore [Pink Floyd], John Bonham [Led Zeppelin], Pete Townshend [The Who], and as many gentlemen of leisure as McCartney could coax out of their mansions.

Since these were all seasoned pros who knew a thing or two about recording, it was disconcerting for some to listen to McCartney dictate how and what they should play. Consequently, because of McCartney's keeping the lid on tight, the performance suffers. Plus, in the context of the times, this is a dinosaur convention. Why not go for broke and invite Billy Idol [Generation X] and Rat Scabies [The Damned] just to see what happens? Not that Paul is a poor ranter and raver, but why not let Johnny Rotten handle the ranting? **B-**

"To You" [Paul McCartney]
Refreshing, but only when compared to the rest of the deadwood. The melody jumps around like popcorn, bouncing off numerous key change [major to minor, then back again], suggesting that McCartney had an idea more sophisticated than he did elsewhere on the album. But the idea remains undeveloped and the tune not especially satisfying. **B-**

"After the Ball/Million Miles" [Paul McCartney]

So Paul, how's things on the plantation? Two half-songs, basically demos shoved together – "Million Miles" allegedly dates from a 1974 session – resulting in a distant relative of "Old Folks at Home." I thought McCartney was so prolific that he could make dozens of songs appear like magic. My mistake. **D**

"Winter Rose/Love Awake" [Paul McCartney]

Evocative title for a lousy track. Make that two lousy tracks, haphazardly smooshed together for a longer track, still lousy. Wait a sec – he also tried this with "After the Ball/Million Miles" and [kind of] "To You." Was he trying for an *Abbey Road* medley? Will somebody please play him *Red Rose Speedway*? **C+**

"The Broadcast" [Paul McCartney]

Harold Margary, a castle landlord and a passing acquaintance of McCartney, recites random passage from library books, including *The Sport of Kings* by Ian Hay, over a nondescript piano. Points for experimentation, penalties for brain failure. **C**

"So Glad to See You Here" [Paul McCartney]

Rockestra strikes again. Semi-interesting the first time, gimmicky the second. McCartney merrily leads them through the murk, hollering over the behemoth behind him, producing neither a memorable moment nor a call for another Rockestra number. By the way, the Ramones did more or less the same thing, consistently, with three musicians. **C+**

"Baby's Request" [Paul McCartney]

Intended for the Mills Brothers, a pop group active in the 1930s. I think John Lennon was right – McCartney had an affinity for "granny music" that he wouldn't give up and his fans had to choke down. A needless rehash of "Good Night" [*The Beatles*], it might be worth a chuckle if his previous 1930s numbers didn't exist, but they do. File it away with "You Gave Me the Answer" "Honey Pie" and all the others that make granny tap her walker. **C**

[bonus]

"Goodnight Tonight" [Paul McCartney]

As *Back to the Egg* wrapped up and with a new tour on the horizon, McCartney decided to launch a new single that wasn't included on the album, though it was recorded more or less at the same time. With a rubbery, virtuosic bass pattern and kindergarten lyrics, the completed track was bouncy fun but a little too close to disco. What am I saying? It *is* disco. An okay track, radiating fizzling sputters with zero to say. [*Pure McCartney*] **B**

"Daytime Nighttime Suffering" [Paul McCartney]

A dazzler seemingly knocked out in the same weekend as "Goodnight Tonight." McCartney and the band sound tough and committed, as if the weak-kneed *Back to the Egg* was all a dream. The only squishy section is the self-conscious choral mush at the beginning. But the rest, impeccable. For a moment, McCartney's gift for melody has risen from the dead. [1993 CD reissue of *Back to the Egg*.] **A**

"Didn't We Meet Somewhere Before" [Paul McCartney]

McCartney originally wrote this Las Vegas number for the 1978 film *Heaven Can Wait* [starring Warren Beatty]. The powers-that-be listened, then showed him the door. The song floated in limbo for a while, until it a few pieces finally showed up in 1979's *Rock and Roll High School* movie [starring The Ramones]. The song wasn't credited, nor did appear on an album. If you're curious, listen to the music under the credits. While you do, consider that "Didn't We Meet Somewhere Before" essentially was rejected both by CBGB and Caesar's Palace. **D**

"Wonderful Christmas Time" [Paul McCartney]

A seasonal non-classic. Such a puny tune, it makes one long for "Jingle Bells." McCartney did it all himself and reaped the rewards, with some reports stating that considering its recurring Christmas airplay around the world, it generates something like half a million dollars every year, forever. Maybe he should have called it "Wonderful Annuity." [1993 CD reissue of *Back to the Egg*.] **D+**

"Rudolph the Red Nosed Reggae" [Johnny Marks]
An instrumental from the retirement home, featuring a sawing violin and some lame one-take reggae. Maybe dread-sporting reindeer like it. [B-side of "Wonderful Christmas Time" single.] **F**

"Get Well Soon" [Kevin Godley and Lol Creme]
[10cc] It's no surprise 10cc and McCartney were joined at the hip for a bit [coming up: "Yvonne's the One," "Don't Break the Promises," "Code of Silence"]. They're smart, they're studio whizzes, and they're precise, pristine performers – this is McCartney's dream band. He lends his voice on the chorus, but it's just another excellently chosen element in this production spectacular. Too eccentric? Only if McCartney's lazier efforts [*Back to the Egg* comes to mind] haven't spoiled you. [*Freeze Frame*] **B+**

CHAPTER THIRTEEN:

McCARTNEY II [1980]

Produced by Paul McCartney
Charted at 3 [US], 1 [UK]

Nothing focuses the mind like a drug bust. After wrapping up *Back to the Egg* and antsy to hit the road, McCartney agreed to tour Japan after a short romp around the UK, all meant as the prelude to an expansive trip to the US. It was a significant moment, as he hadn't been to Japan since the Beatle days of 1966. But Japanese officials warned him to keep out, owing to his prior drug busts and Japan's extremely low tolerance for illegal substances. His advisors told him to take this seriously, but McCartney shrugged them off.

He should've listened. The Japanese customs agents, making a routine search though McCartney's bags, discovered approximately eight ounces of marijuana, not exactly in plain sight, but close. This was serious stuff. This was drug smuggling. This called for a seven-year prison sentence. McCartney's embarrassment turned to confusion, then outright panic as stern-looking officers led him away, deaf to his pleas for compassion.

A defeated McCartney was ushered into a jail cell, the door locked tight, his cries ignored. Meanwhile, McCartney's team frantically made phone calls, held meetings with Japanese personnel, and sped-read law books. After nine days behind bars, McCartney was set free, with a stern warning to stay out of Japan. Shaken and gritting his teeth, he cancelled the tour and returned to Britain.

Why had this happened? Why did he shrug off his advisors' advice? Reportedly, he said that the marijuana "was too good to flush down the toilet." Whatever, the lesson was not taken to heart. He was busted again four years later in Barbados.

Back home, McCartney, sick of listening to the Wings-men grumbling about money and struggling to play what McCartney had already mastered, considered ending the group. The more he thought about, the better it sounded. He could be a solo act, which he practically was anyway.

Secluded again in the Scottish wilderness, McCartney tackled a new project, this one performed, written, and produced entirely by himself. This album would also complete a few tracks he'd been fooling around with, synthesizer instrumentals echoing the New Wave of Talking Heads and the B-52s. Eagerly, using his home as a studio, he set up his equipment using state-of-art devices [among them, the ES80, ERP, and CS-80] and went to work.

McCartney II, a nod to the solo *McCartney* [1970], didn't resemble the Talking Heads so much as it did David Bowie, particularly 1977's *Low* which featured an entire side of electronic instrumentals. But the comparison does McCartney no favours. Where Bowie's tracks were moody and evocative, McCartney's were thin and fluffy, as memorable as, well, *Back to the Egg*. Fans mostly turned up their noses, with discussion boards calling it "self-indulgent" and "hard to listen to." Though the album went gold, it reached only #3 in the US, and Paul was used to #1s. The critics responded accordingly, with the NME saying it "isn't worth the plastic it's printed on." *The Rolling Stone Album Guide* awarded it a mere two stars out of five. *McCartney II* joined McCartney's list of disappointments. And the list was growing.

"Coming Up" [Paul McCartney]
An aberration, so much so that – except for the modern electronics – it seems like a leftover from the Beatles. And a terrific one. So much to like: a bizarre sax that winds around itself, a sped-up vocal resembling a space alien, incessant outer space percussion. Best of all, the stylish forward-looking production tastefully balances the voice, the sax, and the irresistible guitar riff to a whole that feels

perfect. This is light years from the typical McCartney fare, as it's based on recording experiments that actually work. Who needs Wings? **A**

"Temporary Secretary" [Paul McCartney]

Don't get hung up on the iffy title. "Temporary Secretary" seamlessly blends a first-class pop song with electronic nuttiness, creating a fusion that works as an original blend and is definitely not lazy. The grab-you-by-the-throat chorus once again shows that, when he's on, McCartney can do no wrong. The processed vocals and weird drum programming also add to a sense of otherworldly zaniness. Paul often tries to recapture the elusive atmosphere of fun that came so easily to the Beatles, but it's harder than it looks. Here, he comes close. **B+**

"On the Way" [Paul McCartney]

A sub-rudimentary blues swipe, emotion amputated. Also displays McCartney's uncanny knack for making three minutes seem like three hours. **F**

"Waterfalls" [Paul McCartney]

Somebody should investigate why this touching piece failed as a single in the aftermath of the monstrous "Coming Up." Mainly employing an electric piano, light acoustic guitar, and a smear of synthesizer, it sounds like a sad man in a lonely room, isolated from all, dreaming of a yearned for past that's inevitably slipping away. If only the lyrics had received one more re-write, which is needed for ursine removal. **A-**

"Nobody Knows" [Paul McCartney]

If this is legitimate rockabilly, I'm Linda McCartney. Imagine Paul writing songs while sound asleep, with one hand on a guitar, the other poised over a tape machine's "on" switch. It still wouldn't sound this bad. **F**

"Front Parlour" [Paul McCartney]

Doodling on parade, courtesy of a synthesizer played at whatever settings it happened to be on. Compare this to any of the instrumentals on David Bowie's *Low* then see if you can find any sentient being who prefers "Front Parlour." **D-**

"Summer's Day Song" [Paul McCartney]

A throwaway, derived from a snatch of classical music. In the spirit of throwaways, it features an improvised melody with off-the-top-of-my-head lyrics. It's forgettable and in no way a developed song. **C-**

"Frozen Jap" [Paul McCartney]

McCartney probably was still pissed off at Japan for showing him the door, thus the embarrassing title. At least it matches the tune. **D**

"Bogey Music" [Paul McCartney]

"Bogey" translated means "to hurt one's head." Alternate meaning: "past its expiration." **F**

"Darkroom" [Paul McCartney]

Pick a song that's lousy, randomly swap half the notes for different ones, then dash off some lyrics, making sure they remain pointless. Sprinkle with electronic hairballs. You've found the formula for *McCartney II* filler. **C**

"One of These Days" [Paul McCartney]

This acoustic piece is no "Blackbird," but it's not awful, despite the vague lyrics. The chord progression vaguely resembles "When the Saints Go Marching In." Still, "One of These Days" sounds like a masterpiece compared to the previous half-dozen songs on *McCartney II*. **B**

[bonus]

"Check My Machine" [Paul McCartney]

The genesis of "Check My Machine?" My guess: a Tweety Bird cartoon. A mind-numbing riff crawls along for close to six minutes featuring McCartney pestering his synthesizer. As if this wasn't long enough, a long, long 10 minute version also exists, basically recycling itself over and over. Originally the flip side of the "Waterfalls" single, a happy #9 in the UK, a sad #106 in the US. [*McCartney II Remaster.*] **F**

"Secret Friend" [Paul McCartney]
Flip of "Temporary Secretary," resembling a cheesy theme song for a cheap sci-fi film. Plus, it goes on for more than 10 minutes, which I believe is illegal. Synthesized elements all over the place, some interesting, some dull, most empty. **D+**

"Blue Sway" [Paul McCartney]
Written something like 20 years ago, this is background for a surf film. It loses its marginal appeal if you aren't watching the movie. Swirls of sound, periodic vocal drop-ins, and an orchestra rolling and tumbling. Soothing for the easily soothed. Why it was hidden for so long? Sit through all five-plus minutes of it. You'll have a pretty good idea. [*McCartney II Remaster.*] **C**

"Coming Up [Live 1979]" [Paul McCartney]
Recorded in Glasgow, the live "Coming Up" was a smash hit right out of the box, a single that hauled *McCartney II* higher than it deserved. The song is fairly new, bristling with energy, and McCartney seems delighted, maybe surprised, that it works so well. Apparently, US radio was nervous at how their audience would respond to the unconventional studio version, hence, the live version was the one promoted. [*McCartney II Remaster.*] **B+**

"Bogey Wobble" [Paul McCartney]
Ambient music for the deceased. [*McCartney II Remaster.*] **F**

"Mr. H Atom/You Know I'll Get You Baby" [Paul McCartney]
Two demos of two miserable tunes. The first, a cutesy McCartney reciting junk with a chorus of his bored family. The second, an endlessly repeated chanting of the eye-rolling chorus backed by synthesizer belches. This was to be part of a proposed *McCartney II* double album, before the project ran away as fast as is its little legs would go. [*McCartney II Remaster.*] **F**

"All You Horse Riders/Blue Sway" [Paul McCartney]
Over three minutes of a clip-clopping ode to ponies, followed by approximate six minutes of limp reggae tumbling off a cliff. If it were two minutes, tops, then the joke would be valid, though still not funny. But at over ten minutes, it's sadistic, the equivalent of shoving a screwdriver in your ear. **F**

"Got to Get You Into My Life [Kampuchea]" [John Lennon and Paul McCartney]
McCartney performed six numbers at this charity concert for Cambodian refugees. His choices spanned his career, and this one scores a knock out. Live horns copy the original arrangement, Paul sounds thrilled to be performing, and the band plays crisply and tightly. Better than *Revolver*? Don't be silly. [*The Concerts for the People of Kampuchea, 1981.*] **B**

"Coming Up [Kampuchea]" [Paul McCartney]
Home run, courtesy of a lively McCartney and an ace band. But the electronics are missed, leaving this as just another pretty good song. [*The Concerts for the People of Kampuchea, 1981.*] **B**

"Lucille [Kampuchea]" [Richard Penniman]
Incendiary cover of a McCartney fave, rivaling, though not surpassing, the explosive Little Richard track. [*The Concerts for the People of Kampuchea, 1981.*] **B**

"Let It Be [Kampuchea]"
Routine. Time to retire it? Fat chance. [*The Concerts for the People of Kampuchea, 1981.*] **C+**

"Every Night [Kampuchea]" [Paul McCartney]
Paul injects a little pizzazz into this ancient *McCartney* number, responding to a delirious audience egging him on. [*Concerts for the People of Kampuchea,* 1981.] **B**

"Rockestra Theme [Kampuchea]"
A spectacle for the live show, incorporating a host of good-natured artists forced to wear embarrassing suits. Fun for those at the show, a yawner for us stuck at home. [*The Concerts for the People of Kampuchea, 1981.*] **C+**

"Send Me the Heart" [Paul McCartney and Denny Laine; guest performer: Paul McCartney]
[Denny Laine] From Laine's third album comes this mid-tempo cowboy tune, weak and disposable. It has a steel guitar in it, so I guess it's authentic. McCartney plays everything that isn't nailed down, but it doesn't help. [*Japanese Tears*] **D –**

"Weep for Love" [Denny Laine; guest performer: Paul McCartney]
[Denny Laine] Bouncy mid-tempo nothing with McCartney playing it all, more or less. Laine seems to be catching McCartney's lyric ineptitude, not to mention his growing penchant for feeble melodies. [*Japanese Tears.*] **C-**

The End of Wings

Instead of a memorable ending, Wings sort of dribbled away, as McCartney lost interest and the members shuffled away, many nursing their own grudges. The beginning of the end came in the spring of 1981, when Denny Laine called it quits, simmering because the flat fee he received as co-writer of "Mull of Kintyre," missing out on the countless royalties he might have gotten had he been a full or partial partner. McCartney went through the motions of keeping the band alive, but acknowledged the obvious a year later. Wings was no more. Thinking about Wings in 2016, McCartney didn't seem thrilled with the experience, telling the BBC [reported in The Telegraph*], "We were terrible. We weren't a good group." Still, he added, "Looking back on it, I'm really glad we did it."*

Following is a rough breakdown of Wings' come-and-go membership over their blink of an eye life. The years listed are approximate. [PM = Paul McCartney, LM = Linda McCartney, DL = Denny Laine.]
1971-1972: PM, LM, DL, Denny Seiwell
1972-1973 [first half]: PM, LM, DL, Denny Seiwell, Henry McCullough
1973 [last half]: PM, LM, DL
1974: PM, LM, DL, Jimmy McCullough, Geoff Britton
1975-1977 [first half]: PM, LM, DL, Jimmy McCullough, Joe English
1977 [last half]: PM, LM, DL
1978-1981: PM, LM, DL, Laurence Juber, Steve Holley

CHAPTER FOURTEEN:

TUG OF WAR [1982]

Produced by George Martin
Charted at 1 [US], 1 [UK]

John Lennon was murdered on December 8, 1980, a shattering moment not only for McCartney, but for you, me, and anybody else who thinks that passing out guns like Halloween candy is a despicable idea. At an impromptu press conference, a still-shaken McCartney was asked by a reporter to comment. Confused, his mind a thousand miles away, he blurted, "It's a drag, isn't it?" while chomping away on chewing gum. But only a cynic would believe that reflected what McCartney was experiencing. What, really, could he say? Here was a grief-stricken man who'd lost his soul mate in the Beatles, the person with whom he'd shared experiences incomprehensible to the rest of the world.

Politely turning away offers from friends and family to help, McCartney retreated to his studio, locking out unanswerable questions and fixating on his work and his dependable escape, the musical project at hand. His intention: no more fluff, no more fuzzy concepts. Whether responding to a long-simmering discontent with his spotty albums or to the death of Lennon, McCartney began to show a seriousness of purpose he hadn't displayed in years.

McCartney began by hiring a producer. Desiring a father figure both professional and trustworthy, he asked George Martin. Martin considered it, then accepted, but with a few conditions. He wouldn't be McCartney's lackey, a yes man for whatever whim crossed Paul's mind. Martin expected his decisions to be considered and taken seriously. McCartney agreed. The new team set to work.

The first job involved sorting through McCartney's usual bushel basket of demos. In the past, McCartney's strategy was to record more or less everything, assuming that a few songs would take off, the rest would take their place among the forgotten and the what-was-I-thinking. This time, Martin and McCartney critically auditioned each of the demos, picking out the keepers, isolating the maybes for more work, and ditching the losers. The result: a line-up of high-quality material, the most appealing song list McCartney had come up with in a long time.

McCartney's loyal sidemen were politely but firmly dismissed, effectively ending Wings. In their place, Martin encouraged McCartney to select a roster of seasoned musicians who'd not only complement his talent, but whom he would enjoy working with. Thus, *Tug of War* – the tentative title – employed a roster of giants, including Stevie Wonder, Ringo Starr, rockabilly giant Carl Perkins, jazz virtuoso Stanley Clarke, and 10cc mastermind Eric Stewart.

In the past, McCartney had relied on instinct to tell him when a take was acceptable. Now, Martin would be on board to listen intently to every take, diplomatically inform McCartney when he could do a little better, and lo and behold, a better track would come to pass. Gradually, a focused album of impressive performances began to take shape. Both McCartney and Martin suspected they might have a winner.

And they were right. Critics fell all over themselves praising the sparkling new release. *The New York Times* raved. *Creem Magazine* called it "not only fascinating, but quite good." *Rolling Stone* gave it a remarkable five stars out of five. For once, critics and fans were in agreement, with *Tug of War* rocketing to the top of the charts worldwide. Was McCartney back? For the time being anyway, it looked like it.

"Tug of War" [Paul McCartney]

An ominous crowd, mumbling and whispering, signals something thoughtful is coming up, and – what do you know – it is. A dramatic upgrade of the song "London Town" which this track reduces to a Frisbee. The music sways and roars sublimely. McCartney performs at his incredible best, creating an ambitious panorama that effortlessly blows away the competition who might have written him off. As for the startlingly improved lyrics – did Martin chain him to a word processor? "Tug of War" declared that this was an artist who meant business. **B+**

"Take It Away" [Paul McCartney]

Following the impressive "Tug of War" comes this breathtaking pop song, and a serious one from a surprisingly difficult genre. Singing confidently over a solid backing track – thank you Ringo – with a rich melody and lyrics that make sense, McCartney seems born again. Peering into the past, recalling his Beatle days, remembering the miraculous transition from nobodies to deities, he conjures up his old friends in an explosion of joy. Beatle-esque harmonies ping-pong all over the place, as the ever-dependable George Martin unswervingly focuses on the piano, pounding away. Best of all, "Take It Away" explodes in an up-and-down chorus that's both anxious and exciting. An awe-inspiring gem. **A**

"Somebody Who Cares" [Paul McCartney]

It opens with a moody guitar line, a melancholy vocal, then shifts to a major key, all fluttering butterflies. It flops back and forth between genuine emotion and greeting card baloney. What's that you smell? *Eau de Oscar Mayer* **B-**

"What's That You're Doing" [Paul McCartney and Stevie Wonder]

Duets are iffy by definition. Imagine two stars competing for the spotlight, where neither star wants to offer his A-material, preferring to hoard their best for themselves. An example: 1985's "I Do Love You" by Stevie Wonder and the Beach Boys, which has as much to do with Wonder and the Beach Boys as it does with Bugs Bunny and Elmer Fudd. The background funks along nice and cool, and McCartney and Wonder sing like they're kids on the playground, but it boils down to a soft-headed performance by the elderly. Too bad they didn't have something more to work with, but if you think Wonder might offer up another "Superstition," you, my friend, are nuts. **B-**

"Here Today" [Paul McCartney]

No way was McCartney going to commemorate the loss of John Lennon with a press conference, a funeral eulogy, or any format depending on words alone. He chose to, had to, do it in song, a risky proposition considering how easy to would be to mess it up. But thankfully, he by-passes empty romanticism and self-conscious melodrama, and instead, presents a matter-of-fact remembrance of their complex relationship, making a powerful, unforgettable statement about loss and regret. That the song is straightforward, simple, and brilliant is a given. But it's McCartney's delivery that's surprising. And heartbreaking. **A**

"Ballroom Dancing" [Paul McCartney]

Yes, the lyrics are senseless. But the affable surrealism inherent in "Ballroom Dancing" easily trumps the romantic inanity of stupid-on-a-stick "Getting Closer" and "The Mess." Here, McCartney manages to add [a little] depth to his goofy musings by subtly celebrating .... his loss of virginity? Maybe. Speculation aside, "Ballroom Dancing" sports a hooky melody, irresistible and original, creating one of the most striking rhythms yet heard on a McCartney album. Bouncy and genuinely fun, this is a top notch pop tune that rivals "Take It Away" as an example of what McCartney can do when he's on his game. **A-**

"The Pound is Sinking" [Paul McCartney]

Did McCartney get the lyrics from the financial page? Doesn't matter. The song is so compelling, with the vocals soaring into the stratosphere, that it's easy to get sucked into the song's unbridled enthusiasm. A connect-the-sections number, sort of resembling "Uncle Albert/Admiral Halsey," except all the sections are good. Pick your favourite: the unexpected coin roll that sets up the intro, the strange voice – eerie, not dumb – on the bridge, the weary reggae near the end. Mine's the finale, with the best screams since "Golden Slumbers," which sends chills up the spine. **A-**

"Wanderlust" [Paul McCartney]

A majestic, powerful allegory about the resilience of hope, an amazing accomplishment from McCartney, who's usually flippant about heavier concepts. The counterpoint, another rarity from McCartney, is note-perfect, adding yet another gorgeous element to a song already bursting with them. A sparkling classic from a serious man – for now anyway. **A**

"Get It" [Paul McCartney]
Carl Perkins, rockabilly legend, obviously has a deep affection for McCartney, and here's an endearing duet to prove it. A love affair extending back 50 years, when the Beatles recorded his "Honey Don't," "Everybody's Trying to Be My Baby," and "Matchbox," awarding him the second-most covers of anybody. [Chuck Berry was first.] Swapping vocals, trading acoustic licks, and yucking it up, this mini-session ends far too soon. If the song were only more memorable, but alas, it's one of McCartney's light-as-a-snowflake sketches. **B**

"Be What You See" [Paul McCartney]
An outtake from *McCartney II*? With thirty seconds of underdeveloped synthesizer blips, not much here. **C**

"Dress Me Up as a Robber" [Paul McCartney]
A minor song that sounds unfinished, but still worth hearing. A muscular guitar riff sets up a tight rhythm and a strong melodic line that modulates like crazy, sort of like an alien Bee Gees. However, the song collapses when it hits the bridge, a standard flurry of notes that neither elevates nor expands on what's come before. In short, there are too few completed elements to form a top drawer song. Plus the lyrics read like a first draft. **B**

"Ebony and Ivory" [Paul McCartney]
If he fails to tread carefully, McCartney's sincere but obnoxious lecture on race relations might boost membership in the Ku Klux Klan. Stevie harmonizes well. The voices create a pleasant blend. But it's a weak song, old-timey, creaky, and unbelievably embarrassing. The odds of it becoming an anthem, which I suspect would be fine with McCartney, are about the same as *Wild Life* ranking higher than *Abbey Road*. **D**

[bonus]

"Ebony and Ivory [Solo]" [Paul McCartney]
McCartney loses the novelty of having Stevie Wonder along for the ride. What's left is McCartney himself, obliviously crooning this dopey plea for equality. Hearing it adds nothing to one's understanding of the song, as there's nothing to understand. [*Tug of War Deluxe*.] **D**

"Stop, You Don't Know Where She Came From [Demo]" [Paul McCartney]
Edging uncomfortably close to vaudeville, but pulling back in the nick of time. Playful and kind of fun, it's too trite for *Tug of War*, but it would've improved *Back to the Egg* considerably. [*Tug of War Deluxe*.] **B**

"Wanderlust [Demo]" [Paul McCartney]
The absence of a background, crucial to the success of the finished product, is missed more than usual, thanks to the indifferent double-tracking of the voice. Plus, the demo drags here and there, and McCartney tinkers with alternate voices, thankfully ditched. Consider this an experiment, not intended for human consumption. [*Tug of War Deluxe*.] **B**

"Ballroom Dancing [Demo]" [Paul McCartney]
Run-through, revealing nothing. Still a promising tune, but damaged by detached vocalizing. [*Tug of War Deluxe*.] **B-**

"Take It Away [Demo]" [Paul McCartney]
Speed it up, sing it like you mean it, and lose the piano. If not, you might as well let Ringo have it. [*Tug of War Deluxe*.] **B-**

"The Pound is Sinking [Demo]" [Paul McCartney]
The guitar is dreary, the kid's flute has got to go, no funny voice, and no rolling pennies. Skeletal, interesting for its emphasis on simple components, but I wouldn't think a great tune could come out of it. Shows what I know. [*Tug of War Deluxe*.] **B**

"Something That Didn't Happen [Demo]" [Paul McCartney]
A chunk of "The Pound is Sinking." Could this have been a song on its own? Sounds like it, but with

McCartney's love of linking unfinished bits together, it probably didn't stand a chance. Which is too bad, because somewhere in this tangle is a pretty good one. [*Tug of War Deluxe*.] **B-**

"Ebony and Ivory [Demo]" [Paul McCartney]
Rough version accompanied by electric piano, with McCartney gliding over the melody. Stripped even further than the solo take, all that's left is a lounge singer playing to himself as the last drunk patron staggers for the exit. [*Tug of War Deluxe*.] **D**

"Dress Me Up as a Robber/Robber Riff" [Paul McCartney]
Reducing it to the basics shows there's less here than meets the ear. Double tracking enhances it a bit, but not enough to hold anyone's interest, including McCartney's. For extras, we're served up a snatch of fancy flamingo guitar and a few random "ba ba ba"s. The "Robber Riff" is basically the finished track's nifty intro, but it's too short to get excited about. [*Tug of War Deluxe*.] **B-**

"Rainclouds" [Paul McCartney and Denny Laine]
Is this Denny's last gasp? If so, he exits with a whimper. This semi-folk song features a not-particularly-interested McCartney, idly strumming his guitar while checking the clock. A leftover from *London Town*? Could be. [B-side to "Ebony and Ivory," also on *Tug of War Deluxe*.] **C**

"I'll Give You a Ring" [Paul McCartney]
A neat, upbeat number with decent lyrics, tight melody, and a merry McCartney. Another missed opportunity to boost *Back to the Egg*. [B-side to "Take It Away," also on *Tug of War Deluxe*.] **B**

"All Those Years Ago" [Harrison; guest performer: Paul McCartney]
[George Harrison] Harrison, perpetually pissed at McCartney for having the gall to tell him how to play, let bygones be bygones and solicited his backgrounds for this Lennon tribute. [Ringo thumps along too.] This sub-par song with clunky chords, too many lyrics crammed into a short space, and vocals that feel last minute rather than thoughtful, this needed a lot of work before Harrison allowed it to escape. If Harrison was stymied on how to write a genuine farewell to Lennon, he should've listened closer to "Here Today." [*Somewhere in England*.] **B –**

"Maisie" [Juber; guest performer: Paul McCartney]
[Laurence Juber] Simple and charming, this striking finger-picked instrumental threatens to turn country, but veers off toward jazz with such finesse that you're tempted to try it yourself. [Go ahead. You will fail.] A former Wings guitarist, he recruited McCartney to play bass, who rises to the occasion. [*Standard Time*] **B+**

"Private Property" [Paul McCartney; guest performer: Paul McCartney]
[Ringo Starr] This toss-off is at least up-tempo, a pretty good sign the participants were conscious. McCartney doesn't even bother with a serviceable melody this time out, instead coughing up a few notes strung together that Ringo can't screw up. On second thought, judging from the lack of imagination, maybe they *were* unconscious. [*Stop and Smell the Roses*] **F**

"Attention" [Paul McCartney; guest performer: Paul McCartney]
[Ringo Starr] My theory: McCartney tripped and fell on the piano, thus creating this tune. Then he spilled coffee on the lyric sheet, making it unreadable. He turned on his hair dryer, dried it off, and sent it to Ringo. Since the clock was ticking, Ringo said the hell with it and turned what he could read into a record. McCartney added a few anonymous guitar plucks. [*Stop and Smell the Roses*] **D-**

"Sure to Fall" [Carl Perkins, Bill Cantrell, and Quinton Claunch; guest performer: Paul McCartney]
[Ringo Starr] The Beatles performed this Perkins number as part of their usual repertoire before they got a record deal. That this unnecessary cover pales before the Beatles version [*Live at the BBC*] is a vast understatement. [*Stop and Smell the Roses*] **D**

"You Can't Fight Lightning" [Richard Starkey aka Ringo Starr; producer: Paul McCartney]
[Ringo Starr] To beef up a *Stop and Smell the Roses* re-release, this was included as a bonus, supplementing

the already low quality bonus material ["Red and Black Blues," "Take Time to Stop and Smell the Roses, Alternate Version"]. With Ringo on guitar and Paul on drums, this wispy hunk of nothing has no melody to speak of, and basically no lyrics beyond the title. Best part: the simulated thunderstorm. Record it yourself by opening the window on a rainy day. [*Stop and Smell the Roses* bonus] **F**

"The Girl is Mine" [Michael Jackson; guest performer: Paul McCartney]
[Michael Jackson] This pile of goo earned Jackson a platinum single and McCartney a place in the Hall of Panderers. Put aside the creepiness of what is essentially a father-son competition for some poor girl, and note that the duet intentionally avoids discussing a roll in the hay, substituting something like a date for the school prom. Resist the urge to smack them for being so precious. On second thought, go ahead. [*Thriller*] **D –**

CHAPTER FIFTEEN:

PIPES OF PEACE [1983]

Produced by George Martin
Charted at 15 [US], 4 [UK]

Fifteen? *Fifteen*? How could this be? No, it wasn't the end of the universe. And it wasn't *that* bad. Was it? Besides, chart placements were often an inaccurate indication of an album's actual popularity. And many musicians would give their eyeteeth to do this well.

But *fifteen*? In the US! In his entire life, McCartney never – *never*- had a solo album do this bad [unless you count *The Family Way*, where his participation was marginal]. Even the dismal *Wild Life* fared better than this. Plus, he knew the awful truth: there were a lot of pop acts who had a shelf life of a few years while their albums dominated, then declined. Could this be the beginning of the end?

Pipes of Peace, by all accounts, should have performed better. It was hot on the heels of *Tug of War*, one of the best received records of his career. George Martin was still in the driver's seat, his production as solid as ever, giving *Pipes of Peace* an adult sheen that McCartney's records often lacked. The roster of *Tug of War* guest stars – Ringo Starr, Eric Stewart, Stanley Clarke, and Michael Jackson, arguably the most incandescent star in the pop galaxy – was still in place, providing classy performances, just as McCartney counted on them to do. As icing on the cake, *Pipes of Peace* coughed up a number one hit with "Say Say Say," a duet with Jackson. No one would claim it was a masterpiece, but a number one is a number one.

Of course, maybe *Pipes of Peace* wasn't any good. That seemed to be the verdict of critics across the globe. *Rolling Stone*: Two stars out of five. *Something Else Magazine*: " .... definitely not McCartney's strongest effort ..." *NME*: "... dull, tired, and empty ..."

So what happened?

First, there was a lack of quality material. Back in the pre-production days of *Tug of War*, Martin and McCartney sorted through tons of possible songs, keeping the good, setting aside the others. Among those deemed questionable – but recorded anyway for a vaguely defined future project – were "Average Person" and "Sweetest Little Show" which, lo and behold, turned up on *Pipes of Peace*. Filler was not in short supply, evidenced by the trite "Hey Hey" and "Keep Under Cover." "The Man" and "Through Our Love" were hopeless, taking a back seat – way back – to "Take It Away" and "Here Today." How did these mediocrities slip through? One reason: McCartney's chronic lack of self-criticism, where whatever popped into his brain was declared acceptable. And this time at least, he couldn't be deterred.

Second was McCartney's preoccupation with the movie he'd been thinking about for years, now reaching fruition. At war: McCartney's breezy I-can-do-anything self-confidence vs the warnings by professionals that a feature film required an expertise that McCartney had yet to demonstrate. To McCartney, it was merely a big home movie. To the pros, it was an investment of millions of dollars, not casually awarded to a novice, no matter who they were.

What about a script? McCartney had a 20-some page outline written in an off-hand style that betrayed his amateur approach [Generally, a feature script is in the range of 90-120 pages.] Who's going to be in it? McCartney for one – he'd be the star – a neophyte with no experience beyond *A Hard Day's Night* and *Magical Mystery Tour*, where he woodenly portrayed himself. What about pre-production? Direction? Cast readings? Crew approval? McCartney brushed these concerns aside, feeling, apparently, they'd take care of themselves or he'd deal with them when the time came.

And then there was that duet with Michael Jackson. To serious listeners, it was an unavoidable truth that – despite its hit status – it emitted the stench of cold commercialism. McCartney hadn't shown much interest in Jackson before he became a household name. Now they were making records together. Was this acknowledged around the office? Possibly. To McCartney's face? Doubtful.

"Pipes of Peace" [Paul McCartney]

All aboard for Wimp City. A note-perfect but icy voice, gentle backgrounds out of a can, and Mantovani strings, all designed to soothe the troubled soul. But if your troubled soul demands something with more substance, look elsewhere, as you won't find it on this empty track or, for that matter, this wafer-thin album. "Pipes of Peace" goes down like chocolate ice cream drenched in maple syrup with sugar cubes on top. Try eating *that* without barfing. **C+**

"Say Say Say" [Paul McCartney and Michael Jackson]

An undeserving #1. Jackson hams it up, McCartney phones it in. Crooning a whiney love song, the boys compete for the same girl's affection, a bad sign seeing as how McCartney could be Jackson's dad. Jackson, supposedly the primary writer of "Say Say Say," would have opened a few eyes if he'd performed with, say, Twisted Sister. But would it have sold as many copies? **C**

"The Other Me" [Paul McCartney]

Another Poetry from Hell contender as McCartney vacillates between an oblivious lover and a garbage container. As for the slip of a tune, it's a jaunty piano-based head nodder. I wonder, is this McCartney's apology to his wife for diddling with a groupie? And is that a sigh? Or a snore? **C**

"Keep Under Cover" [Paul McCartney]

Nauseous opening with McCartney showing off to his Vegas buddies, followed by a same-note melody as lazy as it is syrupy. **D**

"So Bad" [Paul McCartney]

This slick ballad consists of two disparate elements, a verse and a chorus which, quality wise, have little to do with each other. The verse, a winding melody over a memorable bass line, boasts a pleasing falsetto lead that McCartney pulls off admirably. The chorus, however, drags the song to the bottom, with the lyrics a familiar romantic mudbath. Perfect for Celine Dion. **B-**

"The Man" [Paul McCartney and Michael Jackson]

The McCartney-Jackson team gives it another shot. More poppy than "Say Say Say," which is good, less ballsy than "Beat It," which is bad. Very bad. Polite piano, winsome flute, perfect harmonies, the whole thing lifted out of *Easy Listening for Dummies*. Recall that while McCartney was doing his best imitation of a songbird, Jackson was recruiting guitarist Slash [Guns n' Roses] to shred the curtains on "Beat It." Could this mean that Jackson's audience is harder than McCartney's? And by the way, who is "The Man" anyway? I vote for John Lennon. **C-**

"Sweetest Little Show" [Paul McCartney]

If I didn't know better, I'd swear this tuneless thing was slapped together when McCartney discovered the album was one track short. When would it dawn on him that not every floor scraping was worth releasing? When would one of his meek associates point out that riding on his name alone wouldn't work forever? Since his albums continued to go platinum, the answer to both questions: "Never." **D-**

"Average Person" [Paul McCartney]

I'm sure McCartney wants to identify with the man in the street. But this is a hopeless cause, as I doubt he's had the chance to seriously interact with regular guys for a long time. Note the musical bits seemingly strung together at random, the singer's bored performance, and the condescending tone McCartney takes when ordinary folks discuss their trivial problems. Alternate title: "Sitting Pretty." **D**

"Hey Hey" [Paul McCartney and Stanley Clarke]

I got excited when I thought this was "Hey Hey [We're the Monkees]." No such luck, just a generic instrumental that squanders the talents of bass virtuoso Stanley Clarke. A leftover from *Tug of War*, an album which now seems like a distant dream. **C**

"Tug of Peace" [Paul McCartney]

Like a discard from *McCartney II*, a mostly electronic piece featuring sound effects, clichéd percussion, and a few dopey shouts. A waste of space from a guy who could do this when he was 12. **D-**

"Through Our Love" [Paul McCartney]
Even McCartney's ballads, once his infallible trademark, are sounding insipid. The usual tricks – abrupt modulation, minor to major and back – betray McCartney's creeping exhaustion, or more likely, he just tosses them in here and there. If they work, fine, and if they don't work, also fine. More strings? Why not? **D**

[bonus]

"Twice in a Lifetime" [Paul McCartney]
Thin, cloying ballad, advancing McCartney's march to the middle. Grey haired Muzak. [*Pipes of Peace Deluxe.*] **C-**

"We All Stand Together" [Paul McCartney]
I'm on the fence about the frogs, a cute vocal effect that has somebody – Paul? – croaking merrily away. But after a few seconds, it's like spinach in your teeth. Frogs aside, "We All Stand Together" works as children's song, exactly as intended. [It's from the animated *Rupert and the Frog Song*, a McCartney obsession.] The gentle melody, instantly memorable, miraculously avoids the obnoxious and spreads adorableness all over the place. Grown-ups, those not sympathetic to warbling amphibians, can admire the stylish arrangement, heavy on theme park soundtracks. [*All the Best*, UK and Canada only, and *Pure McCartney.* **B**

"We All Stand Together [Humming Version]" [Paul McCartney]
Flip over the "We All Stand Together" for this oddball, featuring a humming choir and, in there someplace [I think], a humming McCartney. Not half-bad, as the lack of lyrics emphasizes the lullaby-like melody, which fills the bill for those with a higher than average tolerance for *The Lion King* and similar Disney fare. [B-side to "We All Stand Together."] **B**

"Simple as That" [Paul McCartney]
Easy-going reggae with a wandering vocal. Cringe-worthy backgrounds, completely unnecessary, condemn this to McCartney's drawer of dust. [*Pipes of Peace Deluxe.*] **C+**

"Keep Under Cover [Demo]" [Paul McCartney]
He demoed it, listened to it, and decided, yes, it's worthy for the album. Amazing, since "lame" barely describes the paucity of ideas on full display. If pressed, the demo is slightly preferable to the studio version, as it sidesteps the slickness that ultimately sent the studio track to sleep with the fishes. [*Pipes of Peace Deluxe*] **D+**

"Average Person [Demo]" [Paul McCartney]
As with the "Keep Under Cover" demo, this stripped-down version is a tad better than the finished product, though it's still road kill and deserves a quick dump. [*Pipes of Peace Deluxe*] **D+**

"It's Not On [Demo]" [Paul McCartney]
One that never made the cut, although it's strange that "Keep Under Cover" did while this was forgotten. Double tracked voices, one singing, the other talking, make for an odd but intriguing approach that, unfortunately, dribbles away into trite McCartney mannerisms. Towards the second half, it mutates into a distant cousin of "Average Person," which it presumably predates. Wrapping up, an electronically altered monster voice is double tracked with McCartney's normal voice, a little silly this time, but at least he's doing something different, even if it's kid's stuff. A country-western riff [?] dominates the fade. [*Pipes of Peace Deluxe*] **B**

"Simple as That [Demo]" [Paul McCartney]
It's brief, sloppy, and unfinished. But surprise – it's a jewel, albeit a baby one. With an interesting background – forget the limp reggae – and confident vocal, it's strong enough to have us begging, pleading, for more like this and less like the rest of this album. [*Pipes of Peace Deluxe.*] **B**

"Say Say Say [Extended]" [Paul McCartney and Michael Jackson]
A new and longer version, with the backgrounds and arrangement basically the same. Of interest be-

cause McCartney and Jackson reverse roles. That is, it opens with Jackson [McCartney is first on the original], then McCartney, then Jackson. Thus, a new perspective, destined to be forgotten forever after spin number one. [*Pipes of Peace Deluxe*.] **C+**

"Ode to a Koala Bear" [Paul McCartney]

My jaw drops. My eyes bulge. Clutching my throat, I drop to the floor, gasping for air. Then, when all seems lost, salvation. "Ode to a Koala Bear," the song of Satan, has been hunted down and shot. And just to be sure, shot again. [*Pipes of Peace Deluxe*.] **F**

"Christian Bop" [Paul McCartney]

In 1987, McCartney recorded an album called *Return to Pepperland*, an album destined never to be released due its extreme crappiness. The producer was Phil Ramone, who'd also massaged the careers of John Coltrane, Billy Joel, McCartney Simon, Frank Sinatra, and basically any star with a record deal. Could it be that McCartney recruited Ramone because McCartney's bip boppin' career was on life support? Anyway, the album included "I Love This House," "Squid," and "Atlantic Ocean" – all headed for B-sides in years to come – and this one, a song having to do nothing with Christianity or bopping. Instead, it's a percussion-heavy up-tempo instrumental with no serious melody, making it a candidate for vocals which, to date, have never arrived. [*Pipes of Peace Deluxe*] **C-**

"Say Say Say [Instrumental]" [Paul McCartney and Michael Jackson]

With the vocals removed, this becomes a disco record, with a throbbing four-on-the-flood intended to drive you to the nuthouse. [*Pipes of Peace Deluxe*] **C**

"The Honorary Consul" [Paul McCartney]

[John Williams] Graham Green's literary gem *The Honorary Consul* was adapted for the movies in 1983, with McCartney penning the title number. Classical guitarist Williams performed this moody but colourless piece, suitable for the movies, not so much for listening. [Single] **B –**

"Runaway" [Paul McCartney]

[Ivory] More or less a Caribbean lounge band specializing in disco and pop, Ivory had the good fortune to encounter McCartney when he was on vacation in Barbados and was feeling generous. McCartney bequeathed them with "Runaway" and "Freedom Land," with the understanding that he wouldn't be participating himself. The resulting track is an easygoing ballad with pleasant vocals [vaguely reminiscent of Paul's "So Bad"] and light-as-a-tissue keyboards. The soothing track lacks the strong melody necessary to make it memorable. Lost in the clouds, off it goes, floating away. [*Print Out*] **B-**

"Freedom Land" [Paul McCartney]

[Ivory] Not to be confused with the icky "Freedom," this is the second and final McCartney donation to Ivory. It, too, is a pleasant tune, but it's merely pleasant. Make that semi-pleasant. [*Print Out*] **B-**

"Do They Know It's Christmas [B-Side]" [Bob Geldof and Midge Ure; guest performer: Paul McCartney]

[Band Aid] A charity single about the Ethiopian famine of 1983. This became, at the time, the biggest seller in Britain, displacing "Mull of Kintyre." Written by Geldof [Boomtown Rats] and Ure [Ultravox], and recorded by an all-star band that included Bono [U2], Boy George [Culture Club], Sting [Police], Paul Weller [Style Council], and tons more, the earnest anthem inspired listeners of all ages, making it a genuine phenomenon. McCartney couldn't attend the session, but provided a brief spoken commentary for the B-side. [Single] **B**

CHAPTER SIXTEEN:

GIVE MY REGARDS TO BROAD STREET [1984]

Produced by George Martin
Charted 21 [US], 1 [UK]

"... commercially disastrous ..."
Kurt Loder, Rolling Stone
"... underdone plot and self-indulgent staging."
Carol Cling, Las Vegas Review-Journal
"... about as close as you can get to a non-movie."
Roger Ebert, Chicago Sun Times

Why do rock stars want to be movie stars? Mick Jagger tried it in *Ned Kelly* and failed. Bob Dylan tried it in *Renaldo and Clara* and failed. *Paul Simon* tried it in *One Trick Pony* and failed. David Bowie tried it in *The Man Who Fell to Earth* and succeeded. But he was basically playing himself [an alien].

To say that Paul McCartney's *Give My Regards to Broad Street* – meant to evoke "Give My Regards to Broadway" and not funny – was a disappointment to all concerned is being too kind, but it must have been a particular slap in the face to the *auteur*. As a screenwriter, he flunked. As a movie star, he flunked spectacularly. Even playing himself, he was as stiff as a zombie from *The Walking Dead*.

Give My Regards to Broad Street reveals nothing about McCartney as a real human being, instead portraying him as a happy-go-lucky guy whose biggest problem is temporarily losing his master tapes. Blandness abounds. He loves his wife, he loves his friends, he pretty much loves everybody. He portrays himself as master of pop music, knocking off song after song without breathing hard. In the end, McCartney presents himself as a cheerful but brain-dead workaholic, and that's pretty much it.

Of course, there was a soundtrack album. It consisted of a conservative ballad, a couple of throwaway rockers, and – to the audible gasps of Beatle fans worldwide – a basketful of remade Beatles songs. While longtime fans wept, critics piled on. *Sputik Music*: "His new material really is quite boring, empty, and soulless ..." *AllMusic*: Two stars out of five. *Something Else*: "... an album that represents the nadir not just of the decade but quite possibly of Paul McCartney's career."

"No More Lonely Nights" [Paul McCartney]

In 1964, Elvis Presley was discharged from the military and dived back into his movie career. His post-Army films – *Kissin' Cousins*, *Roustabout*, *Harum Scarum*, and many others – not only marked a steady decrease in quality, they encouraged a slide into a pit of musical mush from which he would rarely escape. Witness, from *Kissin' Cousins*, the sorry "Smokey Mountain Boy" and "Barefoot Ballad," having in common a dreary homogenization aimed at pleasing a conservative audience whose idea of a pleasant afternoon at the movies didn't involve a rock star screaming at them.

Was *Give My Regards to Broad Street* sending McCartney down the same path? This was film number four for him – the others being Beatles projects *A Hard Day's Night*, *Help*, and *Magical Mystery Tour* [actually, number five if you count *Let It Be*] – and his insistence on being as inoffensive as possible was dragging him in that direction. The movie, of course, was an empty shell not unlike *Kissin' Cousins*, and the songs betrayed an intention, consciously or not, to be stubbornly unadventurous. Was this his attempt to widen his audience who, he believed, were becoming uncomfortable with the edgy? Or was this his personality, be it real or manufactured?

"No More Lonely Nights," a top ten single and recipient of the project's biggest promotional push, is one of his most inoffensive tracks to date. It serves up the familiar in spades: a soothing melody, a palatable background, a tale of love gone right. The composition, obviously, is soft, but so is the performance – your grandparents would approve. Aggressive production elements, like drums, are mixed down, while the warmer and friendlier instruments, like the acoustic guitar, are out in front.

If *Give My Regards to Broad Street* [the film] had been a hit, it's tough not to wonder: would he have continued a movie career? And if so, would his music become even more bland? And, especially worrisome, would there be any edges left to buff away? **B-**

"Good Day Sunshine [Remake]" [John Lennon and Paul McCartney]
Unlike *Wings Over America*, the composer credits are in the right order. No reason for this, no explanation, and once again makes you wonder: why would McCartney care? Be that as it may, here we have one of *Revolver*'s lesser cuts undergoing an orchiectomy. A barber shop quartet, basically all McCartney, substitutes for the Beatles. The bulk of the track is McCartney doing his best to copy himself and failing. An orchiectomy, by the way, is an operation where the surgeons slice off your testicles. **D**

"Corridor Music" [Paul McCartney]
A wispy non-song lasting a few seconds. Which is too long. **F**

"Yesterday [Remake]" [John Lennon and Paul McCartney]
The inclusion of "Yesterday" is apparently to remind us that McCartney wrote the most popular song in the known universe, except, perhaps *Happy Birthday to You*. Since we all know the original down to our DNA, here was a chance for McCartney to try something different, like a doo-wop version or a surf version or a Devo version. No dice. This is the same thing, only with a small orchestra instead of a string quartet, an insignificant difference. Awful and, for the critically inclined, insulting, **D**

"Here, There, and Everywhere [Remake]" [John Lennon and Paul McCartney]
Perhaps the most beautiful song in the Beatles' catalogue. Lennon liked it, George Martin adored it, and it remains a favourite of all sentient beings, alien or otherwise. So let's redo it and make it worse. The brass adds next to nothing, and makes it crude where the original was delicate. McCartney, so precious, goes out of his way to be winsome, but lands on intolerable. If there's a single sentient being who prefers this to the original, wiggle your tentacle. Just as I thought. **D**

"Wanderlust [Remake]" [Paul McCartney]
Maybe McCartney redoing his own tunes will fare better. You may ask why he didn't use the originals, as getting the film rights shouldn't have been a problem. And since he did them himself, painstakingly, the originals were near perfect. So why did this "Wanderlust" begin, inexplicably, with a tea room take of "Here, There, and Everywhere" [?!?], then glide into the majestic chords of "Wanderlust," as close to the original as he could get? Answer: there is no answer. **C**

"Ballroom Dancing [Remake]" [Paul McCartney]
In *Tug of War*, McCartney skirted the cuteness and went for a measured whimsy that produced grins instead of grimaces. A good trick, one hard to repeat, which, naturally, he didn't. This pointless copy ought to be sent to the shredder. McCartney's inane stage direction leads to prancing children, which reeks of phoniness. An extra verse not heard on *Tug of War* adds zip. **D**

"Silly Love Songs [Remake]" [Paul McCartney]
What is this is doing in the remake pile? Because it was a monster hit? I guess it gave McCartney a suitable background for performing in clown makeup [really]. The disco violins are absent. Other than that, McCartney duplicates the rest and gives a pointless performance. **C**

"Not Such a Bad Boy" [Paul McCartney]
Neat garage-y backup, suitable vocal, so-so song. After remakes of Beatles, anything with a little life in it is bound to be manna from heaven, making this, by default, one of two standouts [the other: "No Values"]. Still, it's a throwaway, dreamed up by McCartney who was, possibly, paranoid about fans dismissing the album as too wimp-ified. Too late. **B**

"So Bad [Remake]" [Paul McCartney]
If you didn't like the single or if you didn't care for it on *Pipes of Peace*, you won't like this either. A note for note recreation of a song that wasn't exactly crying out for a second chance. McCartney sure loves to pile on those lush background harmonies, the sign of an insecure arranger. **C**

"No Values" [Paul McCartney]
McCartney's gotten better at insincere rockers since the days of "Soily." Although this is the album's shining star, it wins because the dullness pervading the rest of the album makes it sound like a *Sgt Pepper* outtake. Adequate verse, fish-flop chorus, and a surprisingly punchy end segment. Is that Barbara Bach on cowbell? **B**

"No More Lonely Nights [Ballad Reprise]" [Paul McCartney]
It's Filler Time! **F**

"For No One [Remake]" [Paul McCartney]
Swamped by strings, making it too quaint for words, McCartney transforms his heart wrenching ballad into something less solid, like an empty garbage bag. Not a chance taken, not even a teeny one. The French horn duplicates the original exactly. Really, why bother? Once a touching, thoughtful ballad, here reduced to a superstar's puffery. **D**

"Eleanor Rigby [Remake]" [John Lennon and Paul McCartney]
The original took an unusual scale [a variant of the Dorian mode], a brutal depiction of loneliness, and a breathtaking choir [Lennon and McCartney with a touch of George] to produce an experimental dazzler that stands as one of the Beatles' best. For this remake, once past a timid start, McCartney sings the song as if he's frightened by it, backing off key phrases that call for power, substituting something oh-so-precious that a bogus clone might attempt. Is a comparison with the Beatles unfair? Well, he picked it. Therefore, he asked for it. **D**

"Eleanor's Dream" [John Lennon and Paul McCartney]
Instrumental retelling of the song's themes, tolerable for a movie background but irrelevant in your house. **C-**

"The Long and Winding Road [Remake]" [John Lennon and Paul McCartney]
At least McCartney dumped the hated Phil Spector band of angels. Beyond that, we get a lounge sax, a lounge crooner and – oh my god – a Spector-lite orchestra. Did McCartney worry that fans of *Let It Be* would demand their money back if there were no violins sawing away, even if he despised them himself? **D**

"No More Lonely Nights [Playout]" [Paul McCartney]
Creature from the Black Lagoon, *Invasion of the Saucer Men*, and *I Married a Monster from Outer Space* all released soundtracks brimming with horror. But they've met their match. All these "No More Lonely Nights" variants makes *Give My Regards to Broad Street* even scarier. **F**

"Goodnight Princess" [Paul McCartney]
This one's for you, Wayne Newton **D**

[bonus]

"No More Lonely Nights [Extended and Special Dance Mix]" [Paul McCartney]
A torture chamber extension, plus a round-'em-up-and-hang-'em edition, both for your disco pleasure. **F**

"On the Wings of a Nightingale" [Paul McCartney]
[Everly Brothers] A customized number for Don and Phil, uncannily mimicking the style of their early hits, notably "Wake Up Little Susie." Harmonies are spectacular and as good as you remember, and guitars are forcefully in front. This should have been a bigger hit than number 50. Apparently the powers that be – that is, radio and record execs – decided their time had come and gone. [*EB 84*] **B**

CHAPTER SEVENTEEN:

PRESS TO PLAY [1986]

Produced by Paul McCartney and Hugh Padgham
Charted at 30 [US], 8 [UK]

Not only did *Broad Street* audiences fall over themselves as they fled the theatres, critics wore out their thesauruses looking up synonyms for "ghastly." Then the creditors came calling. 20th Century Fox had put up real money, essentially as a loan to McCartney's company. Now they wanted repaid. McCartney was in hock for millions.

Meanwhile, as McCartney was shaking his piggy bank, plans for a new album were brewing. Shaken by the dismal *Give My Regards to Broad Street* soundtrack, which managed only a wobbly 21 on the US charts, McCartney swallowed hard and looked for a new producer. George Martin begged off, but suggested Eric Stewart, a stalwart of 10cc who'd co-written the innovative "I'm in Not in Love." Eager to work with a Beatles, as was virtually everybody else on the planet, Eric agreed, and he and McCartney settled in for a songwriting session.

But the partnership was not to be. No sooner had the two shaken hands when McCartney more or less on a whim hired Hugh Padgham, yet another producer. Hugh was no slouch, having guided Phil Collins and Peter Gabriel through successful projects. Was McCartney's association with him a blatant – some might say cynical – attempt at sounding modern? In any event, two producers was one too many. Worse, unlike his relationship with George Martin, who had *carte blanche* to speak his mind and earned McCartney's respect, McCartney wasn't thrilled with Stewart's ideas. Frustrations grew, apparently reaching the point where Stewart felt he'd had enough and, politely but firmly, left the project.

Throughout, McCartney was alternately uncertain, enthusiastic, and indifferent. He seemed to flat-out reject Padgham's diplomatic suggestions that perhaps some of the songs were weak – which they were. McCartney's casual attitude towards songwriting could be maddening. He would, for instance, occasionally write a song on the spot, then insist it be recorded as is, with few, if any, changes, even if the song cried out for another bridge, a stronger opening, or lucid lyrics. Marijuana was another distraction, as was anything that attracted McCartney's attention – TV shows, the weather – other than the project at hand. Bringing in friendly faces, like Pete Townsend and Phil Collins [both for "Angry"], didn't seem to make a lot of difference. Add to this McCartney's apparent difficulty with making musical decisions – a bass part could take forever – and the stage was set for an unfocused and labored record.

To no one's surprise, except maybe McCartney's, *Press for Play* was another disappointment, and worse, it was on a sales trajectory headed straight down. The single, "Press," struggled to reach 21 on the US charts. The UK charts ranked it at a wretched 25. In the US, the album did worse than the single, inching its way to 30 before stopping dead. Fans were disappointed, disillusioned, even betrayed. From *Steve Hoffman's Music Forum*, made up of hardcore fans: "an all-time low," "the production is horrible," "can't stand it." Critics snarled, using whatever synonyms they had left over after mauling *Give My Regards to Broad Street*. *Press to Play* tumbled into the abyss.

"Stranglehold" [Paul McCartney and Eric Stewart]
Reeking of 80s excess, the only pandering element McCartney missed in "Stranglehold" was a burping synthesizer – but that'll come later. The over-emphasized snare whack, the honking Springsteen-ian sax, the cheap pick-up line, it adds up to a by-the-numbers product from a rusted hit machine. Only without the hit part, since McCartney neglected to provide even a semblance of a strong melody. From start to finish, every conceivable edge is smoothed over to a glossy dullness. A disheartening beginning. **C+**

"Good Times Coming/Feel the Sun" [Paul McCartney]

Yet another attempt at linking fragments into a complete composition, resulting in a less than satisfying whole. A shame, because these piecemeal fragments are more appealing than usual. But the concept of fusing two or more little pieces into one big piece was exhausted a long time ago, somewhere around *Ram*'s "Uncle Albert/Admiral Halsey." So we have to settle for pleasant. **B**

"Talk More Talk" [Paul McCartney]

The chorus, all four bars of it, seems solid. The verses? Whatever, throw anything in, like spooky voices and weird synthesizers. It'll sound just like David Bowie! **C+**

"Footprints" [Paul McCartney and Eric Stewart]

A better ballad than the follow-up "Only Love Remains," the melody here is more inventive and a little sinister. But the mood dissipates as the song continues through a hokey build-up of every instrument that happened to be lying around, not to mention a bland coda that's a letdown after the promising beginning. So it starts out ingenious and ends predictable, another strike against an increasingly dreary album. **B-**

"Only Love Remains" [Paul McCartney]

To state the obvious, recent McCartney ballads ["Through Our Love" and "Twice in a Lifetime"] have nowhere near the substance and staying power of old McCartney ballads ["And I Love Her," "Here, There and Everywhere"]. Could it be the oldies are built around soaring melodies and heart-stopping choruses, while the recent ones lie smashed flat on the ground, dead as road kill? An autopsy reveals that "Only Love Remains" features pretty [read: expected] chords, a sad sympathetic narrator, and a blood-curdling bond with Paul Anka. I can imagine a lovesick teenager sighing over "Here, There and Everywhere." Same goes for a lovesick housewife, a lovesick senior citizen, or a lovesick anyone. But I can't imagine anyone sighing over "Only Love Remains," except perhaps fans unfamiliar with his Beatles material. And that's debatable. **C-**

"Press" [Paul McCartney]

Modest, catchy tune, dumber than usual lyrics. The mechanical drums borrow from "Talk More Talk," a production decision that nearly wrecks the song single-handedly. A couple of ridiculous spoken segments also try to wreck it, but they're too short to do much damage. McCartney stands up straight and delivers a decent vocal, unforced and devoid of phony sincerity ["Only Love Remains"]. Since "Press" lacks a punchy chorus, its selection as a single is puzzling, but as an album track, it's passable. Except for the witless lyrics, for which I now withdraw "passable." **B-**

"Pretty Little Head" [Paul McCartney and Eric Stewart]

Shades of "Loup [1st Indian on the Moon]" [*Red Rose Speedway*]. Another serving of electronic oatmeal, with a lyric here, a synthesizer flourish there, a "funny" voice tossed in, and a heaped helping of artificial drums turned up to maximum headache. Undemanding, not really filler, but close. As a bonus, we're served a what-the-hell-was-that astronomy lesson. "Pretty Little Head" offers more melodic pleasures than "Loup," but stops short of attempting an actual song. Whenever McCartney favours noise over notes [see *McCartney II*] beware. **C+**

"Move Over Busker" [Paul McCartney and Eric Stewart]

An easy going track, devoid of electronic clutter, reminiscent of the better work on *Give My Regards to Broad Street* ["No Values," "Not Such a Bad Boy"]. Sabotaged by a clumsy mix – drums way too loud, vocals smothered in echo – the several unrelated pieces arbitrarily bump into each other, making it into a mess similar to the disjointed medley on *Red Rose Speedway*. Needs more work, which is not happening. Lacking that, it needs to be shelved. **C+**

"Angry" [Paul McCartney and Eric Stewart]

I guess he's mad, but about what? Don't know. Who's he mad at? Don't know. What did they do? Don't know. To imply that he's not really mad, just a bit peeved, he softens up the rudimentary arrangement with friendly brass and a staggeringly inappropriate choir. This isn't about anger. It's about a temper tantrum. By the way, Pete Townshend plays on this too. Maybe he dropped by after rehearsing "However Much I Booze." **C-**

"However Absurd" [Paul McCartney and Eric Stewart]
I had hope for this one, imagining it would parody John Lennon's surrealistic experiments like "I Am the Walrus" and "Lucy in the Sky With Diamonds." While not absurd, exactly, the Lennon tunes left room for a poke or two at some of his more extreme images. So does Paul take a swipe at him? Nope. No parody here, although Paul makes an awkward pass early in the verses, which fizzles out. "However Absurd" merely strings together McCartney's random thoughts, none of them particularly interesting let alone extreme. We are left with yet another empty song, devoid of emotion, insight, or humour. As for the song, it begins with a nod to "Strawberry Fields Forever," then meanders off into a series of pedestrian chords and cliché orchestrations, wrapping up with yet another musing on the mystery of love when McCartney couldn't think of anything else. **C+**

[bonus]

"Write Away" [Paul McCartney]
Meandering toss-off, apparently improvised by a guy more preoccupied with the TV schedule than songwriting. The burbling synthesizer instantly dates it, and the vocal is too mawkish for words. Plus, there's a dumb fairy tale reference, which could be a commentary on McCartney's preferred reading material. [*Press to Play Expanded CD*]. **D**

"It's Not True" [Paul McCartney]
Drums bouncing around a king-size bathroom deliver us to a murk-fest, making this an easy call for the worst track associated with *Press to Play*. It crawls along like something you've heard before, only more unpleasant. It's as if McCartney hit a random piano chord, made up some trite passage, hit another chord, more triteness, repeat as necessary until finished. Here's some friendly advice: lay off the echo button. [*Press to Play Expanded CD*] **D-**

"Tough On a Tightrope" [Paul McCartney and Eric Stewart]
Mid-tempo [done it], keyboard heavy [done it], echoed vocal [done it], icky rhymes [done it], dispensable melody [done it], original [are you kidding?]. [*Press to Play Expanded* CD] **D**

"Hanglide" [Paul McCartney]
Filler on a 12" single, evidence that McCartney releases everything he records, good, bad, or brainless. An instrumental sounding like a half-done movie score that should've been filed in a waste basket. A lot of Pink Floyd-ish swoops over a polite drum [machine?] track, and that's pretty much it. ["Press/It's Not True" 12" single] **C**

"Spies Like Us" [Paul McCartney]
For a so-so Chevy Chase comedy, how good does it have to be? Not very, and McCartney rises to the occasion. Plodding verse and kid-friendly chorus – this could be a leftover from *Disney Children's Favourites*. The tag line, thanks to a clever chord, manages fleeting interest, only to be jarred awake by a double-time coda, reminiscent of "Hi Hi Hi." Only it's not "Hi Hi Hi." Not by a long shot. [*Paul McCartney Collection,* 1993]. **C+**

"Once Upon a Long Ago" [Paul McCartney]
Supposedly conceived as a duet with Freddie Mercury of Queen, Mercury bowed out when he became consumed with health issues [that is, AIDS]. Though a McCartney/Mercury duet would have been interesting, it demanded better material than this sentimental mush. McCartney's association with movies is spotty at best – for every "Live and Let Die," we have "Didn't We Meet Somewhere Before" [*Rock n' Roll High School*] – and this continues a downward trend. Doing his best Billy Joel imitation, McCartney warbles his heart out, until every fan of "Helter Skelter" runs for the hills. [*Paul McCartney Collection,* 1993.] **D**

"Get Back [Prince's Trust]" [John Lennon and Paul McCartney]
McCartney helps the prince celebrate his big day with a clutch of oldies. But this great song doesn't get the respect it deserves, as it sounds hastily rehearsed by old guys that could've cared a bit more. [*The Prince's Trust 10th Anniversary Birthday Party*]. **C+**

"I Saw Her Standing There [Prince's Trust]" [John Lennon and Paul McCartney]

Bar band version. If you're a bar band fan, great. If not, keep drinking. [*The Prince's Trust 10th Anniversary Birthday Party*]. **B-**

"Long Tall Sally [Prince's Trust]" [Richard Penniman]

Anyone familiar with McCartney's original attempt [*Long Tall Sally EP; Beatles Second Album*] will automatically make comparisons. One is the tortoise, the other is the Flash. Guess which is which. [*The Prince's Trust 10th Anniversary Birthday Party*]. **B-**

"Let It Be [Ferry Aid]" [John Lennon and Paul McCartney; guest performer: Paul McCartney]

[Ferry Aid] An impromptu group was assembled by *The Sun* newspaper to raise money to commemorate the *MS Herald of Free Enterprise*, a ferry which capsized and killed nearly 200 passengers. As in the Band Aid project, numerous musicians volunteered to participate, including Boy George, Mark Knopfler, and Kate Bush. McCartney donated a vocal for the first verse to this reggae-lite version, though it was rumoured he lifted his voice from the original Beatles track and pasted it in the new arrangement. The record doesn't quite rise to "Do They Know It's Christmas," Band Aid's charity effort, possibly because "Let It Be" lacks the universal sentiments of "Christmas." But the charitable motive is beyond reproach [*Band Aid* single], so be proud to spend your money. [Single] **B**

CHAPTER EIGHTEEN:

CHOBA B CCCP [1988]

Produced by Paul McCartney
Charted at 109 [US], 63 [UK]

Though *Press to Play* hit the UK's Top Ten, it was a major disappointment on most of the rest of the world charts, placing a dismal #30 in Germany, and number #28 in Canada and Switzerland. Sales of singles also foretold of dark clouds ahead. For instance, "Stranglehold" charted at 81 in the US. Even "Mary Had a Little Lamb" charted at 28. Any way you look at it, record sales were on a steady decline, and with rare exceptions, it was hard to find reason to be optimistic.

Perhaps the time had come for McCartney to step away from his conservative persona. Maybe something drastic? Well, maybe. After all, he'd just tried something non-drastic, a full album produced by Phil Ramone, the ill-advised *Return to Pepperland*, with inane songs like "Lindiana" and "I Love This House" that made "No More Lonely Nights" sound like Iggy Pop. McCartney shelved the album, lest he find himself deeper in the hole he was already in.

McCartney had plenty of time to mull over his next move as he puttered around his private studio in the wilds of Scotland, auditioning demos and fooling around with old tapes. With his home recording facilities complete, there was little need to make the journey to London anymore, but this had a downside too. McCartney, basically a social butterfly, felt the occasional pang of loneliness, stuck as he was in the middle of a pastoral wilderness. Invitation-only musicians were friendly and cooperative, but occasionally uneasy with the set-up. In a sense, a formality persisted that, despite McCartney's efforts, never quite went away.

As he toyed with ideas for a new album, he found himself lapsing into a favourite escape, namely, jamming on oldies by the classic rock artists he'd worshipped since he was a youngster. Elvis Presley, Buddy Holly, Fats Domino – he knew them like a preacher knows his hymnal. He enthusiastically urged his current crop of musicians – allegedly there to audition for a touring band – to join in, and they good-naturedly complied.

At some point, he signaled his engineer to record the proceedings. Reviewing the tapes later, McCartney was impressed by the energized performances, and declared they had the basis right there for a new album. He was reminded that John Lennon already had an oldies album on the market [*Rock 'n' Roll*, 1975] and McCartney might be accused of copying him. McCartney thought it over, then announced he'd by-pass any of Lennon's objections and release the album in Russia, with, of course, the full cooperation of the Russian government. Was this in reaction to Lennon's *Rock 'n' Roll*? Possibly.

The album, *Choba B CCCP* [roughly translated, *Back in the USSR*], was an immediate hit overseas, selling out its original Russian pressing, and eventually making its way to record stores around the world. If McCartney was worried about Lennon, he needn't have bothered. Phil Spector, intense and chaotic, produced Lennon's album in an atmosphere of labored misery which Lennon knew was verging toward the out of control.

In contrast, *Choba C CCCP* was start-to-finish fun for the technicians, the musicians, and above all, McCartney. The low-budget ambiance was antithetical to McCartney's past insistence on error-free quality, but this time out, none of that mattered much. In the end, *Choba B CCCP* was relegated to the lower tier of McCartney's catalogue, an entertaining project, but a minor one.

"Kansas City" [Jerry Leiber and Mike Stoller]

An oldie recorded by the Beatles, so trying to beat it – or match it – is begging for trouble. Competing with his own lead vocal on the original, McCartney comes up short. But how could he not? The *Beatles for Sale* version features an electrifying front man and exciting background singers, with George and John gleefully echoing Paul, virtually note for note. On *Choba C CCCP*, McCartney is merely pleasant, with a band [guitarist Mick Green from Billy J Kramer, pianist Mick Gallagher from Ian Dury, drummer Chris Whitten from Julian Cope] that could've been as good as it gets if they hadn't been competing with you-know-who. **B –**

"Twenty Flight Rock" [Eddie Cochran and Ned Fairchild]
Supposedly, this was McCartney's go-to number when he originally auditioned for the Beatles, and he's returned to it repeatedly – from sound checks to impromptu backyard sessions – whenever he needed a comforting jolt. An invitation to a good time, "Twenty Flight Rock" sails along flawlessly, though a bit weary. After all, McCartney's done it about, oh, a billion times. **B**

"Lawdy Miss Clawdy" [Lloyd Price]
McCartney was one of the multitude of teenagers who worshipped at the feet of Lloyd Price. For *Choba B CCCP*, McCartney embraced "Lawdy Miss Clawdy" like a long-lost lover, caressing every syllable with an adoring ferocity. Though a little stiff and an unrevealing photocopy of the original, McCartney charges though it, creating one of the album's best moments. **B**

"Bring It On Home to Me" [Sam Cooke]
Lennon nails this one, belting out a more relaxed and grittier version on his *Rock 'n' Roll* album. McCartney sounds forced by comparison and might as well be singing about reminding his kid to bring home milk. **C-**

"Lucille" [Richard Penniman and Albert Collins]
McCartney rolls out his Little Richard imitation, which he did to perfection with the Beatles on "Long Tall Sally" and later on the *Kampuchea* album. Here, it's too fast, McCartney fights a sore throat, and he takes too many liberties with Richard's stellar inflections, which were unbeatable to begin with. Old McCartney wallops new McCartney, with Little Richard throttling them both. **C**

"Don't Get Around Much Anymore" [Duke Ellington and Bob Russell]
Ellington's sophisticated jazz gets a rock treatment. But it's too much of an afterthought to impress and is largely forgettable. **C-**

"That's All Right" [Arthur Cruddup]
McCartney copies Elvis right down to the last seductive rumble, and succeeds without the embarrassing gimmicks used by the countless Elvises crooning in Las Vegas. Does he top Elvis? Uh, no. **B**

"Ain't That a Shame" [Fats Domino and Dave Bartholomew]
Sorry John. McCartney's intense "Ain't That a Shame" – with a bit of psychedelic echo playfully thrown in – trumps Lennon's lumbering *Rock 'n' Roll* version, easy. Which makes one wonder: were McCartney's duplications of Lennon intentional? Surely – *cough cough* – not. **B**

"Crackin' Up" [Ellas McDaniel]
Bo Diddley is the source for this relatively unheard number. The Beatles used to scrounge record stores for obscurities to cover, and McCartney did the same here. He digs into the comic lyrics, not laughing but coming close, and invents a goofy voice to convey them. This, along with "Ain't That a Shame," will show up soon on *Tripping the Life Fantastic*, demonstrating McCartney's sense of humour is still alive. **B**

"Just Because" [Bob Shelton, Joe Shelton, and Sydney Robin]
Another Elvis, taken from his first album. A feeling of let's-get-over-with permeates the proceedings, though McCartney is competent enough. It would've been a terrific surprise to have a genuine oddball at the end of this album – how about Ronnie Allen's "Juvenile Delinquent"? – but edgy surprises aren't a McCartney specialty. **B-**

"Midnight Special" [Traditional, arranged by Paul McCartney]
Everybody from Creedence Clearwater Revival to Johnny Rivers to ABBA have had a crack at this chestnut,

so McCartney might as well get in line. It concerns a convict on a train ride, has a sticky sing-along melody, and carries a redundant verse that goes on and on. McCartney shows more enthusiasm for this so-so tune than "Don't Get Around Much Anymore" or "Just Because," but it'd been nice if his enthusiasm had been saved for something stronger. **B-**

[bonus]

"I'm Gonna Be a Wheel Someday" [Fats Domino, Dave Bartholomew, and Roy Hayes]
McCartney added this and "Summertime" to satisfy a contract correction. It lacks the marquee value of "Ain't That a Shame" but it's a satisfying time passer. Judging from his over-the-top vocal, McCartney obviously loves it. Dare I say it – McCartney trumps Fats. [*Choba B CCCP Second Edition*] **B**

"Summertime" [George Gershwin, Ira Gershwin, and DuBose Heyward]
A break from the barrage of rockers, McCartney mellows out with a routine run-through of the old standard. It doesn't match Janis Joplin's barrelhouse yowl [*Cheap Thrills*], and isn't within a mile of Brian Wilson eccentric take [*Brian Wilson Reimagines Gershwin*]. [*Choba B CCCP Second Edition*] **B-**

"I'm In Love Again" [Fats Domino and Dave Bartholomew]
Lifted from a B-side ["This One" is the A-side] and plopped onto the 1991 re-release, McCartney doesn't sound like he's got a new girlfriend. Rather, he sounds like a guy at the end of a too-long session, determined to get it up one more time. Adequate, but this time Fats wins. [*Choba C CCCP International Release*] **B-**

"New Moon Over Jamaica" [Johnny Cash, Tom T. Hall, and Paul McCartney; guest performer: Paul McCartney]
[Johnny Cash] "New Music Over Jamaica" emulates a thousand other mind-numbing country songs in that its melody is over-familiar, the instrumentation unimaginative, the platitudes expected. The old-fashioned take detracts from the meager pleasures of hearing Cash and McCartney harmonizing. The pleasure passes quickly. [*Water from the Wells of Home*] **C-**

"Children in Need" [Craig Mathieson and Nicky Hopkins; producer and guest performer: Paul McCartney]
[Spirit of Play] A charitable organization sponsored by the BBC, notable for its fundraising telethons and generous aid to kids needing financial help. Artists as diverse as Lou Reed and the Spice Girls have participated. Here, McCartney, along with ace musicians Craig Mathieson and Woody Woodmansey, performs in *Spirit of Play*. The song isn't much, a "Let it Be"-ish hymn with a flabby melody. McCartney's bass is all but invisible. **C+**

CHAPTER NINETEEN:

FLOWERS IN THE DIRT [1989]

Produced by Paul McCartney, Elvis Costello, David Foster, Neil Dorfsman, Trevor Horn, Steve Lipson, Ross Cullum, and Chris Hughes
Charted at 21 [US], 1 [UK]

It's a given among McCartney aficionados that his primary songwriting dilemma is a near-inability to come up with decent lyrics. In general, the musical community tended to agree. Ignoring his lyric deficiencies and focusing on the music, McCartney's only serious competition was Brian Wilson of the Beach Boys. Wilson matched McCartney in creating gorgeous melodies that seemed like they dropped straight from heaven. But since the early 70s, Brian had personal problems that forced him away from music, leaving McCartney to stand alone, virtually untouchable.

But those lyrics. It was possible for McCartney to come up with the goods if he worked at it, evidenced by "She's Leaving Home" and "Penny Lane" [both *Sgt Pepper* era] that are vivid, deep, and lucid, qualities in short supply during his solo years. Being supremely arrogant – remember the top-of-my-head script for *Give My Regards to Broad Street*? – it's fair to say he believed that lyrics should come as easily as music – that is, instantly. But "Bip Bop," "The Mess," "Getting Closer" and a host of others proved otherwise.

Not only that, but Paul's decline in sales and hostile critical reaction had to be nagging at him. He needed a record to wipe away the relative failures of *Give My Regards to Broad Street* and *Press to Play*, something to earn him the serious respect that had eluded him for an uncomfortably long time.

So anticipation was high when it was rumoured – a rumour that proved true – that McCartney was joining forces with Elvis Costello, a young, brainy, and first rate songwriter whose tunes flowed almost as easily as McCartney's. Only his came with sharp, cynical lyrics that McCartney could only envy. With albums like *This Year's Model* and *Armed Forces*, Costello proved he was a musical force to be reckoned with. As a bonus, his admiration for McCartney [and the Beatles] was unbound. He could barely contain himself when asked to consider a partnership, albeit a temporary one, with McCartney.

In an atmosphere of mutual respect and friendly competition, the relationship got off to a promising start. Initially, there were vague plans of doing an entire album together, but this idea was put on the back burner as premature. Instead, they focused on writing songs. They came in a rush: "Playboy to a Man," "Veronica," "My Brave Face." Their association seemed like a genuine collaboration, two focused professionals, jealousy free and laced with admiration. Where Costello's melodies tended to drift, McCartney would nail them down with memorable passages or boosting them with unexpected twists. And when McCartney's lyrics tended to violate the English language, Costello would come up with pun-laden phrases or clever wordplay.

But as the studio sessions progressed, subtle cracks began to appear. Despite their good intentions, there was no escaping that both McCartney and Costello were established stars, each with their own way of getting their songs on tape. Where Paul was fussy, Costello was devil-may-care. Where Paul was cautiously experimental, Costello tended to go for broke. When Paul was stubborn, Costello could be stubborn too.

Sensing their project was coming to an end, they decided to call it a day. The parting of the ways wasn't bitter, but it was definite. They divided the tracks, most of which would show up on their own albums.

Costello's departure left McCartney in a predicament. The album, once intended as a full-fledged duet, would have to be rethought. More songs, hopefully quality ones, would have to be written and recorded or dug out of the archives. The lengthening roster of producers made the album's consistency uncertain. The difficulties with his fans and critics was also unresolved. And a tour was coming up, a big one, which meant it'd be important, with eyes around the world squarely on him.

Perhaps, just to play it safe and a sure-fire winner guaranteed to rocket his longtime fans into musical nirvana, it was time to resurrect the Beatles.

"My Brave Face" [Paul McCartney and Declan MacManus aka Elvis Costello]

A forceful McCartney, radiating confidence and joy, belting out a strong melody with smart words. It was as close as McCartney had been to the Beatles for an excruciating stretch. Rejoicing fans and shocked critics were near-ecstatic, even as the second or third listen revealed that compared to the Beatles' scruffy aggression, "My Brave Face" was too mannered and too polite. Also, if this was the result of the long-awaited McCartney-Costello meeting of the minds, where was Elvis? Desperately needed in the chorus, his gruff Lennon-like voice was not to be heard, and "My Brave Face" suffered for it. But considering McCartney's recent output, none of this mattered. "My Brave Face" hit the target, a satisfying blend of two masters excelling at their craft.

The lyrics of "My Brave Face" are impressive, glowing with humour, surprise, and insight. It's not clear if Costello kicked McCartney in the pants to make him dig deep for the classy words that John Lennon claimed McCartney always had in him, but it's a reasonable guess that McCartney was unlikely to have done it alone. The folk-ish song mixes faint echoes of "We Can Work It Out" with a hint of *Rubber Soul* and is insanely catchy. The middle section – the Beatles section – is impossible to resist. On the evidence of "My Brave Face," McCartney-Costello was a marriage that deserved to last. It's a shame it didn't.

"My Brave Face" rose to #25 in the US and #18 in the UK, a modest hit, but a hit nonetheless. It'd be McCartney's last hit record for close to a quarter of a century, when his 2014 partnership with Kayne West, "Only One," went to #35 on both the US and UK charts. **A**

"Rough Ride" [Paul McCartney]

A shocker, as "Rough Ride" contains a bit of lyrical edge not usually associated with the happy-go-lucky McCartney. Over a tasteful light funk, McCartney laments his inability to square things with a deceased friend, which sounds to the suspicious like John Lennon. But the melody feels more improvised than composed, and as an improviser, McCartney is middling at best. **B**

"You Want Her Too" [Paul McCartney and Elvis Costello]

The partners trade incisive and clever lines, as McCartney good naturedly lectures and Costello nastily sneers, including an outright insult in the first verse. The snazzy background, good enough for a track by itself, provides an ideal setting for the closest we'll get to a substitute Lennon-McCartney face-off in our lifetime. For the unconvinced, compare this to the McCartney-Jackson duet on Jackson's slick *Thriller* album, then decide which song deals with men and which with boys. **A-**

"Distractions" [Paul McCartney]

Flabby re-do of "Somebody Who Cares" from *Tug of War* with all the accoutrements of a "beautiful" song [intimate vocals, purring background] and imagination on display. That's not to say it doesn't go down easy – it does – but after these empty calories, how about something substantial? **B-**

"We Got Married" [Paul McCartney]

Excavated from the abandoned *Return to Pepperland*, McCartney either was overly fond of it, or found it easier to execute than "So Like Candy" or "Flying to My Home." Poor judgment aside, McCartney earns points for trying harder on his lyrics, this time painting a picture of nuptials that aren't always blissful, ending with a plea – to himself? – to try harder. Beginning in a minor key, to show he means business, he bossa novas his way through a tangle of snapshots depicting honeymoons, kids, and time not always passing the way you want it to. "We Got Married" suffers in comparison to Costello's brainy lyrics, available just a couple of cuts away, but kudos to McCartney for making an effort. **B**

"Put It There" [Paul McCartney]

McCartney's ode to a handshake totters on the brink of silliness, but is temporarily rescued by a deft hook near the chorus that nudges it to safety before it plunges over the cliff. Strange it should be released as a single, lacking as it does a strong melody and a compelling backing track. Since it only rose to number 32 [UK], McCartney would've benefitted from a second opinion. **B –**

"Figure of Eight" [Paul McCartney]

Oddly, McCartney chose to open a few concerts with this sluggish number instead of "Drive My Car" or "Jet" like the lord intended. If the audiences had paid attention instead of waiting for it to end, they might have been exposed to some melancholy lyrics and even a few serious ideas in this semi-obscure discourse on the ambiguity of love. Frustratingly, the cheery music is the flat opposite of what the troubled lyrics seem to intend. **B**

"This One" [Paul McCartney]

The album's obvious single, though it only managed a lackluster 18 in the UK and a gasping-for-air 94 in the US. Too superficial, "This One" chugs along with a heard-it-before chorus and confusing lyrics, a sad step backwards. By the way, is this also about John Lennon? **B-**

"Don't Be Careless Love" [Paul McCartney and Elvis Costello]

A breathtaking McCartney vocal coupled with a plaintive melody and evocative lyrics make this an album highlight. McCartney's voice wavers, pleads, and aches. He hasn't sounded this passionate or this sincere since "Maybe I'm Amazed." The supporting track blankets the piece sympathetically, and if you listen close, you might detect a gentle Costello on the chorus. *A tour de force,* and one of the best McCartney-Costello collaborations, due mainly to Paul. **A-**

"That Day is Done" [Paul McCartney and Elvis Costello]

A thoughtful examination of love gone to hell. Played as a drunken waltz, suitable for the dizzying tune, McCartney sings it like he means it, and at times seems to be on the verge of tears. The chorus swells without the phony sentimentality for which McCartney is too often guilty [see "Motor of Love," coming up]. Best of all, McCartney matures before your very ears, close to an incredible feat. **B+**

"How Many People" [Paul McCartney]

This is the sound of McCartney running out of gas. A shame he couldn't emulate the good old days where an album clocked in at 30 minutes or so, which would've allowed *Flowers in the Dirt* to end with the appropriate finale of "That Day is Done." Instead, two losers – this one and "Motor of Love" – do their best to crush the life out of it. A slow pseudo-reggae serves as the plastic background for a woe-is-us treatise aimed, apparently, at people waking up from a coma. Paul would rather be cheerful than sad. Did you know that people drop dead every now and then? Man, what a bummer! **D**

"Motor of Love" [Paul McCartney]

As on *Tug of War,* McCartney ends *Flowers in the Dirt* with the aural equivalent of a bean fart. Inane lyrics, a sluggish melody, the whole thing drenched in syrupy echo, it's difficult to find anything to like in "Motor of Love." The forgettable presentation moves along on its hands and knees for a painful six minutes, about three times as long as the music deserves. If he was still working on a Linda album, this would've been a good one to palm off on her. **D**

[bonus]

"Ou est le Soleil" [Paul McCartney]

Also available in an instrumental version and several oddball extended versions, none of which improve the song. Translated from French, it's roughly "Where is the Sun." A jam, disco style. How is it? *Ca craint.* [*Flowers in the Dirt Deluxe*] **D-**

"Party Party" [Paul and Linda McCartney, Hamish Stuart, Robbie McIntosh, Paul Wickens, and Chris Whitten]

A jam, disco style yet again, dull, dreary, probably poisonous. That queasy feeling is your natural reaction to McCartney urging you to whoop it up with his kindergarten friends. [*Flowers in the Dirt Deluxe*] **F**

"Back on My Feet" [Paul McCartney]

This is far from McCartney's worst [it doesn't come within miles of "Bip Bop"] but it's nowhere near his best ["Golden Slumbers," to name one of many]. The product of a talented man bored at the piano, inspired by a few chords, eventually coalescing into a heard-it-before tune. Not a great one, but a fair one, probably forgotten within minutes of the tape machine clicking off. [*Flowers in the Dirt Deluxe*] **B-**

"Flying to My Home" [Paul McCartney]
On the other hand, every now and then he comes up with a jewel. Yes, it needs a better verse, and yes, the intro should have been sent to a clip joint. But the rest of it – the irresistible chorus, the crunching guitars, the Bizarro World voice – presents McCartney at his cocky best. Why oh why wasn't this substituted for "Motor of Love?" Or "Figure of Eight?" Or "How Many People?" [*Flowers in the Dirt Deluxe*] **B+**

"Loveliest Thing" [Paul McCartney]
Similar to something McCartney has done previously, maybe more than once, but it's not worth the effort to hunt down. Another mid-tempo piano track, another semi-improvised melody, and empty-headed lyrics. A brief modulation in the middle perks up the ears, but only briefly. You want an impressive demonstration of modulation? See "Penny Lane," written by You Know Who. [*Flowers in the Dirt Deluxe*] **B-**

"The Long and Winding Road [1989 Version]" [John Lennon and Paul McCartney]
Must've been some legal reason for recording this again. For insane collectors. [*Special Package Japanese 1990 Tour*] **F**

"Same Time Next Year" [Paul McCartney]
A *Back to the Egg* outtake. Recorded for a movie of the same name, "Same Time Next Year" apparently was rejected by the producers who didn't care for the lyrics. It's a routine ballad, soaked in strings, for which McCartney supplies a homogenized vocal. Vaguely reminiscent of "Mary Had a Little Lamb" in style if not in content. [*Flowers in the Dirt Deluxe*] **D**

"PS Love Me Do" [John Lennon and Paul McCartney]
What a dumb idea. Linking these early Beatles songs was not inspired, but more of a thumb-in-your-eye from the writer, someone who doesn't revere the originals like the rest of the world. From the opening howl of a dilettante to an echo attack on the pointlessly re-done verses to the show-off guitar solo, this is not an easy ride. If McCartney's goal was to cleanse the originals of their likeability, he succeeded in spades. [*Flowers in the Dirt Deluxe*] **F**

"The Lovers That Never Were [Original Demo]" [Paul McCartney and Elvis Costello]
With a song bursting with melodic invention and a vocalist in full bloom, you don't need more than a piano to carry it. McCartney is so assured, pitch perfect, and in control at all times, even when he's screaming for his life, the demo could've been used as it is on the album. [The studio version is coming in *Off the Ground*.] [*Flowers in the Dirt Deluxe*] **B+**

"Don't Be Careless Love [Original Demo]" [Paul McCartney and Elvis Costello]
A feel-your-way demo with McCartney holding back, the better to rest his vocal cords. [*Flowers in the Dirt Deluxe*] **B**

"Tommy's Coming Home [Original Demo]" [Paul McCartney and Elvis Costello]
This didn't make it to either of the partnership's albums, which is a shocker as it's a good one. Incisive lyric and harmonies to make a statue weep. It peters out towards the end, but nothing that a polish couldn't fix. [*Flowers in the Dirt Deluxe*] **B**

"Twenty Fine Fingers [Original Demo]" [Paul McCartney and Elvis Costello]
The weakest of the collaborations. It's a standard rock tune, Chuck Berry with some fooling around on the chorus and a yawn at the end, provided by the listener. [*Flowers in the Dirt Deluxe*] **C+**

"So Like Candy [Original Demo]" [Paul McCartney and Elvis Costello]
Yes, it's just a demo, but you can't help wishing they'd tried it again to whip those exquisite harmonies into shape. Appears fully developed on Costello's *Mighty Like a Rose* without, unfortunately, McCartney's classy vocals. [*Flowers in the Dirt Deluxe*] **B**

"You Want Her Too [Original Demo]" [Paul McCartney and Elvis Costello]

A sketchy rendition, light on harmonies, background non-existent, made so the composers could get an idea of how it plays. Not for the consumer's ears. [*Flowers in the Dirt Deluxe*] **B**

"That Day is Done [Original Demo]" [Paul McCartney and Elvis Costello]
The treat is McCartney and Costello warbling together, sometimes harmonizing, sometimes not. While waiting for it to end, marvel at the uncanny songwriting skills of two of the best. [*Flowers in the Dirt Deluxe*] **B**

"My Brave Face [Original Demo]" [Paul McCartney and Elvis Costello]
Fun to hear Costello's harmonies, sharp as a razor. As the boys get a real kick out of performing together, who can resist their goofing around? But the band is missed. [*Flowers in the Dirt Deluxe*] **B**

"Playboy to a Man [Original Demo]" [Paul McCartney and Elvis Costello]
The piano doesn't help, pounding away on unsurprising chords as the singers search for a melody that's already left town. [*Flowers in the Dirt Deluxe*] **B-**

"The Lovers That Never Were [1988 Demo]" [Paul McCartney and Elvis Costello]
Little difference, but here the vocal comes across as a hair less confident. [*Flowers in the Dirt Deluxe*] **B**

"Tommy's Coming Home [1988 Demo]" [Paul McCartney and Elvis Costello]
Grand thumps of percussion might be an acceptable experiment, but not for a song as delicate as "Tommy's Coming Home." Of course, demos are intended for experiments, not for purchase. [*Flowers in the Dirt Deluxe*] **B-**

"Twenty Fine Fingers [1988 Demo]" [Paul McCartney and Elvis Costello]
Somewhat bouncier. Big deal. [*Flowers in the Dirt Deluxe*] **C+**

"So Like Candy [1988 Demo]" [Paul McCartney and Elvis Costello]
With a fuller background, "So Like Candy" moves up a notch, but the demo is inferior to the studio in nearly every way, so you can skip this one. [*Flowers in the Dirt Deluxe*] **B**

"You Want Her Too [1988 Demo]" [Paul McCartney and Elvis Costello]
Crude replica of the studio track, including a quirky but disposable bass pattern. [*Flowers in the Dirt Deluxe*] **B**

"That Day is Done [1988 Demo]" [Paul McCartney and Elvis Costello]
More polish, somewhat inferior to the original demo, but an engaging look at an adult song as an infant. [*Flowers in the Dirt Deluxe*] **B**

"Don't Be Careless Love [1988 Demo]" [Paul McCartney and Elvis Costello]
Near carbon copy. Next. [*Flowers in the Dirt Deluxe*] **B**

"My Brave Face [1988 Demo]" [Paul McCartney and Elvis Costello]
The band hesitates here and there, learning the changes as they go. Expected on a demo, but not for home listening. [*Flowers in the Dirt Deluxe*] **B-**

"Playboy to a Man [1988 Demo]" [Paul McCartney and Elvis Costello]
In its early stage, an undistinguished tune, uninspired take. [*Flowers in the Dirt Deluxe*] **B-**

"The First Stone" [Paul McCartney and Hamish Stuart]
Winding up for a kill in the eye-popping verse. But the lame chorus drizzles away like a snowflake in a blast furnace. Save the verse for something better, and chuck the chorus down the disposal. [*Flowers in the Dirt Deluxe*] **B**

"Good Sign" [Paul McCartney]
McCartney compares the love of his life to an electrocardiogram. Awful backing, similar to a half-dozen

lightweight disco tracks he's dumped on us before. The flimsy song sounds like snatches of crap he overheard at Studio 54. Looking forward to the next one when he compares his love to a colonoscopy. [*Flowers in the Dirt Deluxe*] **D –**

"I Wanna Cry" [Paul McCartney]

Blues improv, solid vocal, better than average guitar solo. An unusual McCartney track, worth a listen. ["This One" single] **B**

"Distractions [Demo]" [Paul McCartney]

McCartney rummaged through his kitty litter and came up with three demos that would never have seen the light of day were it not for the demands of the internet. "Distractions" wasn't much of a song in the first place, so one wonders who this for – kitty litter collectors maybe? Nice drum machine. [*paulmccartney.com*] **C+**

"This One [Demo]" [Paul McCartney]

Little more than a ragged practice run. [*paulmccartney.com*] **D+**

"I Don't Want to Confess [Demo]" [Paul McCartney and Elvis Costello]

The least of the collaborations, with conventional chords and unfinished lyrics. Performed as if they gave up on it before the demo was finished. [*paulmccartney.com*] **B-**

"Back on My Feet [Digital]" [Paul McCartney]

The most listenable of the digital tracks – the only one actually. The original was a throwaway. So you can imagine what a throwaway of a throwaway sounds like. [*paulmccartney.com*] **C**

"Coming Up [Knebworth]" [Paul McCartney]

In an album that also features Tears for Fears, McCartney contributes an empty run-through of "Coming Up." Recommended for Tears for Fears fans. [*Knebworth: the Album,* 1990]. **C**

"Hey Jude [Knebworth]" [John Lennon and Paul McCartney]

"Hey Jude," one more trying time. For those having cash in need of quick disposal. [*Knebworth: the Album,* 1990] **B-**

"Shallow Grave [Demo]" [Paul McCartney and Elvis Costello]

Not enough melody to earn a place on *Flowers in Dirt*, though Costello would buff it up and show McCartney how it's done on the stellar *All This Useless Beauty*. [*paulmccartney.com*] **B-**

"Veronica" [Paul McCartney and Elvis Costello]

[Elvis Costello] "My Brave Face" was a treat, but this is better. Leading Costello's 12th album, the forlorn tale of a suffering woman [possibly from Alzheimer's] is shot through with a propulsive rhythm that simmers on the verse and explodes on the choruses. Costello snarls and spits, evocative of pain and frustration, and it stands as one of the best performances of an impressive career. Imagine a duet album: "My Brave Face," "Veronica," "You Want Her Too," "So Like Candy," "That Day is Done" – and grit your teeth because two egos wouldn't let it happen. [*Spike*. A non-essential demo is available on 2001's *Spike Bonus*.] **A**

"Pads, Paws, and Claws" [Paul McCartney and Elvis Costello]

[Elvis Costello] An unfortunate rhythm section, all synthesizer and over-heated slams, uncomfortably reminds the listener of *Press to Play*'s worst. The pedestrian melody isn't helped by the amusing but shallow tale of boy-meets-girl-meets-kitty-meets-something. [*Spike*. A redundant demo is available on 2001's *Spike Bonus*.] **B –**

"This Town" [Elvis Costello; guest performer: Paul McCartney]

[Elvis Costello] An anti-Trump song? With razor-sharp lyrics, Costello slices up the shallow pseudo-zillionaire into teeny pieces while the tough music sticks its tongue out. McCartney offers solid support without getting in the way. Maybe he's wondering if it's in him to write words this well. [It is, kind of.

See "Despite Repeated Warnings" on *Egypt Station*.] [*Spike*. Another version, unneeded, is on 2001's *Spike Bonus*]. **B+**

"So Like Candy" [Paul McCartney and Elvis Costello]
[Elvis Costello] A gorgeous ballad that McCartney was a fool to pass up for *Flowers in the Dirt*. Costello, full-throated and maybe a touch too melodramatic, performs over a tasteful background. For once, it ends too quickly – we softies want it to go on forever. As good as it is, McCartney could have done it better. [*Mighty Like a Rose*] **B+**

"Playboy to a Man" [Paul McCartney and Elvis Costello]
[Elvis Costello] Tuneless, accompanied by a lot of shouting. That's fine, except McCartney can make your bones rattle, where Costello manages only a tickle. A bottom of the barrel collaboration, down there with "Twenty Fine Fingers." [*Mighty Like a Rose*] **B-**

"Shallow Grave" [Paul McCartney and Elvis Costello]
[Elvis Costello] Too good to miss. Sexier than the demo, rumbling at you like a freight train gone bonkers. Scant melody, but on a version this fierce, it's doubtful you'll miss it. [*All This Useless Beauty*] **B+**

"Ferry Cross the Mersey [Remake]" [Gerry Marsden; guest performer: Paul McCartney]
[Gerry Marden and Friends] That's Gerry Marsden of Gerry and the Pacemakers, a British group that were buddies with the Beatles and responsible for several hits, such as "I Like It" and "How Do You Do It" [which the Beatles recorded, but rejected]. This version, roughly identical to the 1964 recording, features McCartney singing a few lines, as do others [Holly Johnson, the Christians]. The single was to raise awareness and money for the families of a disastrous crush of fans at Hillsborough Stadium soccer match, resulting in nearly 100 dead. Charity: noble. Single: blah. ["*Ferry Cross the Mersey*" charity single] **C**

CHAPTER TWENTY:

TRIPPING THE LIVE FANTASTIC [1990]

Produced by Paul McCartney, Bob Clearmountain, and Peter Henderson]
Charted at 26 [US], 17 [UK]

"That was me, all that Stockhausen shit in the Beatles."
- PAUL MCCARTNEY, WORLD TOUR BOOK [1989]

The tour was nearly underway. The new band was primed and ready to go: Chris Witten, drums, from the Waterboys; Robbie McIntosh, guitar, from the Pretenders; Hamish Stuart, guitar, from the Average White Band; Paul Wickens, keyboards, from the Young One. The crowd were already clawing at the fences. And McCartney was determined to visit each and every country that had an extension cord: Norway, Sweden, Germany, France, Italy, Switzerland, Spain, Holland, US, Canada, UK, Japan, New Zealand, Australia, Brazil. If you didn't catch McCartney on stage, it's not because he wasn't trying.

Beyond sharing the spectacle with ravenous fans, there were other reasons to tour. First, the tour would [hopefully] boost the sales of the freshly released *Flowers in the Dirt*, along with the single "[My Brave] Face." Second, the tour would road test the new band. And third, McCartney could gauge the reaction to the set-heavy selection of Beatles songs [four Beatles for 1976's *Wings Over America*, more than four times as many here].

In an act of unprecedented generosity, McCartney gave away, free of charge, a full-colour 95 page tour book to everyone attending the concerts. The oversized book was packed with pictures and stories, including a close-up examination of his career all the way back to the Beatles. If there was a stickler, it was the curious inclusion of McCartney quotes defending himself as the Beatles' promoter of the avant garde, a distinction that usually had gone to John Lennon. Not only was this a reactivation of a feud with a dead man, it was also questionable. McCartney's avant garde contributions tended to be seasoning on pre-existing songs [the buzzing that links the tracks on *Abbey Road*'s medley, the sound effects on Lennon's "Tomorrow Never Knows" from *Revolver*] rather than the full-bore go-for-broke experimentations of Lennon [Revolution 9" from *The Beatles*, "I Want You [She's So Heavy]" from *Abbey Road*.] Strange that this nagged McCartney, a good 20 years later.

As for the concert, the reception was almost beyond description, as if Moses had descended from Mount Sinai with a revised Ten Commandments. Crowds were polite when McCartney delivered "Rough Ride" and "We Got Married," but blasted into the stratosphere when he played "Things We Said Today" and "Get Back." If there was any doubt that his audience came for the Beatles, it was laid to rest at concert number one.

In the tour book, each of the new members of the band was asked to name their favourite McCartney song. Chris Witten picked "The Long and Winding Road." Robbie McIntosh: "Fixing a Hole" [or "Fool on the Hill" or "Penny Lane"]. Hamish Stuart: "She's a Woman" [or "Let It Be" or "Eleanor Rigby" or "The Long and Winding Road"]. Paul Wickens: "I'm Down." All are Beatles songs.

"Showtime" [Paul McCartney]
Gee Paul, is this avant garde? **D-**

"Figure of Eight [Live 1990]" [Paul McCartney]
As the initial frenzy died down, the crowd settled in to feast on ... "Figure of Eight?" Yes, the first song

of a Godzilla-sized concert was a fair-to-middling, easygoing *Flowers in the Dirt* track. "Figure of Eight" refocused attention on the legendary star, not the music, pretty much a given. And yes, McCartney had an album to push. And yes, it served as a pleasant welcome to ease into the long-anticipated proceedings and a tease of things to come. But this? A low-key song that's okay at best? Maybe he should have tried something more up-tempo? Something completely unexpected? Something blow-the-roof-off fun? How about "Why Don't We Do It in the Road?" **B-**

"Jet [Live 1990]" [Paul and Linda McCartney]
Paul the Hoarse clears his throat with this screamer which is obviously a more suitable opening than "Figure of Eight." Of course, it's already appeared live on *Wings Over America*, and knowing McCartney's insistence on reproducing the studio versions as accurately as possible, one might wonder why this is here on yet another live album. One might still be waiting for an answer. **B-**

"Rough Ride [Live 1990]" [Paul McCartney]
Famous song, obscure song, back and forth. An acceptable way to open a show, but as long as there's a Beatle preening in front of us, and as long as re-workings are as rare as Linda keyboard solos, why not go for broke? Given the limitations inherent in a family-friendly performance, a perfect Paul concert would include two or three Wings hits ["Jet" and "Band on the Run" would do it], one show-off number to blow up some fireworks ["Live and Let Die"], a taste of the current album ["My Brave Face"], and the rest of the show, Beatles. Ecstasy. Not going to happen. Or ... is it? **C+**

"Got to Get You Into My Life [Live 1990]" [John Lennon and Paul McCartney]
The opening fanfare ignites the place like a match in a gas tank. Aggressive guitars smack out the beat, McCartney aims for the high notes and – yes! – hits them, and we're transported back to a time when flowers were in bloom and all was right with the world, as the Beatles looked to be eternally intact. That "Got to Get You Into My Life" still sounds fresh is, of course, a tribute to the master who thought it up. The fake "horns," played on a keyboard, is a tribute to the guy too cheap to hire real ones. **B+**

"Band On the Run [Live 1990]" [Paul and Linda McCartney]
Another *Wings Over America* track, proving that McCartney can pull off this moderately tricky number, all the while seeming to be somewhere else while the band dutifully chops through it. **B-**

"Birthday [Live 1990]" [John Lennon and Paul McCartney]
Strong rendition, coming in second after the Beatles, fueled by powerful vocals and a supercharged band, though it seems a bit stiff. Released as a single, which flopped, possibly because every creature in the galaxy knew it inside and out. **B**

"Ebony and Ivory [Live 1990]" [Paul McCartney]
Something for the folks who can't get their ears unstuck from the radio. Worse than the studio version, as Stevie Wonder is absent, taking any semblance of funk that made this endurable. Here and there, McCartney drifts into Vegas crooning. You can almost visualize blackjack dealers rolling their eyes. **D+**

"We Got Married [Live 1990]" [Paul McCartney]
Can't tell if McCartney's melancholy or just pooped. Either way, real or fake, he infuses "We Got Married" with more emotion than he did on *Flowers in the Dirt*, making it intimate and noteworthy. **B**

"Inner City Madness [Live 1990]" [Paul and Linda McCartney, Hamish Stuart, Robbie McIntosh, Paul Wickens, and Chris Witten]
To frustrate bootleggers, McCartney threw in a few extras for deterrence. Did it work? It might have, if he'd added a real song instead of electronic baloney. **F**

"Maybe I'm Amazed [Live 1990]" [Paul McCartney]
Among the reasons for buying this pricey two CD live set: [1] to hear semi-obscure songs in a different context, [2] to collect every morsel McCartney deems worthy to sell, and [3] to hear Beatles chestnuts played by an actual Beatle. Note that being subjected to a previously released live tune performed in exactly the same way, cheesy piano trills and all, is not among the reasons. **B-**

"The Long and Winding Road [Live 1990]" [John Lennon and Paul McCartney]
What is this – four, five, even more versions? I've lost count. Fans who specialize in collecting them all can add another to the pile. Preferable to any of the live versions, the studio efforts remain the keepers, with *Let It Be* the choice for nostalgia buffs, *Anthology 3* the choice for purists. For fans wanting – *needing* – a concert souvenir, let this be an option for no one. **D**

"Crackin' Up [Live 1990]" [Ellas McDaniel]
Vegas-style take on this oldie makes it a time killer, unnecessary and exasperating. **C-**

"The Fool on the Hill [Live 1990]" [John Lennon and Paul McCartney]
A timeless, gorgeous song, one of McCartney's best. And unusual for Paul, it adds something new: a keyboard solo with harmonized voices, easily making it a concert highlight. **B+**

"Sgt Pepper's Lonely Hearts Club Band [Live 1990]" [John Lennon and Paul McCartney]
Uncomfortably resembling a cover band trying hard to please. If McCartney thinks his hired hands can copy the Beatles, he's got another guess coming. Is this the part of the show to remind us that he's the one who wrote "Sgt Pepper," not that other guy in the credits? **B-**

"Can't Buy Me Love [Live 1990]" [John Lennon and Paul McCartney]
The passing of the years is tough, evidenced by middle-age McCartney doing his best to bring back the kid he was when "Can't Buy Me Love" hit the top. He offers show biz schmaltz where passion used to be, reminding us of Elvis dutifully whizzing through "Mystery Train" in Las Vegas. From the original "Mystery Train" to Vegas: about 10 years. From the release of "Can't Buy Me Love" to *Tripping the Live Fantastic*: about 25 years. **B**

"Matchbox [Live 1990] [Carl Perkins]
A pedestrian assault on a Beatles oldie. It's all but unrecognizable as the band cranks up, and a pumped McCartney takes over one of Ringo's rare leads [*Long Tall Sally EP* in the UK, *Something New* in the US]. Then professionalism raises its ugly head. Too slick, too neat, too prissy. It makes Ringo sound like Kurt Cobain. **C**

"Put It There [Live 1990]" [Paul McCartney]
Is this an attempt to revive interest in a single? If so, the patient's long dead. It went to the great beyond after clawing its way to 32 [UK]. If it's to give the crowd a breather after "Matchbox," nobody wanted or needed a breather. If it's to remind the crowd that *Flowers in the Dirt* is still on sale, how about another Elvis Costello tune? Like "You Want Her Too?" Or better yet, a killer surprise, like "Veronica?" **B-**

"Together [Live 1990]" [Paul and Linda McCartney, Hamish Stuart, Robbie McIntosh, Paul Wickens, and Chris Hillman]
A sound check of a crummy reggae jam that goes on and on for an eternal two minutes. Supposedly to thwart bootleggers. [Giggle.] **D-**

"Things We Said Today [Live 1990]" [John Lennon and Paul McCartney]
Ace rendition of a terrific number, spoiled by unnecessary guitar practice. I'm sure it's tempting to show off, but there's no way to upstage McCartney on this song. Or any of his songs, for that matter. **B**

"Eleanor Rigby [Live 1990]" [John Lennon and Paul McCartney]
How much better this would have been if actual strings were used instead of keyboards. C'mon Paul – unlock your money belt and hire the real thing. Either that, or forego the strings altogether and stick with a lone acoustic guitar. The melody is strong enough to survive by itself, and it'd give consumers another reason to invest in this mostly redundant album. **B**

"This One [Live 1990]" [Paul McCartney]
Following "Eleanor Rigby" with "This One" wasn't exactly a brilliant programming decision. Don't tell McCartney, but "This One," an adequate piece of fluff from *Flowers in the Dirt*, sounds older than "Eleanor." **B-**

"My Brave Face [Live 1990]" [Paul McCartney and Elvis Costello]
The high point of *Flowers in the Dirt* not only receives a reverent treatment, it lacks the polish that the studio McCartney usually can't resist, all to the good. The Beatle elements come to the fore, enhancing the billowing charm. **B+**

"Back in the USSR [Live 1990]" [John Lennon and Paul McCartney]
Every bar band on the face of the earth needs to master the tough, gritty Chuck Berry chug so they play credible versions of "Johnny B Goode" and "Rock and Roll Music" to keep the patrons drinking and sustain their career. The Beatles did it in Hamburg before they were signed, and as a consequence, they could churn it out effortlessly. All pros, however, have a tough time unlearning the precision that got them to the top, which is why straight rockers struggling to bring back the good old days tend to sound too slick. They can't help it. This version, though competent, leans towards the bland, a problem bar musicians could solve easily with their garage band style. A round of applause, however, for the plane noise. **B**

"I Saw Her Standing There [Live 1990]" [John Lennon and Paul McCartney]
See "Back in the USSR." In another dimension, McCartney brings out some of his old Liverpool buddies to charge through these old rockers, like Gerry Marsden [Gerry & the Pacemakers] or Colin Manley [Remo Four] or Pete Best [The Beatles]. Or maybe a contemporary bar band of old timers, like NRBQ. Or a left-field choice like Los Lobos. Gosh, isn't life swell in another dimension? **B**

"Twenty Flight Rock [Live 1990]" [Eddie Cochran]
Consumer alert – a notch better than *Choba B CCCP*. Assuming you're going to spring for *Tripping the Live Fantastic,* you'll also have McCartney doing "Crackin' Up" and "Ain't That a Shame," an adequate sample from *Choba B CCCP,* saving yourself a pocketful of rubles. **B**

"Coming Up [Live 1990]" [Paul McCartney]
Funkier than *McCartney II*, Paul fires things up with a screaming vocal that's genuinely exciting. But the synthesized horns sneak in and the song turns thin. Letting the guitarist sing a couple of lines emphasizes what a stellar vocalist Paul is. But the semi-psychedelic section – imagine two cell phones fighting – veers close to disco. **B –**

"Sally [Live 1990]" [Will E. Haines, Harry Leon, Leo Towers]
Spontaneous snippet of a vaguely familiar tune, scooped up from a retirement village. What's it doing in a concert album? Anybody know? You bootleggers have any idea? **D-**

"Let It Be [Live 1990]" [John Lennon and Paul McCartney]
Marred by the synthesizer's fake organ, the annoying pseudo-jazzy piano licks, and one too many McCartney whoop-de-dos, this rock-solid song – which apparently nothing can hurt – comes through loud and clear. John Lennon once remarked that "Let It Be" reminded him more of Wings than the Beatles. Good point, even though technically, this isn't Wings. Remind me – what's the difference between Wings Paul and *Tripping* Paul? **B**

"Ain't That a Shame [Live 1990]" [Fats Domino and Dave Bartholomew]
Indulge McCartney while he tickles himself with a credible Fats Domino imitation. Pass the time by mentally listing Beatles songs you'd rather hear. **B-**

"Live and Let Die [Live 1990]" [Paul and Linda McCartney]
Check out *Wings Over America* when this was relatively fresh. Here, it's more of the same, maybe a bit wearier. But it won't matter to fans of James Bond who like stuff being blown up. Speaking of blown up, the fireworks are more audible here, good news for Beavis and Butt-Head. **B-**

"If I Were Not Upon the Stage [Live 1990]" [Thomas Sutton, Bill Turner, and Stan Bowsher]
Please Paul – resist the bottled charm. Like a little boy armed with his favourite joke, he performed this lame trick every time, playing 30 seconds of this semi-standard before launching into "Hey Jude." **D**

"Hey Jude [Live 1990]" [John Lennon and Paul McCartney]
A standard, wrecked by McCartney's dragging it out forever with an incessant this side/that side routine.

Fine if you're there, tedious if you're home. Too bad, as McCartney's controlled, masterful voice pulls this over the top – that is, until it's turned into a sing-along. **B**

"Yesterday [Live 1990]" [John Lennon and Paul McCartney]
Tolerable, unlike the overblown "Long and Winding Road." Strange that he cut it half when lesser songs, like "Rough Ride" were allowed their full lengths. And instead of a synthesizer, once again, tightwad Paul should've sprung for genuine strings. **B-**

"Get Back [Live 1990]" [John Lennon and Paul McCartney]
McCartney should have an easy time pulling this off – he wrote it, after all – but he messes it up a little. Too speedy, as if he's trying to get it over with, and too smooth, as it takes a man with less technical facility on guitar to copy Lennon's barely there but still charming solos. **C**

"Golden Slumbers/Carry That Weight/The End [Live 1990]" [John Lennon and Paul McCartney]
If you don't own a copy of *Abbey Road*, luxuriate in the aching "Golden Slumbers," bask in the anthemic "Carry That Weight," and wipe the tears as you experience the glorious "The End." Show's over? Now buy *Abbey Road*, and you can trash the inferior *Tripping*. **B+**

"Don't Let the Sun Catch You Crying [Live 1990]" [Joe Green]
Sorry to break the news to Gerry & the Pacemakers fans, but this isn't the 1964 hit by Gerry and friends. Instead, McCartney favours us with a tiny gem recorded by Louis Jordan in 1946. Recorded during a sound check – take that, bootleggers! – McCartney loses himself in this bittersweet tale of a snubbed lover, relishing the gentle chords and dreamlike melody. Despite occasional over-singing and one too many painful howls, McCartney nails it, ending the album on a satisfying note. **B**

[bonus]

"Good Day Sunshine [Live 1990]" [John Lennon and Paul McCartney]
The B-side to the live "Birthday." Probably not included on *Tripping the Live Fantastic* because any semblance of style leftover from *Revolver* is transformed into facelessness. [B-side of "Birthday."] **B-**

"Mull of Kintyre [Live 1990]" [Paul McCartney and Denny Laine]
Unwelcome in the US, explaining its absence on *Tripping*. It popped up on the European leg, however, and it's a pleasing touch, especially with the bagpipe brigade that marched triumphantly across the stage, adding some musical colour. [Import single.] **B**

"All My Trials [Live 1990]" [Traditional, arranged by Paul McCartney]
All of the *Tripping the Live Fantastic: Highlights* tracks were lifted from the double CD, except this one. Ponder the wisdom of keeping the ho-hum "Put It There" on the double CD, in place of "All My Trials" from the *Columbia House Mail Order Highlights Edition*. That aside, enjoy the intimate vocal and warm production featured on "All My Trials," a folk song popularized by Elvis Presley while collecting checks in Las Vegas. An odd choice, but a welcome one for an album that could stand a little more odd. [*Columbia House Mail Order Highlights Edition*.] **B**

"C Moon [Live 1990]" [Paul and Linda McCartney]
Sound check performance, so don't expect stellar musicianship, an off-the-wall performance, or much of anything from this off-handed rehash. [Import single] **C**

"Strawberry Fields Forever/Help/Give Peace a Chance" [John Lennon and Paul McCartney]
Live in Liverpool, McCartney reverently performs this cobbled together medley of songs associated with John Lennon, exquisitely rendered from the opening melancholy of "Strawberry Fields" to the "Give Peace a Chance" sing-along. McCartney slows down the "Help" segment, presumably because grumbling Lennon claimed that the record was too fast. Here, the keyboards, imitating the original's string section, sound thin, and as hard as he tries, McCartney is no substitute for the world-weary Lennon. And why McCartney didn't perform the songs in their entirety is a mystery. Still, an amazing moment. ["All My Trials" single] **B**

CHAPTER TWENTY-ONE:

UNPLUGGED [THE OFFICIAL BOOTLEG] [1991]

Produced by Joel Gallen
Charted at 14 [US], 7 [UK]

McCartney always held acoustic music in high regard, all the way back to his Beatles favourites like "I Will" and "I'm Looking Through You." In the early days, the Beatles often mixed electric and acoustic guitars – "No Reply" and "Run for Your Life," among many others – to produce a key element of their signature sound. McCartney returned frequently to this technique, evidenced by the acoustic set in the *Wings Over America* tour.

MTV, back when it played music, inaugurated a series called *Unplugged*, where stars of the day were given the opportunity to perform without electric instruments. The result was a more intimate setting than they were used to. It also gave their repertoire a fresh spin, allowing the small audience to experience the music as originally conceived, with the occasional wart that made their heroes sound human.

McCartney jumped at the chance to participate as if it were musical catnip, with one condition. Previous acts had taken liberties with the all-acoustic concept and augmented their performances with the odd amplified guitar. But McCartney nixed the pseudo-acoustic exceptions, feeling correctly that it violated the spirit of the program. Therefore, instead of electric pickups that were attached directly to an instrument, he insisted that everything – guitars, bass, keyboards – be miked directly, positioning each microphone a few inches away and allowing them to pick up not only the musical sounds, but the ambiance of the room and bit of natural echo. The resulting sound was warm and clear, perhaps the best the series had offered so far.

Comfortable in the friendly setting and satisfied with the technical adjustment, McCartney gave one of best performances of his career. Possibly because he could gauge the audience's reaction rather than taking a guess necessary at large venues, possibly because his song list featured rarely performed tunes he was eager to try out, or possibly because he had as support the second best band of his life. Consisting of the pro musicians used on *Tripping the Live Fantastic*, with new drummer Blair Cunningham [The Pretenders, Roxy Music], the band actually seemed to be enjoying themselves. Their performance was crystal clear, sensitive, and note perfect. The only exception was poor Linda, who was positioned so that her contributions were barely heard, an arrangement to minimize her chances of an audible screw-up.

Thrilled by an ace show and attentive audience, McCartney decided to release it as an album, an action that other stars would follow. Another plus, he thought, would be to deter bootleggers, which didn't work, as sneaky thieves allegedly issued their own records containing rehearsal takes of "Heart of the Country," "She's My Baby," "Figure of Eight," and "Mother Nature's Son." But sales were unaffected. The official record blazed up the charts.

As for the critics, most were satisfied, some relieved. *AllMusic* called *Unplugged* "a breath of fresh air." From *Entertainment Weekly*: "… after almost 30 years, McCartney still has it and never lost it." The *Rolling Stone Album Guide* awarded it four stars. After the critical drubbing taken for *Give My Regards to Broad Street* and *Press to Play*, McCartney had scored.

"Be Bop a Lula [Live 91]" [Gene Vincent, Tex Davis]
A slinky opener, like a snake ready to strike. However, it risks wimping out when unnecessary harmonies butt in near the end. Otherwise, near flawless. **B**

"I Lost My Little Girl [Live 91]" [Paul McCartney]
The surprise of the set, supposedly the first McCartney song ever, written sometime in his teens. However, in the bridge he spoils the fantasy by including lyrics that look back on good old days, hardly something you'd do as composer who supposedly wrote the whole thing a long time ago. That aside, the song is a pleasant, if clunky, example of pre-Beatles McCartney, a welcome sample from a budding songwriter. He was so pleased with its reception, for a while it became a concert staple. **B**

"Here, There and Everywhere [Live 91]" [John Lennon and Paul McCartney]
Sung in a near-whisper, relaxed as to savour every word, McCartney treats this song like a museum piece, touching up the sound with a perfectly appropriate accordion. And the high notes serve as a reminder that this man remains one of the most amazing singers, ever. **B+**

"Blue Moon of Kentucky [Live 1991]" [Bill Monroe]
Overly polite rendition of ancient Elvis. You don't earn points for perfecting the harmonies. You get them for perfecting the hip wiggle. **B-**

"We Can Work It Out [Live 1991]" [John Lennon and Paul McCartney]
A melody so rich it brings a tear to the eye, a melancholy bridge, an expression of eternal but futile hope that everything will be okay. A silky rendition, exquisitely performed by one of the creators. **A-**

"San Francisco Bay Blues [Live 1991]" [Jesse Fuller]
Paul performs it like he loves it, making it tough to resist. A jangling piano and slide guitar keep things professional, so this retains a touch of a Vegas lounge when it could have used a bit more of a skid row barroom. **B-**

"I've Just Seen a Face [Live 1991]" [John Lennon and Paul McCartney]
Comparing this to the *Wings Over America* take is like comparing a guppy to a dolphin. A note-perfect copy of the original, right down to the guitar harmonic tag at the end. **B+**

"Every Night [Live 1991]" [Paul McCartney]
One of four dips into the *McCartney* album, this one the most obvious candidate for an acoustic concert, "Junk" excluded. Sitting in between two Beatles songs, it comes off a lesser number than it did on his first album, where back in the *McCartney* days, any pearl among the swine tended to shine. Unfortunately, slowing it down makes it resemble the closing theme from a soap opera, not a great move. **B-**

"She's a Woman [Live 1991]" [John Lennon and Paul McCartney]
This is more of a surprise than "I Lost My Little Girl," as it takes an excess of chutzpah to do a sizzling rocker acoustically. Points for trying, but it doesn't really work, kind of like hearing an old timer warble "I Want to Hold Your Hand." **B-**

"High Heeled Sneakers [Live 1991]" [Robert Higgenbotham]
Like "Blue Moon of Kentucky," what was a brassy rocker has been polished until it becomes orthodox and reverent. Listening close, the problem is not so much McCartney's as it is the band, who perform professionally but without a lick of humour. **B-**

"And I Love Her [Live 1991]" [John Lennon and Paul McCartney]
This gorgeous ballad from *A Hard Day's Night* combines McCartney's gift for soaring melodies with his handicap of baffling lyrics. That aside, McCartney seems to know when he's got a good one, caressing the supple number like it's a new lover. A slower speed adds maturity, unlike "Every Night." **B+**

"That Would Be Something [Live 1991]" [Paul McCartney]
New chords and a slide guitar change this old dullard into a sparkler. Almost surreal in spots as the slide careens into the *Twilight Zone*. Not quite a keeper, but closer than it was on *McCartney*. **B**

"Blackbird [Live 1991]" [John Lennon and Paul McCartney]
The *White Album*'s "Blackbird" gave every kid with an acoustic guitar a summer's worth of work. This

casual performance may not be McCartney's best, but the song's so strong that I doubt if anyone cares. **B**

"Ain't No Sunshine [Live 1991]" [Bill Withers]
And yet another left field-er. McCartney takes over the drums, Hamish Stuart handles the vocals. As a drummer's showcase, it's visually striking but audibly bland. **B-**

"Good Rockin' Tonight [Live 1991]" [Roy Brown]
Hearing all the oldies makes one appreciate just how good McCartney is as a songwriter. "Good Rockin' Tonight" is adequate filler, and sure, Paul revels in pretending to be a youngster. But there's no way it compares favourably to "She's a Woman" or "We Can Work It Out." Instead, wouldn't it have been nice to hear "Back in the USSR?" Or "Instant Karma?" **B-**

"Singing the Blues [Live 1991]" [Melvin Endsley]
A yawner. Hey, why not "Mother Nature's Son"? **C**

"Junk [Live 1991]" [Paul McCartney]
Technically, this is "Singalong Junk," but never mind. Too many tentative note plucks, as the band feels their way through a song that may not be that familiar. And [sad face] no vocals. Still, it brings the concert in for an easy landing and an adequate good night to all. **B**

CHAPTER TWENTY-TWO:

PAUL McCARTNEY'S LIVERPOOL ORATORIO [1991]

Produced by John Fraser
Charted at 177 [US], did not chart [UK]

Roger Waters of Pink Floyd [*Ca Ira*], Frank Zappa [*Bogus Pomp*], Elvis Costello [*Il Sogno*], Billy Joel [*Fantasies and Delusions*], Jon Lord of Deep Purple [*Concerto for Group and Orchestra*], and Keith Emerson of Emerson, Lake, and Palmer [*Piano Concerto No.1*] are rock musicians who at one time or another tried their hand at long-form classical pieces. And why not? Whether it comes at the receiving end of a conductor's baton or a screeching Marshall amp, music is music.

But classical music by a rock star can be hit or miss. Too often, a rocker approaches the genre tentatively, like an English guy trying to translate Chinese. The attempt can be painful. And once the novelty wears off, there may not be much worth hearing again. Put another way, next to every promising *Bogus Pomp* lies a moldering stack of *Fantasies and Delusions*.

Which brings us to McCartney. A chance meeting with Carl Davis, a revered composer responsible for the soundtracks of dozens of TV shows, made McCartney's mind race. Perhaps this was the man who could help him realize one of his aspirations: a massive orchestral work that would open him up to a new audience, plus challenge his skills as a composer. That McCartney was unable to read or write a single note of music fazed him not at all. And he had self-confidence to spare, certain he could figure it all out as he went. [Not that his healthy ego always came through. *Give My Regards to Broad Street*, anyone?]

What, wondered McCartney, did Davis have in mind? A symphony? No, said Davis. Something along the lines of an oratorio, a narrative orchestral piece with singers, like Handel's *Messiah*. Their oratorio, obviously more contemporary, could be based on McCartney's memories of a significant locale. Like Liverpool.

Liverpool. McCartney liked that. They agreed to meet whenever the pair had the chance, and would continue to work together as long as the project took.

For the next two years, McCartney dutifully kept every appointment with Davis, and the oratorio began to take shape. Because of his obvious limitations, McCartney would pick out themes on the piano, sometimes simply humming a few bars. Carl took these bits and pieces home, adding flesh and blood to McCartney's skeletal pieces, shaping them into orchestrations.

But like McCartney's collaboration with Elvis Costello, there were problems. At their first meeting, according to *The Telegraph*, McCartney asked Davis to name his favourite Beatles song. The nervous Davis responded with "A Hard Day's Night," a song usually credited to John Lennon. "He seemed rather perturbed," said Davis.

Allegedly, Davis had definite ideas about what would work and what wouldn't. When McCartney calmly objected, Davis politely but firmly insisted. In the end, after a string of disagreements, Davis more or less surrendered to McCartney's sometimes shallow take on classical conventions and did his best to guide him.

And it was decided the work would be formally known as *Paul McCartney's Liverpool Oratorio*. McCartney's name was splashed across the top of the CD package. Davis' name was near the bottom. And so was McCartney's – again.

To the surprise of those who expected retreads of *Ram* or *Band on the Run* and maybe a guitar solo or two, the completed 90 minute work turned out to be a conventional classical work. Even serious aficionados admitted it wasn't half-bad. True, some passages were draggy, a segment here and there was stale and unimaginative, and a good deal of it showcased the errors of a first-time composer. But much of it was engaging, and McCartney's near magical gift for heart-tugging melodies showed through. *Variety* called it "... a graceful, eclectic, if conservative score...." *Gramophone*: " .... well-intentioned, unexceptional yet strangely reactionary..." It wouldn't make anyone forget Beethoven's *Fifth Symphony* or Stravinsky's *Rite of Spring*. But it made for a pleasant afternoon at the concert hall, and in that sense, it was a success.

"War [Andante/Non Nobis Solum/The Air Raid Siren Slices Through/Oh Will It All End Here/Mother and Father Holding Their Child" [Paul McCartney and Carl Davis]

The performance in the Liverpool Cathedral with an orchestra and professional singers – Willard White, Kiri Te Kanawa, Jerry Handley, and Sally Burgess – produced an exquisite recording [technically, a rehearsal] with McCartney not participating but observing, beaming away. The story follows the adventures of a young man named Shanty, who suspiciously resembles Paul. Shanty was born in Liverpool [like McCartney] in 1942 [like McCartney], attended a local school [like McCartney], and endured the horrors of war [like McCartney]. But this was a fairy tale interpretation of the past, with most hardships glossed over or ignored, echoing McCartney's gauzy take on his own life.

Opening with ominous strings and atonal chords, the beginning of "War" is startlingly modern, hinting at the boldness of John Adams and other progressive contemporaries. But much to the chagrin of modern music lovers, this soon dissolves into the superficial. McCartney makes it clear he's on the side of the conservatives, thus reassuring listeners who have no interest in the challenging aspects of modern music. The movement plays out in expected string washes and flute trills. Friendly, yes. Adventurous, no. **B-**

"School [We're in School Today to Get a Perfect Education/Walk in Single File Out of the Classroom/Settle Down/Kept in Confusion/I'll Always Be Here/Boys This is Your Teacher/Tres Conejos/Not for Ourselves]" [Paul McCartney and Carl Davis]

Beginning with an attractive choral reading of a simple but appealing tune, the "School" section features the *Oratorio*'s best moments, although stubbornly sticking to conventions, it feels like it's tied to a tree. The detailing of Shanty skipping school and taking off for destinations unknown nostalgically conjures up memories of the good old days, but it inexplicably cuts into Shanty's encounter with the ghost of his future wife [?] followed by a Spanish lesson [?]. Nothing new here for those of us used to McCartney's torturing of the language. The singers seem to occasionally stumble over the words, an inevitable reaction from professionals used to the more literate librettos of Puccini's *Madam Butterfly* and Mozart's *Don Giovanni*.

Liverpool Oratorio features bits of Romanticism – that is, sort of a low budget Verdi or Schumann – and the occasional 20th century experiment. But "School" is basically a string of pop material with classical decorations. **B**

"Crypt [And So It Was That I Had Grown/Dance/I Used to Come Here When This Place Was a Crypt/Here Now/I'll Always Be Here/Now's the Time to Tell Him" [Paul McCartney and Carl Davis]

After the promising Movement II comes the disappointing Movement III, a head-scratching mish-mash of Shanty's musings in a graveyard, a back-and-forth with a muddled minister, and the reappearance of the pesky ghost that we thought we were rid of. The music rises and falls dramatically, occasionally reminiscent of his better pop songs, but melodrama wins the day, betraying an artist who has yet to figure out how to translate emotions into classical music. **C+**

"Father [Andante Lamentoso, O Father You Have Given/Ah/Hey Wait a Minute/Father Father Father]" [Paul McCartney and Carl Davis]

The narrative stalls as McCartney mourns the loss of his dead father, resulting in adolescent poetry and soggy music. Oddly, considering the closeness of McCartney to the subject – his mother died when he was a young man – he has trouble keeping the story focused. **C-**

"Wedding [Andante Amoroso/Father Hear Our Humble Voices/Hosana Hosana]" [Paul McCartney and Carl Davis]

The wedding of two lovebirds ought to be right up McCartney's alley, even if one of them is a ghost-in-training. His melodies, flowing and sweet, create a texture that could have been romantic, but they're too simple – the words especially – to simulate anything more complicated than a middle school crush. **B-**

"Work [Allegro Energico/Working Women at the Top/Violin Solo/Did I Sign the Letter/Tempo I/When You Ask a Working Man/Let's Find Ourselves a Little Hostelry]" [Paul McCartney and Carl Davis]
Another wobbly movement with less-than-first-rank melodies and a libretto that has too many phrases plucked at random from a romance novel. McCartney again offers protagonists that are two-dimensional at best, blabbering in a superficial dialogue of dumb observations and limp jokes. As for the music, by this time the audience has got to be dead tired of processed sugar and "heavy" themes. I'd vote that this movement is unnecessary and should be introduced to the word "euthanasia" as soon as possible. **C-**

"Crises [Allegro Molto/The World You're Coming Into/Tempo I/Where's My Dinner/Let's Not Argue/I'm Not a Slave/Right That's It/Stop Wait/Do You Know Who You Are/Ghosts of the Past Left Behind/Do We Live In a World]" [Paul McCartney and Carl Davis]
Out of the blue emerges the vocalist Kiri Te Kanawa to perform the centerpiece of *Liverpool Oratorio*, the powerful "The World You're Coming Into." If the complete *Oratorio* were half this good, McCartney might have a full-fledged winner in his hands. But alas, it's not. The majority of motifs in *Oratorio* lack the strength and imagination to be developed into orchestra-worthy themes. A possible solution: Consider re-issuing the album in half its current length, setting aside the weakest movements and polishing the remainder. **B**

"Peace [And So It Was That You Were Born/God is Good/What People Want is a Family Life/Dad's in the Garden/So On and On the Story Goes]" [Paul McCartney and Carl Davis]
Prettied up in a neat package, all conflicts are resolved, love triumphs, instruments soar, and a new child arrives to remind us the family way is the best way. Just like a Disney film.
So what do we have? A competent score from a first-timer, a kid-friendly libretto, and an occasional blip of musical brilliance. We also have a project of interminable length, a basket of insubstantial ideas, and a sprawling work that adds little to the classical library. *Liverpool Oratorio*, unfortunately, is closer, much closer, to *Give My Regards to Broad Street* than *Abbey Road*. **B-**

[bonus]

"It's Now or Never" [Wally Gold, Aaron Schroeder, and Eduardo di Capua]
Elvis' monster single was an easy choice for McCartney's contribution to an Elvis tribute album. The arrangement emulates the original, as does McCartney, giving a mannered performance, though the skating rink solo seems out of place. Will he hit the high note at the end? Of course he does. **B**

124

CHAPTER TWENTY-THREE:

OFF THE GROUND [1993]

Produced by Paul McCartney and Julian Mendelsohn
Charted at 17 [US], 5 [UK]

Was McCartney's conservatism dragging him down? As was depressingly true for the previous decade or so, the formula for *Off the Ground* was predictable: a single [sometimes a hit, most of the time not], the rest hit-or-miss [usually miss] filler. All of it homogenized into a glassy sheen, few chances taken, with radio-friendly production, slick and shallow. No longer in the company of music peers like Bob Dylan, he instead found himself competing with Billy Joel. And occasionally, losing.

McCartney had the time, money, musical resources and fans' ample good will to do anything he wanted. So instead of yet another heard-it-before album, why not, for instance, a series of genuinely experimental pieces with Brian Eno [*Neroli* 1993]? How about a collaboration with unheralded foreign musicians, such as Paul Simon did with South African artists [*Graceland* 1986]? Or when David Byrne partnered with Latin American musicians [*Rio Momo* 1989]? And with the surprise success of his *Unplugged* album, how about an all-acoustic album of just him and his piano? How about tackling an album of just John Lennon?

Not to be. *Off the Ground* was destined to be more of the same.

McCartney decided to record the basic tracks with the band as a unit, rather than overdubbing section after section. Interesting idea, but nothing new, as Paul himself had tried this with the Beatles on *Let It Be* and his own *Wild Life*, with mixed results. He also bravely – for him – added the naughty "f" word to the lyrics of the outtake "Big Boys Bickering." But this was hardly newsworthy in the 1990s where lyrical obscenities were just another arrow in the quiver of on-the-edge artists. And besides, John Lennon had already used the dreaded syllable in "Working Class Hero" way back in 1971.

McCartney stepped up his plea for social justice, coming down hard on animal exploiters in "Looking for Changes" and preaching universal love in "C'mon People." But though sincere, McCartney lacked the patience to dig into these issues and declined to create lyrics that could coax empathy from his listeners. Instead, he settled for vague images [a scientist plunging an unspecified device into a cat's head, which is gross but not much more] and vapid admonishments [we should be nice to each other].

Off the Ground delivered the expected results. There was a sort-of hit single, "Hope of Deliverance," a bomb in the US [charted at #83], but a smash in Europe [Germany, charted at #3]. There was a pretty but routine ballad, "I Owe It All to You." And there was plenty of filler. Any way you slice it, *Off the Ground* was just another album.

"Off the Ground" [Paul McCartney]
More McCartney for kids. Though not sabotaged by overproduction, a recurring flaw of McCartney's, the *Sesame Street* style makes the mature listener clutch his stomach. Dull melody, gentle vocals, and la las galore, just like on "Mary Had a Little Lamb." And by the way, what's with all the feet on the cover? Did he forget "Smile Away?" **C+**

"Looking for Changes" [Paul McCartney]
The one about the poor kitten, the poor bunny, and the poor chimpanzee, "Looking for Changes" stands as a sincere request to give these innocent creatures a break and stop shoving stuff up their sphincters. It would have been far more effective for PETA-inclined people if McCartney had brought in a thoughtful lyricist with a poetic bent, thereby bringing these images to life and rally one and all to the cause. Did he lose Elvis Costello's phone number? **B –**

"Hope of Deliverance" [Paul McCartney]

So close to a deserved hit, it begins weakly, then out of nowhere, explodes with a near-brilliant bridge and chorus, a stunning example of an inspired McCartney. The Latin-favoured rocker features assured vocals, unexpected percussion effects, and a terrific Frank Sinatra salute at the end. More effort on the clipped beginning, and McCartney might've had a monster. **B+**

"Mistress and Maid" [Paul McCartney and Elvis Costello]

A leftover from *Flowers in the Dirt*, this commendable McCartney-Costello collaboration earns high marks thanks to the scheming protagonist's clever way with words. A couple of shaky spots suggest the tune might have gotten away from them before it was ready. That aside, the seductive waltz lurches along like a sad drunk, the melody spirals upward and onward in thrilling twists, and McCartney's vocal is a flat-out marvel. **B+**

"I Owe it All to You" [Paul McCartney]

The album's premiere ballad, "Golden Earth Girl" notwithstanding. A serviceable verse slides into a touching chorus, messed up by trite lyrics. But listen to the heartbreaking instrumental opening – so tender, *Pet Sounds* comes floating by – and all is forgiven. Now, if only McCartney would ... no, he won't. **B**

"Biker Like an Icon" [Paul McCartney]

Best I can tell, a girl loves a motorcycle guy like she loves a Microsoft app, then zips to Los Angeles while the pipes are leaking [?]. Her parents post her image everywhere, but it doesn't do any good because of the pipes, which are leaking [?]. The End. So it's sort of an ultra-low-budget "She's Leaving Home" without a comprehensible narrative. "Biker Like an Icon" putters along like something Bruce Springsteen would reject after Take One, swearing that in the future, he wouldn't drink so much. **B-**

"Peace in the Neighborhood" [Paul McCartney]

Sugary song by a naive man staring out his castle window and singing about peace makes me want to join a gang and start killing people. **F**

"Golden Earth Girl" [Paul McCartney]

Judging from the opening chords, this apparently is supposed to be "Let It Be, Part 10." Melodically, McCartney meanders here and there, winding up in Nowhere Land with the other adult contemporary pap. Whatever modest attributes it has – maybe a couple of brief attractive phrases – are crushed by the stupefying lyrics. Plus, Paul could stand to clear his throat. **C**

"The Lovers That Never Were" [Paul McCartney and Elvis Costello]

It lacks the intensive harmonies that propelled the demo [see *Flowers in the Dirt Deluxe*]. McCartney still offers an outstanding performance, again benefitting tremendously having lyrics that make him sound smart. Compare this to "C'mon People" or "Off the Ground," then try to make a case that McCartney doesn't need a collaborator **B**

"Get Out of My Way" [Paul McCartney]

A tired rocker by an old man. There's nothing here McCartney hasn't done before. Offered in evidence: "Jet," "Hi Hi Hi," and the cherry on the cake, "Helter Skelter." Alternate title: "Get Off of My Lawn." **D+**

"Winedark Open Sea" [Paul McCartney]

Hit a chord, listen, a snatch of melody suggests itself, hit another chord, another snatch, repeat, done. Lyrics? How about my affection for my wonderful lady and the winedark open sea? The word "winedark" comes from Homer, who apparently believed it meant "red oxen." I don't know about you, but I think "Red Oxen Open Sea" is catchier. **C-**

"C'mon People" [Paul McCartney]

McCartney again demonstrates his laziness by apparently jotting down the first thing that pops into his mind. This is twaddle, an unfocused lecture informing us we'd all be better off if ... uh, we got together because, you see ... being bad is ...er, bad. Nearly eight minutes of "Hey Jude" on opiates. **D**

"Cosmically Conscious" [Paul McCartney]

McCartney's memory is so bad that for 25 years he forgot this existed. It does indeed sound like the Beatles, circa 1968, and the hippie-ish lyrics recall the Maharishi in all his psychic glory. Why fans weren't spinning cartwheels over this newly discovered *White*-album-ish tidbit is a mystery, although maybe purchasers of *Off the Ground* couldn't quite get to the album's end. It's a nifty tune, springs along in great leaps, and contains, lo and behold, actually composed A and B sections. Sadly, about a minute and a half, and it's over. But more is on the way in the expanded version coming in the double-CD import. **B+** *[bonus]*

"Long Leather Coat" [Paul McCartney]

When "Hope of Deliverance" became a hit in Europe, McCartney rewarded them with *Off the Ground: The Complete Works*, which added a complete unheard CD, making *Off the Ground* a 2-CD set. The US got zilch, which wasn't a complete disaster, seeing as how this collection of odds and ends is decidedly non-essential. Case in point: "Long Leather Coat," a squishy up-tempo non-song with obnoxious synthesizer diddles and boring guitar breaks, reminding one of a long lost 80s tune that never should have found its way out of the woods. [*Off the Ground: The Complete Works*.] **C+**

"Keep Coming Back to Love" [Paul McCartney and Hamish Stuart]

Painfully uninteresting. If I said you'd heard it before, you'd believe me. Except you haven't. Uh, have you? [*Off the Ground: The Complete Works*.] **D**

"Sweet Sweet Memories" [Paul McCartney]

One gets the feeling that most of this material was churned out on automatic pilot. This has been hailed as proof of McCartney's remarkable skill as a songwriter. Or maybe he has a knack for the ordinary, which would account for why his instant songs tend to stick to the expected, rarely drifting off into the scary unknown where fans don't flock. [*Off the Ground: The Complete Works*.] **D**

"Things We Said Today [Live 1991]" [John Lennon and Paul McCartney]

He already did this on *Tripping the Live Fantastic*, and knowing his obsession with keeping arrangements exactly as we remember them, it's no surprise that this *Unplugged* flotsam is a photocopy, except for fanatics comparing them syllable by syllable. [*Off the Ground: The Complete Works*.] **D**

"Midnight Special [Live 1991]" [Alan Lomax]

A reject from *Unplugged*, rightly so. What's it like? Imagine the residents of an old folks' home circling their wheelchairs around a campfire for the evening sing-along. [*Off the Ground: The Complete Works*.] **D**

"Style Style" [Paul McCartney]

McCartney instructs us how to eyeball women, but never gets to the good stuff. Instead, anything even remotely lustful dissolves into mild admiration, much as a senior citizen might toothlessly slobber over a TV ad for false teeth. So an R-rating turns to PC-13, with a G coming over the hill. [*Off the Ground: The Complete Works*.] **C-**

"I Can't Imagine" [Paul McCartney]

A difference between McCartney and Lennon. McCartney: "I Can't Imagine," self-assured, but feels sympathy for those who haven't experienced true love like him. Lennon: "Don't Let Me Down," also in love, but doubting whether it can last. Which seems more real to you? While you ponder your answer, enjoy this cheery, paper-thin tune by the eternally happy Paul. [*Off the Ground: The Complete Works*.] **C-**

"Cosmically Conscious [Expanded]" [Paul McCartney]

A fragment appeared at the end of *Off the Ground*, but that was just a warm up. Here, the full-blown version combines simplicity, a stylish background of low-key psychedelia, a break right out of *Magical Mystery Tour*, and yes, non-lyrics, but at least they're not about love as defined by *The Bachelorette*. No real complaints with this minor gem, although it could use a solid bridge or lengthier verses with more lyrics. [*Off the Ground: The Complete Works*.] **B+**

"Kicked Around No More" [Paul McCartney]

The lyrics, cryptic as they are, are preferable to the melody, which is so dull you're unlikely to recall a note while you're kicking it. [*Off the Ground: The Complete Works*.] **D**

"Big Boys Bickering" **[Paul McCartney]**
McCartney performs this fugging song for all it's fugging worth, lamenting how the fugging leaders can't fugging get along. It kicks off with a nod to "Old McDonald Had a Farm," then eases along with a nice fugging accordian and good fugging vocals. A pleasure for all you fuggers. [*Off the Ground: The Complete Works.*] **B**

"Down to the River" **[Paul McCartney]**
Reasonable melody, amorphous lyrics, as per usual. Sub-par Neil Young, from whom this was, uh, borrowed. [*Off the Ground: The Complete Works.*] **B-**

"Soggy Noodle" **[Paul McCartney]**
Paul tunes his guitar, and the title writes itself. [*Off the Ground: The Complete Works.*] **F**

"Yeah" **[Eddie Murphy; guest performer: Paul McCartney]**
[Eddie Murphy] Self-indulgent drivel by a superstar pseudo-singing comedian who lured a galaxy of artists – among others, Stevie Wonder, Michael Jackson, Elton John – into recording snippets for this barely existing lightweight funk number, largely consisting of the title word. The prospect of a Michael Jackson-Elton John duet might sound intriguing, but it doesn't happen. Instead, they warble their syllable once or twice, then go home. McCartney is in there somewhere for reasons incomprehensible. [*Love's Alright*] **D-**

CHAPTER TWENTY-FOUR:

PAUL IS LIVE [1993]

Produced by Paul McCartney
Charted at 78 [US], 34 [UK]

*A*nother live album? Didn't we just have *Tripping the Live Fantastic*?

It wasn't as if McCartney didn't have plenty to keep him busy. The massive *Beatles Anthology* was coming, comprising six CDs of unheard material and as many as nine DVDs. McCartney, along with George Harrison and Ringo Starr, had to sort through it all, approving it, recommending changes, and vetoing segments they found irrelevant or embarrassing. Lurking in the background was McCartney's electronic project, *Strawberries Oceans Ships Forest*. Unlike his pop albums, which he could toss off as the mood struck him, *Strawberries Oceans Ships Forest* required an approach that was unfamiliar, drawing the curious McCartney's attention in a way that sifting through live versions of "Biker Like an Icon" could not. In a sense, *Paul is Live* was a marketing decision to keep the fans satisfied while McCartney was occupied elsewhere with an original album.

But is this really a McCartney album? *Paul is Live* features a small chunk of *Off the Ground* material, so on one level, it served a promotional function for an album needing all the help it could get. Oldies are represented, as is a supply of nose-picking ["Robbie's Bit," "Hotel in Benidorm"], a laughable attempt at fending off bootleggers. The oldies in particular smell like filler, and as they're available everywhere from *Beatles Live at the BBC* to *Choba B CCCP*, hardly essential.

So what is it? This is a Beatles album. Or rather, a "new" Beatles album, as close as we'll get since half the Beatles are dead. Clearly, response to Beatles songs in previous McCartney tours was off the charts. Audiences seemed to want more, not less. And Paul is no dummy, "Mary Had a Little Lamb" notwithstanding. The greatest repertoire in the history of popular music was staring him right in the face.

So bring on the Beatles. In the end, the Beatles eat up *Paul is Live*, and McCartney played them as close to the originals as humanly possible. Beatle-lovers responded with tears, screams, and heart failures. That "Penny Lane" got a stronger reaction than "Peace in the Neighborhood" will shock no one. Or that "C'mon People" received polite applause while "Paperback Writer" was showered with hosannas. Maybe this irritated Paul, maybe it disappointed him, but facts are facts, and the ever-pragmatic Paul would respond accordingly.

In subsequent tours, McCartney would see to it that the Beatles would become even more dominant. Fans would get a kick out of "Hope of Deliverance," critics might compliment the accuracy of "Band on the Run." But for everyone, a moment to treasure forever after would be "Hey Jude," performed live by the original singer, right before their eyes.

"Drive My Car [Live 1993]" [John Lennon and Paul McCartney]

Leading the same band as on *Off the Ground*, McCartney lunges into the *Rubber Soul* opener and takes off. But as they easily navigate the original rhythms, it becomes apparent that the band can't quite conjure the energy at its heart. It's not the band's fault. After all, how many hundreds – or thousands – of musicians have tried to copy the Beatles, only to fall short? This will be a chronic problem for McCartney in the years ahead as he attempts to channel his current band into mimicking his old one and failing. For now, enjoy the bouncy "Drive My Car," played by, ugh, pros. **B**

"Let Me Roll It [Live 1993]" [Paul McCartney]

If you've never heard a live version of "Let Me Roll It" – that is, you've never heard *Wings Over America* –

marvel at its simplicity and, especially, McCartney's subtle jabs at John Lennon. If you *have* heard it and liked it, why not send a few royalties to the Lennon estate? **B**

"Looking for Changes [Live 1993]" [Paul McCartney]
Not a rock song, not a slow song, just a notelike-thing struggling to pull itself out of the mud. You kids, be nice to the animals. **C –**

"Peace in the Neighborhood [Live 1993]" [Paul McCartney]
A dreary slog-along performed by a guy whose song-sense is temporarily asleep. **D**

"All My Loving [Live 1993]" [John Lennon and Paul McCartney]
Lacks Lennon's incessant guitar and McCartney's drooling lust. Instead, we get competent professionalism. The crowd? They could care less. **B-**

"Robbie's Bit" [Live 1993]" [Robbie McIntosh]
McIntosh takes a guitar solo while McCartney hits the bathroom. A demonstration of Chet Atkins-influenced picking. How many audience members wanted more of this? Just as I thought. **C**

"Good Rockin' Tonight [Live 1993]" [Roy Brown]
I guess McCartney earned the right to indulge himself with pre-Beatles numbers, regardless of how they pale in comparison to more contemporary material. If you get the rhythm right and the vocalist is on the money, it's nearly impossible to blow it. **C**

"We Can Work It Out [Live 1993]" [John Lennon and Paul McCartney]
The invulnerable "We Can Work It Out" can survive any format in any venue, as long as it's sung by Paul and not you or me. The accordion in front? An understated touch that works. **B+**

"Hope of Deliverance [Live 1993]" [Paul McCartney]
Close but not quite as on the money as in the studio, where various elements could be pushed to the front or back to maximize their effectiveness. Here, "Hope of Deliverance" boosts its acoustic flavor, thanks to the guitars, making it subtly different – not better – than the album track. Still, a song McCartney can be proud of, even with the lyric-poor verses. **B**

"Michelle [Live 1993]" [John Lennon and Paul McCartney]
A beauty. Hearing this and "Here, There and Everywhere" reminds one of why McCartney was so crucial to the Beatles. My wish: he dragged those old skills out of hiding, as records like *Off the Ground* could use some help. **B**

"Biker Like an Icon [Live 1993]" [Paul McCartney]
I wouldn't say this is the dumbest track on *Off the Ground*. On second thought, yes I would. Foregoing the lyrical analysis, we're left with a tuneless melody, a sagging chorus, and the sinking feeling that the band just wants to get through it so they can savor "Here, There and Everywhere." **C-**

"Here, There, and Everywhere [Live 1993]" [John Lennon and Paul McCartney]
More suited to an acoustic setting [like *Unplugged*, its previous home] than a stadium of rabid fans, McCartney gives it a shot, confident that his fans will shut up and listen. They do. A song with a range this wide requires a singer of immense skill to pull off. But McCartney, he of the iron tonsils, polishes it off like he was reading the newspaper. **B**

"My Love [Live 1993]" [Paul McCartney]
For 13-year old girls. You say your heart is broken? You say that Justin Bieber won't return your letters? Fear not. Uncle Paul is here to sing your sorrows away. **C**

"Magical Mystery Tour [Live 1993]" [John Lennon and Paul McCartney]
Coming fresh off the triumph of *Sgt Pepper*, "Magical Mystery Tour" [the song] was bound to suffer by comparison. But here, stuck between "My Love" [ugh] and "C'mon People" [eek], it's a diamond. The middle

break sounds flabby. And what's with the abbreviated coda? But McCartney's transcendent vocals – when he's pumping it out, maybe the best in the business – carry the day. **B**

"C'mon People [Live 1993]" [Paul McCartney]
McCartney tries to fire up this *Off the Ground* loser, but the effort goes nowhere. Fans, the band, and t-shirt pedlars wait it out. **D**

"Lady Madonna [Live 1993]" [John Lennon and Paul McCartney]
Surprisingly enthusiastic performance. McCartney wails and beats the piano till it cries for mercy. **B**

"Paperback Writer [Live 1993]" [John Lennon and Paul McCartney]
A great song, but a studio song, and skeptics had their ears cocked for discrepancies. Which there are: a weak opening acappella, a polite [non-aggressive] lead guitar, and an ending that tries to reach for the stars but settles by reaching for the salt shaker. McCartney, bless him, tries admirably, but he's not a kid anymore, is he? **B**

"Penny Lane [Live 1993]" [John Lennon and Paul McCartney]
Not easy to recreate "Penny Lane' with a relatively small group, and understandably, it's thin. Then you realize the fans aren't all that interested as long as McCartney belts it out on key [which he does], the band hangs in there [which they do], and that incredible chorus comes soaring [which it does]. **B**

"Live and Let Die [Live 1993]" [Paul and Linda McCartney]
Third time up for this pyrotechnics number [*Wings Over America, Tripping the Live Fantastic*], which must've been great to experience if you happened to be in the audience. At home? Not so much. **D**

"Kansas City [Live 1993]" [Jerry Leiber and Mike Stoller]
From *Choba B CCCP* and *Beatles for Sale* comes this warhorse, out of the stable for another ride. McCartney loves it, he loves Little Richard, and especially loves his fans who've parted with their allowances one more time for another copy of what they already own. **C**

"Welcome to Sound Check [Live 1993]" [Paul McCartney]
Oh shut up. **F**

"Hotel in Benidorm [Live 1993]" [Paul McCartney]
Improvised cha-cha seasoned with blather. **F**

"I Wanna Be Your Man [Live 1993]" [John Lennon and Paul McCartney]
A remake of an ancient *With the Beatles* number, originally sung by Ringo and, on a different record, by the Rolling Stones. What will McCartney do? He rocks the hell out of it, effortlessly, and has a blast while the band roars away. **B**

"A Fine Day [Live 1993]" [Paul McCartney]
Wrapping things up with yet another improv, McCartney pontificates about the weather, decides it's okay, then seems amazed that his beloved can read. And he screams a lot. Perhaps he's still mad at the bootleggers. If so, this will show them. Not. **D-**

CHAPTER TWENTY-FIVE:

THE FIREMAN – STRAWBERRIES OCEANS SHIPS FOREST [1993]

Produced by Paul McCartney
Did not chart [US], did not chart [UK]

Youth, a pseudonym for Martin Glover [a member of industrial rock group Killing Joke], was preparing a batch of 12" remixed singles at the request of Paul McCartney. It seemed that McCartney had dreamed up the perfect way to entice the club crowd by serving them fresh dance versions sampled from his current *Off the Ground*, and Glover was just the person to do it. As Glover progressed, McCartney became increasingly intrigued by the startling re-imagining of his songs with the electronic bleeps and synthesized clamor whooshing by and bouncing all over the place. McCartney quickly abandoned his concept of 12" singles and began to envision the project as a full album. He overdubbed new instrumental parts, specifically chosen for electronic manipulation, even adding bits from *Back to the Egg*.

When completed, *Strawberries Oceans Ships Forest* [or for no obvious reason, McCartney's preferred *strawberries oceans ships forest*] had no formal songs and no vocals, resembling an updated *Electronic Sound* [1969] by George Harrison, only beaten into a more recognizable form and not nearly as off-putting as Harrison's project. Because of his fondness for pseudonyms [Percy Thrillington, Apollo C. Vermouth for the Bonzo Dog Band, Bernard Webb for Peter and Gordon's "Woman"] the album was credited to the Fireman [McCartney's dad was a fireman]. A pseudonym would bolster McCartney's fantasy for anonymity. Which, of course, it didn't.

Response? Okay from a few critics. AllMusic: "... solid ambient dance material, with beats and wisps of melody swirling around each other without ever quite coalescing." But generally not good, many complimentary for McCartney attempting something different, but noting how reluctant he was to take real chances. Robert Christgau: One star. *Entertainment Weekly*: "Techno for elevators." Fans raced to the stores, heard it, then raced out. In short, acceptable for dancers, not so much for listeners.

"Transpiritual Stomp" [Paul McCartney with Youth]
A minute of monotonous percussion gives way to a tape loop of a song being murdered, probably "Hope of Deliverance." Followed by more tape loops of drumming accompanied by a single guitar plunk followed by a keyboard riff, all of it supported by that introductory percussion. For 9 minutes. You read that right. **D**

"Trans Lunar Rising" [Paul McCartney with Youth].
I'm all in favour of experimentation, but there's ambitious experimentation and there's lazy experimentation. In high school, my friend experimented on a mouse by holding it underwater to see if it could learn to breathe. That's lazy experimentation. The mouse? As dead as "Trans Lunar Rising." **D**

"Transcrystaline" [Paul McCartney with Youth]
Scary monster belches, followed by tape loops of a Tarzan movie, followed by a robot cleaning its toes. **D-**

"Pure Trance" [Paul McCartney with Youth]
A variant of the piano riff to the Rolling Stones' "We Love You" which I'm pretty sure is accidental. Hardcore McCartney fans might dig out a vaguely interesting keyboard line or marvel at the accuracy

of the tape loop imitating a Martian radio transmission. But this is mostly machines doing all the dirty work, so if I were you, I'd go easy on the praise. **D**

"Arizona Light" [Paul McCartney with Youth]
Wonder why McCartney went ape for this stuff? He subjected himself to "Peace in the Neighborhood" too many times, so naturally this sounded pretty good. **D-**

"Celtic Stomp" [Paul McCartney with Youth]
A sliver of interest from this combination of a single guitar note and somebody whacking his thumb with a hammer. **D-**

"Strawberries Oceans Ships Forest" [Paul McCartney with Youth]
A leftover from *McCartney II*? If this was a track identical to, say, "Pure Trance," would anybody notice? Has anyone on earth ever listened to this more than once? Has Paul? **D-**

"4 4 4" [Paul McCartney with Youth]
The album's shortest track. Therefore, the best. **D+**

"Sunrise Mix" [Paul McCartney with Youth]
Coming soon: *Thrillington: the Ambient Mix*. **D**

[bonus]

"A Leaf [Original]" [Paul McCartney]
Destined to re-appear on 1999's *Working Classical*, McCartney directed a solo piano piece [sensitively performed by Anya Alexeyev] which supersedes the maudlin orchestral remake, capturing more directly an intimate peek at the natural world and avoiding the bombast that has more to do with a forest fire than a single leaf. However, McCartney runs out of quality ideas before the 10 minutes expire, and falls back on ho-hum chording and not particularly imaginative arpeggios. [Single, 1995]. **B**

"Mist Over Central Park" [Paul McCartney]
Sort of a cheat, as McCartney's fooling around on the piano, chatting with host Michael Parkinson on his TV show, and demonstrates a song he's just written, "Mist Over Central Park," heard once and, so far, never again. A companion of sorts to the Sinatra-esque "Suicide," McCartney plays that one too, temporarily turning the Parkinson Show into a Las Vegas lounge. It's lame, and the audience giggles during the opening bars of "Mist," as if McCartney's joking around. He isn't. [Parkinson Show – You Tube] **C+**

"Free as a Bird" [John Lennon, Paul McCartney, George Harrison, Ringo Starr; co-producers: Jeff Lynne, John Lennon, Paul McCartney, George Harrison, Ringo Starr; guest performer: Paul McCartney]
[The Beatles] Prior to the release of the *Beatles Anthology*, the three surviving Beatles thought it'd be a good idea to locate an old Lennon tune, overdub themselves, and create a new "Beatle" single. Not only would it be a creative victory, the promotional value was lost on no one. Yoko supplied a batch of Lennon's cassettes, on which he'd recorded crude demos in various conditions of completion, most of them barely there. The tape included "Real Love," "Grow Old With Me," "Now and Then," and "Free as a Bird." "Free as a Bird" was up first, fragile and fragmented, loaded with technical problems such as wobbling speeds, flopped piano chords, and the absence of a middle eight, for which Lennon mumbled a few half-finished bars. George Martin [wisely] passed on the production job, allegedly citing that if it had been up to him, he'd have started with a few seconds of the demo, faded it out completely, then proceeded with the new recording featuring only the original three. This, however, was not to be, as it ran counter to McCartney's vision of having everybody singing together, just like the real Beatles, except for the inclusion of a ghost.

Ultimately, Beatles fanatic Jeff Lynne accepted the producer's role and did an admirable job of creating a serviceable recording from near-impossible conditions. The result overflowed with ethereal Beatle-esque harmonies, Ringo's signature drumming, and tasteful backgrounds from Paul and George. The newly-composed bridges were of particular notice, as they featured, for the first time, George singing alone on what was essentially a Lennon-McCartney composition [although all four took credit].

Still, Lennon's spectral voice proved to be an unsolvable problem. No amount of dial twiddling could disguise or improve it. The living mixed with the dead was frustrating technically, plus aesthetically creepy. No matter how hard the original three pretended to be the Beatles, they weren't, and no amount of studio magic could compensate. Despite the intense work, the song remained airy and thin. The revived Beatles, uneasy from their forced reunion, needed Lennon's spine, badly. As for the production, Lynne occasionally nudged the Beatles into Electric Light Orchestra territory, with hints of a plasticized and make-it-perfect style that Lennon would've had a hard time swallowing.

The single was a smash, of course, hitting #2 in the UK and #6 in the US. It paved the way for another one, just around the corner. Looking back, however, it seems no one was completely satisfied with the results of this grand experiment. Mixing a half-done cassette with studio gloss, even in the hands of former Beatles, is probably setting yourself up for defeat. "Free As a Bird" now seems less a milestone than a sincere oddity. [*Beatles Anthology 1.*] **B**

"Real Love" [John Lennon; co-producers: Jeff Lynne, Paul McCartney, George Harrison, Ringo Starr; guest performer: Paul McCartney]

[The Beatles] The second of two post-Beatles songs. Though the demo was more or less complete, it was plagued with problems: a hum that wouldn't leave, Lennon's tempo shifts, annoying tape hiss. Lynne struggled mightily and succeeded covering the tape's most blatant flaws, but Lennon's wispy voice, painful to hear due to the existing circumstances, betrayed the sad fact there was something amiss that couldn't be fixed. In spite of the majestic background and sympathetic performance, it's a Beatles record in theory only. As for the song itself, it's a minor Lennon composition, one he was contemplating for *Double Fantasy*, but omitted for more work. [*Beatles Anthology 2.*] **B-**

"Come Together" [John Lennon and Paul McCartney; guest performer: Paul McCartney]

[Smokin' Mojo Filters] This is a long way from the perfection of the *Abbey Road* cut, but as it's for a good cause [the Warchild charity], cut them some slack. Somewhere in the crowd – including Paul Weller [lead singer on what is primarily his track], Noel Gallagher, and Steve Cradock – looms McCartney, banging the drums and vocalizing among the many. [*Various Artists: Help.*] **B**

"My Old Friend" [Carl Perkins and Paul McCartney]

[Carl Perkins] A brief, corny, but undeniably touching goodbye to John Lennon. Perkins sings, and McCartney adds sensitive harmonies. Introduced in the *Tug of War* sessions, "My Old Friend" lingered in the forgotten pile before seeing the light of day, which is a shame as it's one of the most heartfelt songs either man had attempted in a long time [except of course, McCartney's peerless "Here Today"]. Perkins' art is straight-up and to-the-point, and his similarity to Lennon doesn't go unnoticed. And I bet that includes McCartney. A small song, but a beautiful one. [*Go Cat Go.*] **B+**

"Yvonne's the One [10cc Version]" [Eric Stewart and Paul McCartney; guest performer: Paul McCartney]

[10cc] What was left of 10cc – two members of the original four – limped across the finish line with their last album, *Mirror Mirror*, a ragtag collection, half by Stewart, half by Graham Gouldman, recorded in two different countries. But it kicks off with the promising "Yvonne's the One." McCartney strums an uninspired guitar for this unfortunately low-energy run-though. Still, McCartney's fingerprints are all over the writing. He later polished and improved it, transforming 10cc's reggae number into a poignant acoustic ballad, which turned up later, though thus far, not on an album. A demo that sounds like a completed track, McCartney apparently plays everything and sings at his heartbreaking best. Regardless of its murky implications – has Yvonne died at the end? – it remains a tender song of a broken soul and one of McCartney's greats. By the way, "Yvonne's the One" was originally slotted for *Press to Play* then dumped in the end, earning McCartney a free ticket to the mental hospital. [*Mirror Mirror*, 1995] **B** [McCartney's Solo Track] **A –**

"Code of Silence" [Eric Stewart; guest performer: Paul McCartney]

[10cc] Before he parted company with 10cc, McCartney contributed, among other things, percussion and piano to Stewart's vaguely Polynesian ballad. The production excels, as is the case for most of 10cc's work, which lifts the mundane to the not bad. [*Mirror, Mirror*] **B**

"Hiroshima Sky is Always Blue" [Yoko Ono; guest performer: Paul McCartney]
[Ono Ensemble] In addition to McCartney, Ono rounded up assistance from Sean Lennon, Linda McCartney, and McCartney's kids, none of whom are credited on the CD that came with the Japanese book, *The Road of Hope*. The piece was played on Japanese television to commemorate the 50th anniversary of the atomic bomb that decimated Hiroshima. Basically an electronic work punctuated by Yoko's ghostly vocals, McCartney blends into the background so effectively that's nearly impossible to identify him. Pop lovers probably won't enjoy this, but listeners open to the avant garde should appreciate it. [*The Road of Hope*, 1995] **B**

"Battle of the Skeletons" [Allen Ginsberg and Paul McCartney]
[Allen Ginsberg] A true oddity, but unlike many oddities, of ample artistic merit. Ginsberg recites his compelling [and funny] poem, McCartney provides sympathetic accompaniment with organ, guitar, drums, and percussion. And more: also supplying support are composer Phillip Glass, jazz master Marc Ribot, Dylan acolyte David Mansfield, and Lenny Kaye, longtime member of the Patti Smith Group. Despite the all-star cast, it's McCartney who stands out with his warm and moving musicianship. [Single, 1996] **B+**

CHAPTER TWENTY-SIX:

OOBU JOOBU – ECOLOGY [1997]

Produced by Paul McCartney
Did not chart [US], did not chart [UK]

From McCartney's seemingly infinite output came *Oobu Joobu*, a 15-episode radio program featuring Paul as DJ and his impressive tape collection, consisting of rehearsals, outtakes and the occasional unreleased song. Adding to the mix were informal chats with Chrissie Hynde and other guests, Paul's favourite records from other artists, and Linda's cooking segment where she taught listeners on how to make simple vegetarian dishes.

It reads better than it played. Too many of McCartney's much anticipated live segments were disappointing, like "Biker Like an Icon" and "Put It There." Rehearsals were much the same, neither revelatory or particularly fun. As for his beloved hits from other artists, he by-passed his collection of jukebox obscurities and instead rolled out the familiar "Papa's Got a Brand New Bag" [James Brown] and "The Joker" [Steve Miller]. Linda's recipes were helpful for vegetarians, but on rock radio? And the occasional unreleased track – "Cow" and "Endless Days and Lonely Nights," both Linda songs – was welcome but scarce. An unreleased track, at least one of more than incidental interest, was far too rare.

Flash forward to 2006. Bob Dylan initiated his own 100-episode radio series, acting as DJ, much like McCartney, only doing it better. In contrast to the potpourri McCartney favoured, each "Theme Time Radio Hour" began with Dylan announcing the theme of the week – say, "Mother" or "Hair" – followed by records, very seldom his own, that corresponded to the theme. Often, the choices were tongue in cheek, demonstrating a sophisticated sense of humour that eluded fellow novice DJs, McCartney included. For instance, the "Mother" theme would include Randy Newman's "Mama Told Me Not to Come," Memphis Slim's "Mother Earth," and Ernie Kador's "Mother-in-Law." There wasn't a regular cooking segment, but there was plenty of subtle comedy, such as Dylan answering made-up email and offering his housecleaning tips, all broadcast from the fictitious Abernathy Building.

As for *Oobu Joobu*, satellite radio played clips now and then, but as time passed, the series itself was gradually lost in space, and today is seldom heard, particularly in its entirety. However, in 1997, Best Buy released a limited edition *Oobu Joobu – Ecology* CD [edited from Episode 5] for home consumption.

Tracks included on the CD but not discussed here: Chrissie Hynde discusses ecology [superficial], "Wild Life" [the album track which the passing years haven't helped], and Linda McCartney's cooking segment for "Beefless Stroganoff" [which could use some Worcestershire sauce].

"Oobu Joobu Main Theme" [Paul McCartney]
Well, it beats the *One Hand Clapping Theme*. The lightweight call-and-response bit could be the intro to a kiddie show, which, come to think of it, may be the subtext. **C**

"Looking for Changes [Soundcheck]" [Paul McCartney]
A spot-on example of an irrelevant collectible, this one from Las Vegas. Not only does the band perform like the mikes are more crucial than the music [for a soundcheck, they are], McCartney delivers a by-the-books vocal, apparently saving the real thing for the upcoming show. **C-**

"Peace in the Neighborhood [Soundcheck]" [Paul McCartney]
Another Las Vegas entry, identical to the crappy *Paul is Live* version which is identical to the crappy original version. How many copies do you want? Now you have three. **D**

"Mother Nature's Son [Soundcheck]" [Paul McCartney]

For motivations unclear, McCartney decided to omit "Mother Nature's Son" from *Unplugged* and *Paul is Live*, substituting instead "San Francisco Bay Blues" and "C'mon People." Strange world, isn't it? This is more of a folk song than the airy psychedelic take on the *White Album*. Plus we have a distracted vocalist. The accordion, however, adds a charming background, which overshadows McCartney. **B**

"Off the Ground [Soundcheck]" [Paul McCartney]

Laughably awful backing voices make this a kick to hear – once. Otherwise, a leaden run-though of a kill-me-now tune. **C-**

"Cow" [Linda McCartney and Carla Lane]

Overweight farmhands teaching their stomachs to waltz. Linda sings in an echo chamber, stays in key [mostly], and wags a finger at us for not caring enough about cattle. As a singer, she's ... As a composer, she's ... This is an unreleased track. Now you've paid for it. **C –**

"How Many People [Rehearsal]" [Paul McCartney]

You can rehearse this until "Cow" becomes a bull and it won't do much good. Piano-heavy once-over of a number that the band struggles to learn. Are those studio overdubs near the end? Just wondering. **D**

"We All Stand Together [Demo]" [Paul McCartney]

Appealing take of a child's tune, including McCartney's cute/annoying frog burps. If only he'd back off the look-at-me overproduction, "We All Stand Together" could be a minor crowd pleaser. But not to be. **B**

CHAPTER TWENTY-SEVEN:

FLAMING PIE [1997]

Produced by Paul McCartney, Jeff Lynne, George Martin
Charted at 2 [US], 2 [UK]

McCartney was in his mid-fifties, and his outlook was changing. No more "Bip Bop." No more "Mary Had a Little Lamb." *Rupert the Bear* stayed in hibernation. The chronically adolescent McCartney had been sent to his room, and in his place was a maturing artist with his eyes open. With more time behind than ahead, with death not merely a distant fantasy but a cold reality, McCartney could no longer pretend to be a kid.

Reviewing countless hours of composing, recording, and joking for the *Beatles Anthology* forced McCartney to confront his past. The Beatles, though staggeringly successful, seldom were motivated by unadulterated commercialism. Instead, they were driven by a near-obsession to innovate and a pursuit of the new, evidenced by "Tomorrow Never Knows," "I'm Only Sleeping," and the entirety of *Sgt Pepper.* Perfection tended to be irrelevant – when a track *felt* good, it was done. [Listen to *Rubber Soul*'s "I'm Looking Through You" and count the "mistakes."]

In contrast, the solo McCartney fretted constantly about being at the top and staying there. Rather than settling for a good feel, he scrubbed tracks until each and every flaw disappeared. The result: slick, inoffensive to all, and emotion-free. McCartney was producing tracks that too often were forgettable.

But change was in the air, arriving slowly but surely. The new album took a good four years to compose and record, enabling McCartney to discard any tunes that were written hastily or created while the composer wasn't fully engaged.

Lyrics – always McCartney's Achilles' heel – took a turn for the better. Instead of incomprehensible mush ["Soily"], ineffective defensiveness ["Silly Love Songs"], or slabs of pure embarrassment ["Ode to a Koala Bear"], McCartney offered thoughtful ruminations on a variety of subjects that were neither trivial nor purely black and white: a child's grief ["Little Willow"], parental responsibility ["Young Boy"], the relentless passage of time ["Heaven on a Sunday"]. Although no one would mistake him for Bob Dylan, he was trying.

McCartney seemed to be more open to the input of friends and family, who could nudge him in productive directions or subtly prevent him from wandering into the junkyard. For example, this wasn't the first time Ringo showed up [*Tug of War*] but it was the first time he received co-credit on not one but two songs ["Really Love You," "Looking for You"]. Old friend Steve Miller was also on board [co-credit on "Used to Be Bad"]. So was George Martin. So was son James. Most importantly, producer Jeff Lynne, hot off the *Beatles Anthology*, kept the sessions focused.

As evidence of McCartney now fully embracing his Beatles legacy, the title of the album was an affectionate nod to John Lennon, who'd mentioned way back when that the name "Beatles" came to him in a vision, announced by a man on a flaming pie who proclaimed "from this day on you are Beatles with an A."

Flaming Pie was not a complete success, but artistically, it was at least a partial one, heading in a mature direction, and favouring lyrics that exuded genuine effort. Lynne ensured that McCartney would avoid the trite perspective from which he could draw on in his sleep, such as the shallow nostalgia of *Venus and Mars'* "Magneto and Titanium Man" and the first-draft nonsense *of Back to the Egg*'s "After the Ball."

With its hummable melodies and warm ambiance, *Flaming Pie*'s commercial success was almost a foregone conclusion. Adoring fans bought it by the carload, sending it to the top ten all over the world and earning it gold status in the UK and the US, all without the benefit of a hit single. Critics nodded their approval: *Desert News*: " ... a delectable entree ..." *Los Angeles Times*: "... a relaxed, relatively off-the-cuff feel ..." *Rolling Stone*: "... assertive without being defensive ..." *Flaming Pie* was no masterpiece, not with banal tracks like "Beautiful Night," but it was promising.

"The Song We Were Singing" [Paul McCartney]

Flaming Pie kicks off with a waltz, unusual but irresistibly catchy, which features a sentimental look back at McCartney's days with John Lennon. McCartney pulls back when the gee-it-was-great proceedings threaten to get too heavy. Occasionally Lennon comes off as an inanimate object, bereft of thoughts and feelings. But by the end, we're left with a mournful plea from a lonely man who genuinely misses his friend. The sparse arrangement, highlighted by an underplayed acoustic and soft accordion, adds to the wistful atmosphere. **B**

"The World Tonight" [Paul McCartney]

The melancholy established in "The Song We Were Singing" continues with this clenched fist musing about the unfairness of life, specifically as caused by an unnamed person [McCartney's wife?]. If only McCartney didn't feel compelled to keep it all at arm's length – why not name her? – it wouldn't seem so pointlessly unclear. The static melody doesn't help either, but McCartney's delivery does – he's pissed, or at least as pissed as he allows himself to be. **B**

"If You Wanna" [Paul McCartney]

This deals with arrangements for a trip, although it implies something deeper, meaning, possibly, plans for getting through life itself. In any event, the plans aren't specified, beyond hinting that the cross-country trip requires the serious participation of all his riders. Or maybe he's merely planning to poke his honey in the back seat. It's hard to tell. Somewhere, the serious section of McCartney's brain is struggling to take charge, but as he still tends to keep his feelings in another room, lyrical analysis is frustrating. So on to the song itself, a minor key, sadly sung piece that doesn't sound like a friendly outing is coming anytime soon. Call it a work in progress, deserving of more attention from the composer. **B**

"Somedays" [Paul McCartney]

More sadness, a reflection of passing time that won't return. As you listen to this so-so acoustic song, ponder McCartney's dilemma with negative emotions and consider whether his tendency to lock up all the bad feelings might be a way of coping with his mother's early death [cancer at age 47; he was 14]. Basically a continuation of "The World Tonight," McCartney goes back and forth on his emotional state [just like a real person], but flushes it away when he implies it's about "them," not "him." However, before you dismiss McCartney's musings as childish, also consider that the same guy who wrote "Magneto and Titanium Man" might now actually be grappling with difficult concepts. Like a grown up. **B**

"Young Boy" [Paul McCartney]

A would-be Beatles song that's half-Beatles, half-Billy Joel. Lyrics, again, point towards the thoughtful, as he discusses the best way to guide a kid into adulthood. Solution: find a nice girl [or nice boy]. Prognosis: judging from divorce rates, not the greatest advice. Like a deflating Beatle, the composer settles for a melody that starts out promising, then peters out. **B-**

"Calico Skies" [Paul McCartney]

If the anti-war theme, buried toward the end, had dominated "Calico Skies," we might have a winner, seeing as how McCartney's serious political views are few and far between. Maybe "Give Ireland Back to the Irish" still stings, but McCartney's an adult now. So we're burdened with another snoozer about love, telling us, gosh darn it, how much he's in favour of it. The tune? Actually, not bad, pieces of it stick after it's over, and the intro riff, though leaning to the obvious, tastefully compliments the melody. So a nice tune burdened with poor lyrics once again equals a boat that's been missed. **B**

"Flaming Pie" [Paul McCartney]

There's bad nonsense, such as McCartney's "Soily," and there's good nonsense, such as the Beatles' "I Am the Walrus." The former has dull black-and-white images, seemingly strung together at random. The latter sparkles with flights of imagination and an unstrained sense of humour. McCartney's not yet in the good nonsense camp, but with "Flaming Pie," he's getting closer, bolstered by this diverting track's rollicking piano, memorable riff, and off-hand vocal, light years away from "Bip Bop." **B**

"Heaven On a Sunday" [Paul McCartney]
A precarious tilt into squish territory, "Heaven On a Sunday" gets saved in the end by better-than-average-lyrics pondering the ephemeral nature of life. I waited for the inevitable violins, which, thankfully never came. In their place, we're favoured with a subdued background, heavy on electric piano, that gives the track a pleasant lift. **B**

"Used to Be Bad" [Paul McCartney and Steve Miller]
Your tolerance for "Used to Be Bad" depends on how much you tolerate Steve Miller, the Texas blues guy who gave us "The Joker" and "Fly Like and Eagle." "Used to Be Bad" is more or less a Miller track with McCartney poking in here and there. I can take or leave Miller, mainly because there's a limit on how much white boy blues I can sit through. If you're more blue than me, if you think McCartney is deep down a three-chord fanatic, have I got a track for you. **C**

"Souvenir" [Paul McCartney]
With a killer riff, words that mean something, and an insidious melody that won't quit, "Souvenir" is an unexpected stunner. The track bristles with studio flourishes that still dazzle, even after all these years. Witness the imaginative opening that melts a bluesy line into a slinky chorus. And the snarling guitar that underlines a sympathetic vocal, disguising something a bit more sinister. And that ending, with McCartney on the edge of screaming at the girl he's supposedly comforting. The middle eight falters a bit, but it's shoved out of the way pretty fast. A winner. **A-**

"Little Willow" [Paul McCartney]
A minor but endearing song about the death of Ringo's wife, Maureen. With snatches of cliched melody and too many trite lyrics, "Little Willow" longs to soar like "Blackbird," but instead waddles like a duck. **B-**

"Really Love You" [Paul McCartney and Ringo Starr]
Ringo plods away, Paul more or less makes it up on the spot, and the result is what you'd expect from two tired superstars with some tape to fill. Don't get too excited about the admittedly clever riff, since it lasts for about four seconds, then disappears. As for the rest, that's a l-o-n-g five minutes to fill. **C-**

"Beautiful Night" [Paul McCartney]
A re-run from the justly abandoned *Return to Pepperland*, this pretends to be an ode to everything but instead is an ode to nothing. McCartney croons about catching fish, rock climbing, and other blather, all to a joyous tune celebrating, uh, joy. Musically, it's adequate, but undeserving of a talent of McCartney's stature. **B-**

"Great Day" [Paul McCartney]
A gorgeous, haunting melody, reminiscent of "Mama's Little Girl," but melancholic and better. It requires a high level of skill to write a sad song about being happy. McCartney pulls it off spectacularly, demonstrating a level of sophistication he hasn't achieved in quite a while. **A**

[bonus]

"Looking for You" [Paul McCartney and Ringo Starr]
Was this left off *McCartney II*? Could it be the cousin of "On the Way?" Remember "On the Way?" You don't? [*The World Tonight EP*] **D**

"Squid" [Paul McCartney]
A laid-back instrumental, perfect for stroking your squid. Like many of his previous instrumentals, it sounds like a TV theme for a light drama like *Keeping Up With the Kardashians*. Every now and then, McCartney gives the impression that he's so far removed from his own culture, he may as well be writing for Smurfs. [*The World Tonight EP*] **B-**

"I Love This House" [Paul McCartney]

Many of these bonuses [specifically, "Atlantic Ocean," "Squid," "Don't Break the Promise," "Beautiful Night [Original]," "Love Mix," and this one] were included in the *Oobu Joobu* project, so by hunting them down, you can get a taste of what the radio show was like [basically, a lot of semi-interesting radio buzz, emphasis on "semi-"]. Judging from his songs, McCartney loves everything – his family, pets, neighbors, the microbes in his large intestine, and the house he lives in. Grimy, demo-ish, and probably improvised, he details his house's many flaws – water leaks, ratty rugs, holes in the floor – then stubbornly declares he'll stay right there. Sure he will. [*Young Boy EP*] **B-**

"Broomstick" [Paul McCartney]

Featuring Steve Miller on guitar. If you were lukewarm for "Used to Be Bad," get ready to hold your nose when you get a whiff of this paper-thin blues throwaway. [*Young Boy #2 EP*] **C-**

"Atlantic Ocean" [Paul McCartney]

Also rescued from *Return to Pepperland*, but it should have been left to suffocate. The intro sounds like a thousand other disco songs, with a cliched bass, rudimentary snare, and lightweight wheezes. A good chunk of this is McCartney speaking – no orator awards for this – the rest is a grade school couplet repeated endlessly. For twelve hours. Or it seems that way. [*Young Boy #2 EP*] **F**

"Love Comes Tumbling Down" [Paul McCartney]

I suspect "Love Comes Tumbling Down" is composed of chopped up bits of discards. It's well-produced, and non-offensive, plus it features a soothing melody, a musical massage for the non-demanding fan. Like your mom. [*Beautiful Night EP*] **C+**

"Beautiful Night [Original]" [Paul McCartney]

As it lacks George Martin's overproduction, this simpler version exceeds the version on *Flaming Pie*, although the too-loud snare throttles go a long way towards wrecking it. [*Oobu Joobu* portion of *Beautiful Night EP*] **C**

"Same Love" [Paul McCartney]

Straight to lounge land, right where rock lovers do not want to be, ever. If you're not a fan of songs aimed at your parents, prepare to have the skin crawl off your bones. [*Beautiful Night EP*] **D-**

"Love Mix/Waiting for the Sun to Shine" [Paul McCartney]

Written back in 1973, "Waiting for the Sun to Shine" was a minor gem that pummeled junk like "Mary Had a Little Lamb," only to be long forgotten. It's revived here as a chorus for "Love Mix," a putrid sleep-inducer that not quite but almost drains the life from "Waiting." [*Beautiful Night EP*] **C+**

"Hey Jude [Montserrat]" [John Lennon and Paul McCartney]

"Hey Jude" strikes again, this time to benefit the island of Montserrat, smashed to bits by a hurricane. Montserrat was the home of George Martin's studio, also damaged. This "Hey Jude" deviated from the ordinary performance as it included solo vocals from Elton John [thrilled] and Sting [overwhelmed], along with support from a packed stage. McCartney, wisely, left out the call and response nonsense. [*Music for Montserrat*] **B**

"Little Willow [Diana Tribute]" [Paul McCartney]

For a tribute to the late Diana, Princess of Wales, McCartney offers a recent tune, and as always, he's confidently professional. Is it a standard yet? Not while "Blackbird" can still fly. [*Diana, Princess of Wales: Tribute.*] **B-**

"Don't Break the Promises" [Paul McCartney, Eric Stewart, and Graham Gouldman]

[10cc] Sung with a likeable falsetto, this would be okay were it not for the too-far-in-front percussion and the dated synthesizer that comes bumbling in at all the wrong spots. Watered-down sort-of disco. [*Meanwhile*] **B-**

CHAPTER TWENTY-EIGHT:

STANDING STONE [1997]

Produced by John Fraser and Paul McCartney
Charted 194 [US], did not chart [UK]

A gargantuan classical work, *Standing Stone* draws from an equally huge McCartney poem [three dozen verses] describing Celtic philosophy and spirituality as McCartney sees it. The poem doesn't tie directly into the poem, but uses it as inspiration. With EMI's 100th birthday coming up, McCartney felt his poem could be turned into an orchestral spectacular that would be perfect as a commemorative event.

The music itself, as well as the accompanying poem, displayed a hoped-for sophistication unlike anything he'd attempted before, requiring other, more experienced artists, to lend their skills. Although the concepts were McCartney's, David Matthews [friend of Carl Davis, McCartney's collaborator on *Liverpool Oratorio*] gave it a nudge here and there, encouraging him to condense the sprawl into something more listenable. Musician John Harle and composer Richard Rodney Bennett also pitched in. Tom Pickard, a respected poet, edited and polished the lengthy poem. McCartney also solicited electronic assistance from his new Apple Macintosh computer.

Completion ate up four years, on and off. But the finished work accomplished what McCartney wanted, an impressive – in size at least – orchestral *magnum opus*, augmented with a classically trained choir. As a final touch, EMI sliced the work into 19 distinct tracks, for which the overwhelmed listener would be eternally grateful. At approximately 75 minutes, the hulking *Standing Stone* was ambitious, almost staggeringly so.

What's it like? For starters, owing to its episodic structure, it's not a symphony, but more of a tone poem along the lines of Richard Strauss or Bela Bartok. Digging deeper, it reveals itself to be a series of dressed-up songs rather than complex orchestral creations, unsurprising since that's McCartney's forte. Possibly because of its long gestation, it's often rickety, and in spots, it's shallow, sort of a classical echo of *Venus and Mars*. Worn-out clichés pop up all over the place: thundering percussion [to simulate a storm], sweet woodwinds [cue Cupid], ethereal arpeggios [heaven at last!], and ascending major key melodies [love triumphant]. Dull passages go on and on, as if the Macintosh accidently printed identical pages.

That's not to dismiss this as a superstar's vanity project. Bits of *Standing Stone*, particularly in Movement IV, are satisfying, even stirring. There are no blatant missteps; in fact, his major mistake is taking too many tiny steps instead of attempting a couple of big ones. The question of lasting value aside, *Standing Stone* didn't fully satisfy McCartney's classical cravings. Instead, it served as practice for a composer-in-training.

"Movement I: After Heavy Light Years" [Paul McCartney]

More challenging than expected, but still too tame to generate excitement. The chugging violins provide a decent set-up for things to come. Except nothing does, that is, nothing exceptional. A good deal of Movement I feels like walking in place. Through the next, "Cell Growth" and the last, "Human Theme" [best so far], it strikes you that not only aren't these sections developed much [shades of *Pipes of Peace*], they just sort of lie there, comatose. So far, more Broadway than concert hall. **B-**

"Movement II: He Awoke Startled" [Paul McCartney]

The strongest section, but it's strong like *Flaming Pie*, not, say, Beethoven's 5th. Individual chunks sound attractive – "Sea Voyage" should make you sit up – but an overriding theme doesn't exist. Here as elsewhere, *Standing Stone* rides on exaggeration instead of subtlety. That's an acceptable approach for a rock album but not an orchestral piece. "Lost at Sea" sounds like a TV soundtrack. **B**

"Movement III: Subtle Colours Merged Soft Contours" [Paul McCartney]

At times, this movement drifts around so much that you want to grab a violinist by the throat and tell him to stay put. No cohesiveness, no development, nothing unexpected. Motifs come and go for no particular reason. And these stiff melodies are just plain crummy, unsuitable for a virtuoso composer like McCartney. Movement III reminds me of a kid lost in the woods, wandering from tree to tree, getting sleepy, and sitting down for a rest. **C**

"Movement IV: Strings Pluck, Horns Blow, Drums Beat"

It says "Fugal Celebration," but is it a genuine fugue? No more than *Thrillington* is a symphony. Maybe it's a mini-fugue. Whatever. Perhaps you could unravel its fugue-ness on subsequent hearings, but a classical segment this slight is hardly worth the trouble. The odd thing is, considered as a piece of conservative pop, it's not half-bad. "Love Duet," the highlight, is pretty without being trite. "Celebration" modesty brings the piece home, dipping into the Disney pool again, but in a pleasant way.

So is *Standing Stone* too mawkish? Well, yes. For kids and their grandparents, for adults who believe rock music starts and ends with the Eagles, *Standing Stone* is a passable introduction to feather-light classical, nothing more. **B –**

[bonus]

"La De Da" [Ringo Starr, Mark Hudson, Dean Grakal, and Steve Dudas; guest performer: Paul McCartney]

[Ringo Starr] A conscious effort to come up with a Beatle song. Tried, failed. Even with McCartney chipping in with bass and backing vocals [can't hear him], it's second hand, a million miles from "Photograph" [*Ringo*, 1973] and god knows how many light years from "A Little Help from My Friends." The sing-along chorus – the sole reason for the song's existence – has the exact opposite of the reaction Ringo wanted, namely, few warm feelings for Ringo, and next to none for his group. [*Vertical Man*] **B-**

"I Was Walkin'" [Ringo Starr, Mark Hudson, Dean Grakal, and Steve Dudas; guest performer: Paul McCartney]

[Ringo Starr] Awful dreck by a great rock drummer. The song must've taken all of five minutes to write. The freeze-dried ambiance sounds like it was bought in a can at the 7-Eleven. The only redeemable element is the fleeting drum solo, which is nothing spectacular, but you take what you can get. The good-natured McCartney adds distant backup vocals. [*Vertical Man*] **D-**

"What in the World" [Ringo Starr, Mark Hudson, Dean Grakal, and Steve Dudas; guest performer: Paul McCartney]

[Ringo Star] Dreary. A few unexpected chord changes attempt to transform this into something vaguely, sort of, into a Beatles-ish track, but the attempt is DOA. McCartney's backups don't help. This is beyond help. **D**

CHAPTER TWENTY-NINE:

FIREMAN – RUSHES [1998]

Produced by Paul McCartney and Martin Glover
Did not chart

Again assuming the identity of the Fireman, which one more time fooled exactly no one, McCartney rang up his co-conspirator Martin Glover and asked if he was ready to try it again. Glover accepted, and the two began work on what would come to be called *Rushes*, ambient number two. As work commenced, Glover noticed subtle but definite changes in his partner. Ever the workaholic, McCartney was redoubling his efforts, building the tracks with few sections of existing songs like he had before with *Off the Ground* on *Strawberries Oceans Ship Forest*. Instead, he was also using original bits and pieces, some from abandoned tracks like "Plum Jam" and "Let Me Love You Always," and, interestingly, samples from nature, including animal cries and rustling leaves. And McCartney, usually happy-go-lucky, at times seemed preoccupied and melancholy. Neither man acknowledged this. But to Glover, McCartney seemed, at times, like a different person.

Whatever he was, the results were more impressive than they were on the previous ambient project. *Rushes* offers electronic structures derived from human feelings instead of special effects. The music was deeper, giving the impression it'd been worked and re-worked, and not just first draft fluff. Avoiding weak sources such as *Off the Ground*, McCartney chose raw material that could be sculpted into something unique. It wasn't "Strawberry Fields Forever" or "Tomorrow Never Knows," – not even close, really – but it was in the ballpark, all without slavishly copying the Beatles' forays into non-commercial sounds.

Unlike *Strawberries Oceans Ships Forest,* McCartney now had a better grasp of the mechanics of ambient music, enabling him to avoid the self-defeating short cuts cluttering up his previous venture. Could be that he was getting older, and with age came the ability to slow down and take his time? Had he developed beyond the chronic adolescent, and no longer hungered for the hollow satisfaction of beating the competition in chart success? Or it could be that his newfound seriousness was the by-product of frustration and helplessness, leaving him with the sad, unfathomable truth: Linda would no longer be with him?

Critics applauded McCartney's maturity, which had begun to emerge in *Flaming Pie* but now seemed to be in full bloom. *Aural Innovations*: "It's a pleasure to know Paul McCartney is still interested in sound …." *AllMusic*: "four stars out of five." *Rock NYC*: " … both fascinating and different."

"Watercolour Guitars" [Paul McCartney with Martin Glover]

If you're curious about ambient music, *Rushes* is an excellent introduction. "Watercolour Guitars" makes a good start, a gentle repetition of a soothing guitar arpeggio, followed by the swelling of a keyboard, followed by McCartney's eerie voice floating in the background, all of it building and diminishing over the course of six minutes. "Hey Diddle," it definitely is not. Some of it drifts into video game bleeps and blops, which runs counter to the reflective mood. But overall, it's a successful piece, one I didn't think McCartney had in him. **B**

"Palo Verde" [Paul McCartney with Martin Glover]

The end of "Watercolour Guitars" blends into this one, heavier on effects [a horse's snort, somebody – Linda? – mumbling], then blossoms into a dizzying collage of ups-and-downs from a synthesizer. If Lennon's "Revolution 9" was aggressive, even defiant, "Palo Verde" is as reassuring as having your hair brushed. Skeptics will find this dull beyond belief, which is understandable considering it's more or less unchanging for a long 10-plus minutes. But for the patient, able to pick up the gradual changes in tempo and tiny voices appearing here and there, it's calming. Faint praise, to be sure, but praise nonetheless. **B-**

"Auraveda" [Paul McCartney with Martin Glover]
The album's longest and least interesting piece. It opens with a sitar, dating it to the 60s, and synthetic organ chords, dating it to the 80s, not a pleasing combination. It glides along into movie music territory. We're not talking *Gone With the Wind*. We're talking *Robo Vampire*. Not soothing enough to be an electronic lullaby, nor lively enough to be pop music [which it resembles in places]. It picks up near the end, losing both the sitar and the organ, but by then, we've abandoned ship. **C**

"Fluid" [Paul McCartney with Martin Glover]
A broken piano chord, repeating endlessly, sets the stage for a sad guitar and what could be a thunderstorm brewing in the back. Musically, it takes a cue from Kraftwerk for its rhythmic build, but "Fluid" is more melodic, thus more accessible to a newcomer. Majestic, intimate, and strangely reserved, the repetitions suggest a brooding, lonely atmosphere. But just when it's reaching a peak, it breaks to pieces with a woman apparently having an orgasm. I doubt it'll bring you to an orgasm, but hey, you never know. **B**

"Appletree Cinnabar Amber" [Paul McCartney with Martin Glover]
If ambient records had a B-side, "Appletree" would be perfect. A percussion ensemble, not a great change but a change, drives along a brief melody, also an odd choice for ambient, then proceeds with a James Bond guitar and more Linda [I think]. Some organ doodles finish it off, leaving us with an average ambient track, below average if you're feeling grumpy. **B-**

"Bison" [Paul McCartney with Martin Glover]
An admirable attempt at simulating a hairy mammal loping along the plains. A collage of human voices comes spiraling in, followed by an electronic hailstorm from hell, followed by *Psycho*-esque film music, then out. In under three minutes. Too short – an uncommon criticism of ambient music – but fairly impressive. **B**

"7 A.M." [Paul McCartney with Martin Glover]
A second cousin to "Fluid," this simulates a restless sleeper, whose aural dreams consist of a minor chord mellotron, an electronic violin, and something sounding like a ticking clock connected to a time bomb. It ebbs and flows, changing its mind at the last minute, briefly pausing, then charging in again. Who's that? Why, it's McCartney himself, mumbling gobbledygook. **B**

"Watercolour Rush" [Paul McCartney with Martin Glover]
Wrapping it all up is another shot at themes developed in "Watercolour Guitars," most of it played backwards. At under two minutes, there's not much time to do anything – and it doesn't – but it's a stylish ending to a decent ambient record. **B**

[bonus]

"A Room With a View" [Noel Coward]
Ignore the eye-rolling credits for Mellow T. Ron and His Mood Men. This is pure Paul. The guy responsible for "When I'm 64" and "You Gave Me the Answer" is right at home with this toe tapper from the 1920s, one of McCartney's favourite eras, laying it down for an AIDS charity. Slightly tongue in cheek, it'll be right at home in your parents' library where you're unlikely to hear it again. Or will ever want to. [*Twentieth Century Blues: the Songs of Noel Coward*, 1998.] **C**

"T-Shirt" [Jim Imray; producer, guest performer: Paul McCartney]
[The Crickets] Formerly with Buddy Holly, the Crickets have a major fan in McCartney, who claimed the Beatles took their name from them. He jumped at the chance to produce a reunion single. It's slight, an unpretentious look back at a style long gone. But truth be told, it's kind of sluggish which, inadvertently or not, reminds us these guys may be eager to please, but they're teen rockers no more. McCartney's understated contributions neither add nor subtract. [*T-Shirt – The Official Album*] **B-**

Linda McCartney

A good-hearted, peace-loving, and free-thinking woman who loved Paul and succumbed to a vicious death from breast cancer at the age of 56. McCartney tried to save her, but all his ample resources over four long years amounted to little. When the disease spread to her liver, both knew the end was near. She died at the family's ranch in Tucson, Arizona in 1998.

Linda was a devoted wife, loyal friend, loving parent, astute businesswoman, excellent photographer, and tireless champion of animals. But she was not a musician. No matter how much she tried, how much Paul encouraged her, it was not to be, and she retained her status as a talented amateur for life.

Her musical efforts are summarized in Wide Prairie, *a compilation issued in 1998 that collects recordings made with and without the help of her husband, from 1972-1998. Songs from* Wide Prairie *that aren't mentioned here can be found in the following entries:* "Seaside Woman" [Red Rose Speedway], "Cow" [Oobu Joobu], "B-Side to Seaside" [Red Rose Speedway], *and* "Cook of the House" [Wings at the Speed of Sound].

"Wide Prairie" [Linda McCartney; producer and guest performer: Paul McCartney]
[Linda McCartney] From the outset of the title track, Linda's limitations become strikingly clear: thin voice, poor melodic sense, and Paul's ever-present persona, an unstoppable talent on the verge of overwhelming everything his wife tries to do. Recorded in 1973, around the time of the *Venus and Mars* sessions, Linda tries to imitate a backwoods hillbilly, and the results are painful. [*Wide Prairie*] **C-**

"New Orleans" [Linda McCartney; producer and guest performer: Paul McCartney]
[Linda McCartney] You-know-who plunks the piano for this New Orleans travelogue, sort of amiable and sort of clumsy. She's doing the best she can, but ultimately this an amateur effort with assistance from another you-know-who. [*Wide Prairie*] **B-**

"The White Coated Man" [Paul McCartney, Linda McCartney, and Carla Lane; producer and guest artist: Paul McCartney]
[Linda McCartney] Applause to Linda for the incisive words but groans for the dull music. Recorded in 1988, if she hadn't a grasp of composition by then, it probably had passed her by. Co-authorship with comedy writer Carla Lane didn't help much. [*Wide Prairie*] **B-**

"Love's Full Glory" [Linda McCartney; producers: Paul and Linda McCartney; guest artist: Paul McCartney]
[Linda McCartney] That ballads run in the family shouldn't surprise anyone. So in 1980, Linda took a deep breath and gave it a try, knowing that the demands of a ballad require a vocal control that was likely beyond her. Despite desperate multi-tracking, the song proves to be way out of her range, forcing her to concentrate on getting the notes right at the expense of the casual tenderness "Love's Full Glory" requires. As for the song itself, it's nothing special. [*Wide Prairie*.] **C-**

"I Got Up" [Paul and Linda McCartney; producer: Paul McCartney; guest artist: Paul McCartney]
[Linda McCartney] Started in 1973, making it another *Venus and Mars* era relic, this lay dormant until it was dusted off and polished up nearly a quarter of a century later. That it laid in a coma for so long implies either the McCartneys [1] forgot it about it, [2] couldn't figure out how to finish it, or [3] decided it was hopeless and stuck it in a drawer. I vote for the drawer. A suitable vehicle for a non-singer, with a static melody and a I-can't-take-it-no-more lyric that reassures rather than defies. [*Wide Prairie*] **C+**

"The Light Comes From Within" [Paul and Linda McCartney; producer: Paul McCartney; guest artist: Paul McCartney]
[Linda McCartney] The last session before her death, which put her, understandably, in a sour mood. She rails against the creeps who constantly undermined her talent by taking personal swipes at her, which she rightfully insisted wasn't fair. This is far from a Paul McCartney tune. This is a Bikini Kill/ Slits/X-Ray Spex tune, and as such – sneering, contemptuous, dismissive – it shines. Perhaps if her life hadn't been cut short [and she'd had the desire], this might've marked the early stage of a career as a feminist punk, one that could've left a befuddled Paul standing in the dust, clutching his "Ode to a Koala Bear." A standing ovation for having the guts to call out the dicks, complete with four-letter expletives. Somewhere, John Lennon is beaming. [*Wide Prairie*] **B**

"Mister Sandman" [Pat Ballard; producer: Lee Perry and Paul McCartney; guest artist: Paul McCartney]
[Linda McCartney] From the near-sublime [*The Light Comes from Within*] to the headache-inducing ridiculous [this dreck], a 1954 Vaughn Monroe antiquity, updated from somewhere in the vicinity of *Wings at the Speed of Sound*. Right up Paul's alley – remember Mary Hopkin's "Que Sera Sera"? – he lays it on thick, multi-tracking the vocal to high heaven and playing a cute guitar, all to a polite reggae backing. Linda, gamely, goes along. [*Wide Prairie*] **D+**

"Oriental Nightfish" [Linda McCartney; producer: Paul McCartney; guest performer: Paul McCartney]
[Linda McCartney] The partial soundtrack to the Paul-produced *Rupert and the Frog Song* animated film. Recorded during *Band on the Run* [1973], this largely instrumental number – in a minor key with ghostly keyboards – is designed, perhaps unintentionally, to give kids the creeps. If the adult-ish imagery doesn't send them fleeing to the exit, they'll likely be sobbing for mommy. The meandering tune is typical for a soundtrack, meaning it takes a back seat to the film and is practically invisible. [*Wide Prairie*] **B-**

"Endless Days" [Linda McCartney and Mick Bolton]
[Linda McCartney] Linda whimpering about a guy [Paul, right?] who treated her like dirt. Essentially a demo with Paul nowhere in sight, a simple piano carries the mournful tune which, with her sad little voice, Linda actually pulls off. Imagine a contemporary record containing songs like "The Light from Within" and "Endless Days" without a single "Mister Sandman" or "Poison Ivy." It could be a 21st century Mary Hopkin album. [*Wide Prairie*] **B**

"Poison Ivy" [Jerry Leiber and Mike Stoller]
[Linda McCartney] The ten-millionth cover of a web-covered artifact. A clunky rhythm on the verge of collapse, a piano falling asleep, and a vocal searching for a tune. Linda produced this one, proving that production is harder than it looks. [*Wide Prairie*] **C**

"Sugartime" [Charlie Phillips and Otis Echols; producers: Paul McCartney and Lee Perry]
[Linda McCartney] In order to transform Linda into a Muppets version of the McGuire Sisters, Paul foisted this lighter than helium number on his ever-cooperative missus. Deciding the original wasn't quite awful enough, Paul set this to a reggae rhythm, thus making the awful into the ghastly. She tries hard to sing it, the band tries hard to stay awake, and the listener tries hard to find a way out. [*Wide Prairie*] **D-**

"Appaloosa" [Paul and Linda McCartney; producer: Paul McCartney; guest performer: Paul McCartney]
[Linda McCartney] From 1998, a *Band on the Run* build-up with somber recitations and weeping violins, suddenly breaks into a moderately catchy tune performed by what sounds like a 10-year-old girl. That's not an insult, as the child's voice – again, Linda – does a reasonable job of carrying along the nursery rhyme ditty, repeating it over and over until you're humming along. Then it's done. And this is about as good as it gets. [*Wide Prairie*] **B-**

CHAPTER THIRTY:

RUN DEVIL RUN [1999]

Produced by Chris Thomas and Paul McCartney
Charted at 27 [US], 12 [UK]

Just as he'd reacted to Lennon's assassination, McCartney threw himself into his work to ease the pain of Linda's death. The repertoire once again was oldies, both familiar and obscure. They'd be songs he knew as a kid and had loved ever since. Unlike *Choba B CCCP*, which served as a rough draft for *Run Devil Run*, it seemed he wanted the new album to be passionate rather than off-handedly casual. And, almost whether he liked it or not, *Run Devil Run* would be laced with a subtext of grief and loss, giving it a depth ordinarily not associated with Chuck Berry or Elvis Presley.

Ultimately, *Run Devil Run* would stand as one of McCartney's key achievements, better than lightweights like *Off the Ground*, superior to the classical meanderings of *Standing Stone*, and vastly outgunning his pop throwaways like *Wild Life*. It was as if he'd assimilated what it took to be a mature artist, not just a shallow pop star.

For *Run Devil Run*, McCartney recruited first-class musicians, ones that were sympathetic and supportive, and when possible, boasting professional backgrounds comparable to his. He chose wisely. The line-up: David Gilmour [guitar, Pink Floyd], Ian Paice [drums, Deep Purple], Pete Wingfield [keyboards, The Hollies], Mick Green [guitar, Billy J. Kramer], Geraint Watkins [keyboards, Dave Edmunds], and Dave Mattacks [drums, Fairport Convention]. McCartney also employed Chris Thomas [Badfinger, Roxy Music, The Beatles] as co-producer, giving him a strong eye to keep things on track and provide a second opinion.

And he wanted to do it quickly. No fussy production or elaborate overdubs or endlessly laboring over one track, an approach that tended to water down albums like *Press to Play*. The pros rose to the occasion. The entire album was completed in roughly a week.

The title came from an old herbal medicine that McCartney found appealing, possibly believing he could use all the help he could get staving off the bad *juju* floating around [Wisdom Products' "Run Devil Run" claims it can "turn away hexes."] The cover, a photo of an old drug store in Atlanta, Georgia that sold mysterious items, completed one of the strongest albums of McCartney's career.

Fans and critics went nuts. *Entertainment Weekly* gave it an A-. *AllMusic*: four stars out of five. *Rolling Stone*: "…heartbreaking and life affirming." However, *Run Devil Run* failed to hit, ascending to a dismal #27 in the US, a disappointment. But as a creative triumph, and more importantly, as catharsis for a wounded man, it hardly mattered.

"Blue Jean Bop" [Gene Vincent and Hal Levy]

A haunted, instantly memorable vocal explodes into a sizzling recreation of Gene Vincent's seminal hit, both re-inventing and surpassing it. The echo, the rockabilly guitar, and an eccentric mix simultaneously retain the spirit of the original and wed it to a modern day artist who means business. As boldly announced with "Blue Jean Bop," *Run Devil Run* won't be a by-the-books copy job, but an imaginative update from a spot-on McCartney. **A-**

"She Said Yeah" [Roddy Jackson and Sonny Bono]

A lot of competition for this infectious rocker, as the Rolling Stones and the Animals were among the many who took a shot at it. But McCartney jumps on "She Said Yeah" with such force, confidence, and surliness that he tops them all, no mean feat for a guy pushing 60. The flip side of Larry Williams' "Bad

Boy," McCartney probably would've recorded "She Said Yeah" back in the Beatles days if the boys had given their blessings. **B+**

"All Shook Up" [Otis Blackwell and Elvis Presley]
Covering Elvis Presley is pretty much a sucker's bet, as going head to head with Elvis can be asking for trouble. But McCartney does an admirable job of ripping through the familiar "All Shook Up," his vocal alternately friendly, regretful, and snotty. The solid band, exuding reverence for a beloved song, propels him along effortlessly and are a joy to hear. **B**

"Run Devil Run" [Paul McCartney]
The lyrics stink, a futile attempt to channel the swampiness of Credence Clearwater Revival, but flailing all over the place with sloppy images. The music, however, is another matter, a solid rocker that sits confidently with Elvis Presley and Ricky Nelson and matches them both, sneer for sneer. This may be the best "I Saw Her Standing There" clone, ever. **B+**

"No Other Baby" [Dickey Bishop and Bob Watson]
McCartney drifts across the fine line between the tender and the bland in this acceptable but unimproved cover of the 1958 semi-hit by the obscure Vipers. It floats along, barely disturbing the waters, then sinks. The Vipers, incidentally, also recorded an early version of "Maggie May," which the Beatles did on *Let It Be*. **B-**

"Lonesome Town" [Baker Knight]
If this heartbreaker doesn't bring a tear to your eye, you must be Johnny Rotten. Ricky Nelson's rendition was sorrowful enough, but McCartney shreds it, scooping out every last fragment of anguish he, we, or anyone can stand. Consider how this could've been bungled: sappy strings, over-the-top vocals, slick and soulless background. Instead, McCartney offers zero strings, gentle vocals, and backgrounds that are sparse and intimate. If the first time around, you dismissed *Run Devil Run* as just another vanity project, try "Lonesome Town." **B+**

"Try Not to Cry" [Paul McCartney]
A potential throwaway, with the exception of the superlative band who pummel it to submission. But McCartney sounds distracted. Maybe he's hankering for another Elvis tune. **B –**

"Movie Magg" [Carl Perkins]
Such respect McCartney has for Carl Perkins that he performs this like a church hymnal, careful to get every syllable in place, every note exactly where he thinks it should be. Perkins, in contrast, performs "Movie Magg" like a whoop-de-do country ode to his girlfriend, thrilled that she let him hold her hand [or hold something]. McCartney strips away the country trappings, a good move, but sings much too staid, and at times, stiff. **B-**

"Brown Eyed Handsome Man" [Chuck Berry]
Made to order for McCartney. He plays it like he owns it, and for three minutes of sheer bliss, he does. The sparkling backing [sorry, Chuck], the correct tempo [very sorry, Chuck], and the matchless vocal [*really* sorry, Chuck] are all precisely on the money. But the *piece de resistance* is the carnival-esque accordion, an inspired addition to Berry's arrangement that makes the original sound dated. **B+**

"What It Is" [Paul McCartney]
That McCartney is horny seems to be a legitimate reading of the lyrics [he's an insect fluttering around an attractive flower?]. Or possibly McCartney's having a bad day with the pencil. Once again, ignore his words and focus on the music, a mid-tempo shuffle with a sturdy chorus and a clever nod to the 50s. **B**

"Coquette" [Johnny Green, Carmen Lombardo, and Gus Kahn]
McCartney pounds the piano so hard you expect it to crumble to splinters. This isn't Little Richard, but Fats Domino, who's much more reserved. Though McCartney does a fair imitation, the song doesn't do much for the catharsis that fuels *Run Devil Run*. A polite performance of a polite piece. **B-**

"I Got Stung" [David Hill and Aaron Schroeder]

McCartney wails and yowls through this Elvis classic, so savage he's hard to resist. True, it's not the top of his Elvis heap, but Paul decimates it all the same. **B**

"Honey Hush" [Joe Turner]

Back to Louisiana with a visit to Big Joe Turner and his largely improvised [and not great] R&B sizzler. McCartney, on the other hand, sings like his life is at stake. The band smacks the hell out of their poor instruments in a thrilling performance. **B+**

"Shake a Hand" [Joe Morris]

McCartney destroys the first four words with such force, the tune falls to the floor, gasping for air. Of course Linda lurks in the back of his mind as he promises to help her with all her troubles, but of course he didn't, which is a cue to yank the voltage meter into the red. Too bad the song doesn't amount to much, but the blood-curdling singer could make the dictionary sound scary. **B+**

"Party" [Jessie Mae Robinson]

Would you let this maniac into your party? Throttling this Elvis tune transforms McCartney into the Hulk. He tears up the song, the studio, and the countryside as he chomps his way through a killer performance. Here's hoping McCartney's invigorating vocal doesn't require another tragedy to resurrect. **B+**

[bonus]

"Fabulous" [Bernie Lowe and Karl Mann]

From the 1957 Charlie Gracie single comes this light rocker, which McCartney breezes through. Sort of Elvis, sort of Fats Domino, it's too derivative to make much of an impression. Hence, a b-side, the cemetery of the unwanted. [B-side of "Brown Eyed Handsome Man" single, 1999]. **B-**

CHAPTER THIRTY-ONE:

WORKING CLASSICAL [1999]

Produced by Paul McCartney and John Fraser
Did not chart [US], did not chart [UK]

When *Working Classical* tip-toed into record stores, following *Run Devil Run* in less than four weeks, die-hard McCartney-ites couldn't wait to snap it up. But their enthusiasm waned a bit when they got a good look at it. It was, sigh, another classical album, third in a series of who knew how many.

Still, it was easier to get a handle on than the massive *Liverpool Oratorio* or *Standing Stone*. *Working Classical* consisted of fourteen short, easy to digest pieces. Most of the performances came from the Lorma Mar Quarter, a smaller ensemble than the vast orchestras McCartney used before. True, full orchestras were required for three of the pieces, but that left eleven short ones, a relief for classical novices. And many titles were familiar: "My Love," "Maybe I'm Amazed," "Warm and Beautiful." That meant, at best, the album would consist of classical explorations of some McCartney oldies. At worst? Muzak.

Fortunately, McCartney dodged Muzak for the most part. Instead, he offered takes that were easy on the ears, albeit undemanding. Most critics shrugged and found it passable, though some sniffed that it was too slight to take seriously [*Classics Today*: "... sub-par film music ..."].

The picky among us wondered exactly how much of this McCartney actually composed by himself, remembering how he proudly proclaimed he could neither read nor write a note of music, and this lack of formal skill didn't seem to have changed. Examination of the booklet [bottom of page 3] reveals that *Working Classical* benefitted from contributions by Andy Stein, John Fraser, Michael Thomas, Roberto Pansera, and the Lorna Mar Quartet, all seasoned professionals and credited as arrangers.

"Junk [Classical Version]" [Paul McCartney]
On second thought, maybe Paul shouldn't get a pass for avoiding Muzak. This comes perilously close, due to the plastic arrangement and too-sweet strings. "Junk" worked much better in *McCartney*, where you may recall it already received an instrumental interpretation, and better than this one. Since this arrangement adds nothing special, it's forgettable, and a shade embarrassing. **B-**

"A Leaf [Alternate]" [Paul McCartney]
An arrangement from 1995 is tried again, transforming a summer breeze into more of a hurricane, its intimacy washed away in a mass of horns and violins. Not exactly bad, as it offers a genuine alternative to the original, but it's sort of like those alternate takes that artists tack on the end of CDs in hopes of selling a few more copies. **B-**

"Haymakers" [Paul McCartney]
Structured as a song, a form as comfortable to McCartney as a pair of slippers, the violins go up and down like they're supposed to but fail to lock on to a melody, McCartney's specialty. **B-**

"Midwife" [Paul McCartney]
McCartney cranks out tunes like a machine, but they're not supposed to *sound* like a machine. Walking arpeggios support a dull tune, well-played but old fashioned, like a dimly recalled parlor dance of many years back. Like virtually all of McCartney's classical experiments, it's as if the 21st century never existed. **C+**

"Spiral" [Paul McCartney]

Soundtrack music, albeit slightly better than the average soundtrack, but if I discovered it was written, say, in the 1940s, I wouldn't be surprised. Melodramatic, intentionally simple, and if McCartney attempted any musical tricks – say, an inversion or two – they slipped right by me. If 1940 ever rolls around again, McCartney's applying for a job. **B-**

"Warm and Beautiful [Classical Version]" [Paul McCartney]

One of McCartney's best ballads, "Warm and Beautiful" receives a sensitive reading, although there's not much to it here besides a straightforward melody and violins chording along. Again, the main problem with these covers is that they remind you of the originals, and in every case, they come up short. [One exception: "Somedays."] The lack of vocals and the classical settings don't make much of a difference. **B**

"My Love [Classical Version]" [Paul McCartney]

As the theme song of *The Sound of Music Revisited*, it explores – whoops! I got mixed up for a second. **D**

"Maybe I'm Amazed [Classical Version]" [Paul McCartney]

Great song, though this rendition adds little. The skittish cello provides an arresting quirk, and endearingly, the violin attempts a blues riff on the bridge and half-succeeds. **B**

"Calico Skies [Classical Version]" [Paul McCartney]

Stripped of all lyrics and a singer who can sell them, it's too feeble to survive on its melody alone. Though the strings intently saw away, they don't add much. **B-**

"Golden Earth Girl [Classical Version]" [Paul McCartney]

McCartney nears the Pit of Sludge, slips, falls in. A filler cut from a filler album [*Off the Ground*], Linda must've liked this one, or at least Paul imagined she did. I can't think of another reason to include it. **C**

"Somedays [Classical Version]" [Paul McCartney]

Melancholy, sorrow, and regret gush from this simple tune, a perfect candidate for the classical format. Re-listening to the *Flaming Pie* version, you can almost imagine the delicate violins and mournful cello displacing McCartney's voice. This is, in fact, the only remake on *Working Classical* that surpasses [barely] the original. **B**

"Tuesday" [Paul McCartney]

From the score of a children's animated film [really]. Billowing strings, friendly flutes, playful oboe. Played out in multiple parts, it flits from one carefree theme to another. Lovers of flitting, all yours. **B**

"She's My Baby [Classical Version]" [Paul McCartney]

Why orchestrate a song this slight? The violins lurch and shake, struggling to find a tune that isn't there. The cello starts, stops, waits, starts again, producing dopey lines which I guess is the point of this. That it doesn't improve on the *Wings at the Speed of Sound* track isn't exactly a shocker. **C-**

"The Lovely Linda [Classical Version]" [Paul McCartney]

The first song on *McCartney* closes out *Working Classical* with style and welcome brevity. Staccato strings and a smooth violin leading the way makes for a suitable ending to a dubious album. **B**

[bonus]

"Voice" [Heather Mills, Paul McCartney, and Nikko Patrelakis; guest performer: Paul McCartney]

[Heather Mills] It doesn't matter if you're Paul's brother [Mike], wife [Linda], or beloved sheepdog [Martha], sooner or later, there's a chance you'll show up on a track or two of your own. Though Heather wrote the lyrics and Patrelakis manned the electronics, this has Paul all over it [voice, guitar], particularly the electronic-obsessed Paul from *Strawberries Oceans Ships Forest*. Combining snips of Heather praising the benefits of armless women, a few rudimentary electronic sizzles, and a disco beat leftover from *Saturday Night Fever*, "Voice" goes straight to the Frisbee factory. [Single, 1999] **D-**

CHAPTER THIRTY-TWO:

LIVERPOOL SOUND COLLAGE [2000]

Produced by Paul McCartney
Did not chart [US], did not chart [UK]

*M*usique concrete encompasses a range of compositional styles that use non-musical sources, such as spoken words, nature sounds, and electronically modified noises. It's a perfectly valid form of avant garde, having been around since at least 1940 or so, when composer Pierre Schaeffer formalized the basics of the new art form, employing primitive microphones, dissonant chords, and noise collages. Today, *musique concrete* composers use devices ranging from modular synthesizers to 100-speaker monoliths [called Acousmoniums], all to create compositions the likes of which have never before been heard.

In the rock world, the Beatles were among the *musique concrete* pioneers. An early attempt was 1966's head spinner "Tomorrow Never Knows" [from *Revolver*]. A more ambitious effort was the sprawling "Carnival of Light" from 1967, one of the few Beatles productions that have never been heard, due to failed experiments and awkward execution that the group decided was unlistenable.

In 1968, the Beatles had completed their first full-fledged *musique concrete* composition, "Revolution 9," eight-minutes of football chants, tape loops, and other assorted weirdness. McCartney allegedly got the vapors when he heard this, worried that fans would flatly reject a Beatles track without traditional music, while Lennon – largely responsible for "Revolution 9" – dismissed McCartney's objections as nonsense and irrelevant.

Cut to 2000, and who would've thought? McCartney released his very own album-length "Revolution 9, Part Two." Or, as he called it, *Liverpool Sound Collage*, five segments of spoken words, synthesizers, and noises – totally devoid of lyrics and melodies – looped, tweezed, and strangled to form *musique concrete* collages that would make Pierre Schaeffer proud. Or at least would raise his eyebrows.

McCartney allegedly got the idea from artist Peter Blake, the man behind the *Sgt. Pepper* cover, who requested a piece to run in conjunction with an art exhibit. Getting in touch with Martin Glover, his Fireman partner, and Super Furry Animals, an eclectic rock band from Wales, McCartney began assembling the album using tape bits from his collaborators, as well as snips from *Liverpool Oratorio*, virtually unidentifiable after going through numerous electronic transformations.

Notably, the Beatles were listed as collaborators on all but one of the pieces, but this was a bit of a misnomer. A clip or two from discussions during "Think For Yourself" recording sessions were scattered among the chaotic collages, as was a tiny bit of the music from *Sgt. Pepper* on "Free Now." Those hoping for unreleased Beatles music would have to keep hoping.

Liverpool Sound Collage was nominated for a Grammy in the Best Alternative Music Album category. It lost.

"Plastic Beetle" [Paul McCartney and the Beatles]
The flushing of a cosmic toilet. Marching toy soldiers, giggling as they bump into each other. John Lennon's voice, as mystified as you are. "Plastic Beetle" makes "Revolution 9" sound, well, revolutionary. Are we still supposed to be dazzled by a backwards track? Yes, you can tell one *musique concrete* from another, just as you can distinguish quality Sun Ra from lousy Sun Ra. This is lousy. **D**

"Peter Blake 2000" [Super Furry Animals and the Beatles]
If I were Peter Blake, I'd demand my name be taken off this, now. Somebody says the word "rapidly," which

then is repeated and sped up. That's funny? Then, like a 90-year-old comic who doesn't know when it's time to drop dead, throws out another one, then another, and another. This goes on for nearly 17 minutes. And that isn't a typo. **F**

"Real Gone Dub Made in Manifest in the Vortex of the Eternal Now" [Youth]
A flash of *Liverpool Oratorio*, eaten up by a whirlpool of drunken knob twisters. A drummer bangs, a toenail breaks, and it's dawning on you that the performer is tossing on whatever's strikes him as cool for that moment and that moment only. Result: *musique concrete* by the Little League. **D**

"Made Up" [Paul McCartney and The Beatles]
Seeing McCartney and the Beatles' names attached to this makes you wonder if you've slipped into a parallel universe. Yes, there's a Beatle yakking away, but you can get that on *YouTube*, anytime, free of charge. Endless electronic splatters does not add up to something a sane person should be exposed to. I could listen again to hear if that's the *Sgt Pepper* morsel, but I keep nodding off. **F**

"Free Now" [Paul McCartney, The Beatles, and Super Furry Animals]
At last, a segment of reasonable length [3:28] and a surprise cameo by George Harrison, saying an actual sentence. The last hunk of Harrison is repeated over and over – apparently, repetition is McCartney's favourite effect – before being swallowed by junkyard-styled noise. The grunge ambiance works, sort of, as McCartney takes us on a stumbling journey through the bare bones of an actual song, accompanied by a rudimentary drum kit and somebody tickling a chicken. **C+**

[bonus]

"Nova" [Paul McCartney]
[Joyful Company of Singers] *A Garland for Linda* is a tribute album for McCartney's late wife, with proceeds going to the cancer charity Garland Appeal. McCartney joins nine other composers – among them John Tavener and Giles Swayne – who offer original classical pieces for a concert led by conductor Peter Broadbent. The pieces are performed by the Joyful Company of Singers, a choir of virtuosos who've performed around the planet. On "Nova," the choir sings a quietly powerful piece of sorrow, despair, and long nights alone. Considering his hit-or-miss record at classical composition, McCartney's effort is striking and just this side of beautiful. [*A Garland for Linda*, 2000] **B**

"Maybe Baby" [Buddy Holly and Norman Petty]
A cover you've probably never heard, lifted from the film of the same name, which you've probably never seen. McCartney's remake [produced by Jeff Lynne] mainly adds volume, thanks to a heavy metal guitar that grinds out the riff and encourages you to leave the theater, quickly. [*Maybe Baby Soundtrack*, 2000] **C**

"Clean Machine" [John Lennon and Paul McCartney]
A track intended to publicize a vegetarian biking club who in turn supported the Linda McCartney Food Company. "Clean Machine" is a pure McCartney dance track without the assistance of Youth, the Fireman, or anybody else. Cannibalizing – destroying? – "Penny Lane," it's a simple-minded mix of disco clichés: a pounding four-on-the-floor bass drum, endless repetitions of tired riffs, and hopelessly dated electronic scrawls, all of it reminiscent of KC and the Sunshine Band on a bad night. [Internet only] **F**

"God Bless California/Black Gipsy" [Leslie Fradkin; guest performer: Paul McCartney]
[Leslie Fradkin] These two songs by the amiable duo are conservative, not particularly pretty, but competent and professional, vaguely like James Taylor. McCartney adds bass and vocals. He supplies nothing flashy, but to his credit, he doesn't upstage anyone. [*Godzology*; "God Bless California" also appears on Fradkin's solo album *Pass on This Side*.] **B**

CHAPTER THIRTY-THREE:

DRIVING RAIN [2001]

Produced by David Kahne
Charted at 26 [US], 46 [UK]

In addition to McCartney's usual planning problems [Should he cut the questionable songs or record them all? Should he keep them sparse or go for dump-it-all-in arrangements?], dark skies hung over *Driving Rain,* making it difficult to maintain his focus on the record. Namely, how to reconcile his impending engagement with his unresolved feelings for the deceased Linda.

That McCartney believed a new relationship would help him recover from his haunting loss is understandable, but reality remained to be seen. While other artists – John Lennon, Bob Dylan – used their personal turmoil to create compelling art, this was not McCartney's way. Difficult situations were kept at arm's length. For McCartney, recording generally meant escape, not confrontation.

In Linda's place came Heather Mills, a model and activist who met McCartney at a Pride of Britain event in London where McCartney was scheduled to present an animal rights award. At the time, Mills was 33, McCartney was about 59. McCartney was taken with the attractive and intelligent Mills, and soon became full-blown smitten. His family, however, was not impressed, especially daughter Stella, who allegedly accused Mills of wanting his money. Paul listened to his family's objections, but married Mills anyway.

Paul and Heather separated in 2006. Following a bitter court battle, they divorced in 2008. Heather walked away with a settlement reportedly worth over $25,000,000. McCartney told the *Daily Mail* the marriage had been one of the biggest mistakes of his life.

But back to *Driving Rain.* McCartney's refusal – or inability – to focus his talents on the reality consuming him resulted in artistic decisions that weren't the best. Answers to the production questions were often answered in unsatisfying ways. Instead of being objectively judgmental, when in doubt, he did it anyway, failing to veto the jingoistic "Freedom" or the self-indulgent "Rinse the Raindrops." Instead of tightening up the arrangements, McCartney often tossed in any and all marginal elements [see "Riding Into Jaipur"] assuming – hoping? – that some would stick. Songs needing another rewrite ["Lonely Road"] were accepted as fine as they were.

Reception for *Driving Road* was all over the map, most critics declaring it competent but unimpressive. *NME*: "... all the unhinged beatnik wildness of a Neighborhood Watch meeting." " *AV Music*: " ... a few highlights balancing a fair amount of filler." *BBC*: "... a bit of lonely yearning would have made the material a little more challenging and rewarding." As for the fans, the album settled at #46 in the UK charts, McCartney's worst homeland performance to date.

"Lonely Road" [Paul McCartney]

A welcome mat for *Driving Rain*, or more accurately, a half-hearted swamp of maudlin backing, half-written verses, lyrical befuddlement, and non-specific ruminations on being in love with a woman he opts to keep in the shadows. The melody struggles up the scale, contrasting with McCartney's wild, thrilling leaps that used to come so naturally [check *Sgt. Pepper*'s "Fixing a Hole" for a stunning one]. The improv near the end, sort of a "Hey Jude" on arthritis meds, is close to painful. Paul refers to suffering – is this what he had in mind? **B-**

"From a Lover to a Friend" [Paul McCartney]

A cautious venture where McCartney declines to be precise or illuminating. Most likely, this is about thanking Heather for – what? Is he asking for permission to – what? Love them both? Examining this premise would be tolerable – barely – if we didn't have to endure a piecemeal song with a whiney vocal. For further study, I refer McCartney to John Lennon's "Oh Yoko." Maybe that song sucks too, but at least we know who we're dealing with. **B-**

"She's Given Up Talking" [Paul McCartney]

An ominous, somewhat pissed off vocal propelling "She's Giving Up Talking" encourages the repeated listenings that the rest of *Driving Rain* doesn't. Subtle electronic effects add to an eerie ambiance, and "eerie" is not a word often associated with McCartney. During an especially off-beat segment, McCartney sounds less like himself than he does an alien from outer space. And what's that unexpected noise at the end? An outer space toilet plunger? If so, thumbs up for the unexpected plunger. **B**

"Driving Rain" [Paul McCartney]

With a half-speed disco beginning, followed by lyrics that consist of counting to ten [on the same note, same up and down rhythm], this is a ride you might decline. Devoid of anything – words, music, performance, vocals, instrumentation – to catch your ear, it's hard to figure why this exists, except [1] David Kahne was out to lunch, [2] McCartney wanted it, or [3] McCartney's nuts. **D+**

"I Do" [Paul McCartney]

What do Weezer, the Beach Boys, the Castells, Lisa Loeb, and Edie Brickell have in common? All of them recorded songs titled "I Do," and all of them are superior to McCartney's faceless ode to somebody, somewhere. This flabby string of notes is so empty it makes you long for the insanity of "The Mess," which at least provides the entertaining spectacle of McCartney doing battle with the English language. Here, he sounds too sad to battle anything. **C-**

"Tiny Bubble" [Paul McCartney]

Could one of McCartney's inspirations be Don Ho? Purporting to instruct us on how to tell lies from non-lies, it's instead about McCartney's girlfriend [again] whom I guess is Heather [or is it?] and that groovy love [again] is spilling out of his eyeballs [ewww]. Quality-wise, it runs solidly behind "Tiny Bubbles," Don Ho's lounge favourite. **C**

"Magic" [Paul McCartney]

Is this about Linda? Who knows? He could be singing about a dead dog. Worse, McCartney seems distanced and distracted, start to finish. Hasn't he learned to spot filler when he hears it? Hasn't the producer? Or anyone? **D+**

"Your Way" [Paul McCartney]

Pseudo-country employing scrambled gibberish, written this way, I suspect, not because of ideas, but because the words rhyme. Vocally, he recalls the old McCartney in spots, but "Your Way" is so pedestrian, it hardly matters. **C**

"Spinning on an Axis" [Paul McCartney and James McCartney]

If I were an engineer at the *Driving Rain* sessions, I'd be giggling whenever I heard the lyrics to "Spinning on an Axis," so mind-bogglingly weak, they deserve a place in the Bip Bop Hall of Fame. McCartney apparently just woke up when he laid down the sleepy vocal, and the rest of it seems semi-improvised. Note the sloppy style, the spots where he gives up and lazily sings "eee"s and "ah"s, and the two-note dull-as-dishwater riff, courtesy of a superstar sounding like he'd rather be back under the covers. **C**

"About You" [Paul McCartney]

A minor key excursion into Heatherville, and boy, is he mad. But I wonder, about what? Lyrically, it's moon-in-June piffle. Melodically, it's all over the road, nothing special. Come to think of it, maybe he wants to snarl for a bit, if only for a change of pace. Pace-change, noted. **C**

"Heather" [Paul McCartney]

The instrumental section in the first half reminds one of a TV commercial. The vocal section is typical McCartney, sans a memorable lyric or robust melody. If this were removed from every copy of *Driving Rain*, few would complain. Or notice. **B-**

"Back in the Sunshine Again" [Paul McCartney and James McCartney]

A Heather number. Let this be a lesson: Be careful whom you immortalize in a song. Lucky for us all, McCartney chose a tuneless and emotion-free throwaway, too flabby to remember. **D**

"Your Loving Flame" [Paul McCartney]

Into the Jar of Love dips the hand of McCartney, drawing out a random tune that could be about Heather, Linda, or his housecleaner. Falls short, way short, of "The Long and Winding Road," which it resembles both in tempo and the occasional splatter of notes. A sad reminder that in the old days – say, the days of "Let It Be" – McCartney would toss songs like this in the scrap heap, muttering, "What was I thinking?" **C-**

"Riding Into Jaipur" [Paul McCartney]

With exotic instrumentation buzzing away, McCartney takes us back to his days with George Harrison. I can imagine "Riding Into Jaipur" cuddling up to "Within You Without You" [*Sgt. Pepper*] or "Love You To" [*Revolver*], then pushed away by those Beatles songs for being too trite. While you're deciding whether this throwback is worth doing, pay attention to the non-melodic verse or McCartney's attempt at modernizing the affair with electronic effects swiped from a high school science fair. What's that? Why, that's Harrison, spinning in his grave. **C-**

"Rinse the Raindrops" [Paul McCartney]

Looking to "Wild Life" for three-chord ideas is not a good sign. Hollering and whooping as was done on "Morse Moose and the Grey Goose" is not a good sign. Trying to beat "Check My Machine" for the longest filler ever is not a good sign. Of course, this is a textbook example of filler at its most arrogant and self-indulgent, so if McCartney doesn't take home the trophy, it's not for lack of trying. **D**

"Freedom" [Paul McCartney]

A response to the 911 tragedy, McCartney swings for a universal sing-a-long like "Give Peace a Chance," and misses totally, maybe because it's less an anthem and more like a theme song for the Republican National Committee. Making it worse, Paul doesn't sound like his heart's in it, not a good approach when god's lurking in the lyrics. Still worse, the song's aspirations to be an "Imagine"-like classic are pathetic. The swelling applause at the end – which is there because McCartney gave his approval for every detail, like he almost always does – well, les say it doesn't make this awful song endearing. **D-**

[bonus]

"Bip Bop/Hey Diddle [Alternate]"

McCartney's hit packages – *Wings Greatest* [1978], *All the Best* [1978], *Wingspan* [2001], and *Pure McCartney* [2016] – are useless money-wasters for the collector, as virtually all of the material has been played to death on the radio or not worth collecting. As for genuine rarities, forget it. [Where's "Waterspout?" "Yvonne's the One?"]. The redundant hit packages include *Wings Greatest* [1978]. Might casual fans be interested? Maybe, especially if they're teenagers unfamiliar with his early work. But for the hardcore? No.

However, "Bip Bop/Hey Diddle" turned up on *Wingspan: Hits and History* [2001] and to date, it seems to be the only place you can find it. I think. It's hard to find the words to convey the depths to which this track plummets. Maybe it's easier to decide which is worse by hearing them side to side. ["Bip Bop" wins.] Be that as it may, if you want a complete collection, you have no choice but to hold your nose and fork over the cash. [*Wingspan*] **F**

"Vanilla Sky" [Paul McCartney]

The lyrics go a long way in explaining McCartney's workaholic tendencies, as they make a point of how you shouldn't fritter away your time, since you might drop dead any second. Written at the request of Cameron Crowe for the soundtrack of his weirdo film of the same name, it's an understated "Blackbird"-esque acoustic piece, half-friendly half-spooky. It was nominated for an Academy Award and lost, but what do they know? A simple melody, touching lyrics, and overall, a song with enough muscle to reward the listener with his finest song in a long time. [*Vanilla Sky: Music from the Motion Picture*] **A-**

"I'm Down [NYC Version]" [John Lennon and Paul McCartney]

[Various Artists] At a massive fundraiser in commemoration of the 9/11 tragedy – with live contributions by David Bowie, the Who, and a host of others – McCartney favoured the delirious crowd with a mini-set that included the rarely performed "I'm Down." McCartney blasted through the raise-the-roof rocker, yowling and looking like he could play this all night. "I'm Down" rarely has been included on his concert set lists because … ? [*Concert for New York City*] **B+**

"Yesterday [NYC Version]" [John Lennon and Paul McCartney]
[Various Artists] McCartney croons this like a seasoned professional, not meant as a compliment. Maybe he's having a bad night. Maybe he forgot why he wrote it. Maybe he should set it aside for a while and, uh, let it be. [*Concert for New York City*] **C**

"Let It Be [NYC Version]" [John Lennon and Paul McCartney]
[Various Artists] Presenting this at a benefit concert raises the same old dilemma. It's appropriate for the setting, but a drag to sit through at home, one … more … time. [*Concert for New York City*] **C**

"Freedom [Reprise] [NYC Version]" [Paul McCartney]
[Various Artists] If McCartney is confused as to why this never took off, perhaps he should [1] take another look at the lyrics, and [2] scan the audience – is that Donald Trump applauding? [*Concert for New York City*] **D-**

"Receptacle for the Respectable" [Super Furry Animals; guest performer: Paul McCartney]
[Super Furry Animals] McCartney continues his career as a first-call carrot chomper, repaying a favour to the Super Furry Animals for their contribution to *Liverpool Sound Collage*. McCartney began his carrot-munching career with a performance on the Beach Boys' "Vegetables," part of their ill-fated *Smile* project. As on "Vegetables," McCartney is rumoured to chomp celery here as well. [*Rings Around the World*] **B**

"So Bad [Pagano Version]" [Paul McCartney; guest performer: Paul McCartney]
[Lindsay Pagano] A sparse, soothing, almost whispered rendition of the *Pipes of Peace* number, with McCartney vocally floating in and out. Pagano's take isn't particularly dramatic reading, but her simpler, almost childlike approach better suits "So Bad," so she wins. Pagano, by the way, is a member of the band Stellar Mojo who auditioned on the TV show *The Voice*. [*Love & Faith & Inspiration*] **B**

"I'm Partial to Your Abracadabra" [Ian Dury and Chaz Jankel; guest performer: Paul McCartney]
[Various Artists] McCartney, with the Blockheads serving as his band, joined Sinead O'Conner, Wreckless Eric, and others in a tribute to Ian Dury, a mainstay of the British new wave/punk scene circa 1977, who died of colorectal cancer at the age of 57. McCartney, a fan, breezes though one of Dury's most famous numbers, not quite up to the original, but fun all the same. [*New Boots and Panties Collection*] **B**

"That's All Right [Sun Tribute]" [Arthur Crudup; guest performer: Paul McCartney]
[Various Artists] As his tribute to Sun Records – a record featuring Bob Dylan and Jimmy page covering Jerry Lee Lewis, Johnny Cash, and other Sun artists – McCartney chose the song that put Elvis on the map. Elvis burst through the radio-friendly clutter of his conventional stalwarts with a nuclear charged performance that made him sound like he's about to be indicted for assault. McCartney, trying to emulate the breezy tough guy image that made Elvis a star, falls far behind, sounding less like a juvenile delinquent and more like your old uncle screaming at the TV. [*Good Rockin' Tonight: The Legacy of Sun Records*, 2001] **B-**

CHAPTER THIRTY-FOUR:

BACK IN THE U.S. [2002]

Produced by David Kahne
Charted at 8 [US], 5 [UK, for Back in the World]

When in doubt, what the hell, give 'em another live album. This would make four. To put it another way, that's equivalent to 11 vinyl records [and the finish line is not in sight – see *Good Evening New York City*, coming right up]. Or to put it yet another way, with the release of *Back in the U.S.*, there would now be six different recordings of "Hey Jude" for the deep-pocketed consumer [the other five *Knebworth: the Album*, *Tripping the Live Fantastic*, *Music for Montserrat*, *Back in the World*, *Party at the Palace*].

And to make matters more interesting – or more aggravating – McCartney again insisted on reversing credits for all Beatles tracks, changing them from the traditional Lennon-McCartney to Paul's preferred McCartney-Lennon. After all, was it not he who wrote them all, or nearly all? And wasn't his name dropped from 1997's *Lennon Legend* "Give Peace a Chance"? True, but not everyone was convinced these points justified changing a long and established tradition. Allegedly, Ringo was disgusted with McCartney's tactics. Yoko Ono was supposedly so upset that she contemplated legal action. But McCartney was unmoved. The new credits would stay.

Credits aside, *Back in the U.S.* was drifting mighty close to a full-fledged Beatles album, one with a single genuine Beatle holding the fort. Of the 37 songs on *Back in the U.S.*, 22 were Beatles songs. *Driving Rain*, which these concerts supposedly were supporting, was represented by a mere three.

As always, McCartney maintained that all live material would be reproduced as close to the recorded versions as possible. To this end, McCartney's choices for his supporting band hit the mark. In addition to Paul Wickens, a mainstay of previous tours, were Abe Laboriel Jr. [a Berklee College of Music graduate who'd played with Steve Vai and Sting], Rusty Anderson [veteran of Living Daylights and Ednaswap], and Brian Ray [stalwart of Keith Richards]. Not only had these pros helped flesh out *Driving Rain*, they'd continue touring with McCartney for the better part of the next two decades. Longer, in fact, than McCartney's time spent with the Beatles.

"Hello Goodbye [Live 2002]" [Paul McCartney and John Lennon]
The problem with attempting to replicate a song as well known as this one is that cynical fans can immediately spot the differences. It's especially tricky with psychedelic milestones where the studio plays as much a part of the overall sound as the musicians [the Beach Boys have grappled with this for years with "Good Vibrations"]. McCartney gives it his all, but substituting keyboards for strings doesn't help, nor does his attempt at vocally copying the swirling bridge in the middle. The song, of course, is terrific, and makes up for any live deficiencies. Almost. **B**

"Jet [Live 2002]" [Paul and Linda McCartney]
Back in the days when the Beatles were poison ivy – that is, as far as McCartney was concerned – Paul placated the rock-hungry multitudes by performing this rip-roarer on *Wings Over America* and solidified it as a concert highlight. It rocketed then, it rocks now, and the performances and arrangements stay close to the record. Which suggests the question, why do we need it again? Sure, it's fun to hear Paul cheerfully spouting good-natured nonsense, and equally fun listening to the drummer pound holes in his snare. But is it fun yet again? When you're paying for it? **B**

"All My Loving [Live 2002]" [Paul McCartney and John Lennon]
Equivalent to lighting firecrackers under every seat in the house. How could this fail? Well, it could be

rushed. It could be someone other than the Beatles, like Wings Mark II [or III or IV]. Other than that, it's as good as McCartney gets. **B+**

"Getting Better [Live 2002]" [Paul McCartney and John Lennon]
A stunner, a reverent nod to *Sgt Pepper*, and another inducer of sighs. A little soft around the edges, and the backing vocals lack Lennon's sneer, but this one, all by itself, stomps the entirety of *Driving Rain* into the ground. **B+**

"Coming Up [Live 2002]" [Paul McCartney]
As if to prove McCartney is more than the sum of his Beatles days, along comes this imaginative rocker, replete with snaky riff out front and McCartney's playfully contagious vocal. Too bad he's already released a top of the line live version [*McCartney II Remaster*], which makes this redundant. **B-**

"Let Me Roll It [Live 2002]" [Paul and Linda McCartney]
Speaking of redundant, "Let Me Roll It" received a decent treatment on *Tripping the Live Fantastic*, meaning there's hardly a demand for another one. Maybe from the audience, but not from the cash-deprived stay-at-homes. And the jam tacked on to the end suggests that McCartney should lay off jamming. **B-**

"Lonely Road [Live 2002]" [Paul McCartney]
Putting this within three notches of "Getting Better" was not a wise programming decision. Actually, the crunchy guitar livens up the undead version on *Driving Rain*, as does the modest increase in tempo. But it still smells funny. **B-**

"Driving Rain [Live 2002]" [Paul McCartney]
One of the worst tracks on *Driving Rain* gains nothing in a live setting, and I'm betting that after the tour, 'Driving Rain' will join "Spirits of Ancient Egypt" and "Call Me Back Again" in the cemetery. **D**

"Your Loving Flame [Live 2002]" [Paul McCartney]
An unimproved snore-a-thon about – Heather? Who knows? Bottom drawer, locked, key tossed in the ocean. **D**

"Blackbird [Live 2002]" [Paul McCartney and John Lennon]
Motivations for buying this version: [1] failure to purchase a previous live version [*Wings Over America* or *Unplugged*], [2] obsessive completist, [3] a desire to try out your stereo with a new CD. **B**

"Every Night [Live 2002]" [Paul McCartney]
As it did on *Unplugged*, "Every Night" sounds like an also-ran compared to the Beatles tunes surrounding it. It drags less here than it did on *Unplugged*, giving it a mild electric jolt, and the sparse acoustic arrangement shifts attention to the not-bad melody. **B**

"We Can Work It Out [Live 2002]" [Paul McCartney and John Lennon]
Another *Unplugged* retread and a valiant attempt at recapturing the Beatles masterwork, except as an all-acoustic rendition dominated by McCartney, it nibbles around the edges rather than capture the assault of the original. **B**

"Mother Nature's Son [Live 2002]" [Paul McCartney and John Lennon]
McCartney belts out a tune that should be more of a whisper in your ear. Still, the accordion – played by the ever-nimble Paul Wickens – provides a unique support which makes a familiar song sound new-ish. McCartney's vocal, no surprise, is remarkably good. **B**

"Vanilla Sky [Live 2002]" [Paul McCartney]
One of McCartney's best, "Vanilla Sky" doesn't show up on *Back in the World* [see below]. A disappointment, although purchasers of *Back in the U.S.* will have to settle for a slightly inferior version, marred by whistling and a whiff of iffy scat singing. **B**

"You Never Give Me Your Money [Live 2002]" [Paul McCartney and John Lennon]
The music provides more of a challenge than, say, "My Love," but McCartney's got a first-class crew aboard,

and they're up for it. Still, despite the band's versatility and good will, this pales before *Abbey Road*, as it's a bit stiff and much less atmospheric. **B-**

"Carry That Weight [Live 2002]" [Paul McCartney and John Lennon]

There are few songs, perhaps none, more joyous in the face of resignation than "Carry That Weight" from *Abbey Road*. But as presented here, this sacred artifact seems like just another tedious sing-a-long. **B-**

"The Fool on the Hill [Live 2002]" [Paul McCartney and John Lennon]

A stripped-down change from *Magical Mystery Tour* – just piano and a few well-chosen keyboards – places the emphasis solidly on the melody. McCartney has the opportunity to show off his pipes, and why not? His killer voice can make your spine tingle. For the most part, he resists showing off a repertoire of vocal tricks like fellow superstars Celine Dion, Christina Aguilera, Steve Perry – you name them, McCartney vaults over them. [Except, well, see "Maybe I'm Amazed."] **B+**

"Here Today [Live 2002]" [Paul McCartney]

Really, who cares about the awkward lyrics, the rushed bridge, or the semi-clumsy middle eight? McCartney aims for the heart and slices it in two. **B+**

"Something [Live 2002]" [George Harrison]

Tender reading of Harrison's masterwork, performed with a lone ukulele. Poignant, sung beautifully. Problem is, McCartney's version on *Concert for George* with the full band floating in behind him makes this seem a little empty. But I can think of a lot of "Something" covers that are worse than this, including ones by Joe Cocker and Elvis Presley. **B+**

"Eleanor Rigby [Live 2002]" [Paul McCartney and John Lennon]

"Eleanor Rigby" is great for concerts, but robbery for home listeners who've bought *Tripping the Live Fantastic*. And Paul, hire some strings already. **B-**

"Here, There, and Everywhere [Live 2002]" [Paul McCartney and John Lennon]

Unplugged: Excellent. *Back in the US*: How much did you say you paid for this**? B-**

"Band on the Run" [Live 2002]" [Paul and Linda McCartney]

Excepting nostalgia buffs, time has not been kind to the live "Band on the Run." Maybe it's just an easy target for broke consumers mumbling about having to buy it over and over. Am I wrong, or do the dumb lyrics seem dumber? Do the clumsy transitions seem clumsier? And the cheesy opening synthesizer – somebody call Velveeta. The acoustic verses at the end still hold up – for now. This is the seventh [!] version [Studio, Original, *One Hand Clapping*, Live 1976, Live 1979, Live 1990, Live 2002] if you absolutely must have them all. **C**

"Back in the USSR [Live 2002]" [Paul McCartney and John Lennon]

A top-drawer Beatles song demands a top-drawer treatment, which "Back in the USSR" didn't get on *Tripping the Live Fantastic*. Here, it's energized and jet-propelled. It's also a bit faster than before, which means the band is either excited or anxious to get back to the hotel. This time, it's full-blown exciting, as if they don't want it to end. But, you ask, what if I already bought *Tripping the Live Fantastic*? Too bad for you. **B+**

"Maybe I'm Amazed [Live 2002]" [Paul McCartney]

One of the most difficult McCartney compositions to sing effectively, owing to its melodic swoops, a transition of sad contemplation to a near-maniacal frustration, raising shouts, and a vocal cuddle at the end of the bridge. But a song this demanding requires a virtuoso singer, and though McCartney routinely accepts the challenge, there are bits of shakiness in this version that make one wonder if perhaps it's possible that his voice isn't what it used to be: a revision of the bridge that softens the screams on the original, a modest but noticeable drop-off in the wordless cooing, a simplification of the melodic jumps on the second bridge, an elimination of the yell in mid-bridge. All of these changes, subtle as they might be, do in fact make the song easier to sing. This is hardly a crime, and god knows a man of his age [roughly 60] has earned a pass, especially considering his penchant for long concerts. But McCartney has nearly unlimited studio time to correct mistakes, meaning this one is likely to be as good as it gets. It's an applaudable performance, but at the same time a bit disturbing. This could be a preview of coming attractions. **B**

"C Moon [Live 2002]" [Paul and Linda McCartney]
I would've preferred the flip side, ["Hi Hi Hi"], but my request must've got lost in the mail. This time, McCartney approaches "C Moon" with a casual attitude that acknowledges its goofiness, making it more fun to hear than the original. Beneath the bouncy reggae lies the lyrics that portray a fellow mildly pissed at being constantly misunderstood. Misunderstood? Gee, Paul – it's not like you didn't ask for it. **B**

"My Love [Live 2002]" [Paul and Linda McCartney]
A decent version of a blah ballad, one seemingly designed to induce wincing in anyone who's experienced the reality of a love affair gone haywire – it trivializes sincere feelings by just brushing the surface. And it makes McCartney's love object – emphasis on "object" – more ephemeral than usual. **B –**

"Can't Buy Me Love [Live 2002]" [Paul McCartney and John Lennon]
As demonstrated in *Tripping the Live Fantastic*, McCartney has trouble getting rid of the lethargy inherent in this now nearly 40 year old rocker, settling instead for a creakiness that reminds one of an aging Vegas star. A different arrangement might help, say, an acoustic version or a slower tempo. **B-**

"Freedom [Live 2002]" [Paul McCartney]
An intended crowd pleaser that fires up, well, nobody. **D-**

"Live and Let Die [Live 2002]" [Paul and Linda McCartney]
How many versions of a song does McCartney think we should buy? Two? Four? This is the eighth. **C**

"Let It Be [Live 2002]" [Paul McCartney and John Lennon]
Paul McCartney, author of "Hey Jude" and "Golden Slumbers," also wrote and recorded "Spirits of Ancient Egypt" and "Bip Bop" a short time later. A quick analysis would suggest that McCartney functions better [1] in a group, [2] when he's younger, or [3] when he's working with someone who can say "no," [like John Lennon]. By the way, this is McCartney's sixth version of "Let It Be." Credit cards accepted. **B-**

"Hey Jude [Live 2002]" [Paul McCartney and John Lennon]
As close to the Beatles as he can make it, which is ... not very. The sing-along between the boys and the girls has grown beyond irritating to the grating. The compulsion to do the same thing, the same way, over and over, may indicate the possibility of a serious emotional condition. Perhaps McCartney suffers from OCD? **C**

"The Long and Winding Road [Live 2002]" [Paul McCartney and John Lennon]
Before you hear this, ask yourself, "Will he do the sweet Beatles version or the Elvis in Vegas version?" Surprise – it's Elvis! Complete with irrelevant jazzy riffs, vocal gymnastics, and a dollop of quasi-fake sincerity, all for this sixth McCartney version [*Wings Over America*, *Give My Regards to Broad Street*, Live 1989, Live 1990, Anaheim 2002], brought to you by MPL Communications Inc. **C**

"Lady Madonna [Live 2002]" [Paul McCartney and John Lennon]
With a tight focus on the melody, no contest – this version beats *Wings Over America*. The band, at this point earning accolades as the best Paul's ever had, plays loose and muscular. Sore point: backing vocals come from the lounge and not the garage, where they were born. **B**

"I Saw Her Standing There [Live 2002]" [Paul McCartney and John Lennon]
A tune so associated with youthful vigor and lust that a 60-year-old gentleman like McCartney might want to reconsider, regardless of his near-godly power to belt 'em out for three hours at a clip. Given that, this is a laudable performance from somebody's grandpa to somebody's granddaughter. **B**

"Yesterday [Live 2002]" [Paul McCartney and John Lennon]
Alert the I-gotta-have-it-all collector. I lost count – is this version number 98? **C**

"Sgt. Pepper's Lonely Hearts Club Band [Live 2002]" [Paul McCartney and John Lennon]
The band cranks up a semi-grungy, but less druggie "Sgt. Pepper," transforming it into a drink-and-be-merry anthem instead of the psychedelic mind-scrambler as it appears on the original album. But this is a concert, so that's fine, and details would be swallowed up by the ecstatic crowd anyway. It's a little over a minute long, too short to hang on to. So we jump right in to ... **B**

"The End [Live 2002]" [Paul McCartney and John Lennon]
... the conclusion to *Abbey Road*, here turned into something triumphant, or at least, more upbeat. Yes, McCartney sings the intro bit almost exactly like the album, the drummer plays Ringo's solo almost exactly like the album, and the guitars base their solos almost exactly like the album before flying off into parts unknown. Likewise, the coda is close to the same, and in its entirety, makes for a perfect concert finale. That is, a Beatles finale. **B**

[bonus]

"Calico Skies [Live 2003]" [Paul McCartney]
A few months after the release of *Back in the U.S.*, along came *Back in the World*, changed a bit to accommodate the imaginary taste differences elsewhere on the planet. Or maybe it was decided that including the excruciating "Freedom" would drag the whole thing to hell. In any event, gone were "Vanilla Sky" [aww], "C Moon" [too bad], and "Freedom" [lucky Europeans]. In their place came "She's Leaving Home," "Michelle," "Let 'Em In," a modestly different "Hey Jude," and this one, an amiable ballad from *Flaming Pie*, more energetic than the studio track and accompanied by an rubbery accordion. "My Love," "Lady Madonna," and any [or all] of the *Driving Rain* numbers should've been bumped off *Back in the U.S.* for this one. [*Back in the World*, 2003] **B**

"Michelle [Live 2003]" [John Lennon and Paul McCartney]
C'mon! We just had this on *Paul is Live*. The more prominent backgrounds don't make it worth another visit. [*Back in the World*, 2003] **C**

"Let 'Em In [Live 2003]" [Paul McCartney]
If we're bent on reeling off the hit parade, you could do worse than including the slight but masterfully arranged "Let 'Em In." So laid back it needs its pulse checked, McCartney slides though with an exceptional vocal. [*Back in the World*, 2003] **B**

"She's Leaving Home [Live 2003]" [John Lennon and Paul McCartney]
The song, the arrangement, the performance, all magnificent. May the dork who decided this wasn't worth inclusion in *Back in the U.S.* – and "My Love" was? – be haunted for eternity by John Lennon's pissed-off ghost. [*Back in the World*, 2003] **A-**

"Hey Jude [Live 2003]" [Paul McCartney and John Lennon]
Allegedly recorded in Mexico City, not New York City as indicated on *Back in the U.S.*, the microscopic vocal difference on this *Back in the World* version are not worth the trouble it takes to cue it up. [*Back in the World*, 2003] **C**

"India" [Paul McCartney]
Written prior to the *Driving Rain* sessions, about the same time as "Riding Into Jaipur," this obscure track was part of the *Back in the US DVD* "Secret Website," also available on YouTube. Opening with an ominous drone, McCartney enters with a full-bodied vocal, accompanied by lush harmonies and a dreamy melody. Although redundant – it needs a bridge or a chorus to offset the verse – it's an interesting start, one worth developing, and certainly topping the majority of *Driving Rain*. [*Back in the US DVD*] **B**

"Waiting for Your Train" [Paul McCartney]
Another *Back in the US DVD* snippet, apparently performed once. McCartney at the piano, musing dreamily about some woman. Agreeable, but with little to distinguish if, not that different from other McCartney songs of the era. [*Back in the US DVD*] **B-**

"For You Blue" [George Harrison; guest performer: Paul McCartney]
[Various Artists] For a George Harrison memorial concert held at the Royal Albert Hall with an all-star lineup that included Eric Clapton, Tom Petty, and Ringo Starr, McCartney stole the show. Starting with an unexpected but mannered rendition of the Beatles "For You Blue," McCartney's performance was touching, energetic, and flawless, marred only by an arrangement that tried to capture the original, but came up understandably short. A minor criticism of a major moment. [*Concert for George*, 2003] **B+**

"Something [Live 2003]" [George Harrison; guest performer: Paul McCartney]
[Various Artists] McCartney's affectionate tribute to his comrade begins with his controlled, warm voice accompanied by a ukulele, a favourite instrument of George's. About halfway though, the band eases in with Eric Clapton's stately guitar solo out in front, truly breathtaking. McCartney adds his high harmony to Clapton's melody, the band crescendos, then check the film – is that Paul dabbing a tear? [*Concert for George*, 2003] **A-**

"All Things Must Pass" [George Harrison: guest performer: Paul McCartney]
[Various Artists] After trying continually to get the Beatles to record this, most likely for *Let It Be*, Harrison gave up, reviving it on his monster *All Things Must Pass* album. McCartney sings like an angel, the band plays respectfully, but the song can't divest itself of its inherent sluggishness, a compositional impediment that Harrison struggled with for the duration of his career, and in this case, probably obvious to the Beatles from their first hearing. [*Concert for George*, 2003] **B**

"While My Guitar Gently Weeps" [George Harrison; guest performer: Paul McCartney]
[Various Artists] Virtually a note-for-note recreation the original track, with [of course] vocal substitutions, this is the Harrison song that made one wonder if equal billing with Lennon/McCartney was forthcoming. McCartney mans the piano for the unforgettable opening riff, Clapton sings, McCartney harmonizes, followed by Clapton's blazing solo, maybe not up to his Beatles take, but close. Unfortunately, Clapton and McCartney singing the same lines simultaneously is superfluous, as are the vocals over Clapton's extended solo at the end. And horns? Really? [*Concert for George*, 2003] **B**

"Live and Let Die [Alternate]" [Paul and Linda McCartney]
[Various Artists] A lesser, airy version with a so-so vocal, presumably a rejected take. What it's doing in *The In-Laws* movie is anybody's guess, except that since Jeff Lynne is here with "Don't Bring Me Down" and Badfinger supplies "No Matter What," maybe McCartney didn't want to feel left out. [*Music from the Motion Picture The In-Laws*] **B-**

"Calico Skies [Hope Benefit]" [Paul McCartney]
[War Child] An indisputably worthy cause for victims of the Iraq War, sponsored by the War Child charity and the *Daily Mirror*. McCartney's contribution to this concept album is a re-recording of the *Flaming Pie* track. For the casual fan, indistinguishable from the original. Still, anybody who coughed up for more than one live McCartney album ought to be able to fork it over for some genuine goodwill. [*Hope*] **B**

"A Friend Like You" [Brian Wilson and Steve Kalinich; guest performer: Paul McCartney]
[Brian Wilson] When two giants with accomplishments that tower over the competition finally get together, we get ... not much. A love song to McCartney, Wilson sadly sings the where-have-we-heard-it-before melody, sounding like he can use all the friends he can get, while McCartney chimes in irrelevantly. [*Gettin' in Over My Head*] **C**

"A Time to Love" [Stevie Wonder and India Arie Simpson; guest performer: Paul McCartney]
[Stevie Wonder] After a nearly decade-long hiatus, Wonder came back strong with this all-star album featuring Prince, En Vogue, and India Arie. McCartney showed up with his guitar, but strictly for background. Slickly produced and a bit too long at 9-plus minutes, it may not be Wonder at his finest – the honor goes to *Songs in the Key of Life* and *Innervisions* – but it's in the ballpark. [*A Time to Love*] **B**

"Inside Thing/Let 'Em In" [Paul McCartney, Lukas Burton, Billy Lawrie, and Lulu]
[Lulu] The "To Sir With Love" songstress snuggles up with McCartney on this novelty tune. Lulu's "Inside Thing" – a cute track cleverly using the "Let 'Em In" backing – dominates, as does Lulu's playful vocal.

A snatch of irrelevant rap in a feeble attempt to make it contemporary nearly derails it. [*Lulu Together*, 2002]. **B**

"All Shook Up [Elvis Tribute]" [Otis Blackwell and Elvis Presley; guest performer: Paul McCartney]
[Various Artists] A screamer, at least as interpreted by McCartney, who tosses in a sneer or two for good measure. Following Presley is not an easy task, so give Paul credit for avoiding slavish duplication and coming up with a credible track that'd be right at home on *Choba B CCCP*. [*A Tribute to the King*, 2002] **B**

"All You Need is Love [Palace Version]" [John Lennon and Paul McCartney; guest performer: Paul McCartney]
[Various Artists] A concert at Buckingham Palace for Queen Elizabeth's Golden Jubilee, featuring a full orchestra. Rod Stewart kicks off "All You Need is Love" with a shaky first verse, followed by an enthused Joe Cocker on verse two, followed by everybody in the universe. Paul comes in after the chorus, and I wonder if he's thinking, maybe this would be better than "Let It Be" for these charity events? [2002] **B**

"Hey Jude [Palace Version]" [John Lennon and Paul McCartney; guest performer: Paul McCartney]
[Various Artists] The crowd loves it. But do we have to buy it one more time? No-o-o-o! [*Party at the Palace*, 2002] **C**

CHAPTER THIRTY-FIVE:

TWIN FREAKS [2005]

Produced by Paul McCartney and Roy Kerr
Did not chart [US], did not chart [UK]

"I'm really pleased to be working with Fidelity Investments"
PAUL MCCARTNEY, BOSTON.COM. BUSINESS [THE BOSTON GLOBE, SEPT. 8, 2005]

"It was a phenomenally good value for what we paid for it ... I mean, this is Paul McCartney."
KEITH DAUL, LEXUS' NATIONAL MANAGER OF EVENT MARKETING COMMENTING ON THE LEXUS PARTNERSHIP WITH PAUL MCCARTNEY [AUTOMOTIVE NEWS, NOV. 14, 2005]

Back in the 1960s, the era of the Beatles, the reaction from young folk who saw their musical heroes with their arms around international corporations was nothing short of outrage, crying "Sell out!" until their throats were sore. Rock stars were here, corporate bigwigs over there, and never the twain shall meet.

But times changed. These days, everybody – or maybe it just seems like everybody – cozies up to the corporate world and their easy money as fast as you can say "Silly Love Songs." In the eighties, the Rolling Stones struck a multi-million-dollar deal with Jovan, the perfume fellows, to sponsor the Stones' upcoming tour. Beyonce guzzled soda pop for Pepsi. Taylor Swift swallowed Diet Coke. Even Bob Dylan signed a deal to appear in ads for what was surely his favourite company, Victoria's Secret.

Still, eyebrows were raised when during a break in the televised game between the Oakland Raiders and the New England Patriots [September 8, 2005], up popped Paul McCartney in a commercial. As "Band on the Run" played in the background, viewers were treated to a series of photos of you-know-who that reinforced his image as an accomplished guy, climaxing with the Fidelity Investments logo, proclaiming their slogan "Smart Move." Later in a statement, McCartney said about the company, "We have a lot in common – a commitment to helping people, a dedication to the arts, and a belief that you should never stop doing what you love doing."

This was not McCartney's only non-musical brush with the corporate world. Later that year, he agreed to a partnership with Lexus, the luxury car maker. As part of the deal, Lexus became a sponsor of McCartney's upcoming tour, while McCartney gave permission to use an image of his Hofner base to be painted on the side of a one-of-a-kind RX 400h hybrid Lexus. The car was auctioned off in a raffle, the proceeds going to one of McCartney's favourite charities. As a thank you, Lexus presented Paul with a spiffy new LS600H hybrid. Unfortunately, the auto was flown in from Japan, making its carbon footprint many times bigger than if it'd been delivered by ship. Allegedly, the eco-conscious McCartney was not happy, but I suppose that sometimes things take a wrong turn when dealing with corporations of this magnitude.

Meanwhile, as if his business activities weren't enough to keep him occupied, McCartney had a musical project requiring his attention, possibly his oddest album to date, *Twin Freaks*, which slipped into the world as a limited run vinyl release and eventually as a digital download on iTunes and Amazon. For this project, McCartney's partner was Roy Kerr [known professionally as Freelance Hellraiser], a studio wizard of high regard who'd worked with McCartney on his European Tour of 2004. In a pre-show spectacle, Kerr entertained the audience as a DJ, spinning and tweaking McCartney records until they all were unrecognizable. McCartney loved it.

With the tour ending, McCartney suggested they use Kerr's turntable expertise to create an album of remixes – more specifically, dance remixes. Kerr went to work on "Really Love You," an otherwise non-descript *Driving Rain* number, and turned it into a bubbling, throbbing track that thoroughly impressed McCartney.

How much work each man contributed to the project remains unknown, although it's a good guess that Kerr handled the studio work, while McCartney supervised and supplied sections of the original tracks. They worked quickly, completing the project in less than seven days. More focused than McCartney's Fireman records, *Twin Freaks* scored as dance music, embraced by dancers who delighted in the unusual sounds.

The bulk of McCartney's audience, however, would do well to think twice before investing their money in *Twin Freaks*, as it's highly unlikely that dance-o-phobes will find much to like. Instead, may I suggest you look into an investment with Fidelity?

"Really Love You [Freaks Version]" [Paul McCartney and Ringo Starr]
Take one non-descript filler, mix it up with studio prestidigitation, and the result is remix that's formidable, if slight. The always-smiling McCartney sounds like he's in a torture chamber while the simple beat throbs on and on. Monotony comes to visit about halfway though, as there's not a whole lot going on in the last half, and the six minutes begin to seem like six months. **B-**

"Long Haired Lady [Reprise] [Freaks Version]" [Paul and Linda McCartney]
Dullish after the previous track, though it's entertaining picking out the bits and pieces of McCartney's pre-existing repertoire [like the guitar riff from *McCartney*'s "Oo You"]. Too sparse to add up to much, although it adequately serves its purpose for the dance crowd, which of course is the reason this exists. McCartney zooms in with a snatch of "Long Haired Lady" at about the halfway point, which is looped to infinity, or seems that way. **B-**

"Rinse the Raindrops [Freaks Version]" [Paul McCartney]
Curious to see what these guys do with this yawner from *Driving Rain*? What do you know – they channelled Metallica. A blast of pseudo-James Hetfield guitar sets up a barrage of exciting noise. The rest is regular noise. Three minutes and out. **B**

"Darkroom [Freaks Version]" [Paul McCartney]
After the flying saucer picks us up, we're faced with standard dance track conventions that the previous "Rinse the Raindrops" and "Really Love You" avoided. Over a somewhat ordinary drum track, space noises and McCartney's not particularly spacey voice, the sounds swoop in and out for a couple of minutes before dwindling away. **B-**

"Live and Let Die [Freaks Version]" [Paul and Linda McCartney]
A disappointing change of pace. A remix opting for a trance feel, this one features light drums, a banging piano, and McCartney endlessly repeating the same line until you want to strangle him with an Eno tape. McCartney's pinched voice serves as a mood squasher. **C+**

"Temporary Secretary [Freaks Version]" [Paul McCartney]
Opening with a catchy guitar that blends perfectly with the synthesizer squiggle, this eases into McCartney's vocal, here resembling a mad scientist, adding more singing than is usual for *Twin Freaks*. The sum total is a pleasant, unobtrusive track seemingly intended for shy people risking their first dance, unlike "Rinse the Raindrops" which might scare them off the floor. **B**

"What's That You're Doing [Freaks Version]" [Paul McCartney and Stevie Wonder]
The grunting piggy bass introduces Wonder's vocal, which quickly moves into McCartney's harmony, essentially making it a variant of the original track instead of a complete reimagining. An okay update, but it sidesteps the promise of the album's more adventurous cuts. **B-**

"Oh Woman Oh Why [Freaks Version]" [Paul McCartney]
A variety of old tracks show up for dissection, including tidbits of "Venus and Mars," "Band on the Run," and

[possibly] "Another Day," plus McCartney babbling about babble. Spacey effects give way to an interesting combo of the vocal from "Oh Woman Oh Why" and the guitar riff from "Band on the Run," which stays just long enough to be noticed by the sharp-eared before whizzing away in a blur of science fiction sound. **B**

"Mumbo [Freaks Version]" [Paul and Linda McCartney]

Possibly the album's best – "Rinse the Raindrops" is right up there – this crazy quilt of a noise fest may usurp McCartney's "Let 'Em In" as his premiere drug song. [Mind you, he just describes them.] The mind-sizzle jumble sounding like a short-circuited *Twilight Zone* gets your attention, then drops you in the middle of a robotic ant invasion. All this in the first 15 seconds. What follows: a sped-up chanting McCartney [the leader of the ants], which builds and buzzes over a broadside of synthesizers and keyboards. About this time, you realize the original "Mumbo" wasn't a goofy time-waster, but a blueprint for a hostile takeover by insects. Alas, the problem sets in: a magnificent set-up needs a suitable climax, which this lacks. Otherwise, you'll have turn off your ears and let your feet do the listening. **B**

"Lalula [Freaks Version]" [Paul McCartney]

The only original track, "Lalula" combines an inventive percussion opening with an aggressive keyboard, a pinch of "Old Siam Sir," and [possibly] the riff from "Oh Woman Oh Why." It's brief, which is good. Altogether, it sounds like hungry cannibals dancing around a pot full of explorers. **B**

"Coming Up [Freaks Version]" [Paul McCartney]

This should have been called "Morris Moose and the Gray Goose, Part Two," since it uses that backing track to support the original "Coming Up" vocal. Not a whole lot of excitement here. Take away "Morris" and "Coming," you're left with a lot of percussion pinging and ponging. **B –**

"Maybe I'm Amazed [Freaks Version]" [Paul McCartney]

The ultra-romantic "Maybe I'm Amazed" gets ripped to shreds, a nod to the celibate. Sped up with the percussion reinforced, it stands in place until a few screams are superimposed near the end, which is about it. More of a trance piece than a dance extravaganza. **B-**

[bonus]

Never Stop Doing What You Love

Is McCartney rich enough? Apparently not. In conjunction with his tenure as a spokesperson for the international multi-billion dollar Fidelity Investments, McCartney issued *Never Stop Doing What You Love*, an hour-long album of old tracks intended specifically for Fidelity employees and clients. Among the songs included for the rockin' stock watchers were "Silly Love Songs," "Live and Let Die," and "Bluebird." Said Paul at the time, "Fidelity and I have a lot in common." **D**

CHAPTER THIRTY-SIX:

CHAOS AND CREATION IN THE BACK YARD [2005]

Produced by Nigel Godrich
Charted at 6 [US], 10 [UK]

With *Twin Freaks* out of his system, McCartney bounced back with *Chaos and Creation in the Back Yard*, a surprisingly strong album that left the lackluster *Driving Rain* in the dust. What accounted for the resurrected McCartney? Maybe it was just the luck of the draw, in that this batch of songs, by good fortune, were simply better than usual. Or maybe now that his emotional turmoil had more or less passed, with divorce just a bad memory, he could focus on his music with less distraction. Or perhaps the passage of time had blessed him with perspective.

One factor, a positive one for sure, was McCartney's decision to hand the production reins to a new and younger person, one attuned to the current record market and not quite as dazzled by the Beatles legend as others of McCartney's age. In his early thirties, Nigel Godrich was a seasoned producer and anything but an amateur, having produced all of Radiohead's albums, and also having worked with Beck, Roger Waters, and Pavement. Introduced to McCartney with high praise from George Martin, Godrich was amiable, confident, and knowledgeable. He also knew what he wanted. And he knew how to say no.

McCartney began with an idea to make an album based on Indian music. Godrich listened, then dismissed it. McCartney could do better – try again. McCartney had his new band in tow, ready to go. Godrich sent them home. They weren't needed.

Most importantly, Godrich was upfront in his opinions of McCartney's music. He told McCartney which songs could stand improvement and what they needed. On "Riding to Vanity Fair," for instance, McCartney wanted it fast, Godrich wanted it slow. In the end, slow it was. Godrich told him which songs were unworthy to be considered. "I really was getting a bit pissed," McCartney told the *UK Observer*. "But then, I have to realize, well, why work with a producer if you don't want his opinion?"

Owing largely to the clash of ideas and the resultant compromises, the album was a remarkable success. Godrich achieved a sparse, yet powerful sound that solidified McCartney as a thoughtful artist, placing him once again in the vanguard of contemporary music.

Fans agreed, pushing *Chaos and Creation* into the top ten of both the US and UK, even without the promotional push of a hit single. *Rolling Stone* called it "the freshest sounding McCartney album in years." *The Guardian*: " ... a sense of purpose, lovely tunes in abundance, and charm." *Time*: "McCartney's first album that matters since the Beatles broke up." It was nominated for several Grammy Awards: Album of the Year, Best Pop Vocal Album, and Best Male Pop Performance. Godrich was nominated for Non-Classical Producer of the Year. And "Jenny Wren," the stillborn single, won for Best Male Pop Performance.

To date, Paul McCartney and Nigel Godrich have never worked together again.

"Fine Line" [Paul McCartney]

A smidge of dissonance popping up in the aggressive piano line signals a change ahead, one more serious and more bleak than usual. A rock song, rare for this album, carries the riveting vocal, cushioned by a stylish instrumental ensemble, all of it supplied by McCartney, drums included. A flop single? Yes, as it inched its way to #22 in the UK and #31 on the US's Adult Contemporary, the booby prize for high-stature musicians. A smart track like this deserved better. **B+**

"How Kind of You" [Paul McCartney]

A forlorn McCartney wandering in the darkness, helpless and despairing. He sings as if hadn't slept in days, his eyes glazed, his voice weary – the performance is startling. If only the melody was as deep as the lyrics imply, but it seems improvised, at times drifting into the unstructured. Still, overall, this is damn good. McCartney's pained vocals, plus the spooky sustained keyboard chords, make it a haunted winner. **B+**

"Jenny Wren" [Paul McCartney]

Despite his insistence to the otherwise, "Jenny Wren" – named [accidentally?] after a character from Charles Dickens' novel *Our Mutual Friend* – did not evolve from "Blackbird," as only the picking style is familiar. In fact, it's more like "Eleanor Rigby," with its personality profile of a glum female and her despairing life. This is a gorgeous and intelligent masterpiece that has inspiration written all over it, a one-of-a-kind, straight from the heart example of McCartney's best. The fresh melody is based on a thrilling switch from major to minor in the last two bars of the verse, while the bracing chorus carries us into the atmosphere, still in a minor key, before gently setting back to a major. The clever arrangement features a *duduk*, an Armenian woodwind instrument related to the oboe which produces a warm, ghostly sound, one that's seldom, if ever, used by rock musicians. It's straight from the Beatles playbook. So is this song. **A**

"At the Mercy" [Paul McCartney]

Melancholic in the beginning, increasingly sad in the middle, and unexpectedly strong at the end, a restrained McCartney by-passed the temptation to dump strings all over it, which would have made it more friendly and far less effective. Despite its being lyrically muddled, the gorgeous melody overflows with human emotion, this from a guy that many of us figured didn't have any. **B+**

"Friends to Go" [Paul McCartney]

Allegedly about the late George Harrison [who died from cancer in 2001], the lyrics are too vague to be certain. On the other hand, the brief but effective reflections on his own mortality are surprisingly poignant. The okay melody doesn't come close to matching the power of the lyrics, and I never thought I'd write that sentence either. **B**

"English Tea" [Paul McCartney]

Defiantly, McCartney slaps down a challenge to join him for a dainty cup of tea. Challenge declined. **C**

"Too Much Rain" [Paul McCartney]

In "Too Much Rain," if he's soothing a friend or lover, it's basically meaningless. But if talking to himself, he may be saying something. Dig a little, you'll discover a man confused by the unpredictability of an indifferent life. Too musically thin to be considered a classic, even a minor one, but McCartney's aching voice brings it close. **B**

"A Certain Softness" [Paul McCartney]

With "Here, There, and Everywhere" and "Yesterday," McCartney has set the bar impossibly high for love songs. "A Certain Softness" offers bit of samba, a restrained vocal, and a modest lyric to make it more of a grown-up effort than on albums past. But does it belong in the Hall of Fame? Nope. I wonder, as he studies his old Beatles material, is he ever jealous of himself? **B**

"Riding to Vanity Fair" [Paul McCartney]

Maybe this is what McCartney had in mind when he wanted to nudge the album in an India direction. This qualifies, with its exotic arrangement and drone-like melody, coupled with the welcome self-analytical lyric. The music swells and echoes, pushing against thick waves of strings and keyboards, making for one of McCartney's more unusual tracks. Just for fun, compare this to "Loup [1st Indian on the Loup]" on *Red Rose Speedway* for a stark difference between the man and the boy. By the way, Godrich was right – an all-India album wouldn't have made the grade, as it makes a tasty seasoning but not a whole meal. **B**

"Follow Me" [Paul McCartney]

Another love song. This one, however, features an affecting vocal, almost pleading. The song, itself a little weak, works as a platform for a suffering romantic, begging for a glance, a nod, anything from the idealized woman of his attention, which may not be forthcoming. **B**

"Promise to You Girl" [Paul McCartney]
An up-tempo, piano-based musing on … something. Not up to snuff, lyric-wise, and also deficient in the melody department. Though this would've been passable 20 or 30 years ago, *Chaos and Creation* has raised the songwriting standards considerably. **B-**

"This Never Happened Before" [Paul McCartney]
Speaking of fine lines, there's also a fine line between the romantic and the stupid. This doesn't plummet to the depths of "My Love," but it's too close for comfort, what with the this-time-it's-real psycho-babble. Noodling precedes a too-precious vocal straight from the movies, say, a soundtrack number that occurs during the smooching scene in *Cinderella*. **C+**

"Anyway" [Paul McCartney]
Is that Curtis Mayfield? Rod Stewart? Is "People Get Ready?" the grandfather? McCartney's already tackled romantic uneasiness more eloquently elsewhere on the album, "At the Mercy" for one. And really, are you in the mood to hear about the all-conquering power of wonderful love one more time? Still, the melancholy track stays with you, owing to McCartney's sincere performance, as he appears to believe what he's singing, which he didn't always manage in the days of "Magneto and Titanium Man." An acceptable, slightly disappointing, end to an exceptional album. **B**

"I've Only Got Two Hands" [Paul McCartney]
An afterthought instrumental, tagged to the conclusion of "Anyway," composed of two distinct parts. Part one is a major key exercise in arbitrary doodling, though it's still fun to follow along as McCartney's musical brain wanders here and there. Part two is a minor key excursion into dreamy psychedelia. The second part is the more successful of the two, earns a medal for its successful blending of straightforward catchiness and weirdo spacey-ness, indicating that, perhaps, those naughty drugs still linger in his blood vessels. **B**

[bonus]

"Comfort of Love" [Paul McCartney]
McCartney does Gilbert and Sullivan, sort of. He begins with the universal complaint that material possessions don't add up to peace of mind, then forgoing the obvious [that there's no answer], he dribbles off into some nonsense about romance. It sounds like a couple of others from *Chaos and Creation*, only duller. Much duller. ["Fine Line" CD single] **B-**

"Growing Up Falling Down" [Paul McCartney]
After a few mundane verses, a right-field twist – which is: you'll be dead before you know it. Not a surprise, but hearing McCartney say it out loud is enough to raise eyebrows, possibly depressing you for the rest of the day. A creepy tune, which nails your attention and never lets go. Should have been on *Chaos and Creation* instead of – yuck – "English Tea." ["Fine Line" CD single] **B**

"Summer of 59" [Paul McCartney]
A song about getting laid. In 1959, McCartney was around 17, which seems about right, and was a guy who admired plants, which seems, uh, odd. A carefree ditty, roughly 50s-ish, inconsequential. ["Jenny Wren" vinyl single] **B-**

"This Loving Game" [Paul McCartney]
Acceptable piano riff, but slides into Boring Town, fast. As for the lyrics, they're so crude they might as well be cave paintings. ["Jenny Wren" CD single] **C-**

"I Want You to Fly" [Paul McCartney]
A Chuck Berry clone, performed on electric piano, slowly, with McCartney seemingly making it up as he goes along. Well-sung but a snoozer. ["Jenny Wren" CD single] **B-**

"She is So Beautiful" [Paul McCartney]
With a title like this, you can bet we're not in for an innovative *magnum opus*. What's that sound? Why, it's the ghost of John Lennon, giggling. [Japanese pressing of *Chaos and Creation in the Back Yard*] **C-**

"Jenny Wren [Live Abbey Road Studio]" [Paul McCartney]
Stripped down, "Jenny Wren" retains its beauty but misses out on the attractive studio arrangement that provided a surplus of charm. Still a wonder. [*paulmccartney.com*] **B+**

"Line Art" [Paul McCartney]
Rambling instrumental. The longer it plays, the more irrelevant it becomes. [*Chaos and Creation Special Edition*] **B-**

"Whole Life" [Paul McCartney and Dave Stewart]
[Paul McCartney and Dave Stewart] Suspiciously similar to "No Values" [*Give My Regards to Broad Street*], not exactly a recommendation. The static melody, surprising lazy for McCartney, drags and sputters until a winning chorus brings it to life. This, incidentally, was part of an AIDS project in Africa, and 46664 was Nelson Mandela's Robben Island prisoner number. [*46664: One Year On*] **B-**

"Sgt. Pepper's Lonely Hearts Club Band [Live 8]" [John Lennon and Paul McCartney; guest performer: Paul McCartney]
[U2] Short and startling. Plus they even threw in a live brass quartet wearing Sgt Pepper uniforms. You thought U2 was wimpy? Me too, but maybe I was wrong. [*Live 8*] **B**

"Drive My Car [Live 8]" [John Lennon and Paul McCartney]
[Various Artists] Is that darn ol' cowbell too loud? With a dapper George Michael adding harmony, pulling it down a notch. [*Live 8*] **B**

"Get Back [Live 8]" [John Lennon and Paul McCartney]
[Various Artists] Not the same without Lennon's crappy solos, but still fun. [*Live 8*] **B**

"Helter Skelter [Live 8]" [John Lennon and Paul McCartney]
[Various Artists] Electrifying, thanks to the best band Paul's ever had [er, second best]. Vocals sizzling, guitars like chainsaws, and Paul on top, joyously screaming his lungs out. [*Live 8*] **B+**

"The Long and Winding Road/Hey Jude [Live 8]" [John Lennon and Paul McCartney]
[Various Artists] A generic "Road" leads seamlessly into the semi-grand finale of "Hey Jude," which goes on forever and makes you glad you stayed home. [*Live 8*] **C –**

"Hurt Myself" [Rusty Anderson; guest performer: Paul McCartney]
[Rusty Anderson] Anderson, a stalwart of McCartney's *Back in the U.S.* touring band, gets a helping hand from bandmate Abe Laboriel Jr, David Kahne [who helped produce], Wix Wickens, and McCartney himself [bass, guitar, and backing vocals], along with a host of others, for an good natured solo disc. Released on his own Oxide Records, picked up later by Surfdog Records, the production flirts with the bombastic but backs off before things get too heavy. Though Anderson sings well and performs like the pro he is, the songwriting – evidenced by "Hurt Myself" – is too frail to sustain a single, much less a full-length album. [*Undressing Underwater*] **B-**

CHAPTER THIRTY-SEVEN:

ECCE COR MEUM [2006]

Produced by John Fraser
Did not chart [US, UK]

Sometimes, being the best pop melodicist in the universe isn't enough. It leaves you feeling a little empty. You want more.

Choices galore. Do you want to align yourself with a grungy contemporary band for a couple of years, nurture them, guide them through the minefield of show biz? [Nahh]. How about starting a record company, focusing on worthy musicians who can't get a break? [Nahh.] Maybe sign up for night school? An intense study of poetry might do wonders for your lyric writing. [B-o-r-i-n-g.]

But when all is said and done, what you want is to compose classical music. Maybe out of curiosity. Maybe out of a long-standing love of the genre. Maybe to win the respect of the classical community who scoff at the Clash but admire the works of Mozart. [Memo to McCartney: You have this already].

Whatever the reason, the time had come for classical album number four, the others being *Liverpool Oratorio* [1991], *Standing Stone* [1997], and *Working Classical* [1999], none of them receiving the acclaim of, say, *Band on the Run*. But maybe this time would be different.

McCartney eagerly accepted the offer of Anthony Smith, an associate of Oxford's Magdalen College, to compose a piece inaugurating the school's new concert hall. As McCartney still couldn't read or write a single note of music, he enlisted professionals like John Fraser [who also produced *Working Classical*] to give advice and guidance when necessary. The project, off and on for eight years, was sprawling and, without argument, ambitious. The approximately hour-long oratorio, *Ecce Cor Meum* [Latin for *Behold My Heart*], required an orchestra, a classical vocal group [including a choir of boys], and a soprano soloist [Kate Royal, acclaimed for her performance in the Glyndebourne Festival Opera]. As *Ecce Cor Meum* came together, McCartney allegedly envisioned it as comparable to Handel's *Messiah*.

If so, he was wishing for the stars. Though containing the usual supply of McCartney's deft melodies, *Ecce Cor Meum* came up wanting. Instead of inventive classical ideas, the work sounded more like collection of churchy pop songs that had little to do with each other.

Critics, generally speaking, were not sympathetic. *The New York Times*: "Mr. McCartney has too much sense, and has had too much success, to aspire to classical forms." *AllMusic*: "[McCartney] is still the classical naif who, by dint of his supreme self-confidence, believes he has the technical skill and artistic imagination to set his rambling, sentimental text with enough interesting material to hold the listener's attention ..." *The Telegraph*: "[The] musical substance is just not strong enough to support the piece's expanse." *Gramophone*: "... a creakily Victoria four-parter ... both short-winded and constipated ..."

"Spiritus" [Paul McCartney]

Opening with a too-serious choir, reminiscent of a synagogue with battered hymnals, "Spiritis" crawls along without any obvious direction, channelling Brahms, Prokofiev, and second-rate Broadway musicals. Timpani pound and trumpets blare, all mushed together, producing a sum less than the parts. There are some pretty passages but it takes five minutes to say what could be said in one. As I struggled to stay focused on this long movement [12 minutes], I wondered: instead of McCartney aspiring to be Handel, couldn't he try harder to be the Pixies? **C+**

"Gratia" [Paul McCartney]

A string ensemble evokes "Eleanor Rigby," making the second movement a lot more palatable. But by the time the woodwinds, choir, and soprano slink their way in, "Eleanor Rigby" is eased aside in favour of a third-tier Disney movie, which seems to be an inspiration for all of McCartney's classical efforts. Still, Kate Royal is a joy, but then, sadly, we're again trudging through a mud puddle that seemingly has no end. It's obvious, depressingly so, that when it comes to classical McCartney, much less is much more. **B-**

"Interlude [Lament]" [Paul McCartney]
At three minutes, the shortest. And with its song-like structure, the most satisfying. But it still feels way too long. **B**

"Musica" [Paul McCartney]
Better, not great. Seems more unified than previous movements, but at 15 minutes, that's a lot of ground to cover and not much to cover it with. As the music drifts this way and that, Disney again rears its cobwebs, surrounding us in a gush of moderately pleasant but ultimately shallow passages. A few intriguing bits of actual songs emerge, but that's not what this is about, is it? **B-**

"Ecce Cor Meum" [Paul McCartney]
Garbled and in dire need of editing, the final movement too often resembles a handful of light film scores that McCartney tossed in the air, then taped together. Worse, the tone throughout is straight-jacketed by self-imposed historic restraints which he dare not go beyond, as if he automatically associated classical music with the Romantic era, period. Given that, there are a few nods to contemporary composers that slip in, such as the occasional static progression that's [sort of] Steve Reich-ish, and there are a few passable melodies that have McCartney's fingerprints all over them. But overall, the material that should be muscular is flabby. Either McCartney's in over his head or he lost his focus. Or both. **C+**

[bonus]

"Bring It On Home to Me [Jarreau Version]" [Sam Cooke; guest performer: Paul McCartney]
[Al Jarreau and George Benson] McCartney tried this on *Choba B CCCP*, playfully and quickly, but only marginally better. Again, McCartney heads for the middle of the road, drawn like a magnetic attraction, draining the life out of this classic. When Jarreau nudges him, the duo sleepwalks to the finish, wrapping up this slice of lightweight jazz. [*Givin' It Up*] **C+**

"Heal the Pain" [George Michael; guest performer: Paul McCartney]
[George Michael] For what is essentially a greatest hits package, Michael added a re-recorded duet of "Heal the Pain" with his pal Paul. It's a weak song that McCartney can't find much to do with, but he gives it a shot anyway, ending up with a track that's far too slick for rock lovers [read: Beatles lovers]. [*Twentyfive*] **C+**

"The Very Thought of You" [Ray Nobel]
[Tony Bennett] Popularized by Bing Crosby in 1934, this late-night set-'em-up-Joe piece epitomizes Bennett's world-weariness. McCartney's, who can transform like a chameleon from balls-out rocker to lounge crooner, slithers right up beside him. Bennett sounds smooth but old, so between the two, the winner is golden-throated McCartney, who sings like it's the easiest thing he'll do all day. But this is grandpa stuff. [*Tony Bennett – Duets: An American Classic*] **B**

CHAPTER THIRTY-EIGHT:

MEMORY ALMOST FULL [2007]

Produced by David Kahne
Charted at 3 [US], 5 [UK]

Following the blueprint laid out in *Chaos and Creation in the Backyard*, David Kahne, overseer of *Driving Rain* and *Back in the U.S.*, again filled the producer's chair, all by himself, just like Nigel Godrich did on *Chaos*. A few tracks tinkered with prior to *Chaos* got another look, including "Only Mama Knows," "Vintage Clothes," and "House of Wax." Adding their skills were members of McCartney's touring band, making for a tough, slightly slicker sound, but always sympathetic to the boss's intent.

Most striking is the album's sober tone, an unflinching, occasionally self-critical look at his life and the honest reflections of the memories they stirred up. *Memory Almost Full* presents a closed artist in a rare moment of candor, not as graceful as Bob Dylan or as frank as John Lennon, but impressive in his own reserved way. Clumsy? Occasionally. Lazy? Sometimes, too often falling back on unfocused images and forced couplets. Musically, too, he tends to be all over the place, one minute endearing ["That Was Me"], another minute trite ["Dance Tonight"]. And now and then, vague lyrics [the semi-surreal "House of Wax"] require a cryptographer to figure them out.

Still, McCartney's openness is startling, always interesting, and leagues away from the man who began his solo career mired in nursery rhymes and superficial observations about next to nothing. How far has he come since "Spirits of Ancient Egypt"? How about "The End of the End," featuring musings on his own death?

"Dance Tonight" [Paul McCartney]
A bit of fluff that has more to with its mandolin track than the wisp of tune it supports. Establishes the tone of a party album, a tone that will be blown to bits about three minutes later. A reason for the existence of "Dance Tonight": [1] a practical joke from Paul, [2] shoddy sequencing by an intern, or [3] he thought it sounded like a sure-fire single. It wasn't. It topped out at #26 in the UK and a miserable #69 in the US before it crawled away. **B-**

"Ever Present Past" [Paul McCartney]
McCartney gets down to business with a rumination of a quickly passing life going down the drain. He sounds bewildered by it all, formulating vague plans to make the remainder of his days substantive and meaningful. The music, fairly standard pop stuff, isn't quite as angry or confused or sorrowful as the lyrics suggest. As it progresses, however, McCartney seems to resolved to his fate, and the relatively upbeat tune responds accordingly. This is a lot for a single song to carry, and though he stumbles here and there, it's amazing that he tries. Points docked for echoing Duke Ellington's "Don't Get Around Much Anymore." **B**

"See Your Sunshine" [Paul McCartney]
Horny McCartney lusts after an unnamed woman, drool soaking his shirt. The opening shower of voices, similar to the Beach Boys, means McCartney's been listening to *Pet Sounds* again. That, frustratingly, is the only passage of interest in this routine tune, which otherwise features McCartney – about 64 years old – leering at girls while squinting. **B –**

"Only Mama Knows" [Paul McCartney]
Baby Paul is abandoned by his mom in a ghost-faced town, left by himself to push up daisies. Yikes!

Suitably up-tempo, sort of "Jet"-like [not as good], and a tough McCartney growling away. Is that a funeral dirge at the beginning? Double yikes! **B**

"You Tell Me" [Paul McCartney]

Beatle-ly backwards instruments introduce this maudlin ballad, with its images of a crimson bird in Arizona where Linda spent her last days, suggesting it's about his deceased wife. Dreamlike, almost unbearably sad. The stony melody is uncharacteristically McCartney at his most lethargic. **B**

"Mr. Bellamy" [Paul McCartney]

Multiple listenings don't do much to reveal the secrets of Mr. Bellamy, other than he's busy, easily scared, and high [as in, up in the air – I think]. In the same vein as "Maxwell's Silver Hammer," "Lovely Rita," and McCartney's other imaginary oddballs, it's half Lennon and McCartney, half Gilbert and Sullivan, coupled with a neat piano riff and an eye-opening ending. With more definite lyrics, it'd earn higher marks. **B**

"Gratitude" [Paul McCartney]

No names mentioned, but "Gratitude" seems like a bouquet to Heather as the oodles of appreciation, all past tense, imply. That he can be this sweet to somebody with whom he engaged in a bloodthirsty divorce is either admirable or dumbfounding. That said, the song reflects his sincerity, although it's hard to understand what all the shouting's about. A surprisingly powerful performance by a guy who never met a wife he didn't like. **B**

"Vintage Clothes" [Paul McCartney]

The first of five loosely linked tunes in which McCartney takes a look – actually, more of a glance – at an exhilarating life that's over before you can say "Beatles reunion." With out-of-nowhere effects that are fresh and imaginative, plus flawless Freddie Mercury-ish vocal ensembles, the song is a treat. A reminder that even with hundreds of songs under his belt, McCartney's uncanny musical skills can still amaze. **B+**

"That Was Me" [Paul McCartney]

A list of unimaginable experiences that can only belong to him and three other guys You can practically see McCartney's I-can't-believe-it expression as he recalls TV appearances and sitting room rehearsals, events that can never be duplicated or, as he implies, can never really be appreciated by anyone else. A personal song that, what it lacks in poetic description, makes up in honest incredulity. All of this against an effortless rockabilly, which doesn't accomplish much melody-wise. But considering how a lesser artist might succumb to drowning it all in string-laded nostalgia, still a minor triumph. **B**

"Feet in the Clouds" [Paul McCartney]

Look, just ahead – it's a vast Field of Corn! And – oh no – it's Paul McCartney, blindingly trotting toward it! Go back Paul! Go back! His loyal dog Cutey Tunes is trying to pull him away! But they're pounced upon by – oh god! – Man-Eating Bip Bops! **B-**

"House of Wax" [Paul McCartney]

Intense, minor key, images of destruction – this is a long way from "Magneto and Titanium Man." McCartney sounds defeated and too tired to run, as if the lightning storm the band emulates not only zapped the neighbors, but got him too. Consider this McCartney's take on programme music, sort of feather-weight Debussy. **B**

"The End of the End" [Paul McCartney]

Kudos to Paul for staring down the Grim Reaper in this tale of a reticent artist in a rare moment of candour. What does he want on that fateful day he journeys to the great beyond? Kids frolicking, funny stories cracking up friends, maybe his songs wafting through the hills. And like a lot of the elderly facing the inevitability of an abrupt stop, he professes – hopefully? – the existence of a life-after-death so he can, uh, whatever. "The End of the End" proclaims all of the preceding, and if he sounds frightened – which he does, even when trying to whistle – who can blame him? **B+**

"Nod Your Head" [Paul McCartney]

Bizarre opening, atonal backing, insane vocal. Working at cross purposes, reminiscent of "Angry" on

Press to Play, by including bits of multi-track harmony and friendly keyboard lines amid the unusual elements, McCartney seems reluctant to go full-out nuts and settles for mildly deranged. Consider this an experiment, undercooked. **B-**

[bonus]

"Why So Blue" [Paul McCartney]
Static melody that fumbles, trips, and falls, at which time it threatens to get up and take off, but soon wanders back into the sleepy verses and a soggy middle. Fragments of value are sabotaged by a semi-engaged composer. Plus the lyrics are dumb. [*Japanese Memory Almost Full* bonus track] **B-**

"Dance Tonight [Acoustic]" [Paul McCartney]
Resist this, or "Mumbo for String Quartet" will be next. [*iTunes Store* bonus] **C**

"In Private" [Paul McCartney]
A modest instrumental with a modest melody and a tempo best described as modest. [*2CD Limited Edition Memory Almost Full* bonus] **B-**

"222" [Paul McCartney]
A song about his two-year-old daughter, Beatrice, walking. Similar to Vince Guaraldi's "A Charlie Brown Christmas" from the *Peanuts* TV special. McCartney fiddles with a piano riff, moans brief endearments to his kid, and waits for inspiration that's on vacation. [*2CS Limited Edition Memory Almost Full* bonus] **B-**

"Only Mama Knows [Live 2007]" [Paul McCartney]
McCartney showcased several new numbers and one oldie at the iTunes Festival [also called the Apple Music Festival], a free arts event staged for lucky winners who were members of Apple Music via Apple TV, iPhone, iPad, and other Apple devices. McCartney's five live songs were released on an EP. On "Only Mama Knows," he comes across more reserved than he does on the studio track, but that aside, it's a near-duplication, right down to the synthesizer flourishes in the introduction. [*iTunes Festival EP*] **B**

"That Was Me [Live 2007]" [Paul McCartney]
The band rocks like they mean business, and for that matter, so does McCartney. Equal to the studio cut, though not its superior. [*iTunes Festival EP*] **B**

"Jet [Live 2007]" [Paul and Linda McCartney]
Despite their best efforts to get it airborne, "Jet" barely gets off the ground. Tired, waning enthusiasm, adequate at best. [*iTunes Festival EP*] **B-**

"Nod Your Head [Live 2007]" [Paul McCartney]
Odd choice for the live band, owing to its twisty structure and off-kilter effects. A bland attempt. [*iTunes Festival EP*] **B-**

"House of Wax [Live 2007]" [Paul McCartney]
A sparse rendition, nearly funereal. McCartney sings somberly, like an old guy who's seen it all. Unusual, making it interesting. [*iTunes Festival EP*] **B**

"I Want to Walk You Home" [Fats Domino]
With Allen Toussaint on piano, McCartney does an imitation, literally, of Fats Domino. Marvel at his uncanny abilities as a mimic while reminding yourself how much better the original is than a copy. [*Goin' Home: A Tribute to Fats Domino*] **B-**

"Shoes" [Paul McCartney]
An odd one. During a friendly interview, McCartney was asked to improvise a new song, for which the interviewer would also participate. She gave him the title "Shoes," chosen at random. McCartney picked up his acoustic guitar, strummed a few chords, and sang a not-very-good tune about footwear, roughly a verse long. Later, the song was picked up by an enterprising blogger who overdubbed a bunch of

instruments, thus producing a "new" McCartney song. Except it wasn't, despite a few naive fans who claimed it was. A crummy tune, but not really Paul's. [Internet Only] **D**

CHAPTER THIRTY-NINE:

AMOEBA'S SECRET [2007]/AMOEBA GIG [2019]

Produced by David Kahne
Amoeba's Secret: [US] 119, [UK] did not chart; Amoeba Gig: 4 [US], [UK] 82

Amoeba Music is a disc lover's dream. An independent record store that opened in Berkeley, California in 1990, it branched out to Hollywood in 2001. Currently, Amoeba stocks in the neighborhood of 100,000 CDs and god knows how many vinyl records, cassettes and other paraphernalia. In the current environment of dwindling sales of physical media, it's amazing the store has survived, let alone prospered, at least to date.

As Amoeba grew, so did its outreach to the professional community. Live in-store performances became a staple. The roster of performers, both well-known and obscure, is impressive: The Remains, Nancy Sinatra, Tokyo Police Club, Jenny Lewis. And in a coup for Amoeba, they hosted a June 2007 performance by Paul McCartney.

Yes, he was great. Fans squealed with delight, and McCartney beamed throughout. But to some, it was an opportunity lost. It's hard to imagine a better venue – this was "secret" after all – for McCartney to dig deep into his catalogue, and take a shot at songs he'd neglected in his stadium concerts. How about "Take It Away," "Uncle Albert/Admiral Halsey," or "Souvenir"? Or a Beatles tune he'd missed, like "Oh Darling" or "Rocky Raccoon"? Or a left-fielder like "Come and Get It" or "Goodbye"? His ace band could play anything, and even if they stumbled, the receptive Amoeba audience would likely be far more forgiving than critical. But alas, it was not to be. Instead, in addition to a couple of *Memory Almost Full* numbers – "Dance Tonight" and "Only Mama Knows" – we got "Blackbird" and "Hey Jude" and other staples of his standard stadium concerts.

Of course, it's possible McCartney had other things on his mind besides remembering the chords to "Goodbye." He was on the verge of his third marriage. Through mutual friends, he'd met wife-to-be Nancy Shevell at East Hampton, then commenced serious dating in 2007. She seemed ready made for McCartney – gorgeous, vice president of the Metropolitan Transportation Authority, well to do, stylish and – most importantly – approved of by McCartney's family. Fingers crossed – third time's a charm.

Live Re-Releases
In the summer of 2019, McCartney re-released a clutch of live albums, including an upgrade of *Amoeba's Secret EP* titled *Amoeba Gig*, featuring a ton of songs omitted from the 2007 EP. Other re-releases at this time – *Wings Over America, Paul is Live, Choba B CCCP* – featured sonic upgrades but no unheard material.

Amoeba's Secret EP
"Only Mama Knows [Live Amoeba] [Paul McCartney]
Just okay, as it basically recreates the album track. **B**

"C Moon [Live Amoeba] [Paul and Linda McCartney]
A frisky throwaway. McCartney has a fine time with this one, a lively version of a lower-tier tune. **B**

"That Was Me [Live Amoeba] [Paul McCartney]
Bouncy and playful, though the band tends to drag it down, betraying, perhaps, their unfamiliarity with the relatively new tune. I bet if McCartney could clone himself, he'd have an army of compliant Pauls prancing around on stage. **B**

"I Saw Her Standing There [Live Amoeba]" [John Lennon and Paul McCartney]
Hey Paul – kinda hard to pull off teenage lust when you're 65, isn't it? He tries, the band tries, the audience pretends. **B**

Amoeba's Gig [released in 2019, includes previous songs, plus the following]

"Drive My Car [Live Amoeba]" [John Lennon and Paul McCartney]
Casual performance, reasonably entertaining, and for the consumer, definitely superfluous. **B –**

"Dance Tonight [Live Amoeba]" [Paul McCartney]
This threatens to be the 21st century answer to "Hey Diddle," only with better words. Take away the mandolin, and what you have left: an eager-to-please guy singing a monotone tune. **B-**

"The Long and Winding Road [Live Amoeba]" [John Lennon and Paul McCartney]
The setting actually improves this warhorse, making it more personal and thus, in theory, more affecting. But McCartney performs on automatic pilot, making this tender tune just another entry on his endless hit parade. **B-**

"I'll Follow the Sun [Live Amoeba]" [John Lennon and Paul McCartney]
Rushed but charming, exquisitely sung, and as comforting as having him perform in your own bedroom. If it were only a smidgeon more relaxed … **B**

"Calico Skies [Live Amoeba]" [Paul McCartney]
Once wistful, now it's a sea shanty. **B-**

"Blackbird [Live Amoeba] [John Lennon and Paul McCartney]
Why is it here? Why, when it's been on live albums since *Wings Over America*? Why hasn't anyone played him "Unplugged" and see if that'll cage "Blackbird" for a while? **B-**

"Here Today [Live Amoeba]" [Paul McCartney]
Jesus. Is he crying? **B**

"Back in the U.S.S.R. [Live Amoeba]" [John Lennon and Paul McCartney]
The sluggish tempo brings this perilously close to life support. What's left is a generic bar band rendition of a Beatles classic, which I believe is a federal offense. **B-**

"Nod Your Head [Live Amoeba]" [Paul McCartney]
Another shot at a strange track. It doesn't work, but that may be due to the odd structure of the song rather than screw-ups from the band. Still, the composition's inherent weirdness – weird for McCartney that is – is refreshing. **B-**

"House of Wax [Live Amoeba]" [Paul McCartney]
Solid performance, nothing special. Preferable, however, to "My Love" and any of its snooze-inducing cousins ["Dance Tonight" springs to mind]. **B**

"I've Got a Feeling [Live Amoeba]" [John Lennon and Paul McCartney]
The concert McCartney has transformed "I've Got a Feeling" into a live standard, rightly so, as the interplay between his and Lennon's parts never fails. This take is more aggressive than usual, adding to the atmosphere of sheer pleasure it's all but guaranteed to generate. Still, when you copy the Beatles verbatim, comparisons are inevitable, and the copier is doomed to lose. Even when the copier is Paul. **B**

"Matchbox [Live Amoeba]" [Carl Perkins]
Sloppy but engaging rendition of a rockabilly fave. Kudos to Paul for not bothering to make the guitar more radio-friendly, instead letting it spew and sputter all over the place. Marred by crappy synthesizer horns. **B**

"Get Back [Live Amoeba]" [John Lennon and Paul McCartney]
The rhythm of a chugging train makes this perfect for a concert, but merely running through it isn't the way to go. In one sense, the Beatles fancied this as a song about slide-off-your-drawers seduction. By himself, gentleman McCartney turns it into slide-on-your-drawers, your-bus-is-here. **B-**

"Baby Face [Live Amoeba]" [Harry Akst and Benny Davis]
Since McCartney's performed this at least from the *Band on the Run* days, he seems determined to continue until we get the joke. Okay, what *is* the joke? **C-**

"Hey Jude [Live Amoeba]" [Paul McCartney]
Who likes this better than *Knebworth: the Album*, *Tripping the Live Fantastic*, *Music for Montserrat*, *Back in the U.S.*, *Back in the World*, *Party at the Palace*, or *Live 8*? Anyone? Anyone? **C**

"Let It Be [Live Amoeba]" [John Lennon and Paul McCartney]
He will never let it be. Even though "All You Need is Love" is ready to take its place. **C**

"Lady Madonna [Live Amoeba]" [John Lennon and Paul McCartney]
I never get tired of hearing this. Okay, I'm lying. **B-**

"Coming Up [Live Amoeba]" [Paul McCartney]
Rehearsal run-though. Passable, but passable only. [*Amoeba Gig* LP] **B-**

"Get Back" [Live Bridge Street]
The Bridge Street Concerts, a charity for handicapped children sponsored by Neil Young and Pegi Young, are major fund raisers for the organization. Each year Young recruits the planet's biggest stars to perform. This 2011 collection highlights participants from the first 25 years, among them Bruce Springsteen, the Who, Pearl Jam, and Paul McCartney, who contributes a loose, energized version of "Get Back." Nothing special, but it's hard to argue with a record jammed with everybody under the sun, all of them – McCartney included – in top form. [*Bridge Street Concerts 25th Anniversary Edition*] **B**

CHAPTER FORTY:

THE FIREMAN – ELECTRIC ARGUMENTS [2008]

Produced by Paul McCartney
Charted at 67 [US], 79 [UK]

The third collaborative album of Paul McCartney and contemporary studio wizard Martin Glover [Youth] finds them once again mining the cosmos for sonic knick-knacks, the results guaranteed to frustrate McCartney fans who long for the good old days of "Listen to What the Man Said." However, before skeptics toss this on the life's-too-short pile, they might consider the following:

- Songs. Instead of unrecognizable fragments and warped wisps of tunes, *Electric Arguments* bases its soundscapes on structured [and semi-structured] songs, more so than *Strawberries Oceans Ships Oceans Forests* and *Rushes*. Not to say this is *Memory Almost Full Part Two*, but rather a different and preferable method [for an ace songsmith like McCartney] of approaching an electronic album.

- Vocals. On the previous Fireman projects, McCartney's voice was used as another source of raw sound, to be stretched and mutated as he saw fit. Here, however, he's mostly on terra firma, singing actual lines from actual tunes. This is not from the cautious artist who rarely settles for less than finely tuned, carefully perfected vocals, but from a liberated man willing to go for broke, wailing blissfully, forcefully, even ferociously.

- Ambience. Those who consider ambient music on par with water dripping from a kitchen faucet should be pleased to hear that *Electric Arguments* dials the ambient elements down a notch. There are fewer wafts of spacey chords drifting through the clouds or lethargic slurpings of a synthesizer. *Electric Arguments* generally showcases a tighter focus on developed motifs that have a beginning and an end.

Unlike its predecessors, *Electric Arguments* actually charted, rising to a respectable #67 in the US, #79 in the UK, not bad for an experimental album. Still, although McCartney allowed his name to be featured on the cover rather than conceal himself as The Fireman, it's surprising he was reluctant to promote the album as part of his on-going catalogue. After all, with *Chaos and Creation in the Back Yard* and *Memory Almost Full*, McCartney the formidable songwriter and stylish producer, the Cute Beatle was experiencing a renaissance.

"Nothing Too Much Just Out of Sight" [Paul McCartney]
The compelling vocal aside, this is overstuffed with noisy effects. Plus it drags and plods on to the five-minute finish line, a journey that takes forever. How to improve it? One minute, tops, to showcase the weird textures, then over-and-out would've done the trick. This serves the same unfortunate function as "Dance Tonight" did on *Memory Almost Full* – a listless and misleading introduction to an album that's much better. **B-**

"Two Magpies" [Paul McCartney]
A sleepy but intense vocal anchors this unusual finger-popper. Simultaneously mature and goofy, it's a winner, albeit a modest one, from a guy who apparently can do anything. Explain to me again why a fan might prefer "Silly Love Songs." **B+**

"Sing the Changes" [Paul McCartney]
How a straightforward pop song – that is, a slightly skewed pop song – slipped in here is anybody's guess. It's enlivened by a clever arrangement that gradually pumps itself, turning a deflated balloon to a neon spaceship. That aside, the song would have improved with a stronger melody, a nagging flaw

shared by much of the *Electric Arguments* material. "Sing the Changes" was reportedly composed and recorded the same day, as were all of the songs, but that *que sera sera* approach might have lost in polish what was gained in spontaneity. **B**

"Travelling Light" [Paul McCartney]
McCartney's voice is electronically altered to make him sound about 100 years old, a riveting effect. In a shadowy waltz, the creaky voice glides over a thick fog of echoed piano, sinister flute, and a dinner bell from hell. Unfortunately, a shift to a major key transforms it into a pub sing-along, changing the dark, melancholy tone into something friendlier. A shame, because hell was cool. **B**

"Highway" [Paul McCartney]
This incendiary snarler with a blazing electric guitar and bone-rattling rhythms would've made a much better album opener than "Nothing Too Much Just Out of Sight," but they forgot to ask me. Yes, the melody is missing in action, at least in the verse, but it explodes in the chorus, with an incessant chant that's among McCartney's finest hooks. Strip it of the electronics and examine it as a mere song, it comes up short, as is true of *Electric Arguments* in general. But the electronics define it. Songs recorded in a studio don't always have to be soundtracks for live performances. A track that can never be duplicated outside a studio setting – no longer benefitting from elaborate special effects and wizardly studio magic – is not only perfectly acceptable, but in some cases, preferable. Anyone who prefers any of the numerous live versions to the original studio complexity of the Beach Boys' "Good Vibrations," might consider having his ears examined. Ditto for "I Am the Walrus." And ditto for the studio-born "Highway." **B**

"Light from Your Lighthouse" [Paul McCartney]
A country ditty from Venus, backed by robots. A stronger melody for this legitimate song would have made it more memorable, but it's still head, shoulders, and rivets ahead of McCartney's ambient rivals. **B**

"Sun is Shining" [Paul McCartney]
More ambient than usual, with an airy beginning that wants to lull you to sleep. McCartney enters, normal voice for a change, sings an easy rhyme over a pleasant background. But this is *Electric Arguments*, and we don't want pleasant, do we? If you disagree, and if you're longing for an "Off the Ground," here's a gift. **B-**

"Dance 'Til We're High" [Paul McCartney]
Hmm ... do I hear "Be My Baby?" This could be an audition for Phil Spector, but last time I checked, Phil was busy in prison. Which is a shame because McCartney knocks it out of the park by underplaying the melodrama in this busy piece, and offering a full-bodied vocal. What does this have to do with the experimental *Electric Arguments*? Honestly, not much. **B**

"Lifelong Passion" [Paul McCartney]
A wispy ballad-ish throwaway, made palatable by some space-age sound effects. Although it's hard to see what the sci-fi clamor has to do with the song, at least it provides semi-interesting ear candy to hold your attention for a couple of listens. **B**

"Is This Love" [Paul McCartney]
Well, they can't all be gems. Dull flute intro over recycled ambient slush, augmented by whatever percussion happened to be lying around. The rest of it consists of bits of McCartney swooning about something no one cares much about, least of all him, an electronic wind threatening to blow it all away, and an irrelevant hum at the end. Remember how Paul supposedly came up with a new song every day? He should've taken the day off. **B-**

"Lovers in a Dream" [Paul McCartney]
The sound of someone strangling a whale gives way to elves frolicking in a slaughterhouse. The effects overtake whatever song fragments McCartney dug from his scrap bag. So this more of an ambient experiment – though darker than most – and less of a sing-able track. For those still on board, "Lovers in a Dream" makes a nice soundtrack for a siesta. **B**

"Universal Here, Everlasting Now" [Paul McCartney]
The tinkling piano, the yipping dog, the too-cute alarm clock – here lies *Electric Arguments'* fluffy side. The tune, which takes its time getting started, attempts a light rock mode, fails, continues anyway. The son of Brian Eno and A Flock of Seagulls. **B-**

"Don't Stop Running" [Paul McCartney]
Heavy on atmosphere and light on songwriting, the lyrics remind us of the title admonishment over and over, dotted with a few random comments that mean nothing. Apparently, this was assembled from snatches of airhead poetry. *"Chomping chocolate fur." "Cows dressed like ballerinas." "Chimes of hot dogs."* See? I can do it too. **B-**

"Road Trip" [Paul McCartney]
Hidden a couple of minutes after "Don't Stop Running," this postscript consists of sustained keyboard chords, electronic bleeps, and screaming birds falling out of their nests. If you like listening to screaming birds falling out of their nests, you'll like this. **B-**

[bonus]

"Solstice Ambient Acapella" [Paul McCartney]
The lighter side of Pink Floyd. But for 15 minutes? [*Electric Arguments Bonus*] **C**

"Travelling Light Instrumental" [Paul McCartney]
Remember Mike Oldfield in his *Tubular Bells* days? Too reserved to keep your attention from wandering. [*Electric Arguments Bonus*] **C**

"Wickerman Ambient Dub" [Paul McCartney]
Electronic filler is still you-know-what. [*Electric Arguments Bonus*] **C**

"Equinox Instrumental" [Paul McCartney]
Not a song, nothing memorably ambient. A cut above radio static. [*Electric Arguments Bonus*] **C**

"Sawain Ambient Acapella" [Paul McCartney]
A new mix of "Lifelong Passion" – no bass, no drums – has little substance, and therefore merits no one's attention. [*Electric Arguments Bonus*] **C-**

"Sawain Instrumental Dub" [Paul McCartney]
A *sawain* is an ancient Celtic spiritual celebration during which the celebrators meet up with their otherworldly brothers and sisters. This piece goes out to the Sawain Planning Council, Junior Division. [*Electric Arguments Bonus*] **C+**

"My Soul" [Nitin Sawhney; guest performer: Paul McCartney]
[Nitin Sawhney] A multi-talented musician from India, Sawhney has written and performed around the world, collaborating with artists as diverse as Brian Eno, the London Symphony Orchestra, and Sinead O'Connor. On this cut from his eighth studio album, he features friend McCartney as vocalist on this pretty, delicate piece. Paul performs reverently, with a voice purposely made to creak like an elderly sage. [*London Undersound*] **B+**

CHAPTER FORTY-ONE:

GOOD EVENING NEW YORK CITY [2009]

Produced by Paul McCartney
Charted at 16 [US], 28 [UK]

In 1965, a concert landmark was set in New York City's Shea Stadium. The headliners, naturally, were the Beatles, and 55,600 delirious fans were there to scream, drool, and pass out as the boys rocked their way through "Ticket to Ride" and "I Feel Fine." Not that you could hear them, but who cared? Being in their presence was satisfying enough.

In 2009, 43 years later, McCartney agreed to perform a sort of an anniversary tribute to the Beatles' performance and to informally launch the opening of the new Citi Field, essentially Shea Stadium's replacement. Ticket sales blasted to Pluto and beyond, as if the promoters were selling diamonds for a dime. For the three-night stand, attendance topped a staggering 180,000.

In preparation for these concerts [part of his summer tour] McCartney faced an obvious and inarguable fact: with extremely few exceptions, Beatles songs were more popular than his entire catalogue. Put another way, material roughly generated from 1963 to 1969 [six years] crushed the material from 1970 to 2009 [close to 50 years]. It was irrefutable. Why pretend otherwise? And, for all practical purposes, he *was* the Beatles. Two were dead, and one was, well, one was [sorry] Ringo. The legacy of the Beatles belonged to McCartney.

When audiences filled the sold-out stadium, they'd be primed to be dazzled by Paul McCartney and to experience an event they were unlikely to forget. But were they actually seeing him? Weren't they, in an understandable fantasy, actually seeing the Beatles? Then again, for a concert featuring Beatle music and one real-life Beatle, was there anyone who cared?

Paul, accommodating as always, was there to please. Of the 36 songs immortalized on *Good Evening New York City* [including "Foxy Lady," "Give Peace a Chance," and "The End," all added to other songs], 22 were by the Beatles. Almost two out of three.

"Drive My Car [Live 2009]" [Paul McCartney and John Lennon]
Brought to you by Worldwide Photocopiers. *"If you loved it then, you'll love it now."* **B-**

"Jet [Live 2009]" [Paul and Linda McCartney]
A song that stands shoulder-to-shoulder with Beatles numbers, this pounds the walls as good as it ever has, despite its wearing out its welcome a couple of live albums back. **B**

"Only Mama Knows [Live 2009]" [Paul McCartney]
Picks up power the more it's played, turning from a friendly kid rocker to a riveting growl-a-thon. It's no "Helter Skelter," but it's miles away from "Bip Bop." **B**

"Flaming Pie [Live 2009]" [Paul McCartney]
Tougher than it was on the *Flaming Pie* album, and tougher is better. Details of the song get lost in the live performance, however, so it's a toss-up if this exceeds the studio version. **B**

"Got to Get You Into My Life [Live 2009]" [Paul McCartney and John Lennon]
Heavenly father, thank you for the strength to forgive others, as they know not what they do. Specifically, thank you for the guidance I needed to change "Lennon-McCartney" to "McCartney-Lennon." I know

"Lennon-McCartney" caused my fans unnecessary confusion, which led to nightmares and over-eating. Or it would eventually. Or it should eventually. I know John would agree. Right, John? John? **B-**

"Let Me Roll It [Live 2009]" [Paul and Linda McCartney]
How has this changed since *Wings Over America*? Or *Tripping the Live Fantastic*? Or *Back in the U.S.A* ? **B-**

"Highway [Live 2009]" [Paul McCartney]
For this live recreation, begin by trashing all the studio sorcery that made "Highway" close to a keeper. Here's what's left: an undercooked stew of head-scratching lyrics, too-simple melodies, and pedestrian instrumentation. On *Electric Arguments*, "Highway" zapped from the sky like a lightning bolt from Zeus. On *New York*, it slurps like an old dog's tongue. **B-**

"Foxy Lady" [Jimi Hendrix]
A polite jam on the familiar riff, giving the musicians a chance to show off. The band does itself no favours by comparing themselves to Hendrix, but before this dawns on the audience, it's over. **C**

"The Long and Winding Road [Live 2009]" [Paul McCartney and John Lennon]
"The Long and Winding Road" appears on *Wings Over America, Give My Regards to Broad Street*, Live 1989, Live 1990, Anaheim 2002, and *Live 8*. That's a lot of winding roads. **C-**

"My Love [Live 2009]" [Paul and Linda McCartney]
Zombie approved. **C**

"Blackbird [Live 2009]" [Paul McCartney and John Lennon]
Have you heard of those hologram performances, where a three-dimensional image of manipulated light plays the tune, exactly the same every time? Just wondering. **B-**

"Here Today" [Live 2009]" [Paul McCartney]
Will his voice waver tonight? We ghouls want to know. **B-**

"Dance Tonight [Live 2009]" [Paul McCartney]
In what alternate universe has this become a concert staple? Possible reasons for its continued existence: [1] The composer still thinks it'll be a hit with enough exposure. [2] The composer heard from a few fans proclaiming how wonderful it is, and he extrapolated this to mean most of his fans feel the same way. [3] It's easy to play, a nice rest before the relatively demanding run of songs coming up. I vote for number three. **C**

"Calico Skies [Live 2009]" [Paul McCartney]
Maybe it's intended to join "Blackbird" and "Here, There, and Everywhere" in McCartney's throng of acoustic classics. That would account for its appearance his concert repertoire yet again. But "Calico Skies" is a minor piece, one doomed to ride in the back of the bus. How about the superior "Vanilla Sky" instead? **B-**

"Mrs. Vandebilt [Live 2009]" [Paul and Linda McCartney]
Enthusiastic rendition of an oldie with Paul flexing his muscular voice. Too bad about the cheesy synthetic sax – that should bring on a few chortles. **B**

"Eleanor Rigby [Live 2009]" [Paul McCartney and John Lennon]
Here's an idea. "Eleanor Rigby" is stuck on this concert disc for the poor souls who didn't catch the first, second, or third time McCartney sold it to you. Therefore, he should put "Golden Slumbers" on reissues of *Revolver* for all the folks who missed it. And while he's at it, he should add a synthetic orchestra. Cha-ching! **B-**

"Sing the Changes [Live 2009]" [Paul McCartney]
Probably started life as an innocent little song before McCartney and his pal Martin Glover sunk their claws in, turning it into a downpour of ragtag psychedelia and one of *Electric Arguments*'s least successful experiments. Back to the basics here, with every trace of psychedelia sent to the dressing room. But with

not much melody to sustain it, and lyrics of no use to anyone other than students of primitive poetry, McCartney might invite – or beg – the psychedelia to return. **B-**

"Band on the Run [Live 2009]" [Paul and Linda McCartney]
Gosh it's swell of Paul to sell this to us again. Now we can compare it to the other numerous versions of the same thing. Hold it – did he go a semitone flat on the twelfth note? See, this one's different! **B-**

"Back in the U.S.S.R. [Live 2009]" [Paul McCartney and John Lennon]
An audition for *Beatlemania: the Live Experience*. **B-**

"I'm Down [Live 2009]" [Paul McCartney and John Lennon]
Paul's in top notch voice for this scorcher. He blasts through like he's just remembered how good it is. If you're sitting still, somebody must've super glued your butt to your chair. **B**

"Something [Live 2009]" [George Harrison]
McCartney sidesteps the obvious – the Beatles version is superior, easy – by strumming the ukulele and changing the tempo a bit. It's charming but it's a notch worse on *Concert for George*, which featured the band majestically breaking in halfway. Still, this gives one and all the chance to bask in McCartney's mind-boggling voice, on full display. **B**

"I've Got a Feeling [Live 2009]" [Paul McCartney and John Lennon]
McCartney tip-toes around this for some reason – maybe his afraid of the high notes. So this is less a rock number than a recital for his relatives. "I've Got a Feeling" is roughly a quarter John's, so somebody other than him, obviously, has to sing his part. Guitarist Rusty Anderson handles it, but it's hard not to feel a little bit cheated, plus – again – it stirs up sympathy for a guy who'll never be here again. Next time, maybe McCartney can rent a hologram. **B-**

"Paperback Writer [Live 2009]" [Paul McCartney and John Lennon]
Another perfectly played Beatles tune. No wonder they love this guy. I love him too, my love growing exponentially as each new Beatles heart grabber rolls off the stage. But what's this? "My Love"? "Dance Tonight"? The wedding is off. **B-**

"A Day in the Life [Live 2009]" [John Lennon and Paul McCartney]
The Beatles masterwork, which means rock music's masterwork. Though Lennon originally sang it, here McCartney gives it a shot, his first time in public. He begins like a pastor opening a Bible – carefully, reverently, lovingly. Over the first two verses, his voice is hypnotic. The pre-taped orchestra eases in seamlessly. Then, abruptly – what the hell? "Give Peace a Chance?" Blasphemy! Depending on your regard for "A Day in the Life," the amputation of the last verse ranges from a big-deal shrug to a jaw-dropping outrage for a violating an anthem, and a sacred one at that. It's almost as if McCartney's interest dwindled after performing his segment of the track. **B**

"Give Peace a Chance [Live 2009]" [John Lennon and Paul McCartney]
Despite the fact that it swallowed "A Day in the Life"'s final verse, this comes a nice surprise, with the entire audience joyously singing along. But McCartney needs to shut up with those cringe-worthy asides. **B**

"Let It Be [Live 2009]" [Paul McCartney and John Lennon]
A certain segment of the audience would go home feeling cheated if they didn't hear the core of McCartney's songbook, which includes "Let It Be" and "Hey Jude." That's fine. But their pals might point out these songs are available all over the place, live and, even better, in the studio. Want a concert souvenir? Buy a t-shirt. **C**

"Live and Let Die [Live 2009]" [Paul and Linda McCartney]
Before you blow your paycheck on this largely useless artifact, I got news for you: fireworks not included. **C**

"Hey Jude [Live 2009]" [Paul McCartney and John Lennon]

I'm pretty sure there's some great marketing strategy behind including "Hey Jude" for whatever go-round this is. But that belongs in business school, not your record collection. **C**

"Day Tripper [Live 2009]" [John Lennon and Paul McCartney]

Add this to "A Day in the Life" as a second draw, deservedly so, as it's a Beatles atom bomb, never sung – at least start to finish – by Paul. His energetic performance, plus the band on fire, transforms it into a show stopper, with the ascending middle sending shivers from one end of the stadium to the other. Plus, we're treated to the whole thing, unlike the hacked in half "A Day in the Life." **B+**

"Lady Madonna [Live 2009]" [Paul McCartney and John Lennon]

Loses its luster in the wake of "Day Tripper." And more luster, fading away, with each subsequent run-though on each subsequent live album: Live 76, Live 93, Live 02 ... I'm sick of listing them. **B-**

"I Saw Her Standing There [Live 2009]" [Paul McCartney and John Lennon]

Its hair is turning gray. Alternate title: "I Saw Her Standing There, But I Can't Be Sure With These Bifocals." **B-**

"Helter Skelter [Live 2009]" [Paul McCartney and John Lennon]

Something about this metallic monster seems to bring McCartney back to life. Perhaps it's the tidal wave of praise it's gotten him over the years, dubbing him as the Godfather of Heavy Metal, suggesting that maybe he likes the Godfather of Heavy Metal better than "Bip Bop" dubbing him the Prince of Porridge. So you'd think there'd be scores of new heavy metal-ers in his solo repertoire. You'd be wrong. **B+**

"Get Back [Live 2009]" [Paul McCartney and John Lennon]

While McCartney and band walk through this for the umpteenth time, let's take the opportunity to name a few Beatles songs he has thus far ignored: "I Want to Hold Your Hand," "She Loves you," "Nowhere Man," "Hold Me Tight," "Maxwell's Silver Hammer." And oh yes: "The Ballad of John and Yoko." **B-**

"Sgt. Pepper's Lonely Hearts Club Band [Live 2009]" [Paul McCartney and John Lennon]

The original sounds like it was recorded on Popeye's spinach juice. This one sounds like it was recorded on cheap lemonade, complete with seeds. The shout-outs by lounge lizard McCartney don't help, and neither does cutting it down to a minute. It's not like we didn't have a couple of extra minutes to spare. **C**

"The End [Live 2009]" [Paul McCartney and John Lennon]

Still a masterpiece. Still glorious. I'm referring to the live version on *Tripping the Live Fantastic*. Or better yet, on *Abbey Road*. This is pointless. **B-**

[bonus]

"Cosmically Conscious [Live 2009] [Paul McCartney]

A three-for-one Beatles-era oddity: [1] McCartney performs it live for the first and last time. [2] He's joined in the festivities by Ringo Starr. [3] An all-star cast – including Ringo, Eddie Veder, Mike Love [?] and many more take part in the sing-along coda. The event is the Change Begins Within PETA concert, sponsored by the David Lynch Foundation, held at Radio City Music Hall in New York City. The once-in-a-lifetime show featured lengthy sets by Sheryl Crow, Donovan, Ringo, and others, all of whom were also part of the "Cosmically Conscious" finale. McCartney, starting the number with an acoustic guitar, is in fine voice, and the music makes up in enthusiasm what it lacks in the studio's psychedelic pizzazz. [Internet Only] **B**

"I Want to Come Home" [Paul McCartney]

McCartney composed this for the film *Everybody's Fine*, starring Robert De Niro. Apparently the movie's theme hit close to home. De Niro's character was on a nationwide trip to reconnect with his offspring, possibly reminding McCartney of the long stretches he's spent on the road. In any event, this delicate piano piece finds McCartney in a sentimental mood, occasionally wandering into a field of corn. Fine vocal and a tasteful arrangement, but a stronger tune would've helped. [Single] **B-**

"Meat Free Monday" [Paul McCartney]

McCartney is a big-time supporter of the vegetarian life, throwing his support [including cash] behind various meat-free causes, and this song is one of them. A simple, piano-based tune with partially sung/ partially spoken lyrics encouraging his fans to skip meat one day a week. It feels improvised, and the arrangement is nothing special, so I wouldn't lament its lack of commercial exposure. It exists online, apparently with Paul's blessing, making it relatively easy to find. In the meantime, do him a favour and ditch the hamburger. [Internet Only] **B-**

"Peace Dream" [Richard Starkey, Gary Wright, and Gary Nicholson; guest performer: Paul McCartney]

[Ringo Starr] Typical Starr minor league pleasantry. Its eyebrow-raising moment comes with a nod to John Lennon, awkward but sincere. McCartney's bass lingers somewhere in the background. [*Y Not*] **C+**

"Walk With You" [Richard Starkey and Van Dyke Parks; guest performer: Paul McCartney]

[Ringo Starr] Ringo joins forces with the illustrious Van Dyke Parks, co-author with Brian Wilson of the milestone *Smile* project, to produce an attractive duet with McCartney about the power of friendship. Touching lyrics coupled with a pedestrian melody hints at what could have been but doesn't achieve. Starr and McCartney, however, can't help but make this gentle outing more than a little moving. [*Y Not*] **B**

"I'm in Love Again [Voorman Version]" [Dave Bartholomew and Fats Domino; guest performer: Paul McCartney]

[Klaus Voormann] A mainstay on the Beatles' periphery, having contributed to projects as diverse as the cover for *Revolver* and bass duties on John Lennon's *Plastic Ono Band*. On his first solo album, he rounds up cohorts past and present, including McCartney who handles bass and vocal chores on Fats Domino's "I'm In Love Again," with Ringo Starr on drums. It's a serviceable track, brief and punchy, with McCartney and Starr in fine form. [*A Sideman's Journey*] **B**

"Boots and Sand" [Yusuf Islam aka Cat Stevens; guest performer: Paul McCartney]

[Yusuf Islam] Because of cowardly US policy, Islam and his daughter were denied entrance to America because of a piece of crap called a "No-Fly List." Instead of a bitter tirade, which Islam would've been perfectly justified in doing, the song remains thoughtful and dignified, rising above the creeps who supported and promoted such a petty law. McCartney sings subtle background. The song fades to an instrumental touch of "Peace Train," an appropriate ending. [*Roadsinger*] **B**

"As It Comes" [Fran Healy; guest performer: Paul McCartney]

[Fran Healy] Lead singer of Scottish band Travis, Healy is the spokesman for depression, at least he sounds that way on this track, a look back at a love gone down the tubes. A compelling, sensitive singer crooning a maudlin tune. McCartney's bass is low-key and just right. [*Wreckorder*] **B**

James McCartney

James is one of five McCartney kids, the only male. His sisters – Heather and Mary [the older] and Stella and Beatrice [the younger] – were more or less indifferent to a show biz career. But James was up for it and cautiously gave it a shot. His early efforts included guitar on "Heaven on a Sunday" on Flaming Pie *and co-writing "Spinning on an Axis" and "Back in the Sunshine Again," both on* Driving Rain. *Buoyed by the experience and encouraged by his father, James left home to polish his skills. In his early-to-mid-twenties, he worked as a waiter to make ends meet while he practised in his room.*

About four years later, when James was around 27, he began to record his own music, assisted by producers David Kahne and, not surprisingly, his father. Two EPs were accompanied by brief tours. His thoughtful songs and low-key style animated fans and critics alike, citing a promising new talent who, thankfully, didn't sound like dad.

Still, it was hard to escape the shadow of the most famous man in music, and possibly, the world. James seemed to be endlessly bombarded with the same old questions: Will your dad show up tonight? Are you tired of being compared to your father? What's your favourite Beatles song? He shrugged it all off, seemingly unfazed, and continues to soldier on.

"Angel" [James McCartney; producer: Paul McCartney with David Kahne]

[James McCartney] After accompanying his dad on his 2005 tour, James issued his first EP, a modest move for someone so ridiculously famous. The first track, "Angel," serves as an in-your-face introduction with a Byrds-like guitar supporting a not particularly supple but expressive voice, employing incisive lyrics that ought to make dad envious. By the way, Paul might have played a note or two on this and subsequent tracks, but if so, his contributions are too indistinguishable to make a difference. Considerer this James' art, all the way. [*Available Light EP*. This and the following four tracks were also issued on *The Complete EP Collection* in 2011] **B**

"Glisten" [James McCartney; producer: Paul McCartney with David Kahne]

His voice trails off into parts unknown and just about the entire tune feels improvised [chords first, melody dripped on top]. But it's better than average filler. [*Available Light EP*] **B-**

"My Friend" [James McCartney; producer: Paul McCartney with David Kahne]

An anthem for lost souls. I want to comfort this guy, right now. Not fond of the hiccups though. [*Available Light EP*] **B-**

"Denial" [James McCartney; producer: Paul McCartney with David Kahne]

[James McCartney] Back to the Byrd-ish guitar. When James rockets to the top of his range, it's chilling. With his a deeply pained persona just below the surface, he reminds me more of John Lennon than he does his dad. Now if he can just get more explicit with his lyrics and let us know exactly what he's feeling, rather than falling back on dad-like finger exercises. [*Available Light EP*] **B**

"Old Man" [Neil Young; producer: Paul McCartney with David Kahne]

[James McCartney] He's got some Lennon in him, but his world-weary what-can-you-do personality makes him a born-again Neil Young. A sharper, more intense take than the original track, plus the way he wraps his voice around these haunted lyrics reveals a man who means business. [*Available Light EP*] **B+**

"As It Comes" [Fran Healy; guest performer: Paul McCartney]

[Fran Healy] The singer of the Scottish group Travis recruited McCartney to add bass to this dream-like pop song, featuring Healy's smooth voice and an incessant, sticky riff that makes the song better than average. McCartney, ever the professional, is in there too, somewhere. [*Wreckorder*] **B**

CHAPTER FORTY-TWO:

OCEAN'S KINGDOM [2011]

Produced by John Fraser
Charted at 144 [US], did not chart [UK]

You've hung in there through McCartney's previous orchestral extravaganzas – are you up for one more? *Ocean's Kingdom*, a ballet based on a love story between ocean and earthly empires, falls victim to the worst of classical Paul [sprawling feel-your-way passages, warmed over Disney-derived sleepers] and comes up short on his strongest [memorable melodies, stylish arrangements]. As before, the musically handicapped McCartney, still unable to read or write music, called on outside help, utilizing the skills of composer John Wilson and orchestrator Andrew Cottee.

If nothing else, like the previous efforts, it's ambitious. But although the concept is interesting [water vs. earth], its execution is not. It's 50 minutes of underdeveloped ideas that some editing and rewriting could've shaped it into a tolerable, much shorter piece. But *Ocean's Kingdom* simply wafts in one ear, out the other. Inevitably, it's forgotten.

Generally, critics held their noses. *BBC Music*: "... McCartney well and truly floundered with this one." *Entertainment Weekly*: "A little watery." *The New York Times*: "... bland, thin, and occasionally incompetent." There was occasional encouragement: *PopMatters*: "... pleasant and moderately engaging classical music." But not much.

Meanwhile, on the home front, Paul and Nancy Shevell tied the knot on October 9, 2011 in a lavish London ceremony. She was 52, he was 69.

"Movement I: Ocean's Kingdom" [Paul McCartney]
Opening with a soothing impression of a rolling ocean, the trademark McCartney's coziness with melody promises interesting, though conservative, things to come. But it more or less stays put, not really going anywhere interesting and short-changing sections begging for development. It builds to a relatively energetic middle, but falls back on the not-that-intriguing ideas introduced in the beginning. More ebbs, more flows, more inoffensive meanderings. A dime store variation of Debussy's *La Mer*. **B-**

"Movement II: Hall of Dance" [Paul McCartney]
Listener friendly, "Hall of Dance" livens things up a little: hushed then high-spirited, jolly then ominous. But it sputters on its way to its 16-plus minutes conclusion [the longest of the four movements]. McCartney seems to reach for inspiration in snatches of vaguely recalled classical works from the past, making the movement mildly entertaining but second hand. Still, if you're interested in McCartney's classical ambitions, this melodic, albeit longish, movement is as good a place as any to start. **B-**

"Movement III: Imprisonment" [Paul McCartney]
Despite an occasional appealing morsel, "Imprisonment" is muddled and unadventurous. If this becomes part of the accepted ballet repertoire, I'll eat my dance card. **C**

"Movement IV: Moonrise" [Paul McCartney]
As we head for home, the strings swell, the horns appear, the orchestra looks around for Walt Disney as we float away on *La Mer*-isms that seem empty and not as beautiful as the composer has hoped. Now it's happy? Sad? What the hell is it? The spring-loaded woodwinds pop away, the strings add plastic melancholy. Too wearisome to be annoying, *Ocean's Kingdom* is a mild time-passer, sometimes poignant,

too often corny. For McCartney, master of the three-minute single, writing orchestral music is like hunting dinosaurs if you only have a pea shooter. **C**

[bonus]

"Ocean's Kingdom [Live]" [Paul McCartney]
The version considered above was performed by John Wilson conducting the London Classical Orchestra. Another version – the "live" version – was performed by conductor Faycal Karoui and the New York City Ballet Orchestra. As of now, it's available for those with a code card [found on either of the physical formats] to access the digital version from iTunes. All four movements are included. The attentive listener might pick up a more stately performance in this one, though "stately" could also mean "draggy," depending on your tolerance for conservative classical music. But the differences are minimal, and the stately/draggy-ness doesn't affect the ballet in any significant way. More to the point – does anyone want two versions? **C**

"I Only Want to Be Alone" [James McCartney; producer: Paul McCartney with David Kahne]
On his second EP, James sounds angrier, more frustrated, and even less like dad. A tough rocker, slightly sabotaged by James' tired vocals, the serviceable melody takes a back seat to the in-your-face-lyrics. Good stuff from an artist who's on his way – to greatness? Too early to tell, but it should be fascinating to watch. [*Close at Hand EP*. This and the following five tracks also appear on *The Complete EP Collection*. The extra tracks beginning with "New York Times," appear only on *The Complete EP Collection*, not on *Close at Hand*]. **B**

"Wings of a Lightest Weight" [James McCartney; producer: Paul McCartney with David Kahne]
As close to romantic as James gets. He keeps sentimentality at arm's length, a defense appropriate – as far as James is concerned – to the ups and downs of cold reality. Put another way, he takes a mature position, as opposed to a fluffy one often taken by a certain relative of his. He lacks Paul's musical facility and seems uncertain as how to compose a confident melody, an obvious flaw in "Wings of a Lightest Weight." Can he learn? I wouldn't bet against it. [*Close at Hand EP*] **B**

"The Sound of My Voice" [James McCartney; producer: Paul McCartney with David Kahne]
A majestic guitar opening, followed by a King Crimson-ish gathering of musical darkness, followed by not much of anything but routine vocals and mushy support. [*Close at Hand EP*] **B-**

"Else and Else But Dead" [James McCartney; producer: Paul McCartney with David Kahne]
James attempts a recipe for depression with this moody sigh-inducer, tenderly sung against resonant chords that border on the gorgeous. Not a recommended choice for weddings, but near-perfect if you're convinced the end is coming. [*Close at Hand EP*] **B**

"Jesus Be My Friend" [James McCartney; producer: Paul McCartney with David Kahne]
If a God-fearing man can't count on Jesus, he's got problems. After exposure to James' budding repertoire, there's no escaping the fact that James is an unhappy and confused fellow, somebody who desperately could use some cheering up, or at least needs a few spins of *Band on the Run*. Meanwhile, enjoy [?] yet another wistful, plaintive soul searching from a sad guy whose outlook seems to be the dead opposite of his father's. [*Close at Hand EP*] **B**

"Fallen Angel" [James McCartney; producer: Paul McCartney with David Kahne]
A masterful piano intro, played by James, introduces a powerful ballad with chilling vocals, demonstrating that singing prowess can indeed be inherited. It's been tough for dad to come up with a song this haunting, a high compliment to his talented son who, unfortunately, has the albatross of Paul hanging around his neck. [*Close at Hand EP*] **B+**

"New York Times" [James McCartney; producer: Paul McCartney with David Kahne]
If James had a good time in New York, the gloom hanging over this tune doesn't show it. A turgid, Neil Young-like guitar showcase, it peppers us with random images, ranging from street dwelling down-and-outers and self-serving stock brokers. But the melody doesn't go much of anywhere, making this a rare throwaway for James [*The Complete EP Collection*] **B-**

"I Love You Dad" [James McCartney; producer: Paul McCartney with David Kahne]
An up-tempo semi-bluegrass throwaway where the kid pledges his love for Paul. Like we doubted that? [*The Complete EP Collection*] **C+**

"Moonstar" [James McCartney; producer: Paul McCartney with David Kahne]
A catchy chorus weighed down by bland verses, but all of it intelligent. In spite of this hit-or-miss number – James has more imaginative songs elsewhere – how refreshing to hear an artist who's not afraid of his IQ. Hear that, Mr. Bip Bop? [*The Complete EP Collection*] **B-**

"Spirit Guides" [James McCartney; producer: Paul McCartney with David Kahne]
If regular folks disappoint, you can always appeal to the dead. This vague [and dumb] idea is about all that "Spirit Guides" has to offer lyrically. Musically, also negligible. I see why James and his producer felt the project needed more memorable rockers. This isn't it. [*The Complete EP Collection*] **C**

"Your True Love" [Carl Perkins; producer: Paul McCartney with David Kahne]
Knowing how dad loves Carl Perkins, this has Paul written all over it. But James not only handles it like an expert, he sounds supremely confident and, dare I say, sexy. [*The Complete EP Collection*] **B**

"Best Love" [Steve Martin; guest performer: Paul McCartney]
[Steve Martin] Martin, the comedian, has abandoned his arrow-through-the-skull routine [for now] to concentrate on bluegrass. This is his second music album. Vocalist McCartney manfully pitches in, Martin cranks up the banjo, and his band provides subtle support. Attractive blend, but McCartney sings like he's somewhere else. [*Rare Bird Alert*] **B**

"Rain Came Down" [Matt Berry]
[Matt Berry] Matt Berry is best known as a comic actor, appearing in *The Mighty Boosh* and *The Toast of London*, but he occasionally dabbles in albums, such as Music for Insomniacs. So who's the mystery background singer on "Rain Came Down?" Why, it's our boy Paul, providing nutty support on this light as a feather ditty. Not exactly a milestone, but fun all the same. [*Witchazel*] **B**

"I Saw Her Standing There [Billy Joel Version] [John Lennon and Paul McCartney]
[Billy Joel] For the most part, the Shea Stadium concert was enjoyable for the spectacle, not for musical performances. Sure enough, the stiff "I Saw Her Standing There" felt like Old Timers Night at the Ball Field. Easier to watch than to hear. [*Live at Shea Stadium: The Concert*] **C**

"Let It Be [Billy Joel Version] [John Lennon and Paul McCartney]
[Billy Joel] One more time. With each passing minute of "Let It Be," I feel thirty years older. [*Live at Shea Stadium: The Concert*] C

CHAPTER FORTY-THREE:

KISSES ON THE BOTTOM [2012]

Produced by Tommy LiPuma
Charted at 5 [US], 3 [UK]

Imagine buying this with no indication of what it's about. Instead of a fresh "Jet" or "Coming Up," the very un-rock, un-danceable, un-young disc introduces McCartney's takes on "Ac-Cent-Tchu-Ate the Positive" and "Bye Bye Blackbird," tunes from ancient times you recall from your great uncle's third wedding. None of them are penned by McCartney, except for two. The copyright date for the majority hovers somewhere in the 1930s, close to a hundred [a *hundred*?] years ago.

Paul McCartney is again on an archeological expedition. The man who gave us "You Gave Me the Answer," "When I'm 64," and "Honey Pie" – not to mention the un-thrilling *Thrillington* – has dug up a clutch of lounge crooner/martini swigging numbers to take us back to a different time, when "rock concert" referred to "prisoners hammering granite." For fans of the era, ecstasy. But for the indifferent, appalled by the very mention of Bing Crosby, they might want to slip this back in the rack.

Aside from McCartney's vocals, sumptuous as always, the rewards come not from the song selection, but from the interpretations of a crack band. Leading the proceedings: Diana Krall, arranger, jazz pianist, and three-time Grammy winner [and Elvis Costello's wife]. Also on board: John Clayton [jazz and classical double bassist], John Pizzarelli [guitar, 20 solo albums], Tommy LiPuma [who worked with Miles Davis, Barbara Streisand, and Natalie Cole], Eric Clapton, and Stevie Wonder. All good-naturedly dive in, performing in a suitably mellow mood.

Fan response was gratifying, as were the sales, indicated by the high positions *Kisses on the Bottom* reached in both the US and UK charts. Reviews were supportive, though few were enthusiastic: *Los Angeles Times*: "... a more satisfying listen if treated as a footnote in McCartney's repertoire." *Chicago Tribune*: "... this slow-dance with the misty past can't help but feel like a letdown." *NME*: "... if anyone on earth has earned the right to make the dreaded *Stuff I Loved When I Was Little* cover album, it's Paul McCartney."

Still, it seems reasonable to believe that the primary audience for *Kisses on the Bottom* isn't critics or fans or, for that matter, other human beings. Most likely, it's McCartney himself.

"I'm Gonna Sit Right Down and Write Myself a Letter" [Fred E. Ahlert and Joe Young]
Kisses on the Bottom kicks off with this leisurely stroll through Fats Waller's amiable hit from 1935. McCartney effortlessly nails a song nearly a century old, admirable on one hand, yet puzzling on another. As "I'm Gonna Sit Right Down" has been done so many times it's practically engrained in our DNA, why another version that adds little, except the novelty of a Beatle crooning away? Does McCartney's fondness for the era translate into an obsession to do it himself? **B-**

"Home [When Shadows Fall]" [Peter Van Steeden, Jeff Clarkson, and Harry Clarkson]
Another hit from the 30s, this one courtesy of co-writer Peter Van Steeden and sweetened by a petite orchestra. Here, it sounds like a template for "Baby's Request," the *Back to the Egg* track [coming up on a *Kisses* bonus]. McCartney's an expert at conjuring up records from the [very] distant past, demonstrated since "Till There Was You" [from the musical *The Music Man* by Meredith Wilson] on 1963's *Meet the Beatles*. But aside from marveling at his skill at mimicry, I'm at a loss as to what a typical McCartney fan – a lover of "Jet," "Band on the Run," even "My Love" – is supposed to do with this. One or two of them, say, "I'm Going to Sit Right Down and Write Myself a Letter" and "The Inch Worm," would have proved

McCartney's point and made for an acceptable B-side here and there. But a whole album? Maybe he wanted to broaden his audience. Do you feel broadened? **C**

"It's Only a Paper Moon" [Harold Arlen, E.Y. Harburg, and Billy Rose]
Ella Fitzgerald, among others, popularized this standard, yet another remnant of the 30s. Andy Stein adds some appropriately old-time violin, and McCartney is too precious for words. Three songs in. Uh, how much is left? **C**

"More I Cannot Wish For You" [Frank Loesser]
From the musical *Guys and Dolls*, McCartney approaches this soothing piece like a lullaby and succeeds in that respect. That is, until an unnecessary orchestra drifts in, squashing any subtleties having to do with the dreamy melody and turning it into middle-of-the-road mush. McCartney, meanwhile, goes blissfully on his way, as if he's singing into a mirror. **C**

"The Glory of Love" [Billy Hill]
Dean Martin and Jimmy Durante, who also sang this, welcome Paul with open arms as he clinks his cocktail, straightens his tuxedo, and eases into this sentimental standard. Elsewhere, the ghosts of John Lennon and Kurt Cobain roll their eyes and race for the door. Will your dad like this? Or does he prefer Dean Martin? **C+**

"We Three [My Echo, My Shadow, and Me]" [Sammy Mysels, Dick Robertson, and Nelson Cogane]
"We Three" was a number three hit for Frank Sinatra in 1940, defining for all time the word "smooth." A lot for Paul McCartney to live up to and, no surprise, he doesn't. Praise goes to Diana Krall's silky piano, and it probably tallies high for folks unfamiliar with Sinatra. But seniors – the obvious audience for *Kisses* – who remember this fondly may turn up their noses at the remake. **B-**

"Ac-Cent-Tchu-Ate the Positive" [Harold Arlen and Johnny Mercer]
McCartney comes to life, sort of, on this 1945 hit from the film *Here Come the Waves*, making room for a spirited solo by Diana Krall, the easy highlight. McCartney gets a kick out of the word play, almost giggling between the convoluted phrases. This one doesn't demand sexiness, just playfulness, making it ripe for Paul. **B**

"My Valentine" [Paul McCartney]
A song for wife Nancy. It's simple and pretty, featuring a sympathetic Eric Clapton guitar. So far so good, but then the superfluous violins come sneaking in. If only McCartney would've set aside the useless strings, this could've stayed out of the cornfield. But he didn't, and it lacks the substance to be more than a footnote to his catalogue. **B**

"Always" [Irving Berlin]
Back to the 20s for this Berlin ode to eternal love, sung by Frank Sinatra among others. Though it calls for a light touch, McCartney comes lumbering in like Frankenstein's monster. Sinatra makes it sound like a proposal. McCartney makes it sound like a threat. Of course, if this is what Franken-Paul intended – not impossible, considering the creepy "Loup [1st Indian on the Moon]" and "Catcall" – my apologies. **C**

"My Very Good Friend the Milkman" [Harold Spina and Johnny Burke]
Passing for *Kisses'* novelty song, it's another Fats Waller ditty from what apparently is McCartney's favourite decade, the 30s. He whistles in this one. The rest of the time, he sings like a 90 year old man. Intentionally. I think. Is that scary? **D+**

"Bye Bye Blackbird" [Ray Henderson and Mort Dixon]
When Ringo Starr attempted this on his *Sentimental Journey* album [1970], he could barely handle the melody, but compensated somewhat by imbuing the tune with an easygoing sense of humour. No humour here, or anywhere else on *Kisses on the Bottom* for that matter. It could've used some. McCartney might have studied the Bonzo Dog Band, one of his own production projects from 1968 , to see how a few good-natured laughs – check out "By a Waterfall" [*Tadpoles*] or "Mickey's Son and Daughter" [*Gorilla*] – can make these oldies more palatable to fans not normally sympathetic to the musical museum. **C-**

"Get Yourself Another Fool" [Frank Haywood and Ernest Tucker]
Sam Cooke recorded this in 1963, making it *Kisses'* most modern covers at a mere 50-plus years old. McCartney sings as cool as always, but he sounds reserved, locking the tune's sexiness in the closet. Eric Clapton's leisurely guitar, a voice in itself, is the track's highlight. **B-**

"The Inch Worm" [Frank Loesser]
In 1968, McCartney produced Mary Hopkin's *Postcard* album which included a gorgeous rendition of this 1952 song, complete with an ethereal accordion and a chilling children's chorus. By comparison, his own version sounds empty and half-done. Worse, his old man voice – virtually the same one he uses on the entire album – pales before hers, which sounds vibrant and young. **B-**

"Only Our Hearts" [Paul McCartney]
This McCartney original finds him slipping into his grandpa pants, confirming that, for this album anyway, he doesn't want to be Mick Jagger. He wants to be Tony Bennett. Longtime pal Stevie Wonder adds a modest solo, channelling "I Just Called To Say I Love You," with "Superstition" a distant memory. **C**

[bonus]

"Baby's Request [2012 Version]" [Paul McCartney]
The backing improves on the original [*Back to the Egg*], thanks to the pristine mini-combo under Diana Krall's direction, and McCartney's half-whispered vocals. All provide an up-all-night ambience lacking in the original. But the song remains a so-so effort. [*Kisses on the Bottom Deluxe*] **B-**

"My One and Only Love" [Guy Wood and Robert Mellin]
Lounge lizard McCartney accepts the challenge for this tricky song that swoops and dives like a drunken acrobat, unusual, to say the least, for a popular tune from the 50s. Will he pull it off? Yes he will. Of course, "Jet" has already proven he's got the goods, as does his killer live "Helter Skelter." C'mon, admit it – doesn't the mere mention of "Jet" tempt you to bury "My One and Only Love" in a hole? A deep hole? Covered in concrete? [*Kisses on the Bottom Deluxe*] **B-**

"The Christmas Song" [Mel Torme and Bob Wells]
Good luck going up against Mel Torme on this Christmas classic. Correct me if I'm wrong, but I believe McCartney owns this one, as he does the Buddy Holly catalogue and hundreds of others. McCartney does his best Torme impression, which is a mistake as it comes off exactly like, well, an impression. A perfect opportunity to show us an old song in a different way, like, perhaps, reggae. On second thought, we all remember "Rudolph the Red Nosed Reggae," so forget it. [*Kisses on the Bottom – Complete Kisses*] **B-**

"My Valentine [Original Arrangement]" [Paul McCartney]
Inconsequential differences from the original, although if I had to choose one at gunpoint, I'd go for this one. Still, the Johnny Mandel version is slightly more eccentric, hence, more interesting. But like Paul's version, it's burdened by too many sappy strings. [*Kisses on the Bottom – Complete Kisses*] **B**

Complete Kisses [Kisses on the Bottom Live in the Studio]
I have the perfect birthday present for McCartney: *The Complete Fun House*, a 7 CD set that details the making of *Fun House* by the Stooges. It features the same band attempting the same arrangements over and over again. For example, the band attempts 15 takes of "Down in the Street" and 28 takes of "Loose." McCartney ought to be tickled pink, knowing his fondness for issuing multiple takes of the same song over and over again, like "Hey Jude," which is up around nine.
So in the tradition of the Stooges, here we have *Live Kisses*, a bonus album featuring the entire [all but one] *Kisses on the Bottom* album – plus a bonus track ["My One and Only Love"], which we've already heard once before. All of it is live in the studio, with more or less the same musicians, arrangements, and lead vocalist. Difference range from the minor to the next-to-nothing. For instance, some of the song lengths differ ["Get Yourself Another Fool" rambles on forever], and occasionally, McCartney sings less intimately, which is sort of interesting. Sort of.
So who's the audience for this? Three possibilities: [1] The fanatic collector who demands copies of McCartney's every cough, wheeze, and belch. [2] The crazed fanatic who buys everything automatically.

[3] The surprised recipient of a gift from his kindly but clueless aunt. As for the omitted song, how come "The Inch Worm" got booted? Not that we need it – again. [*Kisses on the Bottom – Complete Kisses*] **D**

"Cut Me Some Slack" [Paul McCartney, Dave Grohl, Krist Novoselic, and Pat Smear; guest performer: Paul McCartney]

[Nirvana] Or what's left of them. Noisy, no melody, and surprisingly terrific. This collaboration between McCartney and Nirvana should've been a disposable mess, and in a way, it is. But those screeching guitars prod McCartney into rising to the occasion and screaming his balls off. Supposedly from a jam session, but who cares? If Nirvana needs a new front man, I have a suggestion. [*Sound City: Real to Reel*] **B+**

"He Ain't Heavy, He's My Brother" [Bob Russell and Bobby Scott; guest performer: Paul McCartney]

[Justice Collective] The Hillsborough Disaster, where a crush at a Sheffield football game left nearly 100 dead, spawned this response: an overproduced maudlin weeper, not dissimilar enough from the Hollies or original enough to make you lunge for your wallet. A flock of musicians [Peter Hooten, Melanie C, Tony Hicks, among others] take turns on pieces of the song, with a sincere McCartney doing his dullest. Send these folks some money and tell them to keep the record. [*He Ain't Heavy* 7" single] **D**

"Helter Skelter [Sandy Relief]" [John Lennon and Paul McCartney]

[Various Artists] McCartney joined the Rolling Stones, the Who, and Bruce Springsteen and other superstars at a New York City benefit concert for victims of Hurricane Sandy, a killer storm that wiped out areas of the northeastern United States. "Helter Skelter" isn't up to par with his *Good Evening New York City* take, thanks to his vocals [a bit weary], but it's still a scorcher. [*12-12-12 The Concert for Sandy Relief*] **B**

"The Christmas Song [Alternate]" [Mel Torme and Robert Wells]

[Various Artists] No strings, at least none audible, always a plus. But a Torme imitator, no matter how good, makes for a low budget holiday. **B-**

"Scrambled Eggs" [Gerard Bradford, Mike DiCenzo, John Lennon, and Paul McCartney; guest performer: Paul McCartney]

[Jimmy Fallon] From a collection of *Tonight Show* sketches, this consists of Fallon and McCartney singing stupid lyrics to the melody of "Yesterday." McCartney plays along, Fallon follows nervously. Amusing once. Twice, not so much. [*Blow Your Pants Off*] **C-**

CHAPTER FORTY-FOUR:

NEW [2013]

Produced by Giles Martin, Paul Epworth, Mark Ronson, and Ethan Johns
Charted at 3 [US], 3 [UK]

After clearing his tonsils on *Kisses on the Bottom*, McCartney was chomping at the bits to head back to the studio for a new rock album. He came up with a memorable one, the sparkling *New*, a disc that fondly examines his past while keeping both feet planted in the present.

His planted feet owe a good deal to his choice of producers, of which there were four, all of them hot, all of them sharp. Giles Martin, son of George Martin and executive producer of *New*, handled most of the album, adding a cautious, reserved sheen to McCartney's tunes, much as he'd done for the *50th Anniversary Editions* of *Sgt Pepper* and *The Beatles [White Album]*. Paul Epworth, producer of Adele and Rihanna, added contemporary and occasionally aggressive touches to "Queenie Eye" and "Save Us." Producer of Bruno Mars, Mark Ronson kept an eye on the old days, moulding "Alligator" and "New" to fit comfortably beside latter day Wings. Ethan Johns, the most traditional of the four and collaborator with Tom Jones and Ryan Adams, stressed an acoustic simplicity appropriate for "Hosanna" and "Early Days."

Rather than four disparate approaches, the multiple producers succeeded in nurturing a rainbow of styles that complimented each other, an appealing tactic that inadvertently echoed the Beatles in their waning years. Whether intentional or accidental, it worked, especially in creating the kaleidoscopic feel that McCartney was after.

Dazzled by McCartney's musical brilliance, it's easy to overlook his deft talents at marketing. But evidenced by his efforts since the beginning of his solo career, he's proven himself to be a promoter *par excellence*. In 1970, right after the Beatles split, he issued a clever "self interview" which not only addressed the Beatles' problems, but also functioned to announce his first album, *McCartney*. No stranger to the power of television, practically every album has been accompanied by a flurry of TV interviews and performances, which serve to introduce his new music to a Paul-hungry world, as did a barrage of music videos that never seemed to end. *New* continues in the same vein, adding previews on Instagram, a chat on Twitter, and a clever mini-concert – staged like a drive-in movie- in New York City, featuring songs from you-know-what.

Nimble as a kid, McCartney was 71.

"Save Us" [Paul McCartney and Paul Epworth]
Rushing through the melody like his shorts are on fire, McCartney, beneath the usual lovey-dovey platitudes, cries out in near-desperation for somebody, anybody to throw him a lifeline, making this oddly compelling tune more attractive than usual. The despairing vocals, weary in spots, add to the razor-edged performance of this solid [but not stellar] tune, suggesting that those of us still paying attention could be in for an interesting ride, almost unimaginable for a McCartney album. **B**

"Alligator" [Paul McCartney]
The album's oldest song. I guess he's been uneasy about life stuff for some time, although he's too crappy a lyricist to flat-out say what's specifically bugging him. Okay, fine. On to the melody, a light reggae featuring a chirpy synthetic flute, a static vocal, and a disparate bridge, all of it adding up to a song in need of a lot more work. **C+**

"On My Way to Work" [Paul McCartney]

McCartney examines a moment in time when he was a youngster, pre-Beatles, working for a delivery service. On that particular day, he bought a cheap periodical featuring an attractive nude, then picked up his delivery stuff and went on his way, the nude reminding him, I guess, that he had yet to locate the nude of his dreams. Too vague to inspire like-minded memories from his listeners, except that we had crummy jobs as kids and salivated over naked women when adults weren't looking. So we listen, shrug, and move on, wondering how a talented lyricist – say, John Lennon – might have brought this to life. On to the melody, which supports a wishy-washy tune with a routine acoustic guitar. Despite the promising title, this is close to filler. **B-**

"Queenie Eye" [Paul McCartney and Paul Epworth]

On the heels of the single "New," "Queenie Eye" also took a shot at the charts. With the exception of Japan [where stunningly, it hit the Top Ten], it too belly-flopped, continuing McCartney's dismal chart performance since the turn of the century. Like "New," "Queenie Eye," inspired by a children's game of the same name, lacks a memorable melody in the verses, but comes alive on the chorus, a sing-along that's both imaginative and irresistible. **B**

"Early Days" [Paul McCartney]

Where "On My Way to Work" falters, "Early Days" succeeds, painting a picture of the embryonic Beatles complete with slicked down hair, a trudge down streets while stylishly dressed in black, and an envious gaze at the photos of superstars pinned to the wall. What makes these images come alive is McCartney's reaction: he felt strange and uneasy, consciously laughing it all off lest the chaos of the Beatles times drove him batty. Wisely, McCartney confined the accompaniment for this folky number to primarily acoustic backing so as not to draw attention away from his story. Simple, starkly effective, and – who would have thought? – a winner. **B+**

"New" [Paul McCartney]

A bright, keyboard-driven pop killer, exactly what McCartney does best, sans all the smarmy lyrics that make similar [and inferior] efforts hard to digest. Beatle-y? A bit, but not so much that it seems warmed over [although the tempo and tone are reminiscent of "Good Day Sunshine"]. The clever mix of instruments give it colour, as bright as a spring day, with only the middle section lacking the propulsive melody inherent in the verses. Vocally superb and the production flawless, "New" is the stuff of Beatle dreams. **B+**

"Appreciate" [Paul McCartney]

McCartney talks to himself in "Appreciate," wondering if he might consider fixing things [things unnamed] before he's six feet under. Any serious ideas, however, are lost in the murky production, and the omnipresent electronics overwhelm the human dilemma McCartney struggles to explore. But he's trying, so good for him. Not only is there nothing wrong with writing about death, but for artists over 70 shouldn't it be required? It's got to be on their minds more than another dopey love affair. **B**

"Everybody Out There" [Paul McCartney]

A simple tune and a complicated subject [death] that McCartney circles around but unfortunately never quite tackles head on. Beneath the happy-go-lucky persona he stubbornly insists on presenting to the world lies a troubled guy whom he struggles – or refuses – to acknowledge. Of course, McCartney's lazy attitude regarding anything poetic makes his lyrics the usual confusing mess. For all I know, he could be singing about rerooting his house. But "Everybody Out There"'s startling climax doesn't sound like he's misplaced his shingles. It sounds like he's just spotted the Grim Reaper. **B+**

"Hosanna" [Paul McCartney]

Don't you just hate love? "Hosanna" is the tune McCartney and his sweetums warble together at dawn. What kind of woman goes for this stuff? Maybe the same kind who finds this turgid crud romantic. **C-**

"I Can Bet" [Paul McCartney]

Whereas "New" and "Everybody Out There" are fresh and surprising, "I Can Bet" is as inert as a dead guppy. McCartney sounds restrained, as if he's having trouble connecting with a song that, admittedly, doesn't offer much in the way of substance. Plus, the you're-gonna-get-it lyrical subtext makes it somewhat uncomfortable. Couple that to the aggressive, borderline metal background on the intro and bridges, what's left is a song that needed a critical eye that McCartney had firmly shut. **C+**

"Looking at Her" [Paul McCartney]

A love song swimming in self-doubt, adding an unexpected depth that makes it superior to all the "Silly Love Songs" tripe he's cranked out for years. That's the good news. Bad news – the tune sucks. Whether it was actually improvised on a first take is beside the point, because it sounds like it was. Somewhere, amid the puzzling phrases, the musical wanderings, and the surprising loud/soft segments, lurks a passable track. This is not it. **C+**

"Road" [Paul McCartney and Paul Epworth]

Sort of a throwback to the days of the *Fireman*, this spacey improv/jam offers to take the listener to a distant place where synthesizers roam free. McCartney opines about whatever wanders through his head while polite electronics swirl and pop, snare drums rattle away, and a catchy keyboard riff emerges periodically, only to be whooshed away by a chorus of cooing Pauls. Have I made this sound better than it is? Yes I have. **B-**

"Scared" [Paul McCartney]

He's not particularly afraid of dying, losing loved ones, or his career. So what's he afraid of? Why, commitment. This should come as no surprise to McCartney scholars who time and again have read of McCartney's voluminous exploits in the lust department, seldom getting closer than arm's length to his intended lover. So here's his king sized sorry, dressed up in a "Let It Be"-ish ballad, all sincere and lovely, before he jets away. **B**

[bonus]

"Turned Out" [Paul McCartney]

So melody-free it practically qualifies as a rap song, McCartney opines about ... oh, who cares? In the tradition of Paul releasing everything he decides is finished. Which generally speaking, is everything. [*Deluxe New*] **D-**

"Get Me Out of Here" [Paul McCartney]

McCartney is pissed that the tax collector is pounding on the door, hence the basis of "Get Me Out of Here." Did he notice the homeless guy in the alley down the street, the one gobbling dog food? Of course McCartney has the right to be indignant, but fortunately, the royalties from this nondescript tune – which lacks even a glimmer of the humour prevalent in George Harrison's "Taxman" – should take care of at least a piece of his tax bill. [*Deluxe New*] **D**

"Struggle" [Paul McCartney]

Need an idea for how to get with that cute girl? How about comparing yourself to strychnine? If you thought the title promised more McCartney introspection, boy, were you wrong. It's another shallow love song with inane lyrics and an inappropriate electronic background going back to *McCartney II*. [*Japanese Edition New*] **C**

"Hell to Pay" [Paul McCartney]

"Hell to Pay" is to *New* as "Maxwell's Silver Hammer" is to *Abbey Road*. [*Collector's Edition New*] **C –**

"Demons Dance" [Paul McCartney]

With two chords toggling back and forth, McCartney improvises a quasi-melody which morphs into a gospel-ish flopper. No demons, dancing or otherwise. [*Collector's Edition New*] **C**

"Save Us [Live 2013]" [Paul McCartney and Paul Epworth]

Minus the electronics of the original, what's left is a grown-up concert piece, tight and to the point, and a surefire crowd pleaser, rightly so. Makes the days of "Rock Show" [*Wings Over America*] seem long ago. [*Collector's Edition New*] **B**

"New [Live 2013]" [Paul McCartney]
A great album track doesn't necessarily translate into a live wonder. Witness "New," boasting a strong melody that McCartney has trouble navigating as smoothly as he did on the album. Plus the backup vocals are obtrusive and unnecessary. If he reworks this – that is, practice – it'd could easily find a home on the set list. I mean, "Biker Like an Icon" did. [*Collector's Edition New*] **B**

"Queenie Eye [Live 2013]" [Paul McCartney and Paul Epworth]
Adequate recreation of the album track, energetic and punchy. Maybe too intimate for these show biz spectacles? Probably. So give the edge, if only a slight one, to the album. [*Collector's Edition New*] **B**

"Everybody Out There [Live 2013]" [Paul McCartney]
Reasonably solid presentation of the album track. But more of the screaming coda is needed, immediately. [*Collector's Edition New*] **B**

"Hope for the Future" [Paul McCartney]
From the video game *Destiny*. Yes, a video game. As video game soundtracks go, it's – wait a sec. Did I say *video game*? [*Hope for the Future* single, including various remixes] **D**

"Destiny [Soundtrack]" [Michael Salvatori, C Paul Johnson. Martin O Donnell, and Paul McCartney]
The full video game soundtrack [which doesn't include the previously mentioned "Hope for the Future"] comprising dozens of orchestral fragments, about half of which McCartney had a hand in ["The Hope," "The Rose," and "Tranquility," among others]. Though attractive in a conventional way, overall, they're mostly too overwrought and borderline pretentious to pay off. Recommended to admirers of *Standing Stone*. [*Destiny Original Soundtrack*] **B –**

"In the Blink of an Eye" [Paul McCartney]
McCartney is a sucker for cartoons, so this heart-tugging animated movie was catnip to him. Performed over the closing credits, it's a melancholy piano piece with sweeping harps, an army of violins, and a sincere McCartney who croons a familiar melody; meaning, it's a melody he's sliced and diced in a variety of ways in a variety of settings, more times than I care to consider. Plus, those strings reek. [*Ethel & Ernest Original Motion Picture Soundtrack*] **C**

"Another Girl [Live 2015]" [John Lennon and Paul McCartney]
This Japanese concert was showcasing the usual when, out of nowhere, McCartney debuted this oldie from *Help*, a song neither he nor the Beatles had ever played live before. One reason: It's not much a song, padding for the soundtrack, and the movie's most forgettable. McCartney duplicates it precisely, but seems distant and detached from the vocal. As such, after the initial thrill of hearing the opening, which takes maybe 15 seconds, impatience begins to bloom. Maybe a better one is coming? Maybe "Tell Me What You See"? [*Live in Japan*] **B-**

"Out of Sight" [Paul McCartney; guest performer: Paul McCartney]
[Bloody Beetroots] Electronic combo from Italy, specializing in spacey dance music. McCartney whines like he's trying to dig a splinter from his toe, while the impressive group swirls and darts around him, then gives up and goes home. [*Out of Sight* single] **B-**

"All of Me" [Gerald Marks and Seymour Simons]
[Eric Clapton] Inspired [maybe] by *Kisses on the Bottom*, Clapton assembled his own album of standards, recruiting pals like Steve Winwood, Taj Mahal, and Paul McCartney to pitch in. McCartney adds vocal harmonies and bass to this inconsequential excursion to Nowhere Land. [*Old Sock*] **C**

"Wonderful Christmastime [Remake]" [Paul McCartney; guest performer: Paul McCartney]
[Straight No Chaser] Fans of white bread acappella groups will be delighted with this non-daring cover of one of McCartney's worst. The band ooos and ahhs, as McCartney does his best to recreate the original. Awful. [*Under the Influence: Holiday Edition*] **D**

"Only One" [Kayne West, Paul McCartney, Kirby Lauryen, Mike Dean, and Noah Goldstein; guest performer: Paul McCartney]

[Kayne West] West paused on his way to world domination to record this ode to his daughter, with musician McCartney helping out. A Kayne effort through and through, it makes one inclined to ask, who's doing who the favour? [*Only One* single] **B**

"Fourfiveseconds" [Kanye West, Paul McCartney, Kirby Lauryen, Mike Dean, Ty Dolla Sign, Dave Longstreth, Robyn Fenty, Elon Rutberg, and Noah Goldstein; guest performer: Paul McCartney]

[Rihanna, Kayne West, and Paul McCartney] The powerfully sung "Fourfiveseconds" makes your head swirl when Rihanna takes over. Kayne holds his own, barely, but the song belongs to Rihanna. And McCartney? Acoustic guitar? Is he there? [*Fourfiveseconds* single] **B**

"All Day" [Kanye West, Paul McCartney, Tyler Bryant, Kendrick Duckworth, Karim Kharbouch, Ernest Brown, Cydel Young, Allan Kyariga, Mike Dean, Che Pope, Noah Goldstein, Allen Ritter, Mario Williams, Charles Njapa, Patrick Reynolds, Malik Jones, Rennard East, and Noel Ellis; guest performer: Paul McCartney]

[Kanye West] Interesting work from West, but McCartney's inclusion is a head-scratcher. Lyrically, it's not his style, and West's effortless electronics make McCartney's attempts at the same [like his *Fireman* experiments] seem like something from the Paleolithic Age. McCartney's evident on the coda, but it's brief and nothing special. This is West all the way. [*All Day* single] **B**

"Love Song to the Earth [Natasha Bedingfield, Paul McCartney, Tony Gad, and John Shanks]

[Friends of the Earth] For the worldwide environmental group Friends of the Earth, Paul collaborates on a tedious song that squanders its good will on a lame melody and lousy production. Is this any way to treat your favourite planet? [*Love Song to the Earth* single] **D-**

"We're On the Road Again" [Ringo Starr and Steve Lukather; guest performer: Paul McCartney]

[Ringo Starr] When I first spotted this on the track list, I mistakenly thought it was the Willie Nelson song. Or maybe the Canned Heat song. No such luck. Ringo and Steve [of Toto] clawed their way through ancient clichés, shoved a few together, and came up with this dull tune. Built around a routine guitar riff, the simple melody poses no challenge for Ringo, always a plus for him, and the forced enthusiasm from the band isn't going to move many tickets. So where's McCartney? In the chorus, hiding. [*Give More Love*] **D**

"Show Me the Way" [Ringo Starr and Steve Lukather; guest performer: Paul McCartney]

[Ringo Starr] Polish your ear trumpet and listen closely for Paul's bass, a minor element of this pedestrian ballad. [*Give More Love*] **C**

"Come and Get It [Remake]" [Paul McCartney; guest performer: Paul McCartney]

[Alice Cooper/Hollywood Vampires] Is this a meeting of the minds? Or of the cash registers? Cynics may suspect the latter, as this gathering of Hollywood superstars – Aerosmith's Joe Perry, Foo Fighters' Dave Grohl, actor Johnny Depp [?] – emits a suspicious odor. On the other hand, there are worse ideas than having a bunch of old guys [Alice is around 67] blast through tunes by dead stars, including Jimi Hendrix's "Manic Depression," John Lennon's "Cold Turkey," and Nilsson's "Jump Into the Fire." McCartney drops by for a heavy metal re-do of Badfinger's "Come and Get It." With an in-charge Alice guiding the proceedings, all concerned, McCartney included, are thoroughly non-offensive. Though this version of "Come and Get It" comes off less like an end-of-the-world anthem and more like a cartoon theme song, the results are charming. An example of feather-light metal? [*Hollywood Vampires*] **B**

"If I Take You Home Tonight" [Paul McCartney]

[Diana Krall] Written during the *Kisses on the Bottom* session, left for dead by McCartney, then dug up by Krall, "If I Take You Home Tonight" is a gorgeous ballad that McCartney was crazy to abandon, as it surpasses his other *Kisses* material, including "My Valentine." While it's no "For No One" or "Waterfalls," the intimate vocal makes it worth a listen. [*Wallflower*] **B**

"Sunday Rain" [Foo Fighters; guest performer: Paul McCartney]
[Foo Fighters] McCartney plays drums, not bad at all, on this pop-grunge piece, which is sort of reggae, but not enough to offend metal purists. [*Concrete and Gold*] **B**

"Songbird in a Cage" [Paul McCartney; guest performer: Paul McCartney]
[Charlotte Gainsbourg] Gainsbourg, daughter of renowned musician Serge Gainsbourg [pop music giant] and actor Jane Birkin [1966's *Blowup*], is a French film star and singer who reportedly came to the attention of McCartney when over lunch she asked if he had any unused tunes lying around, and he offered this one. Not much of a gift, as it relies on a fluff of a melody and electronic doodles. McCartney supplies elementary instrumental support, so routine that, except for fanatic collectors, it makes the record useless. [*Rest*] **D+**

CHAPTER FORTY-FIVE:

EGYPT STATION [2018]

Produced by Greg Kurstin, Paul McCartney, Ryan Tedder, and Zach Skelton
Charted at 1 [US], 3 [UK]

Paul McCartney spent the five years after the release of *New* touring the planet [*Out There Tour* and *One on One*], sharing his interpretations of Beatles songs and contemplating his future days, of which there was an increasing short supply. At the same time, his loyal fan base were clutching their pearls, fearful that even though live performances of "Hey Jude" and "Let It Be" were enjoyable, there was reason to believe that new material was but a distant memory. McCartney was, after all, roughly 76 years old.

They needn't have worried. McCartney came back with an album of generally solid material in the unusually named *Egypt Station* [which shared a title with a McCartney painting]. And further, picking up where *New* left off, he unleashed an onslaught of public relations consisting of a barrage of special performances, breezy interviews and special events that would put McDonalds to shame.

In mid-2018, McCartney began the *Egypt Station* campaign with a flurry of teaser spots on various social media platforms, implying that he was about to unleash something big. Which could mean anything, though hopeful fans were crossing their fingers for something brand new. Time passed. Lo and behold, the finger-crossers were right, evidenced by not one but two videos from McCartney's forthcoming project, "I Don't Know" and "Come On to Me." Though the tunes were on the thin side, the performances were appealing and, more importantly, demonstrated that the old man could still sing.

Next, McCartney announced a secret – that is, a not-secret – micro-concert at Abbey Road Studios, featuring a few of his new songs [and scads of publicity], followed by another non-secret gig at the Cavern Club, McCartney's go-to spot for all things Beatle. To further placate his starving fans, he slipped in another new song, "Who Cares."

These shows preceded a dizzying array of videos, one after the other, turning home computers into Paul-O-Vision. McCartney's video singles marched across screens worldwide, including "lyric videos" [read while you watch!] for the naughty "Fuh You," and another new one, "Back in Brazil." Elsewhere, McCartney patiently endured a lengthy *YouTube* chat where he explained the back stories to a clutch of Beatle songs, primarily tired retellings for the umpteenth time, though the always professional McCartney told them as if they'd just occurred to him. An hour-plus talk at the Liverpool Institute for Performing Arts became an online hit. And if you left the screen, there he was, profiled in *GQ* magazine for an entertaining story that also managed to squeeze in a reference to *Egypt Station*.

And there was more. A blitz of television appearances included interactions of all stripes, with a nod to *Egypt Station* slipped in whenever possible. A show biz powwow with Jimmy Fallon on *The Tonight Show*. A one-to-one on *The Howard Stern Show*. A stint *with Late Late Show* host James Corden for his "Carpool Karaoke" segment, after which McCartney popped over to Liverpool's Philharmonic Dining Room and performed an impromptu "Come On to Me." Care for more? How about a subway ride using a Metropolitan Transportation Authority set of *Egypt Station* Metro Cards?

McCartney's most impressive coup was another not-secret performance at the smartly chosen Grand Central Station in New York City where, with his band, he performed a short but hit-heavy concert for swooning fans. The song list included Beatle faves, such as "Can't Buy Me Love" and "Blackbird," as well as *Egypt* excerpts "Come On to Me" and "Fuh You." Available on *YouTube*? Of course.

So did all this publicity actually help the album? Kind of. According to *Billboard*, McCartney sold more albums during the week of the *Egypt Station*'s barrage than he had since *Memory Almost Full* in 2007.

More significantly, it was McCartney's first #1 album which impressively debuted at the top spot.

The triumph, however, was short lived. He remained at the top for only a single week. Again, according to *Billboard*, the second week found *Egypt Station* hemorrhaging customers with sales plunging a depressing 76 percent. Who knocked him off? Carrie Underwood, the country queen, with *Cry Pretty*.

"Opening Station" [Paul McCartney]
More coherent and less dumb than "Loup [1st Indian on the Moon]" [*Red Rose Speedway*] or "Reception" [*Back to the Egg*], similarly tossed-off montages, this works as a moody but shallow introduction for things to come. *Sgt. Pepper* boasted a comparable opener which at the time seemed revolutionary. But that was then. **B-**

"I Don't Know" [Paul McCartney]
He's depressed, but nobody said being elderly was easy. Minor chords, a barely audible acoustic guitar, and a guy who sounds on the verge of doing something awful, then talks himself out if it right before he steps into the pit. Although musically lacking, the painful lyrics make it a fascinating treatise on McCartney's woebegone state of mind. If this opener – forget "Opening Station" – established the intent of *Egypt Station*, this could be McCartney's *Plastic Ono Band*, and his most adult effort since the days of "For No One." Of course … **B+**

"Come On to Me" [Paul McCartney]
… it isn't. A stripped-down lightweight pop song, intentionally commercial and aimed at the McCartney-starved masses. But it only made it to #10 on the Adult Contemporary Chart [read: Easy Listening] before it drowned in the drink, possibly because of its thin melody and routine arrangement. Plus, positioning it immediately after the brooding "I Don't Know" deflated and trivialized its already juvenile pick-up lines. **C+**

"Happy With You" [Paul McCartney]
Pretending for the moment that "Come On to Me" doesn't exist, McCartney returns to the introspection of "I Don't Know" with the casual confession that, essentially, he once was a druggy and a possible drunk. But now, he's cheerful again, presumably because of Nancy, though she isn't mentioned. If I were Paul's muse, I'd have whispered in his ear that the song would opened a few more eyes if he'd explored his relationship with drugs and booze a little more, maybe backing off Nancy, just for a minute. As is, this is a pleasant song with stripped-down "Blackbird"-ish acoustic accompaniment, startling honest words – half of them anyway – and a "Help Wanted" ad for a stronger lyricist. **B**

"Who Cares" [Paul McCartney]
McCartney implies that his critics are imbeciles. His brutal honesty makes him sound like John Lennon, as right before your ears, a normally two-dimensional personality [all smiles, all the time] becomes a snarling and snapping three. Whereas "Angry" [*Press to Play*] made him sound whiney, "Who Cares" reveals frustration, a sour temper, and a guy who might actually belt you. McCartney sings intensely, spitting out the snotty lines, over a tough backing of staccato guitars and a great cheesy organ. **B+**

"Fuh You" [Paul McCartney and Ryan Tedder]
In 1969, Apple Records released a single by Brute Force [Stephen Friedland assisted by The Tokens] called "King of Fuh," with the enthusiastic support of John Lennon and George Harrison. Middle school kids all over the world giggled. That is, they would have if chicken-hearted record execs had released it beyond a token pressing of about 1,000 copies. Now, a half-century later, McCartney does it again, presenting a brand-new tee-hee tune. The crappy adolescent joke now seems even lamer. The gosh-did-I-say-that lyric reflects McCartney's mousy artistic courage. He dares not utter the forbidden syllable but can dance all around it, winking and playing dumb. In other words, he fuh-ked us. **D**

"Confidante" [Paul McCartney]
There are few pleasures as pure to a music fan as discovering a McCartney song buried in an album that unexpectedly combines a strong but simple melody, creative production, and – well, maybe not first rank lyrics, but acceptable ones. "Souvenir" [*Flaming Pie*] comes to mind, as does "Wanderlust" [*Tug of War*]. And so does this one, a heartfelt ode to, of all things, his guitar. Interesting that an inanimate object

brings out the poetry in Paul. If we're lucky, someone will suggest he turn his poet's pen to his piano. Or his drum set. Or any other instrument that might stir his artistic soul. Still, I wonder, could it be that the instrument represents a person? **B+**

"People Want Peace" [Paul McCartney]

A sincere plea for peace, a sentiment I doubt will generate much disagreement. A dull melody has many of us pacing around the living room, hoping it will end, quickly. Chalk it up to CDs requiring an hour of music. **C+**

"Hand in Hand" [Paul McCartney]

Sad, melodic song about a long-time romance, not as starry eyed as McCartney's usual love letters, because, possibly, he's taking the role of someone his actual age, with hand holding being about all he can muster. Like most of *Egypt Station*, the arrangement is tasteful, the vocal attempts to be genuine, and the lyrics ... he's trying. **B**

"Dominoes" [Paul McCartney]

The engaging melody arcs to parts unknown as the guitar slinks though a hooky motif. The lyrics are puzzling rather than insulting, making them tolerable. Better than the classy guitar is the achingly nuanced vocal, a gift from an aging man who can still summon his strengths when he's come up with a song that snags his imagination. Consider how a track of this quality would have elevated *Venus and Mars* or *Off the Ground*. **B+**

"Back in Brazil" [Paul McCartney]

McCartney cues up a samba, chokes a couple of birds for sound effects, and cranks out this ho-hum tale reminiscent of a less entertaining "Ob-La-Di Ob-La-Da." To pull this off, Paul needed to lose himself in the smart irreverence of the Beatles, which apparently he finds next to impossible to do. **C**

"Do It Now" [Paul McCartney]

A power-to-the-people number. Only about halfway through, McCartney splits, leaving us to fend for ourselves [sort of]. This bizarre ambivalence owes more to Paul's lyrical ineptitude than his lack of conviction. Beyond that, "Do It Now" rumbles along at snail speed, reminding you of a half-dozen other Paul songs you can't quite put your finger on, all along knowing that the time spent contemplating lightweight filler like this could be better off spent dancing to "Jet." **C+**

"Caesar Rock" [Paul McCartney]

Nothing here about Caesar. Maybe McCartney likes the word. A distant cousin of "Tomorrow Never Knows," only without even a note of its intellect. Of course, what do you expect from an on-the-spot improv? [Which he admits.] One of these here-and-gone snappy riffs could've been the spine of a decent song, but on "Caesar Rock" it's one among many incidental toss-offs. **C+**

"Despite Repeated Warnings" [Paul McCartney]

Though the villain goes unnamed, it's probably Donald Trump, so the song's got a guaranteed audience. Off we go on the ship of state, smack into the iceberg dead ahead. With several disparate song segments seamlessly tied together mainly by McCartney's compelling voice, the just-under seven minutes go by in a blur, leaving the listener pining for more, an unqualified victory for Paul. Even when faltering, the segments stand head and shoulders above the nursery rhymes of the similarly structured "Uncle Albert/ Admiral Halsey," proof of a grown up at work. As a bonus, the lyrical subtleties zap this to the top of McCartney's political song list, especially as he urges us on to stop this boneheaded nitwit, all the while harboring doubts as to the power we actually have. **A-**

"Station II" [Paul McCartney]

Filler, to keep you waiting for the song with naked in it. **C**

"Hunt You Down/Naked/C-Link" [Paul McCartney]

Three fragments glued together, beginning with "Hunt You Down," a generic rock tune featuring the shorter vocal lines McCartney tends to favour on *Egypt Station*. Next is "Naked," slower and jerky in 6/8 with an enthusiastic vocal but a forgettable melody. Then, on to an instrumental called "C-Link," a long guitar solo in a blues style we're not used to hearing from McCartney. Though out of character, it's good-humoured and enjoyable. And except for a vocal whoop at the end, that's it. It could be worse. **B**

[bonus]

"Get Started" [Paul McCartney]
Amiable tune, but wispy, due to short musical phrases. Plus the usual lyrical crud. [*Egypt Station II*, which compiles the "*Traveller's Edition*" and *Explorer's Edition*" bonus material] **B-**

"Nothing for Free" [Paul McCartney and Ryan Tedder]
An English teacher is recommended for McCartney so he can learn, once and for all, the difference between general nouns ["she"] and specific nouns ["Yoko"]. Using specific nouns will go a long way toward eliminating hazy sludge evidenced by "Nothing for Free" which, on the surface, reads like a tight-fisted Republican's call-to-arms, but on closer inspection reveals itself to be about some woman who wants to borrow or steal or rent-to-own, an object or feeling or whatever. Musically, it's a modest electronic experiment with next to no melody. In other words, air. [*Egypt Station II*] **C-**

"Frank Sinatra's Party" [Paul McCartney]
Polite reggae in a minor key. McCartney and the rest of the Beatles did indeed meet Sinatra at a Brentwood Party in 1964, which was apparently the inspiration, loaded with references to said night – there's Dean Martin! – and a what-the-hell attitude that makes this tossed-off tune more palatable than it would be ordinarily. [*Egypt Station II*] **B**

"Sixty Second Street" [Paul McCartney]
Flypaper-catchy acoustic riff backs a so-so tune about a promise to fill Paul's dream girl with ecstasy in only one minute [?]. Abruptly, it breaks into a faster scat singing section, light on the scat. [*Egypt Station II*] **B-**

"Who Cares [Full Length]" [Paul McCartney]
Approximately double the length of the original, elongated with a not bad guitar solo at the end, making it a time killer except for those who enjoy guitar solos. [*Egypt Station II*] **B**

"Get Enough" [Paul McCartney and Ryan Tedder, and Zach Skelton]
Cows fly, pigs whistle, and Paul uses Auto-Tune to repair his off-key vocals. In his own defense, he mumbled something about the Beatles being unafraid to use the latest technology, except that Auto-Tune is hardly the latest. It's been around at least since 1998 [Cher's "Believe"]. Half-done non-song. [*Egypt Station II*] **C**

"Come On to Me [Live at Abbey Road Studio]" [Paul McCartney]
This mediocre song gains nothing played live. McCartney sings perfunctorily, the band plays likewise. The crowd patiently waits for "Love Me Do." [*Egypt Station II*] **C**

"Fuh You [Live Cavern Club]" [Paul McCartney]
I suppose the majority of the audience has never heard the 50-year-old "King of Fuh" [or "Big Boys Bickering," McCartney's semi-lewd bonus track from the *Off the Ground* sessions]. So maybe this'll drag out a few giggles. A few. [*Egypt Station II*] **D**

"Confidante [Live LIPA [Liverpool Institute for Performing Arts]]" [Paul McCartney]
Indistinguishable from the studio track, only without the intriguing details. Therefore, who needs it? [*Egypt Station II*] **C+**

"Who Cares [Live Grand Central Station]" [Paul McCartney]
McCartney is so distracted, he might as well be singing about ham sandwiches. Also, turn up the organ. [*Egypt Station II*] **C+**

CHAPTER FORTY-SIX:

WINGS OVER EUROPE [2018/1972]

Produced by Paul McCartney
Bonus album included in the Paul McCartney and Wings: 1971-1973 box set

A mere 46 years after the fact, McCartney got around to releasing this souvenir disc of his first tour. The ensemble included Denny Laine, Henry McCullough, Denny Seiwell, Paul, and Linda, bopping their way through a smattering of small European locales, as secret as a Paul McCartney project could be. As of now, the CD commemorating the event is available only as part of the massive *Paul McCartney and Wings: 1971-1973* box set [known formally as the *Paul McCartney Archive Collection Limited Super Deluxe Edition*] which also includes three CDs of *Wild Life* [with alternate mixes, practices, and fooling around], 3 CDs of *Red Rose Speedway* [including a double album re-arrangement of what-might-have-been, plus miscellaneous singles], three DVDs, a Blu-ray, a couple of books, and assorted curios [lyrics, notes, and sketches]. And the unreleased *Wings Over Europe*.

McCartney assembled the compilation from several discreet concerts, including Newcastle upon Tyne, UH; The Hague, Netherlands; Berlin, German Antwerp, Belgium; Groningen, Netherlands. For this album, McCartney presumably used the best takes, which was not easy considering the band's nervousness, the inevitable comparisons with the Beatles, the newness of the material, and poor Linda fighting the keyboards, an amateur among professionals. Worse, the set list included not a single original Beatles tune, bound to baffle, even anger fans who demanded more than McCartney's mere presence and a supporting group of relative unknowns.

In spite of the generous sampling, several songs are nowhere to be found, owing, supposedly, to technical glitches or lousy performances: "When the Night," "C Moon," "Little Woman Love," "Go Now," Live and Let Die," "Cotton Fields," "Will the Circle Be Unbroken," and "Help Me." On the plus side, considering the age of the tapes, the mix and fidelity are surprisingly good.

By the way, the box set featuring *Wings Over Europe*, available only on McCartney's website, is currently sold out. As of this writing, there are no plans to re-release it.

Note: A live "1882" can be found in the bonus section of *Red Rose Speedway*.

"Big Barn Bed [Live 1972]" [Paul and Linda McCartney]
"Big Barn Bed"'s appeal doesn't derive from the enthusiastic performance or the defiantly dumb lyrics, but from its infectious bounce, a studio achievement that may have been accidental as much as intentional. Could it be duplicated on stage? Not really. McCartney plays cautiously, the band uncertain, and instead of a rubber ball, the tempo resembles a rotten apple falling from the tree and splatting on the ground. Would it be inappropriate to point out that merely a couple of years prior, McCartney was playing with the Beatles? **B-**

"Eat at Home [Live 1972]" [Paul and Linda McCartney]
Borrowing a bit from Buddy Holly and merging it with clever vocal flourishes made "Eat at Home" a highlight of *Ram*. This attempt captures some of the original's charm, but it's in need of a lighter touch, which Wings struggles to supply. And as elsewhere, they seem uncomfortable with the material. **C**

"Smile Away [Live 1972]" [Paul McCartney]
An ode to stink. Whatever its shortcomings, the studio "Smile Away" had a reasonably strong lead guitar and not bad background vocals. This has neither, sounding instead like your neighborhood garage band rehearsing in the driveway. **C-**

"Bip Bop [Live 1972]" [Paul and Linda McCartney]
Strange but true: Jefferson Starship's "We Built This City" hits Number One, Donald Trump is elected President of the U.S., and McCartney performs "Bip Bip" live. **F**

"Mumbo [Live 1972]" [Paul and Linda McCartney]
It takes balls to perform this throwaway studio nonsense in concert. But give McCartney credit for attempting a re-arrangement that turns it into something vaguely resembling a song with something vaguely resembling lyrics. However, it's still a jam, albeit one that lumbers along like your feeble grandma on her way to the grave. **D**

"Blue Moon of Kentucky [Live 1972]" [Bill Monroe]
This Elvis tune is so simple it's impossible to screw up, making it a good choice for this not-always-there band. That leaves it up to Paul to do the heavy lifting. It's not bad, aided by Denny Laine's lively harmonica. but not strong as, say, *Run Devil Run*, when Paul had more time to, you know, practise. **B**

"I Would Only Smile [Live 1972]" [Denny Laine]
Denny Laine performs this friendly but faceless composition. The band steps up and plays beautifully, and Laine sounds relaxed. As Laine is more convincing as a rocker than a folkie, a tougher tune would've been nice. Replaced on *Wings Over America* by "Go Now," a wise choice. **B**

"Give Ireland Back to the Irish [Live 1972]" [Paul and Linda McCartney]
Since the single was essentially a demo, standards for the live version have been lowered substantially. Still too high. The tempo is listless, McCartney [for once] has trouble singing the opening bit, and somebody's guitar needs its tuning checked. **C-**

"The Mess [Live 1972]" [Paul and Linda McCartney]
A simple tune, perfect for an inexperienced band. McCartney carries it without breaking a sweat, resulting in a competent performance of a blah song. **C –**

"Best Friend [Live 1972]" [Paul McCartney]
McCartney was the guy responsible for "Can't Buy Me Love" and "All My Loving." Instead, he hands the band "Best Friend," more grousing about John Lennon doing him wrong. Sort of a stumbling copy of Buddy Holly, which leaves behind the Holly and keeps the stumbling. This is McCartney at his worst, skating by on charisma and not much else. **F**

"Soily [Live 1972]" [Paul and Linda McCartney]
Sleepy take of a second-rater. Make that a third-rater. No, fourth. No, fifth. **F**

"I am Your Singer [Live 1972]" [Paul and Linda McCartney]
If we're here to promote *Wild Life*, of which this CD includes approximately half, why not "Tomorrow" or "Dear Friend" instead of this audio Ipecac? Too slow, an arrangement on the verge of imploding, an ugly guitar solo, and what sounds to me like errors galore. **F**

"Seaside Woman [Live 1972]" [Linda McCartney]
Linda stays on key, the band's elementary reggae remains unobtrusively light, and overall, the feel is pleasant though nothing special. **B-**

"Wild Life [Live 1972]" [Paul and Linda McCartney]
A bargain basement McCartney tune from the album of the same name. The original left a lot to be desired, and it's no better here: a practically melody-free, chord-free, and insight-free brain-dissolver. That it's a breeze to play may be the reason McCartney chose it. It is, however, shorter than the album track, an inadvertent improvement. **D**

"My Love [Live 1972]" [Paul and Linda McCartney]
An awful take of an awful song. Henry McCullough's gutsy guitar solo on the original here sounds like a first try. Paul sings like Vegas is just around the corner. Linda's new background vocals should've stayed

in her throat. As for the composition, what once came easily with "And I Love Her" now arrives with cut-and-paste romanticisms and why-try lyrics. **C**

"Mary Had a Little Lamb [Live 1972]" [Paul and Linda McCartney]
For pre-schoolers. Make that fetuses. **F**

"Maybe I'm Amazed [Live 1972]" [Paul McCartney]
The roller coaster melody on this flawless song makes it a killer to sing, but McCartney pulls it off with jaw-dropping virtuosity, his vocal laden with pleading and pain. That, of course, refers to the studio take on *McCartney*, his first solo. Here, the band drags, and McCartney can't resist showing off his listen-to-this vocal. The same guy? Hard to believe. **B**

"Hi Hi Hi [Live 1972]" [Paul and Linda McCartney]
The new rhythm is interesting but stiff. Plus somebody's out of tune. This is concert-ready? From a Beatle? **D**

"Long Tall Sally [Live 1972]" [Richard Penniman, Enotris Johnson, and Robert Blackwell]
Echoes of the Beatles, who often used this as a show-closer, radiate from this Little Richard fireball. That this version falls short is no surprise, as it lacks the energy of his original group, as well as the unbelievable exuberance he must have been feeling in the early Beatlemania days. *Now* we know why he didn't include any Beatle songs. **B-**

[bonus]

"Home Tonight" [Paul McCartney]
From the *Egypt Station* reject pile comes this jaunty also-ran with horns, which McCartney hasn't used in a while but here sound perfectly in place. Melody wise, it's moderately catchy but nothing out of the ordinary, which at this stage is all we can expect from this cautious man. [Black Friday vinyl picture disc] **B**

"In a Hurry" [Paul McCartney]
Yet another leftover from *Egypt Station*, this one a bit better than "Home Tonight." An enthusiastic McCartney barrels though this word barrage, not bad for a guy his age. Tasteful horns, neatly produced, and a clever ending. [Black Friday vinyl picture disc] **B**

"I Saw Her Standing There [Live 2017]" [John Lennon and Paul McCartney]
[Little Steven and the Disciples of Soul] Owing to his legendary stint with Bruce Springsteen's E Street Band, Steven Van Zandt is made to order for McCartney, who's also a lover of old rockers. This live cut from Van Zandt's London show features a backing reminiscent of Little Richard's "Lucille" and two veterans in the throes of ecstasy. It's sloppy fun, so much that you want it to go all night. [*Soulfire Live*] **B**

"Grow Old With Me" [John Lennon; guest performer: Paul McCartney]
[Ringo Starr] Lifted as a demo from Lennon's *Milk and Honey*, this is a tender version by the nearly 80-year-old Ringo. Sterile around the edges, but still stylish and crisply produced, with McCartney adding a delicate harmony and understated bass that can't help but remind you of days gone by. A milestone from Ringo. [*What's My Name*] **B+**

"Made for You" [Thelma Black, Paul Kelly, and Paul McCartney; guest performer: Paul McCartney]
[Thelma Black] McCartney popped into the studio, heard the song, and asked the astonished Ms Black if she'd mind if he'd add a little guitar. Gasping for air – a real Beatle! – she said yes. Her gentle voice is more attractive than the somewhat generic tune, although the track's contemporary enough to earn radio play. As for the guitar, I know it's in there somewhere. [*Better in Black*] **B**

APPENDIX

[SUPPOSEDLY] RECORDED AND UNRELEASED

The prolific McCartney has generated a backlog of unreleased material that's basically just sitting there. Whether any of these songs will ever see the official light of day is anybody's guess. The following partial list includes a substantial number of them, all of which allegedly exist as artifacts in various stages of development. Some of these, of course, exist under different titles, and it's possible that some may not exist at all. The indicated years are an educated guess.

1970-1979
"Cavendish Parade," "Blackpool" [1970]; "Nutwood Scene," "Henry's Blues" [early 1970s]; "Love is Your Road," "Partners in Crime," "She Got It Good," "Sunshine in Your Hair," "Upon a Hill," "Sea," "Sea Melody," "Sweet Little Bird," "Storm," "Walking in the Meadow," [previous ten, approximately 1974; all or some intended for the *Rupert the Bear* project]; "You've Got to Help Me" [possibly performed during 1972 tour]; "All It Needs is a Darn Good Song," "Find a Way" [circa *Wings At the Speed of Sound*, 1976]; "S.M.A.", "Twelve of the Clock," "Waterspout," "Praying Mantis [*London Town* outtake, 1978]; "Cage," "Robbers Ball," "Flying Horses," "Ranachan Rock," "Tippy Tippy Toes" [previous five circa *Back to the Egg,* 1979]; "Newt Race," "Norfolk Broads," "Beautiful Dream," "Crazy Fool," "Bucket of Water," "Memories," [previous six circa 1979]; "Reverse" [unknown, probably 1970s].

1980-1989
"Juggle," "Nature is Calling," "Old Man Loving," "Your Lucky Day" [sometime in the 1980s]; "Stealin' Back to My Same Old Used to Be," "That" "You're Shaking the Hand," "The Unbelievable Experience" [previous three recorded during sessions/rehearsals for *Flowers in the Dirt*, 1989]; "Your School" [near or during 1986's *Press to Play*, a brief segment featured on an Oobu Joobu broadcast]; "Politics of Love" [with Peter Gabriel, 1986]; "So Long Blacky" [1988, played on Oobu Joobu broadcast].

1990-1999
"Stella May Day" [mid-90s instrumental used as background music at daughter Stella's fashion shows]; "Hot Pursuit," "Maybe May Time" [circa 1991]; "Angel in Disguise" [co-written with Ringo Starr, omitted from Ringo's 1992 album *Time Takes Time*]; "In My Dreams" [probably close to 1992]; "Island in the Sun," "I Ain't Never" [about 1993]; "Wedding Invitation," "Hurricane Bob," "On a Pedestal," "Simple Song," "Wish You Were Mine," "If You Say So," "In Liverpool," "Is It Raining in London Again," and "Magic Lamp" [all considered for *Off the Ground*, 1993]; "Someone Rocking My ..." [1994]; "Pull Away" [circa 1995];"All For Love," "Hey Now," "Little Daisy Root" [circa 1995]; "Oh Mama," "You Know You are Such an Incredible Thing" [possibly 1995, both had excerpts played on Oobo Joobu]; "Cello in the Ruins," "Peacocks" [previous two probably outtakes from *Flaming Pie*, 1997]; "They Call My Baby Baby" [possibly 1997]; "Sweet Home Country Girl" and "Soul Boy" [both with Steve Miller, leftovers from *Flaming Pie*]; "Tomorrow's Light" [1998]; "Plum Jam" [1998]; "Me Love You Always" [late 90s]; "Though the Marshes" [1998]; "Fools Like Me" [1999]; "Big Day" [unknown, probably in the 1990s].

2000 and After
"You are Still Here," "Washington," "Always Be There," "If This is Wrong" [previous four circa *Driving Rain*, 2001]; "Secret Life of a Party Girl," "Build a Bridge," "Seventies with a Twist," "By Night Dark Clouds," "Sexual Ealing" [previous five are *New* outtakes]; "Church Mice" [around 2002, part of a pre-show tape]; "Perfect Lover," "A Modern Dance," and "Watching My Fish Drown" [previous three from *Chaos and Creation in the Back Yard* sessions, 2005]; "Purple Daddio" [2000]; "Diving Song" [2003]; "That Seems to Make No Sense," "A Song to Us," "It's Time for My Massage," "Stately Horn" [previous four circa 2004]; "Miami Beach" [2005] "Rain Go Away Song" [2005]; "The Church We Never Went" [also known as "Never Went to Church," possibly 2006]; "Juggler Fanfare" [2006]; "Us" [2006]; "Long To Hold You," "50th Birthday, "Fred," "I Can't Wait," "Your Song Belongs to You" [previous five approximately 2010]; "Path" [2013]; "Prison" [2013]; "Blankit" [2014]; "Gonna Set This Town on Fire Tonight," "Swimming in the Milk with Anne," "Shadow Cycle" [date unknown].

REPORT CARD

Below are all of the "As" and "Bs" listed in this book. If you're interested in making your own best-of collection, here's a suggestion: begin with the entirety of your favourite album [mine is *Band on the Run*], adding all the "A"s and selected "B+"s, finishing with as many "B"s as you like. Of course, feel free to omit any tracks that rub you the wrong way.

Songs in these lists are only mentioned once. This excludes live versions, alternates, and demos. Songs attributed to someone other than McCartney – like Elvis Costello or Mary Hopkin – are also excluded, though you can't go wrong with "Veronica" or "Those Were the Days."

If you're looking for hits, check out the compilations: *Wings Greatest*, *All the Best*, *Wingspan*, *Pure McCartney*. But be forewarned: they're iffy. There's not enough recent material on the early ones, and even on the massive *Pure McCartney*, a 4-CD set, some tracks are questionable ["Bip Bop"? Really?]. The relatively inexpensive *Wings Greatest* is probably your best bet, although it goes no further than "Mull of Kintyre."

A [and A-]
Maybe I'm Amazed [*McCartney*]
Back Seat of My Car [*Ram*]
Jet [*Band on the Run*]
Let Me Roll It [*Band on the Run*]
Warm and Beautiful [*Wings at the Speed of Sound*]
Daytime Nighttime Suffering [*Back to the Egg Reissue*]
Coming Up [*McCartney II*]
Waterfalls [*McCartney II*]
Take It Away [*Tug of War*]
Here Today [*Tug of War*]
Ballroom Dancing [*Tug of War*]
The Pound is Sinking [*Tug of War*]
Wanderlust [*Tug of War*]
My Brave Face [*Flowers in the Dirt*]
You Want Her Too [*Flowers in the Dirt*]
Don't Be Careless Love [*Flowers in the Dirt*]
That Day is Done [*Flowers in the Dirt*]

Souvenir [*Flaming Pie*]
Great Day [*Flaming Pie*]
Blue Jean Bop [*Run Devil Run*]
Vanilla Sky [*Vanilla Sky: Music from the Motion Picture*]
Jenny Wren [*Chaos and Creation in the Backyard*]
Despite Repeated Warnings [*Egypt Station*]

B+
Oo You [*McCartney*]
Eat at Home [*Ram*]
Oh Woman Oh Why [*Special Edition Ram*]
A Love for You [*Special Edition Ram*]
When the Wind is Blowing [*Wild Life Archive Edition*]
Bip Bop Link [*Wild Life*]
Tomorrow [*Wild Life*]
Mama's Little Girl [*Wild Life Remaster*]
Little Lamb Dragonfly [*Red Rose Speedway*]
Hi Hi Hi [*Red Rose Speedway Deluxe*]
Band on the Run [*Band on the Run*]
Bluebird [*Band on the Run*]
Helen Wheels [*Band on the Run*]
Nineteen Hundred and Eighty Five [*Band on the Run*]
Junior's Farm [*Venus and Mars Deluxe*]
Let 'Em In [*Wings at the Speed of Sound*]
Beware My Love [*Wings at the Speed of Sound*]
Temporary Secretary [*McCartney II*]
Tug of War [*Tug of War*]
Hope of Deliverance [*Off the Ground*]
Mistress and Maid [*Off the Ground*]

Cosmically Conscious [*Off the Ground*]
She Said Yeah [*Run Devil Run*]
Run Devil Run [*Run Devil Run*]
Lonesome Town [*Run Devil Run*]
Brown Eyed Handsome [*Run Devil Run*]
Honey Hush [*Run Devil Run*]
Shake a Hand [*Run Devil Run*]
Party [*Run Devil Run*]
Fine Line [*Chaos and Creation in the Backyard*]
How Kind of You [*Chaos and Creation in the Backyard*]
At the Mercy [*Chaos and Creation in the Backyard*]
Vintage Clothes [*Memory Almost Full*]
The End of the End [*Memory Almost Full*]
Early Days [*New*]
New [*New*]
Everybody Out There [*New*]
I Don't Know [*Egypt Station*]
Who Cares [*Egypt Station*]
Confidante [*Egypt Station*]
Dominoes [*Egypt Station*]

Ten Best Albums [In Order, Excluding Classical and Experimental]
1. *Band on the Run*
2. *Tug of War*
3. *Chaos and Creation in the Backyard*
4. *Run Devil Run*
5. *Flowers in the Dirt*
6. *Egypt Station*
7. *New*
8. *Flaming Pie*
9. *Memory Almost Full*
10. *Ram*

Ten Best Tracks [In Order]
1. Maybe I'm Amazed [*McCartney*]
2. Jet [*Band on the Run*]
3. Coming Up [*McCartney II*]
4. Jenny Wren [*Chaos and Creation in the Backyard*]
5. Back Seat of My Car [*Ram*]
6. Daytime Nighttime Suffering [*Back to the Egg Reissue*]
7. Great Day [*Flaming Pie*]
8. My Brave Face [*Flowers in the Dirt*]
9. Let Me Roll It [*Band on the Run*]
10. Wanderlust [*Tug of War*]

Ten Worst Tracks [Worst First]
1. Bip Bop [*Wild Life*]
2. Mary Had a Little Lamb [*Wings Remaster*]
3. Gotta Sing Gotta Dance [*James Paul McCartney TV Special*]
4. Ebony and Ivory [*Tug of War*]
5. Hey Diddle [*Special Edition Ram*]
6. Ode to a Koala Bear [*Pipes of Peace Deluxe*]
7. Freedom [*Driving Rain*]
8. Cook of the House [*Wings at the Speed of Sound*]
9. Sprits of Ancient Egypt [*Venus and Mars*]
10. Sweetest Little Show [*Pipes of Peace*]

Three Best Classical Pieces [In Order]
1. Nova [*A Garland for Linda*]
2. A Leaf [Original] [*Single*]
3. School [*Liverpool Oratorio*]

Three Worst Classical Pieces [Worst First]
1. Father [*Liverpool Oratorio*]
2. Spiritus [*Ecce Cor Meum*]
3. Movement 3: Imprisonment [*Ocean's Kingdom*]

Best Beatles Covers [In Order]
1. Helter Skelter [*Live 8*]
2. We Can Work It Out [*Unplugged*]
3. I'm Down [*Concert for New York City*]

Worst Beatles Covers [Worst First]
1. Eleanor Rigby [*Give My Regards to Broad Street*]
2. The Long and Winding Road [*Give My Regards to Broad Street*]
3. Good Day Sunshine [*Give My Regards to Broad Street*]

GLOSSARY

A-Side, B-Side. When records were made out of plastic, the single was a popular format, especially for teenagers on a limited budget. Played at 45 rpm [albums played at 33 1/3], a single had one song on one side, a different song on the other. The hit side [or the side hoped to be a hit] was the A-side. The song on the other side was the B-side. Occasionally, both sides received airplay, making the A and B sides interchangeable in regards to their potential commercial success. [Example: The Beatles' "Something" and "Come Together."]

Alternative Take. A take [or partial take] of a song deemed unacceptable for a variety of reasons: somebody made an error, the performance is flat, the singer thought he or she could do better. In the CD age, alternative takes often show up as bonus tracks.

Auto-Tune. A device that electronically repairs off-key vocals. Often, experienced sound engineers can tell when the device is in use – it sounds mechanical or artificial – but experienced listeners can too, evidenced by McCartney's voice modifications on "Get Enough" from the *Egypt Station* sessions.

Backing. Informal term referring to the part of a song that stays in the back of the mix, usually drums, bass, and a rhythm guitar. It can also be a vocal chorus – or even a single singer – that supports the lead vocal. Put another way, strip a song of the lead vocal and any other prominent elements, in general what's left is the backing.

Chops. A compliment, meaning the recipient has an unusually high mastery of his instrument or of music in general. Paul McCartney has chops galore. A 10-year-old piano student does not.

Cover. A song that an artist hasn't written but performs live or on a recording. Example: "Roll Over Beethoven," written by Chuck Berry, recorded by the Beatles.

Demo. A practice recording to give a hint as to how the finished piece might sound. Demos can be recorded just about anywhere – a living room, bathroom, outdoors – but most professionals prefer a studio. Occasionally, the demo is so good, it's used on the final recording as is.

Dive. A hellhole where live music is played. Noted for dirt, vomit, and drunks. It's been a while since McCartney played in one of these establishments, but played them he has. In his early Beatles days, many of the Hamburg *Tangungsort* seem to have qualified.

Editing. The process of physically or electronically eliminating sections of a track to get rid of mistakes, unnecessary pauses, chunks of music deemed irrelevant or unacceptable, or to change the length of a track. Example: A piece of "I'll Cry Instead" [*A Hard Day's Night*] was electronically copied and added to the song to make it longer.

Filler. Musical [or non-musical] junk used to pad an album where the performer has run out of recordable songs, but still needs something bring the album up to a reasonable length. Filler can be anything from alternate takes to instrumental jams to talking.

Garage Band. Informal term for a beginning group, named for the location in which they are forced by circumstance to practice. "Garage band" is commonly used as a derogatory moniker, although beginning in the 60s, being known as a garage band was often a term of honour, symbolizing an anti-corporate stance and being unashamed – even proud – of their amateurism. In those days, a surprising number of garage bands received substantial radio play for some terrific records, including Count Five ["Psychotic Reaction"], and the Mysterians ["96 Tears"], and the Castaways ["Liar Liar"].

Gig. A place to perform, hopefully for money, sometimes, maybe. McCartney's gig: A night at Shea Stadium. Count Five's gig: A night at *der Tangungsort*.

Improvisation. Spontaneous playing by one or more musicians, who make it up on the spot. Can be exquisite [Miles Davis] or painful [your neighborhood garage band]. Entire songs are occasionally spawned as the result of improvising.

Jam. Spontaneous improvised instrumental piece that can be based on a 12-bar Chuck Berry song, a funk riff, randomly selected chords, or anything that'll result in passable filler. Though fun for musicians, it can be exasperating for listeners.

Key. A group of notes identifying a musical piece's tonal center, generally defined by a scale. The key of C major, for example, consists of the scale C-D-E-F-G-A-B-C.

Mastering. The transfer of a completed, mixed track to a final tape or digital medium. This is essentially the final chance an engineer has for last minute editing, adjusting the ambiance, or otherwise fiddling with the recording before it's locked in and ready for duplication.

Mellotron. An organ-like instrument where each key on the keyboard corresponds to a particular piece of pre-recorded magnetic tape. When a particular key is pressed, the tape plays. Probably the most famous use of the mellotron is the otherworldly introduction of "Strawberry Fields Forever," played by Paul McCartney.

Mix. Placement of the various elements of a recording in the stereo spectrum; for instance, a finished mix might place a sax on the right, a guitar on the left, the lead vocal in front, drums in the back, etc. Because modern recording allows for a distinct track for each element of the song [voice one track, guitar on another, tambourine on another, and on and on], the tracks and the associated musical elements can go just about anywhere. And then there are all the electronic modification to be considered, like echo, compression, and frequency trimming. Mixing choices are nearly infinite. An art in itself, a good mix can save a song, a bad mix can wreck it.

Middle Eight. In a song, an informal designation for the middle section. It can be eight bars, but can also be more or less.

Modulate. An abrupt key change – a song in the key of C might modulate to the key of C# near the end – giving the tune an aural boost. McCartney occasionally uses modulation, sometimes subtle and brilliantly [throughout "Penny Lane"], sometimes obvious and formulaic [the end of "Mull of Kintyre"].

Motif. A short flurry of notes, developed or repeated throughout a musical piece, which may be modified and lengthened later in the piece.

Movement. Musical section of a larger piece that can be performed on its own, due to specific moods, techniques, and textures, with the tempo generally being a primary consideration. For instance, Movement I might be fast, Movement II might be slow, and so on. Because a single movement is part of a whole, composers tend to prefer their works to be played with all movements in order and intact.

Multitrack. In the old days, an engineer placed the microphones and adjusted the level, then let her rip. Recording utilized a single track, and everyone – singer, band, everyone – recorded at the same time. Today, the number of tracks has exploded, with some studios offering equipment that accept dozens of them, one for each singer and instrumentalist. The end product is a marvel, but juggling a plethora of tracks generally requires a professional.

Noodling. Improvised messing on an instrument, in general sounding like aimless practice. McCartney has released examples of noodling, like "Soggy Noodle" [*Off the Ground: The Complete Works*].

Oratorio. A lengthy composition for an orchestra and singers. Unlike an opera, an oratorio has few, if any, theatrical elements. McCartney's *Liverpool Oratorio* is an example.

Overdub. The process of adding a new part to an already existing whole. If a completed track consists of a vocal, a guitar, and a bass, the producer might decide that the last verse could use a flute. So while listening to the track, a musician adds a flute. The addition is an overdub.

Riff. Catchy guitar [or bass] part, repeated throughout the song. Example: The bass riff percolating through "Silly Love Songs."

Rough Mix. When the recording is more or less finished, the rough mix is the first playback before the musical elements receive serious tinkering.

Soundcheck. Prior to a concert, the audio elements [vocals, band, effects] are checked and modified to ensure everything works and to ensure the best quality sound for the concert goer. This requires the headliners – or suitable stand-ins – to perform a mini-concert for an audience of engineers and technicians. Devious headliners might deny their opening acts a soundcheck, forcing them to accept crummy sound, and – as a bonus for the big shots – make the headliners sound even better by comparison.

Synthesizer. Device for producing and modifying electronic sounds. Synthesizer sounds range from traditional instruments to atonal noise, occasionally appearing in the same passage.

Timbre. The tone of an instrument or voice. It's what makes a piano and trombone sound different, even when playing the identical note.

Tone Poem [Symphonic Poem]. An orchestral work, usually one continuous movement, intended to evoke a particular poem, artwork, literary piece, or natural wonder. McCartney's *Standing Stone* could be considered a tone poem.

Vamp. A part of a song, such as a guitar riff, played endlessly, over and over. One could say that McCartney's too-long ending to the live "Hey Jude" is a vamp.

BIBLIOGRAPHY

Books

Blackwood, R.L. *A Man's Guide to Surviving Divorce*. CreateSpace Independent Publishing, 2011

Brown, Peter and Steven Gaines. *The Love You Make*. New American Library, 1983

Carlin, Peter A. *Paul McCartney: A Life*. Touchstone, 2009.

Davies, Hunter. *The Beatles*. W.W. Norton and Co., 2010.

DiLello, Richard. *The Longest Cocktail Party*. Alfred Music, 2014

Doggett, Peter. *You Never Give Me Your Money: The Beatles After the Breakup*. Harper, 2011.

Doyle, Tom. *Man on the Run: Paul McCartney in the 1970s*. Ballantine Books, 2014

Du Noyer, Paul. *Conversations with McCartney*. Harry N. Abrams, 2016

Emerick, Geoff. *Here, There, and Everywhere: My Life Recording the Beatles*. Avery, 2007.

Lewisohn, Mark. *The Complete Beatles Recording Sessions: The Official Story of the Abbey Road Years 1962-1970*. Hamlyn, 2018.

Lewisohn, Mark. *Tune In: The Beatles: All These Years*. Three Rivers Press, 2016.

McNab, Ken. *And in the End: The Last Days of the Beatles*. Polygon Books, 2019

Miles, Barry. *Paul McCartney: Many Years from Now*. Holt, 1998

Norman, Phillip. *Shout! The Beatles in Their Generation*. Touchstone, 2005.

Trafford, Abigail. *Crazy Time: Surviving Divorce and Building a New Life*. William Morrow, 2014

Selected Magazine and Newspaper Articles

Christgau, Robert. "Living Without the Beatles". *The Village Voice*. September, 1971

Gambaccini, Paul. "Paul Won't Rest His Wings". *Rolling Stone*. December 16, 1976

Gambaccini, Paul. "The Rolling Stone Interview: Paul McCartney". *Rolling Stone*. January 31, 1974

Ghosh, Palash. "40 Years Ago, Paul McCartney Saved His Career With An Album Made Under Duress In Nigeria". *International Business Times*. July 16, 2013

Goodman, Joan. "Playboy Interview: Paul and Linda McCartney". *Playboy*. December, 1984.

Hilburn, Robert. "McCartney Generation Nears Middle Age". *Los Angeles Times*. June 4. 1989.

Hilburn, Robert. "McCartney's One-Man Show". *Los Angeles Times*. 7 June, 1980

Hochman, Steve. "More intimate, but still cautious". *Los Angeles Times*. September 4, 2005

Holden, Stephen. "Paul McCartney hits new low — again". *Rolling Stone*. July 24, 1980

Mulholland, Garry. "Paul McCartney and Wings – Wings Over America". *Uncut*. June, 2013

Murphy, Kim. "Life for a man on the run". *Los Angeles Times*. June 3, 2007.

Racine, Martin. "Nice & friendly: mushy Paul McCartney finally gets off the ground and Wings it". *Houston Chronicle*. February 9, 1993)Williams, Mark. "Wings: Taking off at Last". *Melody Maker*. June 16, 1979

Willman, Chris. "Paul McCartney's Gets Saucy, and Slightly Serious, on Egypt Station." *Variety*. September 6, 2018

Internet Sites

Sites devoted to icons like the Beatles and Paul McCartney take on a religious fervor that make the slightest hints of criticism as popular as poison ivy. In most cases, lacking editors or anyone insisting on accuracy, the internet acts a receptacle for wild fantasies and bizarre speculations. [Did you know Jimi Hendrix was the author of "Sgt. Pepper?" Me neither.] That said, here are a few sites that seem reasonable:

https://www.imdb.com/name/nm0005200/ [*IMDb*, film work]

https://www.the guardian.com/music/paulmccartney [*The Guardian*, good source for reasonable editorializing]

https://www.nme.com/artists/paul-mccartney [*NME*, recent news]

https://www.nytimes.com/topic/person/paul-mccartney [*New York Times*, more news]

https://ultimateclassicrock.com/tags/paul-mccartney/ [*Ultimate Classic Rock*, thoughtful commentary and news]

CPSIA information can be obtained
at www.ICGtesting.com
Printed in the USA
BVHW011429201020
591409BV00009B/197